S0-AEN-541

DISCARDED

SHELTON STATE COMMUNITY
COLLEGE
JUNIOR COLLEGE DIVISION
LIBRARY

DG
678.235
.F56

Finlay, Robert,
1940—

Politics in
Renaissance
Venice

DATE			
AUG 5 '83			

© THE BAKER & TAYLOR CO

Politics in
Renaissance Venice

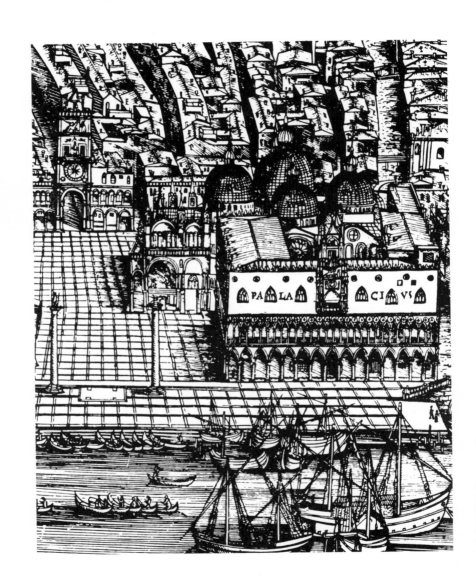

DISCARDED

Robert Finlay

Politics in
Renaissance Venice

Rutgers University Press
New Brunswick, New Jersey

Publication of this book was aided by a grant from the
Gladys Krieble Delmas Foundation.

Library of Congress Cataloging in Publication Data

Finlay, Robert, 1940–
    Politics in Renaissance Venice.

    Bibliography: p.
    Includes index.
    1. Venice—Politics and government.
I. Title.
DG678.235.F56   320.9′45′3105   79-20012
ISBN 0–8135–0888–6

Copyright © 1980 by Rutgers, The State University of New Jersey
All rights reserved
Manufactured in the United States of America

To Constance

Contents

List of Illustrations

Acknowledgments

It is a pleasure to acknowledge a debt of gratitude to many persons who gave me encouragement and advice in the writing of this book: Christopher and Mary Cooley, Gaetano Cozzi, Philip Geraldi, Felix Gilbert, Hanna H. Gray, Vincent Ilardi, Patricia H. Labalme, Martin Lowry, Richard Mackenney, Michael Mallet, Edward Muir, and Robert Smith. David Chambers, John R. Hale, Margaret L. King, Brian Pullan, and Donald Queller read the typescript soon after its completion, and their criticisms have greatly improved the book. David Chambers also spent valuable time in the Mantuan archives trying to track down for me a rumor concerning the sexual predilection of Marino Sanuto, a key figure in this study.

William H. McNeill introduced me to the study of Venice, guided my first research on the subject, and has continued to be a source of help and encouragement. Frederic C. Lane suggested that the diaries of Sanuto were a fruitful and neglected source for a student of Venetian politics; this book, the final product of his advice, has benefited greatly from his scrutiny and kind interest. Marilyn Perry's assistance was invaluable. There is little in the book that is not partly hers, for she read the manuscript as it was written, suggesting many revisions that improved the style and structure of the final work; in addition, she shared with me her extensive knowledge of Venetian art and helped gather the illustrations for the book. I could not have completed the work without a research grant from the Gladys Krieble Delmas Foundation that enabled me to spend a year in Venice. Scarcely less important was the personal support and gracious hospitality of Gladys Delmas and her husband, Jean, during that year. I trust that this book reflects, however inadequately, the deep affection they feel for the city of Venice.

The librarians and archivists of Venice have always been courteous and helpful, and I would like to express my gratitude to the staffs of the Archivio di Stato di Venezia, the Biblioteca Nazionale Marciana, the Biblioteca Querini Stampalia, the Museo Civico Correr, and the Istituto di Storia della Società e dello Stato of the Fondazione Giorgio Cini.

I also wish to thank Marcel Tetel, the editor of the *Journal of Medieval and Renaissance Studies*, for permission to incorporate my article, "The Venetian Republic as a Gerontocracy: Age and Politics in the Renaissance," *JMRS* 8 (1978):157–178, into Chapter III of this book.

Abbreviations

ASM   Archivio di Stato di Mantova. Carteggio estero; carteggio ad inviati.

ASMo.   Archivio di Stato di Modena. Archivio Segreto Estense, Cancellaria Estero: ambasciatori a Venezia.

ASV   Archivio di Stato di Venezia.

Barbaro   Marcantonio Barbaro. *Genealogie delle famiglie patrizie venete.* BMV. MSS. It. Cl. VII, 925–928 (8594–8597).

BMV   Biblioteca Nazionale Marciana, Venice.

Capellari   Girolamo Capellari. *Il Campidoglio Veneto.* 4 vols. BMV. MSS. It. Cl. VII, 8306.

Consegi   "Raccolta dei Consegi (Nomine, ballotazioni ed elezioni alle cariche della Repubblica di Venezia)." BMV. MSS. It. Cl. VII, 813–871 (8892–8950).

Malipiero   Domenico Malipiero. *Annali veneti dall'anno 1457 al 1500.* 2 vols. Edited by T. Gar and A. Sagredo. Archivio storico italiano, 1st ser., vol. 7. Florence, 1843–1844.

MCC   Museo Civico Correr, Venice.

Michiel   Marcantonio Michiel. "Diarii." MCC. MS. Cod. Cicogna, 2848.

Priuli   Girolamo Priuli. *I diarii di Girolamo Priuli.* Vol. 1. edited by Arturo Segre. Vols. 2 and 4 edited by Roberto Cessi. Rerum Italicarum Scriptores, vol. 24, pt. 3. Bologna, 1912–1938. Idem. "Diarii." Vols. 5–8. MCC. MSS. Prov. Div., 252-c.

Sanuto   Marino Sanuto. *I diarii di Marino Sanuto.* 58 vols. Edited by Rinaldo Fulin and others. Deputazione R. Veneta di Storia Patria. Venice, 1879–1903.

Glossary of Governmental Terms

CENSORS. Two officials, elected to one-year terms by the Great Council, who were commissioned to guard against illegal electoral activity in the Great Council and the Senate.

COLLEGIO. The steering committee or cabinet of the Senate, which set the agenda and made proposals to that assembly; elected by the Senate, it was composed of the *savi grandi, savi di terraferma,* and *savi agli ordini.*

COUNCIL OF TEN. The special executive council for secret affairs and state security; elected by the Great Council, it was composed of seventeen men: the ten ordinary members of the Ten proper, six ducal councillors, and the doge.

DOGE. The head of state and supreme magistrate, elected for life by a committee of forty-one men drawn from the Great Council; as the central figure of the Signoria, he presided over the Great Council, and, along with the Signoria, he sat with the Collegio in the Senate.

DUCAL COUNCILLORS. Six advisors of the doge on the Signoria; elected by the Great Council to eight-month terms, with each councillor drawn from a different district of the city; the doge needed the accord of at least four councillors to take any action, and at least four councillors had to be present at all meetings of the Council of Ten.

FORTY, CHIEFS OF THE. Three heads of the Court of the Forty, who were elected by that tribunal; during their two-month terms, they sat on the Signoria, except when that council formed part of the Council of Ten.

FORTY, COURT OF THE. The *Quarantia criminal,* the supreme appeals court for criminal cases; it was composed of forty judges who had served on the other two *Quarantie* during the previous sixteen months; it formed part of the Senate.

FULL COLLEGIO. The union of the Signoria and Collegio, both for the daily business of government and to preside over the Senate.

GREAT COUNCIL. The sovereign assembly of the Republic, made up of all patricians over the age of twenty-five; by means of four nominating committees and a general election, it elected most officials; it voted on legislation dealing with offices and administration and occasionally convened as a court.

PROCURATORS. Nine men elected for life by the Great Council, who acted as treasurers for the government and as fiduciaries for private individuals; the doge was usually chosen from among their number.

Quarantia civile nuova. The supreme appeals court for civil cases originating outside the city of Venice; after serving for eight months, the forty judges became members of the *Quarantia civile vecchia.*

Quarantia civile vecchia. The supreme appeals court for civil cases originating in the city of Venice; after serving for eight months, the forty judges became members of the Court of the Forty and, hence, the Senate.

savi agli ordini. Five members of the Collegio, elected by the Senate to six-month terms, who were responsible for maritime affairs; by the Cinquecento, they were the lowest-ranking members of the Collegio.

savi di terraferma. Five members of the Collegio, elected by the Senate to six-month terms, who were responsible for military affairs on the mainland.

savi grandi. Six members of the Collegio, elected by the Senate to six-month terms, who were responsible for general governmental affairs and were the highest-ranking members of the Collegio.

SENATE. The central council of debate and decision; it was composed of four groups: sixty ordinary senators, sixty extraordinary senators (the Zonta), the Court of the Forty, and about 140 magistrates who entered by virtue of their offices.

SIGNORIA. The ducal council, which ceremonially represented the Republic; it was composed of the doge, six ducal councillors, and three chiefs of the Forty; it presided over and set the agenda of the Great Council, and it presided with the Collegio over the Senate; with the exclusion of the chiefs of the Forty, it constituted part of the Council of Ten.

STATE ATTORNEYS. Three *avogadori,* elected to sixteen-month terms by the Great Council; they were the state prosecutors in the three supreme courts or *Quarantie*, and at least one state attorney was required to be present in all councils to guard against violations of the law.

TEN, CHIEFS OF THE. Three of the ordinary members of the Council of Ten, who were elected to one-month terms by the ten ordinary members of the council; they were responsible for convening the council on special occasions and acted as the executives of the council.

TEN, *zonta* OF THE. A group of fifteen men who regularly met with the Council of Ten; the men of the *zonta* were co-opted by the Council of Ten before 1529, and after that date they were nominated by the Great Council and then approved by the Ten.

ZONTA. A group of sixty men elected to the Senate every September 29; the Senate made nominations to the Zonta, and the Great Council selected sixty of them.

Well might it seem that such a city had owed its existence rather to the rod of the enchanter, than the fear of the fugitive; that the waters which encircled her had been chosen for the mirror of her state, rather than the shelter of her nakedness; and that all which in nature was wild or merciless—Time and Decay, as well as the waves and the tempests—had been won to adorn her instead of to destroy.

John Ruskin

Introduction

This book is an attempt to fill a critical gap in Venetian studies by examining the political life of the Republic during the Renaissance. Venetian politics has usually been viewed through the distorting lens of the myth of Venice, a complex of notions regarding the Republic's self-image and reputation. As early as the fifteenth century, Venice was renowned for its political stability and civic harmony, and even as late as the eighteenth century it was widely believed that Venetians had discovered the secret of a perfect constitution, that they had constructed a political system reconciling the demands of power and justice, order and freedom.[1]

Until recently the *mito di Venezia* was dominant in historical study, and its continuing attraction is evident in discussions of the harmony of Venetian institutions, of the extraordinary devotion of the patriciate, and of the city as an emblem of fraternity.[2] Today, a counter-myth, an old tradition of viewing Venice as corrupt and tyrannical, holds the field and gives impetus to debunking exercises.[3] However, there are very few studies of Venetian politics and no overall, detailed examination of the Venetian political system. Indeed, the literature on the influence of the myth far outweighs that on the politics of Venice.[4] The myth was widespread and successful, and the scant attention paid to the domestic politics of the Republic reflects that fact.

1 For a discussion of the myth of Venice, see Chapter I. 2.

2 William Roscoe Thayer, *A Short History of Venice*, p. x; Charles Diehl, *Une République patricienne*, pp. 116–119; R. Guerdan, *L'oro di Venezia*, pp. 144, 211, 247, 311; cf. Giuseppe Maranini, *La costituzione di Venezia dopo la serrata del Maggior Consiglio*, p. 403.

3 For debunking exercises, which also add considerably to understanding of Venetian politics, see Donald E. Queller, "The Civic Irresponsibility of the Venetian Nobility"; Felix Gilbert, "Venetian Diplomacy before Pavia"; Giorgio Cracco, *Società e stato nel medioevo veneziano;* Charles J. Rose, "Marc Antonio Venier, Renier Zeno and 'the Myth of Venice.'"

4 See the discussions and bibliography in Myron Gilmore, "Myth and Reality in Venetian Political Theory," and William J. Bouwsma, "Venice and the Political Education of Europe," in *Renaissance Venice*, ed. J. R. Hale (Totowa, N.J.,

I

Only a Cinquecento patrician at the end of his career could have
adequately explained the complexities of Venetian politics and the
constitution.[5] A number of questions might have been addressed to
such a veteran: How did a patrician exert influence on his fellows?
How did electoral procedures affect political life? What was the
nature of familial and factional interests within the ruling class? What
influence did the mass of the patriciate have on those in positions of
power? How were dissent and opposition expressed within the government? What was the political relationship between the councils of
state? Answers to such questions lead one ineluctably back to problems
posed by the myth of Venice: What were the sources of the Republic's stability? How finely ordered was the constitutional structure?
What was the relationship between constitutional prescription and
political reality? How devoted to the state was the patriciate? Was
the ruling class really so united and congenial? Why does the patriciate present so anonymous and faceless an appearance?

This study is addressed to both sets of questions. It was begun with
two assumptions: first, that the undeniable stability, harmony, and
longevity of Venice must somehow be related to its political system;
second, that Venice possessed the usual quotient of flaws and confusion, imperfection and wickedness, shared by all human communities. Although this examination depicts Venice's rulers as often grasp-
ing, faction ridden, and lacking in public spirit, a desire to debunk
Venice played no part in its inception. Indeed, the myth of Venice is,
so to speak, approached by the back door, for a fundamental theme
of the study is that Venice's stability and harmony owed much to its

---

1973), pp. 445–466. On Venetian politics: Gaetano Cozzi, "Authority and the Law
in Renaissance Venice"; Felix Gilbert, "Venice in the Crisis of the League of
Cambrai"; M. J. C. Lowry, "The Reform of the Council of Ten, 1582–3"; Aldo
Stella, "La regolazione delle pubbliche entrate e la crisi politica veneziana del
1582"; Mario Brunetti, "Il doge non è 'segno di taverna' "; idem, "Due dogi sotto
inchiesta." The best general description of the Venetian constitution is in Frederic
C. Lane, *Venice*, pp. 86–117, 250–273. The basic history of the constitution
remains Maranini's *Costituzione di Venezia*. A useful general discussion on Venetian politics is in D. S. Chambers, *The Imperial Age of Venice, 1380–1580*, pp. 73–
107. Several works not directly concerned with day-to-day political life are also
useful: James Cushman Davis, *The Decline of the Venetian Nobility as a Ruling
Class*; Brian Pullan, *Rich and Poor in Renaissance Venice*; Gaetano Cozzi, *Il
doge Nicolò Contarini*; Federico Seneca, *Il doge Leonardo Donà*; Vittorio Lazzarini, *Marino Falier*; William J. Bouwsma, *Venice and the Defense of Republican Liberty*.

5 Cf. Chambers, *Imperial Age of Venice*, p. 74.

commonplace political life. The nature of power, factionalism, electoral competition, and political corruption in the Republic fostered modes of compromise, consensus, conciliation, and conformity within the patriciate. In short, the reality of Venetian politics is wholly relevant to the myth of the perfect republic.[6]

The first chapter is an introduction to the city, the myth, and the government. The second chapter is an analysis of the relationship between the Venetian populace and the patriciate, the divisions that ran through the patriciate, and the role of family relationships in binding the ruling class together. The subject is the nature of political action in the sovereign assembly, especially the influence of elections on aspects of the political scene. The third chapter is an examination of the political power of the doge, the elected head of state, emphasizing the substantial importance of the dogeship in Venetian politics and administration. In contrast to the second chapter, emphasis is on competition among the most powerful politicians for the highest office of the Republic. The fourth chapter concerns the effect of the War of the League of Cambrai (1509–1517) on politics and the constitution, a topic that permits an analysis of the patriciate reacting to a crisis in ways that transformed Venetian politics. This chapter is concentrated on the more exclusive councils of government: the Senate, the Collegio, and the Council of Ten. The fifth chapter concerns the place of dissent in Venetian politics shown through an examination of the careers and interests of some outspoken patricians, including the diarist Marino Sanuto, a principal source for this study. Many of the themes of previous chapters are taken up again in this final discussion.

Any of these chapters—in fact, a section of any chapter—warrants a book-length study of its own. Moreover, much that is important for Venetian politics is not dealt with, such as the nature of the non-patrician (cittadini) secretarial class; the fiscal apparatus of government, especially the taxation system; and the role of central magistracies, for example, the water and salt offices, the state attorneys, the procurators of San Marco. This book touches on the principal aspects of Venetian politics, but it still remains a first step toward making sense of the political order of the Republic.

6 A broadly similar approach may be found in Lane's *Venice* and in essays by Stanley Chojnacki, "Crime, Punishment, and the Trecento Venetian State"; "In Search of the Venetian Patriciate"; "Patrician Women in Renaissance Venice"; and "Dowries and Kinsmen in Early Renaissance Venice"; and by Margaret Leah King, "Personal, Domestic and Republican Values in the Moral Philosophy of Giovanni Caldiera"; and "Caldiera and the Barbaros on marriage and the family."

The 180 years from 1450 to 1630 may be regarded as the Renaissance phase of Venetian domestic politics. This study is concentrated on the late Quattrocento and early Cinquecento, by which time Venetian government had assumed the form it was to retain until the end of the Republic in 1797. From 1297 to about 1450, the structure of government was taking shape; from 1450 to 1797, the Venetian constitution underwent slight alteration, although the early seventeenth century saw significant changes in the politics of the patriciate. Thus the late fifteenth century marks the emergence of the Venetian constitutional system in its final form. The period was crucial for another reason. Venetian wealth, power, and self-confidence remained great into the last decades of the Quattrocento. A program of urban renewal and embellishment launched in the 1480s was only one indication of Venice's prosperity and power at that time.

But then Venice went on the defensive. In the Mediterranean the Ottoman Turks cut away portions of Venice's *stato di mar*. A turning point in Venetian history was reached in 1503, for in that year Venice signed a costly peace with the Turks, relinquishing key cities in Albania and Greece, in order to defend its territory on mainland Italy.[7] Attacks by the Turks were coupled with Portuguese entrance into the spice trade soon after the turn of the century, and Venetians feared that their commercial prosperity was at an end. The threat in Italy culminated in 1509 with the War of the League of Cambrai, in which Venice was attacked by an alliance of the leading powers of Europe. In the space of a few weeks, the Republic lost the *terraferma* empire it had built since the early Quattrocento. By 1517 Venice had succeeded in regaining its mainland possessions, but Italian and European politics were dominated by France and the Spanish-Hapsburg empire. The northern kingdoms drew Venice into their battles; Venice found itself once more involved in wars and suffering the inevitable commercial and financial difficulties. Crowded by the Turks in the East, hemmed in by foreign powers in the Italian peninsula, Venice became a second-rate power in the first half of the Cinquecento.[8]

Venetian patricians were aware that they were living in critical

7 The Venetian year began on March 1; all dates in this study are according to the modern calendar. On the significance of 1503, see Lane, *Venice*, p. 242.

8 Lane, *Venice*, pp. 225–237, 241–249, 285; cf. Robert Finlay, "Venice, the Po Expedition, and the End of the League of Cambrai, 1509–1510"; Alberto Tenenti, "The Sense of Space and Time in the Venetian World of the Fifteenth and Sixteenth Centuries." On the Portuguese and Venetian reaction: Fernand Braudel, *The Mediterranean and the Mediterranean World in the Age of Philip II*, 1:543–545.

times, and some of them kept diaries to record the great, often distressing events rushing in around them. These diaries, particularly those of Marino Sanuto and Girolamo Priuli, permit a unique and revealing look at the politics of the patriciate, a fleshing out of the skeleton of the constitution. No attempt to penetrate the surface legality of Venetian politics can be wholly successful; much of what went on behind the scenes is lost forever. Even in the face of historical scrutiny, Venetian patricians preserve their veil of restraint and decorum. The diaries permit one, ever so slightly, to lift the veil and observe patricians in search of place and power.

Government records are generally silent about the unofficial, informal aspects of Venetian politics. For example, the records of the censors, a magistracy charged with combating electoral corruption, are skimpy and unrevealing for the early Cinquecento, not because vote seeking and fraud during elections were insignificant but because the very nature of Venetian electioneering inhibited action by the censors—a political reality recorded by the diarists. In a Senate register for June 26, 1499, there appear proposals regarding the creation of special commissioners for maritime affairs (*provveditori sopra le cose marittime*), who would take on some of the tasks normally performed by the *savi agli ordini* ("sages of the marine"). The proposal as put forward passed with eighty-seven votes, whereas a contrary proposal by the *savi agli ordini*, which stipulated that they should continue their duties as usual, received eighty-four. Obviously, the Senate was deeply divided over creating a new office and limiting the responsibility of its own maritime supervisors. Sanuto's *Diarii* confirm this and add more information, noting which *savio* drew up each proposal and who spoke in favor of each, as well as what was said; they also reveal reasons for the proposals that are not apparent in the legislation itself. In another case, the records of legislation passed by the Great Council show that in the last four days of July 1527 a measure concerning electoral procedures was voted on a number of times and finally passed. It is clear from both the narrow votes and the large attendance that the measure excited considerable interest; but only by supplementing this austere record with Sanuto's account does one realize that the legislation was the focus of intense parliamentary maneuvering for weeks and that it was considered an "affair of the greatest importance for these times."[9] Official records, unlike the

9 On 1499: ASV, Senato, Mar, Reg. 14, fol. 190r; Sanuto, 2:852–853. On 1527: ASV, Maggior Consiglio, Deliberazioni, Liber Diana, Reg. 26, fols. 87r–88v, and the discussion in this book, Chapter II. 4.

diaries, do not contain information about the tone of debates in the councils, the impact of popular opinion on public policy, or the motives behind proposals and decisions. As always, a host of considerations never found their way onto paper and into the archives of the government.

Although other sources were extensively used—archival material, elections lists, genealogical records, and (where applicable) seventeenth-century commentaries on the government—the diaries were the basis of this study. It is, in part, an examination of a unique and unusually personal sort of evidence not otherwise available in the study of Venetian history.

Of course, the diaries must be used critically, as with any other kind of historical evidence. The intentions, assumptions, and whims of the diarist determined what he recorded. Everything a chronicler says cannot be believed, anymore than one would accept a columnist's word for what was really happening in Washington or Rome. More often than not, there is no way to check the accuracy of the diarist's assertion. The recorder's view of an event or of an individual must not be confused with an objective assessment; his notions about politics must not form an interpretive framework. Using due care, the diaries can be made to yield an intelligible portrait of Venetian politics.[10] Venetians expended their subtlety in the practice of commerce and politics, and the diarists were practical men little given to extensive analysis or to profound thought. Their records of daily occurrences do not contain discourses on the nature of politics; their generalizations about Venice, ranging from expressions of patriotism to protests against corruption, are rarely original or of great value. Instead, a picture of Venetian political life must be built up from the innumerable and often elusive notices that comprise the diaries. Almost all the themes in this study are products of such syntheses.

The judgments a diarist makes about his contemporaries may be based on political disaffection, personal spite, or simple ignorance; but they are not thereby rendered useless for analysis. For example, if Sanuto attacks someone for lobbying for office, what is relevant for a study of politics is that patricians sought votes and that Sanuto thought the practice worthy of condemnation. If Priuli complains

---

10 Frederic C. Lane has made extensive and cautious use of the diarists in his many essays on finance, shipping, and trade (collected in *Venice and History*, Baltimore, 1966), as well as in his "Naval Actions and Fleet Organization, 1499–1502."

that government leaders failed to check political gossip because they were cowardly and weak, what is useful is not so much Priuli's personal judgment as the widespread nature of and concern about political rumor. The social and political environment of the patriciate slowly emerges from reading the diarists skeptically and seeking a pattern in their records.

Five diarists survive from the early Cinquecento: Marino Sanuto, Girolamo Priuli, Pietro Dolfin, Marcantonio Michiel, and Domenico Malipiero. Of lesser importance because less extensive are the works of Dolfin, Michiel, and Malipiero. Pietro Dolfin (1427–1506) was a failure in commerce and as a galley captain. His diary, which runs from March 1500 to April 1501, was the fourth and final part of his chronicle of Venice from its origins. Dolfin may have intended to integrate the notes of his diary into his chronicle, but there is no indication that he did so.[11] Marcantonio Michiel (1486–1552) was the son of Vittore, a politician of middling importance. Marcantonio never followed a political career. In 1525 he was banished from the Great Council for one year because of violence against a relative in a squabble over an inheritance. He is best known for the valuable catalog of contemporary collections of art that he put together well after he ceased keeping a diary. His diary covers the period from January 1511 to February 1520; after October 1518 he spent most of his time in Rome as a secretary to Cardinal Domenico Pisani and had to rely for news on his father and brother.[12]

Domenico Malipiero (1428–1515) was an experienced and highly regarded naval commander, whose involvement in a defeat in 1499 may have prevented his being elected captain general of the fleet (*capitanio generale del mar*). After tours of duty as a captain of towns in Dalmatia and at Rimini, he died while serving as general at Treviso. His *Annali*, covering the period from 1457 to 1499, is a problematic document surviving only in a much-altered version edited posthumously. Malipiero reports events in Venice when he was serving in the fleet off Greece, and he places himself in Venice when he was clearly

11 On the diarists: Rinaldo Fulin, *Diarii e diaristi veneziani*. On Pietro Dolfin: see Roberto Cessi's introduction to Dolfin's *Annalium Venetorum* (*pars quatro*).
12 On Michiel's difficulties in court: MCC, MSS. Prov. Div., 2115; Sanuto, 39:371, 376, 396, 424, 442–443. On Michiel: Emmanuel A. Cicogna, *Intorno la vita e le opere di Marcantonio Michiel, Patrizio veneto della prima metà del secolo XVI*. Michiel's catalog has been published as *Notizie d'opere di desegno nella prima metà del secolo XVI*, ed. T. Frimmel (Vienna, 1880); cf. Jennifer Fletcher, "Marcantonio Michiel's Collection."

in Pisa. His notations are not always contemporaneous: He mentions a patrician as winning the dogeship nineteen years before the event; another, he identifies as a procurator twenty-one years before his election and refers to as dead before the fact. Whether Malipiero or his editor, Francesco Longo (d. 1584), brought the *Annali* up to date is unknown. Although it must be used with special caution, Malipiero's "diary" is valuable because it contains information on certain events not available elsewhere. It is also disappointing because Malipiero rarely mentions himself, despite the key role he played in some of the events he records.[13]

Girolamo Priuli (1467–1547) was the only one of the diarists from an important political family. The family home was a costly palace at Santa Fosca rented from a fellow banker. Girolamo's father, Lorenzo (d. 1518), was a leading politician, and much of Girolamo's inside information came from him. An uncle, Alvise di Pietro, was mentioned for the dogeship in the 1520s. A brother, Vincenzo, married a daughter of Alvise Pisani, a powerful man and rich banker. A considerably less important and rather distant relative by marriage was Sanuto.[14]

Priuli spent from 1493 to 1498 as a merchant in London. In 1507 he opened a small bank, but his timing was unfortunate. War came two years later, and the bank folded in 1513. Although he stayed aloof from politics, he was called on by the government during the war in his capacity as a banker with access to ready funds: "I am often with the doge and the Fathers [*Padri*] of the Collegio in these difficult times for Venice, with letters coming in from all over with the bad news of cities, fortresses and men lost, of fire, destruction and violence."[15] He was thirty-three when he wrote this; his experience with

---

13 Malipiero gives detailed information on events in Venice when he was at Zonchio (1:179–180). Lane ("Naval Actions and Fleet Organization," p. 168, n. 6) points out Malipiero's confusion in his records about his presence in Venice and Pisa. On the patrician winning the dogeship: Malipiero, 1:213–214. On the procurator and his death: Malipiero, 2:661. For information on Malipiero, see Agostino Sagredo's preface in Malipiero, 1:xiii–xxv.

14 For comments on Priuli, see Segre's introduction to the first volume of the *Diarii* and Cessi's introduction to the fourth; also see Rinaldo Fulin, "Girolamo Priuli e i suoi Diarii (I Portughesi nell'India e i Veneziani in Egitto)." The "Giornale Lorenzo Priuli" (MCC, MSS. Prov. Div., 912/1-2) describes the operations of the Priuli family in commerce and banking. On Priuli's home: Sanuto, 44:24. On Sanuto's connection with the Priuli: Sanuto, 7:672; 26:54; 37:13.

15 Priuli, 4:369; cf. ASV, Consiglio di Dieci, Parti Miste, Reg. 34, fols. 16v, 20v, 21v–22r, 70r, 84r–84v.

the government in time of crisis, and its subsequent unwillingness to bail out his bank, may have soured him on politics permanently.

Priuli started his diary when he returned to Venice in 1498 (although his record of events begins with April 1494) and continued it until July 1512; the volumes from August 1506 to June 1509 have been lost. Priuli kept his diary secret and intended to release it to the public only after a hundred years. He fondly hoped that when the Venetian state was at an end his books would be consulted to see how the Republic was governed. Unfortunately for those future readers, his diary is a tiresomely prolix work. He rambles on, through eight huge volumes, careless of repetition and redundancy; he suffers, he informs the weary reader, from a poor memory. Because his composition was secret, his diary is uninhibited in its criticisms of government leaders. Yet because he was impetuous and sorely lacking in political sagacity, his criticisms are usually overstated, superficial, and malicious. His condemnation of the city's leaders for stupidity, cowardice, corruption, inefficiency, and sexual excess is made no more convincing by his lack of specificity. One must resist the temptation to quote him on these matters. He does not name names but issues sweeping indictments; he is equally general when moved to sympathy by the plight of those in power. He was an inveterate puritan, with a paucity of common sense and responsibility. His suggestion for solving the problem of licentious convents was to burn them to the ground, along with the nuns in them![16] There is, at least, no difficulty in pinpointing Priuli's prejudices and how they influenced what he recorded.

Yet his diary is invaluable. It contains a vivid portrait of political life and conveys a sense of personality and immediacy usually missing in other diaries. As he points out, he did not have access to the secrets of the government, so he recorded what was said in public places. He was assiduous in writing down the popular opinion and gossip that flourished at the Rialto, where he kept an office. A merchant, not a historian, his businessman's contempt for politics was matched by his regard for hard facts. He was proud of seeing things at firsthand. At the siege of Padua in September 1509, he counted the patricians serving there and insisted, not without some satisfaction, that official records of their number were inaccurate. Business affairs often did not permit him the leisure to make daily entries in the diary, and some

16 On his diary being secret: Priuli, 2:397. On consulting the diary: Priuli, 4:367. On his poor memory: Priuli, 4:332. On convents: Priuli, 4:369; cf. 2:115. On Priuli's intemperate character, cf. Sanuto, 24:492, 630; 27:260.

pages represent final drafts, not his original notes. On occasion he predicts the outcome of an event or a policy well after it was evident—antedated entries that particularly highlight his self-righteous character and concern for accuracy. To be fair to Priuli, he was acutely aware of the faults of his work. He knew that many of the rumors he recorded were mere "packs of lies," and he urges future readers to ignore whatever they find displeasing or improbable. Although intending to revise the diary to correct error and eliminate repetition, he ingenuously notes that it is far preferable to write something with flaws than not to write at all. Moreover, those who consult the diary "only have the labor of reading, while I had the work of writing, which is much greater."[17]

Marino Sanuto (1466–1536) kept his *Diarii* from January 1496 to June 1533. The text, in fifty-eight volumes and forty thousand pages, is an immense source book of political, social, and economic history from which Sanuto intended one day to write a history of Venice. It includes synopses of government documents, transcripts and summaries of private letters, accounts of debates and elections, notes on life in Venice, and reports on happenings from Persia to Greenland. It combines aspects of a newsletter, a society column, a political digest, and a stock report. The labor involved in compiling the diary was tremendous, especially when one considers that Sanuto attended the Ducal Palace almost every day and was engaged for years in writing his massive *Vite dei dogi*, "the final basin where so many of the earlier streams of Venetian historiography eventually merged."[18] He was, however, an undiscriminating collector of facts and could not construct a coherent, extended narrative. His discourse on Venice, the *Cronachetta*, is essentially a list of noteworthy sights and government offices. In his history of Charles VIII's invasion of Italy, amid an account of Venice's hectic preparation for war, he pauses to note that three whales had been sighted off Venice, the first in twenty-five years.[19] As his history of the doges nears his own time, miscellaneous

---

17 On recording rumor: Priuli, 2:112, 268. On having an office at the Rialto: Sanuto, 24:492. On being a merchant: Priuli, 2:117, 396. On seeing things at firsthand: Priuli, 2:19. On the number of patricians in Padua: Priuli, 4:280, 296, 412. On recopying pages: Priuli, 2:396. On predictions and premonitions: Priuli, 1:116, 167; 2:313. On rumor as lies: Priuli, 2:397. On his intention to correct errors and his desire to write: Priuli, 2:200. On the labor of reading: Priuli, 4:95.

18 Hans Baron, "Early Renaissance Venetian Chronicles," p. 191.

19 Marino Sanuto, *La spedizione di Carlo VIII in Italia*, pp. 331–332; cf. Guglielmo Berchet's preface, Sanuto, 1:35.

information overwhelms his theme until one has, inevitably, a diary. Although Sanuto regretted that he never produced the history of Venice for which he accumulated so much material, his talents in fact found natural and fitting expression in the *Diarii*.[20]

Sanuto took notes on everything: sermons, festivals, lotteries, freak shows, processions, building projects, marriage feasts, murders, executions, plays, costumes, assaults, fires, bank failures, galley arrivals, market prices, foreign visitors, accidents, religious relics, weather, and the occasional earthquake. He was most interested in political affairs; and his diary is replete with accounts of elections, vote peddling, infighting, foreign policy, and state administration. He collected information from a variety of sources other than his personal observation. When Venice suffered a defeat at Brescia in 1512, Sanuto interviewed a soldier who had made his way to Venice from the battle. In 1515 he drew an account of the battle of Marignano from the courier who brought the good news to the Ducal Palace. He had a standing arrangement to copy letters sent to Venice by men abroad on private and public business. For example, a letter to Marcantonio Michiel from his brother describing the Venetian reconquest of Brescia in 1516 appears in the diary. Secondo Pesaro, an official in Dalmatia, wrote a long letter to Benedetto Guoro on his activities and appended an injunction to show the letter to Sanuto. When Pietro Bragadin, consul at Constantinople, was unable to complete reading his report to the Senate when he returned to Venice, Sanuto copied it in full, with additional information that Bragadin gave him.[21] Much of Sanuto's time at the Rialto and the Ducal Palace must have been spent buttonholing patricians for their letters and personal accounts; it was probably something of an honor to have one's private correspondence included in his well-known volumes.

In addition, Sanuto transcribed official documents of the Senate. Indeed, some judicial records now in the Venetian archives are in his hand. Twenty-two years after beginning his diary, he obtained permission to examine, and in some cases copy, material in the archives of the Ten. On occasion his records proved to be better than the government's. He was able to provide state secretaries with a copy of a law they could not find in the archives. When the Rialto burned in

---

20 Chapter V.2. deals with Sanuto's background, career, opinions, and the motivations behind his keeping a diary for thirty-seven years.

21 On the soldier from Brescia: 13:514–518. On the courier from Marignano: 21:111, 116–117. On Michiel: 23:248–250. On Pesaro: 18:361. On Bragadin: 41:524–534, 534–535.

1514, he presented the tax officials with abundant copies of their destroyed records—an act that may not have endeared him to his fellow citizens. Somewhat later he cited a legal precedent regarding an election to the Signoria, the documentary source for which had been lost by fire in the archives. In 1531, when a legal procedure was at issue, he gave Doge Andrea Gritti a detailed written report of trials held in the Great Council in 1500 and 1510, boasting to himself in the *Diarii* that his account was more complete than that found in the chancellery. Sanuto also apparently referred to his diary to prepare for debate in the Senate or Great Council. Few patricians had so thorough a command of the law, and none had so formidable a source available.[22]

Sanuto's reliability must be judged according to the different types of material he recorded. When his synopses of government documents have been checked against archival records, they have been found to be faithful and fair, nothwithstanding occasional minor inaccuracies and omissions.[23] Moreover, he records copies or extracts of official letters and dispatches no longer extant and lists a large number of elections not in archival sources.[24] The private correspondence he copied has been entirely lost, but it seems a reasonable assumption that he was as faithful with these as with official documents. Doubt about his reliability increases when the realm of documents is left behind. Reporting council debates and political conflicts, he probably emphasized the views he supported, favoring the opinions of those with whom he was friendly or with whom he agreed. When friends were disgraced, he is clearly prejudiced and tends to discount either the seriousness or the validity of the charges against them.

In general, Sanuto is most untrustworthy in two matters. First, he exaggerated his own importance. He liked to imagine himself as a courageous defender of republican liberty; and when concerned over an issue, he was no less sparing of his opponents, if less verbose, than was Priuli. In all likelihood, most of his contemporaries regarded Sanuto as an indiscreet troublemaker, overly rigid in principle and

22 On judicial records in Sanuto's hand: Andrea da Mosto, *L'Archivio di Stato di Venezia*, 1:24, 64, 220. On permission to use the Ten's documents: Sanuto, 20:532; cf. 31:383. On finding a law for the secretaries: Sanuto, 23:301. On the tax records: Sanuto, 17:527. On the copy of a document lost in a fire: Sanuto, 23:495. On the trials in the Great Council: Sanuto, 55:211, 214. On using the diary in debate: cf. Sanuto, 42:718–719.

23 This view, confirmed by personal experience, is shared also by Pullan (*Rich and Poor*, p. 643) and Gaetano Cozzi ("Marin Sanudo il Giovane," p. 353).

24 Philip M. Giraldi, "The Zen Family (1500–1550)," p. 53.

obstreperous in character. Second, Sanuto's diary was not a secret enterprise, so he suppressed events that seriously embarrassed the government, which was very sensitive about its reputation. He was at pains to advertise his labor, and important visitors to Venice often asked to examine his volumes. One tourist wished to see the buildings of the Arsenal, the jewels of San Marco, and the library of Sanuto.[25] In 1530 the diary even assumed a quasi-official character when the Council of Ten gave Sanuto a pension to continue it. Ironically, for all the material that he collected, the greatest flaw in his diary is what he left out of it. When placards condemning the government were posted in the city, Sanuto makes no mention of them. When rumors circulated that a new law against sodomy was part of a political vendetta, he does not report them. When a mercenary general was openly insubordinate to the government, hardly an echo of his actions appears in the diary. Similarly, he does not record a call for rebellion against the ruling class to the people of Venice in 1511.[26] Such a list could be extended at some length. Although the *Diarii* are an incomparable source for the history of Venice during the Renaissance, they were shaped by obvious restraints and prejudices. A study of politics based principally on the diaries cannot pretend to flawlessness, even if a coherent and animated portrait of the Republic may be drawn from them. One finally must take refuge in Priuli's justification that it is better to proceed despite flaws than not to proceed at all.

---

25 Rawdon Brown, *Ragguagli sulla vita e sulle opere di Marin Sanuto*, 2:65; cf. Sanuto 53:173.

26 On the placards: Priuli, vol. 5, fol. 77v. On the rumors: Michiel, fol. 255r. On the mercenary general, Bartolomeo Alviano: Michiel, fols. 152r, 166r–167r. On Maximilian's call for rebellion: Antonio Bonardi, "Venezia città libera dell'Impero nell'immaginazione di Massimiliano I d'Asburgo."

Chapter I

Reality and Myth in Renaissance Venice

1. *The City*

Marino Sanuto left his home about the same time every morning. His modest palace lay in the Santa Croce *sestiere* of Venice, not far from the Grand Canal and around the corner from the church of San Giacomo dall'Orio. A short distance from his home were the granaries of the city, as well as a magnificent palace, the *Casa del duca di Ferrara*, in which visiting dignitaries were lodged by the Republic. These important buildings brought the out-of-the-way neighborhood of San Giacomo into some contact with the commercial and political life of Venice. But for firsthand news, Sanuto had to go to the Piazza di San Marco, where his fellow patricians congregated outside the Ducal Palace, the political center of Venice. There he could gather the most important notes for the immense diary he kept from 1496 to 1533. Everything interested him: electoral competition, political squabbles, casual gossip, council debates, marriages and deaths, public and private eccentricities. As inquisitive as he was tireless, Sanuto thus earned for himself a historical importance far greater than that he enjoyed in his own time.[1]

On his way to San Marco, Sanuto passed through the Rialto, the

1 For information on everyday life in Venice, some of it drawn from Sanuto, see Pompeo Molmenti, *La storia di Venezia nella vita private*. Guglielmo Berchet's preface to Sanuto's *Diarii* and Rawdon Brown's compilation of notices from the *Diarii* (*Ragguagli sulla vita e sulle opere di Marin Sanuto*) contain much information on Sanuto.

commercial center of the city, about a ten-minute walk from San Giacomo dall'Orio. The marketplace was at the western foot of the shop-lined Rialto bridge, a fifteenth-century wooden structure whose decrepit state was a cause for concern. The Rialto was crowded with vendors, pawnbrokers, and merchants. Tables of bankers packed the portico of San Giacomo di Rialto, considered the oldest church in Venice, where an ancient inscription exhorted merchants to be honest and faithful in their bargaining. Involvement in commerce was a hallmark of Venetian patricians, who, as a commoner complained in 1553, were not above using their status to gain an advantage in business negotiations: "Note well, when you have to do with noblemen, how we are treated and how they haggle." A Milanese priest shared this impression: "For the most part they are tall, handsome men, astute and very subtle in their dealings, and whoever has to do business with them must keep his eyes and ears well open."[2] Whether honest or not, the merchants apparently did their bargaining in hushed voices, for an observer in 1500 was surprised that those in the marketplace were so quiet and restrained, so little given to boisterous display.[3] The affairs of international trade and finance may have been conducted in an atmosphere of restraint, but others could not afford to stand on their dignity. Bankers and merchants aside, the Rialto was thronged with the poor, who comprised as much as a third of the city's population, from beggars and itinerant peddlers to street sweepers and water sellers. There was also a huge number of prostitutes in Venice, about one for every ten persons. A quick count of the population in June 1509 revealed that there were more than eleven thousand prostitutes, an occupation recently swollen by war on the mainland but still, as Girolamo Priuli remarked, "It seems to me a truly large number, and one can scarcely believe it."[4]

Sanuto held partial ownership of the Campana, a hostelery and tavern with two shops on the ground floor, in a prime location at the Rialto. Although not actively engaged in running the family business, Sanuto did represent its interests to the government when higher taxes were being levied on wine sales.[5] The property provided enough

2 Ugo Tucci, "The Psychology of the Venetian Merchant in the Sixteenth Century," in *Renaissance Venice*, ed. J. R. Hale (Totowa, N.J., 1973), p. 360; M. Margaret Newett, *Canon Pietro Casola's Pilgrimage to Jerusalem in the Year 1494*, pp. 142–143.

3 M. A. Sabellico, *Del sito di Venezia città*, p. 17.

4 Priuli, 4:91; cf. Sanuto, 8:414.

5 Sanuto, 13:458; 18:147, 185.

income to allow him to devote his time to politics and writing. After looking in on the Campana, Sanuto would join his fellow patricians in the loggia at the base of the bridge, where they gossiped, conducted affairs, and heard the government proclamations read from the stone column in the church square known as the "Rialto hunchback" (*Gobbo di Rialto*). On occasion an anonymous placard would appear there, slandering an important patrician, complaining about taxes, or even casting doubt on the nobility of Venice's rulers; and Sanuto would note it for his diary.[6] Near the loggia were government offices for trade and navigation, facing the German warehouse (*Fondaco dei Tedeschi*) across the Grand Canal. Tax and customs magistrates had their offices at the Rialto in palaces built in the 1520s; the treasury office (*Camera dei Camerlenghi*) also housed a prison on its ground floor. Patricians seeking office came to the Rialto to solicit votes amid the barges, fish stalls, and drapers' shops; the business of buying and selling provided cover for what was, after all, illicit activity.

With its mixture of trade, finance, and politics, the Rialto was the busiest part of Venice, surpassing San Marco in its diversity and tempo. Perhaps because they were removed from immediate super-vision by the Ducal Palace, the government officials who worked at the Rialto were especially fond of their locations. After the disastrous Rialto fire on January 1514 (only the church escaped destruction), when some insisted that the Rialto magistracies should be transferred to San Marco, "the universal affection for the place prevailed, and the [officials at the Rialto] wished to continue their public and private affairs amid the ruins rather than leave so precipitately."[7]

The walk from the Rialto to the Piazza di San Marco runs along the narrow and twisting street of the Mercerie, dominated by shops dealing in exotic and expensive items that testified to Venice's role as the principal entrepôt between Europe and the Levant. Canon Pietro Casola, a pilgrim on his way to the Holy Land, marveled at the goods available: "And who could count the many shops so well furnished that they also seem warehouses, with so many cloths of every make—tapestry, brocades and hangings of every design, carpets of every sort, camlets of every color and texture, silks of every kind; and so many warehouses full of spices, groceries, and drugs, and so much beautiful white wax!" The shopkeepers of the Mercerie and the traders of the Rialto prospered or failed according to events in Arabia and India. In

6 Sanuto, 45:333; 56:78; 57:247, 288.
7 Michiel, fol. 104r.

1519 a Venetian patrician wrote to his father from Egypt: "Things are not going very well because the prices of spices tend to rise in the East while at Venice they are on the decline, but the arrival of the caravan which is expected will bring everything to rights and the galleys will depart well laden." By the end of the Cinquecento, some four thousand Venetian families were said to be living in the Levant, maintaining the flow of goods back to their native city.[8]

Because of its prominence in international trade and its site in the lagoon, Venice was a cosmopolitan and fabulous place. Philippe de Commynes, French ambassador to Venice at the end of the fifteenth century, wrote, "It is the most triumphant city I have ever seen, does most honor to all ambassadors and strangers." Priuli agreed: "The city of Venice, to whomever lives here, appears to be a terrestrial paradise. . . . One can only say, '*non est vivere extra Venetiis.*'" Commynes, after his lavish praise, added the odd comment that "most of the people are foreigners," a statement echoed by Priuli in his observation that, except for the patricians and some citizens (*cittadini*), "all the rest are foreigners and very few are Venetians."[9] These impressions undoubtedly reflect the perspective of the writers, for, as ambassador and banker respectively, they spent most of their time in the centers of the city. Their notion that the majority of Venetian inhabitants—numbering some one hundred thousand in the early Cinquecento—were foreigners is comprehensible, for they often must have been surrounded by people not speaking the sibilant Venetian dialect.[10]

Indeed, Venice boasted large colonies of foreigners, especially Germans, Greeks, Jews, Flemings, French, Slavs, and mainland Italians. Foreigners ran many of the shops at the Rialto and on the Mercerie. Traders from north of the Alps, especially the south German cities, and from Italy, especially Milan, bought the Eastern goods carried to the city in Venetian galley convoys. Immigrants brought a wide range of skills, as well as some social movement, to their adopted city.[11]

8 On Casola's statement: Newett, *Canon Pietro Casola*, p. 129. On the 1519 letter: Tucci, "Psychology of the Venetian Merchant," p. 358. On Venetian families in the Levant: Ugo Tucci, "Mercanti Veneziani in India alla fine del secolo XVI," in *Studi in onore di Armando Sapori* (Milan, 1957), 2:1089–1111. On news of the East in Venice: M. Nallino, "L'Egitto dalla morte di Qā'it Bay all'avvento di Qānsūh al-Gūri (1496–1501) nei *Diarii* di Marino Sanuto."

9 Philippe de Commynes, *Mémoires*, 2:208–209, 213; Priuli, 4:101, 331.

10 On Venice's population: Frederic C. Lane, *Andrea Barbarigo, Merchant of Venice, 1418–1419*, p. 14. On keeping track of foreigners: ASV, Consiglio di Dieci, Parti Secrete, Reg. 5, fols. 147r–148r.

11 Stephen Ell, "Citizenship and Immigration in Venice, 1305 to 1500."

Germans were housed and did their trading in "a sort of miniature Germany" at the *Fondaco dei Tedeschi,* a huge building maintained by the government and decorated with frescoes by Giorgione and Titian. "The Germans living in Venice," Priuli emphasizes, "all have wives and children and are destined to die in Venice; they love the city of Venice more than their native land." Greeks in Venice may have numbered almost eight thousand by 1494, when they were allowed to draw up a constitution for their community. They congregated in the *sestiere* of Castello, near the Riva degli Schiavoni, where they had their own church and fraternal society. Albanians, Slavs, and Armenians also lived in particular neighborhoods, although without the internal cohesion enjoyed by the Greeks. From 1516 Jews had their own quarter in the district of Cannaregio, the Ghetto Nuovo ("New Foundry"), where they were locked in at night at their own expense.[12] A colony of Turks, later installed in the *Casa del duca di Ferrara,* may have made possible the school for teaching Arabic that Sanuto saw when passing along the Mercerie in October 1517.[13]

At the end of the Mercerie, the entrance to the Piazza di San Marco is marked by the Clock Tower (*Torre dell'Orologio*), built in the first decade of the Cinquecento as part of major renovations in the civic center. During Sanuto's lifetime, numerous improvements were visible throughout the city. Beginning in the 1480s, bridges were rebuilt in stone, alleys paved, canals excavated, and palaces increasingly faced with brick and stone. (Sanuto approved of the project to widen the streets, but he thought replacing wood with marble was often ostentatious.)[14] The eastern facade of the Ducal Palace was restored after a fire in 1483. In 1505, the same year in which the Clock Tower was completed, three bronze standards were erected in front of the Basilica di San Marco. Along the north side of the piazza, the *Procuratie Vecchie* was wholly rebuilt after a fire in 1512. The immense bell tower, or Campanile, was restored in 1513; Sanuto saw it crowned

12 On the "miniature Germany": Fernand Braudel, *The Mediterranean and the Mediterranean World in the Age of Philip II,* 1:209. On German love for Venice: Priuli, 4:148. On the Greeks: Deno John Geanakoplos, *Greek Scholars in Venice;* Giorgio Fedalto, *Ricerche storiche sulla posizione giuridica ed ecclesiatica dei Greci a Venezia nei secoli XV e XVI.* On the Flemings: Wilfred Brulez, *Marchands Flamands à Venise, 1568–1605.* On the Jews: Brian Pullan, *Rich and Poor in Renaissance Venice,* pp. 476–482; and Frederic C. Lane, *Venice,* pp. 300–302.

13 Sanuto, 25:20. On Turks in Venice: Paolo Preto, *Venezia e i Turchi,* pp. 126–137.

14 Marino Sanuto, *Cronachetta,* pp. 23, 31; Sanuto, 55:435; Malipiero, 2:683.

by a statue of a golden angel, while trumpets blared and wine and milk were exuberantly poured from the top.[15]

The piazza in Sanuto's time is best known from Gentile Bellini's late fifteenth-century painting of the *Procession in the Piazza di San Marco*, in which magistrates and members of religious fraternities (*Scuole*) parade around the square in orderly ranks. This is misleading. Most of the time, San Marco was as bustling and commercial as the Rialto. Money-changing booths clustered at the base of the Campanile, and a butcher's shop was nearby. Cheese shops fronted the lagoon side of the Mint (*Zecca*). Run-down huts housed vegetable stalls on the southern side of the piazza. Herbs were sold in the piazzetta, the extension of the piazza toward the harbor. Notaries worked in the arcades of the Ducal Palace, where latrines also rimmed the massive columns. Peasants wandered about hawking hair hung on long poles, stuff for the wigs of patrician women. Freaks were exhibited in front of the basilica; beggars, showing sores and mutilations, were everywhere. Criminals were hung in cages from the Campanile, and beheadings were carried out between the columns on the piazzetta. In 1531, Jacopo Sansovino, the government's architect, suggested clearing the vendors from the piazza to create a vista in keeping with the beauty of the surrounding buildings.[16] His proposal was ignored. The piazza did not become merely a proscenium for ceremonies staged by the government; it remained a place of business and disorderly display.

On special occasions jousts were held in the piazza—an exotic entertainment, for few Venetians owned or knew how to ride a horse. On Fat Thursday (*Giovedì Grasso*) in 1519, Sanuto and a large crowd watched a raucous parade of the butchers' guild, followed by their traditional pig hunt in the piazza. When an earthquake struck Venice in 1511, bells rang in the swaying Campanile, and the city was terrified; the devotional processions called up to appease divine anger were probably not as calm and stately as Bellini's *Procession*.[17] To celebrate a victory, bonfires were lit in the Campanile and the piazza, where crowds also gathered when news of a defeat filtered out of the Ducal Palace. Sanuto claims that over sixty thousand people jostled into the piazza in 1495 when an alliance against France was proclaimed. An-

15 Sanuto, 6:214–215; 15:541; 16:467.
16 Deborah Howard, *Jacopo Sansovino*, pp. 13–14.
17 On horses in Venice: Priuli, 4:339. On the pig hunt: Sanuto, 27:12. On the earthquake: Sanuto, 12:80, 84–85; Priuli, vol. 6, fol. 129v. On public celebrations in Venice: Bianca Tamassia Mazzarotto, *Le feste veneziane*.

other anti-French alliance in 1511 was celebrated with a sumptuous five-hour parade of the *Scuole* and clergy past the basilica and Ducal Palace, which were covered with tapestries and gold cloth. On display were hundreds of silver vessels and enormous gilded candles; children dressed as angels; effigies of Spain, England, and the pope; poems praising their Holy League; satires on the French monarch; floats depicting the cardinal virtues; women dressed as Justice; pantomimes of Saint Mark speaking with Christ, the Virgin, and Justice; as well as numerous relics: the hand of Saint Theodosia, the foot of Saint Lorenzo, the arm of Saint George, and the newly discovered head of Saint Ursula.[18]

Prestige and honor were at stake in these spectacles; violence, sometimes just beneath the surface. A *Scuole* procession in 1513 was marred by a fight between fraternities over which had precedence entering the piazza. When the doge, as the newly elected head of state, was carried around the piazza, the mob fought for the money he flung to them; order was kept by workers from the Arsenal armed with hefty staves. On Antonio Grimani's election in 1521, Sanuto watched his excursion through the piazza: "One of those from the Arsenal hit a foreigner in order to make room, so he struck off [the guard's] head, saying, 'Now go and beat with your cudgel!'" The intemperate foreigner was captured and shortly after lost his own head on the piazzetta. Strangers in Venice had to learn Venetian ways.[19]

The smallest bell in the Campanile, called the *Maleficio*, announced that an execution was imminent, although often the discovery of a body on the piazzetta early in the morning was the only signal that the Council of Ten, the special council for state security, had executed its justice.[20] The bells of the Campanile also had the more mundane task of calling the patricians of Venice to assemble. The *dei Pregadi* summoned the Senate (*Consiglio dei Pregadi*), the central council of debate and decision, which met in the afternoon three or four times a week. Runners shouting "Pregadi per la terra" were also sent around the city to announce meetings to the approximately three hundred men who had the right to attend.[21] The *Marangona*, the largest bell, announced the Sunday meetings of the Great Council (*Maggior Consiglio*), the sovereign assembly, to which all male patri-

18 On 1495: Marino Sanuto, *La spedizione di Carlo VIII in Italia*, pp. 299–301; cf. Sanuto, 21:111, 123–124. On 1511: Sanuto, 13:132–141.

19 On 1513: ASV, Consiglio di Dieci, Parti Miste, Reg. 35, fols. 160v–161v. On 1521: Sanuto, 31:5; cf. Priuli, 4:101, 385.

20 Cf. Sanuto, 1:917–918.

21 Priuli, 4:104.

cians belonged. The *Trottiera*, a sharper bell, hurried laggard patricians along. The only sizable assembly not to be called by bells was the Court of the Forty (*Quarantia criminal*), the supreme appeals court for criminal cases. Because this body met every weekday morning and Saturday afternoon, and was also part of the Senate, the judges of the Forty did not need a reminder to assemble. Additionally, the judges of the Forty received a salary, a substantial inducement to promptness and regularity of attendance.[22]

The Forty, then, generally had its full complement of members, but the same was not true of the larger councils. Only about 180 of 300 men habitually attended the Senate, and only 70 were needed for a quorum. Of about twenty-five hundred eligible members—and a required quorum of six hundred—the Great Council usually had from one thousand to fourteen hundred in its chamber, although certain issues or elections drew several hundred more.[23] There was always a large number of patricians out of Venice on public or private business. Administration of Venice's mainland empire (*stato di terraferma*), stretching from the Adda river to the Adriatic, occupied about 150 patrician officials; the maritime empire (*stato di mar*), along the Adriatic and in the eastern Mediterranean, took almost as many.[24] Patricians were resident merchants in the great trading cities of Europe and the Levant. Sanuto, however, rarely left Venice; and except for illness, he never missed sessions of the Great Council. Still, there were patricians who remained in the city and never ventured to the Ducal Palace. In 1527 Sanuto counted forty-six patricians in the Great Council who had not been there for twenty years; and in 1509, when twelve hundred men were present, he notes that "of more than 2,000 patricians in the city who may come to the Great Council, some have never attended."[25] This aversion to politics was shared by Priuli, who, as he boasted in 1509, seldom attended the assemblies:

> It is most certain that I am of a very dignified family and of the most noble blood; my father, my uncle, and all of my relatives, including those by marriage, are very highly honored in the Republic. And

22 Sanuto, 32:426–427; idem, *Cronachetta*, pp. 138–139, 190–191. Francesco della Torre (?), "Relazione della Serenissima Republica di Venezia."

23 Sanuto, *Cronachetta*, p. 222; Sanuto, 42:562. Cf. James Cushman Davis, *The Decline of the Venetian Nobility as a Ruling Class*, p. 135.

24 Marino Sanuto, "Cronica di Marino Sanuto," MCC, MS. Cod. Cicogna, 969, no pagination; cf. Sanuto, 8:469–472.

25 Sanuto, 8:496; 45:560–561.

since I am rich, according to my rank and situation, I would not lack the honors and dignities due any other Venetian patrician. Yet my spirit has always been estranged and distant from such honors, and it has been ten years since I have been in the Great Council and other councils of the city.[26]

To be sure, Priuli was among the minority; most patricians had sufficient interest, leisure, need, or ambition to go to the Ducal Palace at least once a week. There they gravitated toward the small loggia, the Loggetta, at the base of the Campanile facing the Ducal Palace, which had been elegantly redesigned for them by Sansovino in 1537. Even more important was the stretch of the piazzetta alongside the Ducal Palace called the *piazza del broglio* or *brolo* ("orchard"), where patricians promenaded exchanging gossip, discussing elections, and soliciting votes. Apart from the hall of the Great Council, this was the central political exchange of Venice, and no doubt it was Sanuto's penultimate destination, when he left San Giacomo dall'Orio. According to a sixteenth-century rhyme, the *broglio* was the pond where a patrician, born to the lagoon, navigated the shoals of politics, gratifying this powerful man, sensing the temper of that one, whispering in this one's ear, tugging that one's robe.[27] On the *broglio* the powerful and the lowly staged a courtly pavane, exchanging favor for votes in precisely calculated measures of condescension and servility. An influential patrician could not afford to seem stiff backed; his bow had to be sufficiently low, an adequate tribute to the honor of his supposed peers. It was customary, at least in the early seventeenth century, to kiss the sleeves of others as a greeting.[28]

A politics of ceremony and simulation had to be learned if a patrician were to be successful in his pursuit of office. A man was eligible to enter the Great Council at the age of twenty-five, although most gained entrance a few years earlier—to fail to do so was to be classed among those known as "the sad ones" (*i tristi*). Every December 4, the Feast of Saint Barbara, about forty-five patricians at least twenty years old were selected by lot to enter the Great Council. In addition, twenty legal posts, called *avocati pizoli*, were available for patricians of at least twenty years. The office, though insignificant, provided an apprenticeship of sorts in Venetian law; and patricians were "happy to

26 Priuli, 4:38.
27 L. C. Borghi, "Del Broglio," pp. 3–8.
28 Peter Burke, *Venice and Amsterdam*, pp. 63, 68.

be elected, in order to go to the Great Council."[29] On the day that a young man was to enter the Great Council (his matriculation into the patriciate), he would hover at the edge of the *broglio* until an elder motioned him into the promenade. By this act the youngster was said to *entrar in broglio*.[30] He became part of a new world of favors and intrigue, deference and dependence. As a member of the sovereign assembly, he was the equal of all other patricians by virtue of his single vote; as a stroller on the *broglio*, he was at the bottom of the pecking order, expected to be respectful of the powerful, deferential to his elders, and obedient to his family's patriarch. A seventeenth-century tutor to Venetian patricians instructed young men at the *broglio* to divine the thoughts of others "in order to accommodate oneself the better to their humors."[31] The political novice was obliged to be attentive.

The young man entering public life was also wearing a unique costume for the first time. Patricians donned plain black robes or togas to attend the Ducal Palace, although most wore other and fancier clothing at home. These long robes, as well as the advanced age of leading politicians, gave Venetian patricians their characteristically restrained and stately demeanor. "Certainly," wrote Canon Casola in 1494, "it is a dress which inspires confidence and is very dignified. The wearers all seem to be doctors in law, and if a man should appear out of the house without his toga, he would be thought mad."[32] The robes were the political work clothes of the patriciate and were identified with its function as the ruling class of the Republic. A change of costume marked the line between public and private, duty and pleasure. A seventeenth-century patrician posted a sign at the entrance of his holiday retreat on the mainland: "You are off duty here; take off your robes."[33] Venetians evidently saw a significance in clothing beyond mere fashion: What one wore indicated, and perhaps influenced, one's character. Young patricians were not considered politically responsible, so their cavorting about the city in multicolored hose was regarded as appropriate to their immaturity, even if an unfortunate waste of money. Nor was it surprising when a quar-

---

29 Sanuto, *Cronachetta*, pp. 218, 221–222; Sanuto, 21:349.
30 Borghi, "Del Broglio," pp. 3–4.
31 Burke, *Venice and Amsterdam*, p. 64.
32 Newett, *Canon Pietro Casola*, p. 143; cf. Burke, *Venice and Amsterdam*, p. 63.
33 Burke, *Venice and Amsterdam*, p. 69.

relsome patrician appeared for a ceremony with his robe on askew.[34]

In 1525 the prospect of patricians dressing as women in order to sail with the doge's granddaughter on the state ship was alarming enough for the Council of Ten to forbid the transvestism. Likewise, the trimming of robes with ermine "in the ducal manner" was forbidden by law as a sign of overweening ambition. A passion for foreign finery, especially French, swept Venice (and Italy) in the early Cinquecento; government leaders and tradition-minded patricians were upset over what they considered a slur on Venetian values. The popularity of French costumes, it was thought, incited sexual appetite, destroyed marriage, harmed the economy, weakened the state, and presaged defeat and conquest. Legislation was passed in 1506 restricting this "evil and damnable habit," although Priuli predicted that the new law "will last a short time and will not be obeyed, as is the custom." He was right, and three years later during the war with France, he reports that "foreign dress reigns in this city, which in ancient times would have been disgraceful and shocking and not tolerated." The *habito ultramontano* was outlawed—one might almost say exorcised—and for a brief time Venetian patricians abandoned foreign fashion for their native styles, both private and public.[35]

Patrician regalia gave Venetian political ideals visible expression: The ruling class valued uniformity, solidarity, anonymity, tradition, dedication, frugality; it frowned on eccentricity, faction, self-interest, novelty, frivolity, ostentation. The robes were a statement of republicanism, patriotism, puritanism, and communality. They also served to emphasize the exclusivity of the patriciate as a closed, hereditary body. It was fitting that a patrician caste should wear a distinctive costume to set it off from the rest of the community, especially as Venice had so large a foreign population, and that the costume should be worn when the patriciate was fulfilling its essential function.[36] The caste status of the patriciate was defined by its political activity in the Great Council. To allow foreigners to enter elections was to impugn the integrity of the caste and the security of the state. However,

---

34 On the young men: Lionello Venturi, "Le Compagnie della Calza (sec. XV–XVI)." On the quarrelsome patrician: Sanuto, 56:242.

35 On men dressing as women: Sanuto, 37:470–471. On robes in the ducal manner: "Le vesti e maniche ducali" (103). On Venetian and foreign costume: Pompeo Molmenti, "La corruzione dei costumi veneziani nel Rinascimento." On the legislation of 1506: Priuli, 2:391; 399–400. On 1509: Priuli, 4:37, 39; Sanuto, 7:163.

36 Cf. Lane, *Venice*, p. 253.

Venice sometimes extended honorary membership in the Great Council to visiting dignitaries and to mainland subjects who had rendered extraordinary service to the Republic. In 1509 Girolamo Savorgnano of Friuli was given such an honor; but many patricians were shocked when he was subsequently elected to the Senate, whereupon he was immediately sent abroad on an errand by the Ten, "for he is of an alien land and not born in the salty water." In the mid-Cinquecento, an expert on fortifications thought that only Venetians could defend the city, "for considering men born on the *terraferma*, who have never been in the lagoon, it would seem to them, seeing only water and sky, that they had entered a new world." Francesco Barbaro, a Quattrocento humanist, stressed the same point when he wrote that patricians are the "walls" of the city.[37]

Only those born to the patriciate and "the salty water" were eligible to elect and be elected. It follows that to lose the right to engage in electoral activity was effectively to be deprived of nobility, to be evicted from the caste, as Priuli asserted in 1503 when patrician state debtors were turned away in the Great Council. Moreover, for the city of Venice to be conquered, as was feared in 1509 and 1513, meant the death of the patriciate; that is, the doors of the Great Council would be shut and patricians would be dispersed and ruined, facing "an exile worse than that of the Jews."[38] Patricians had no doubt that the lagoon, "the walls of the city," preserved their political order as well as their state. In September 1513 Sanuto climbed the bell tower in the piazza to see the ravages of enemy forces at Lisa Fusina (he reports that the sun was "so red it seemed bloody because of the smoke of so many fires"); and he joined a crowd at Cannaregio, the district closest to the mainland, to watch the white-clad enemy cavalry burn Mestre. Despite such extremities, Sanuto complains, patricians did not cease haggling over offices and elections.[39] But even if they could be complacent about enemy troops on the mainland, their concern for the lagoon was constant. Preventing the lagoon from being filled in, a task the Ten took charge of in 1501, "was an enterprise of the very greatest importance for the benefit of Venetian liberty and

37 On Savorgnano: Priuli, 4:418; 370–371; Sanuto, 9:256, 257, 259, 265, 266, 269, 276. On defending the lagoon: Michiel di San Michiel's report, ASV, Consiglio di Dieci, Parti Secrete, Reg. 5, fol. 95r. On Barbaro: Margaret Leah King, "Caldiera and the Barbaros on marriage and the family," p. 33.

38 On 1503: Priuli, 2:325; ASV, Senato, Terra, Reg. 18, fol. 186v. On the prospect of conquest: Priuli, 4:135.

39 Sanuto, 17:103, 105, 113.

the welfare of the Venetian Republic."[40] The oddity of the city's site
—"surrounded by water yet needing to buy water," as Sanuto put it—
made possible a unique political system, in particular, rule by a patrician caste.[41] Venetian insularity, both geographic and political, was
epitomized by the black robes of the ruling class.

Within the patriciate, further political distinctions were expressed
through costume. Members of the Signoria (the ducal council that
represented the Republic) wore scarlet robes, as did those on the Ten;
senators wore purple, and members of the Collegio (the steering
committee or executive council of the Senate) wore violet or blue,
depending on their rank in the council. The men who occupied the
twenty-eight key positions on the central executive councils of the
Ten, the Collegio, and the Signoria constituted part of the "governing
circle" of the ruling class, which numbered from one hundred to two
hundred individuals.[42] Venetians referred to the governing circle in
several ways: "the Fathers" (*Padri*), "the Great Ones" (*Grandi*), "Important men" (*Homeni di conto*), and the "First" (*Primi*), as in
i Primi di la terra ("the first ones of the city"). *Primi* moved from
council to council, changing their robes as they assumed different responsibilities. When not on one of the executive councils or in a post
outside the city, they were usually in the Senate; when not in the
Senate, they once more donned the anonymous black robes of the
ordinary patrician. The political regalia expressed an essential value of
the patriciate—that only election to office raised a man above his
fellows.

Of course, whatever the official values of the ruling class, political
realities were neither so simple nor so ideal. The *Primi* were almost
invariably *ricchi* ("rich ones"), who had the education, social standing, and resources to devote themselves full time to politics. Strengthened by marriage alliances and bolstered by patrician clienteles, they
dominated the *piazza del broglio* and had the favored seats in the
Loggetta. With money and influence, they dictated Venetian tax laws
and commercial policy. A rich patrician circulated through the executive councils, went on important diplomatic missions, served as a
general on land and sea, and represented the Republic in Padua,
Verona, and Vicenza. If he were fortunate, he would climax his career
by election as a procurator of San Marco, an influential lifetime post
that entitled him to a scarlet robe and rent-free lodging in the *Pro-*

---

40 Priuli, 2:169; 380–381.
41 Sanuto, *Cronachetta*, pp. 63–64; cf. p. 66.
42 Cf. Lane, *Venice*, p. 256.

curatie Nuove along the south side of the piazza. The doge, the only patrician allowed to wear cloth of gold, was almost always elected from among the nine procurators. By contrast, the ordinary patrician wore a black robe throughout his political life; and if he were "without money, influence, friends or relatives," he moved in a different political world from the great men of the city. He could vote against one of the *Primi* in the Great Council, perhaps temporarily discomfiting a powerful man; but in the daily political life of the city, in the business of seeking votes, making decisions and administering justice, the *Primi* ruled Venice. "Big fish," says Priuli, "eat the smaller."[43]

2. *The Myth*

The clash between reality and ideal in the Venetian Republic was epitomized in the juxtaposition of the *piazza del broglio* and the Ducal Palace. The *broglio* presented politics as it was: the jostling for position, the pursuit of ambition, the dispensation of favors, the petitioning for largesse. Naturally, these activities were not limited to the *broglio* but spilled into the Rialto, the piazza, the basilica, and the Ducal Palace. Sanuto frequently witnessed men soliciting votes in the courtyard of the palace and on the stairways to the council halls.[44] They chanted the names of their favorites, whispered entreaties and threats, made deals, exchanged money—and placed bets on the election results. Lobbying continued in the chamber of the Forty, in the Senate, and in the Great Council, where patricians moved from seat to seat with messages and gossip. If admonished to remain silent, they signaled to one another whom they supported or opposed. The men appointed to maintain order in the Great Council—the three heads (*capi*) of the Ten and two censors (*censori*)—had their hands full trying to keep more than one thousand patricians quiet and on their benches. The Signoria (comprising the doge, six ducal councillors, and the three heads of the Forty) presided over the Great Council but was usually helpless to stop the lobbying for votes. Little inclined to take action—after all, they or their relatives might be up for election that Sunday—they sat on the tribune at the head of the immense hall, a subdued frieze of color looking down on a bustling mass of black robes. The Great Council was a singular combination of electoral assembly, permanent convention, exclusive club, and job market. Patricians met together week after week, nominating, electing, and

43 Priuli, 4:36, 40.
44 Sanuto, 23:523, 489, 528, 530; 32:354.

competing with one another. Everyone knew everyone else, so contacts were easily kept and nominations for office traded across the years. Effectively, the *piazza del broglio* extended into the Ducal Palace. In fact, the Venetian term for lobbying or electioneering, and in its widest application, for corruption and intrigue, was *broglio*, from the promenade where so much of the city's political business was negotiated in blatant disregard for the laws and values of the Republic.[45]

In contrast to the reality of politics on the *broglio*, the Ducal Palace symbolized the Venetian state and politics in their ideal form and was decorated accordingly. The palace of the doge was identified in Venetian minds with the palace of Solomon, and the virtue that gave them a common bond was justice.[46] A statue of Venice as Justice gazes on the harbor of San Marco from the facade of the Ducal Palace; and another, seated on Solomon's lion throne, looks down on the *broglio*. Sculpted on the corner of the arcade near the Porta della Carta, the main entrance to the courtyard, is the Judgment of Solomon, representing the Old Law, with a statue of the archangel Gabriel announcing the New Law directly above. Gabriel was of special import because the city was thought to have been founded on Annunciation Day in 421; Venice, "the virgin city," received special protection from the Virgin. On the piazzetta corner of the palace, the archangel Michael, bringer of God's justice, is depicted above a sculpture of Adam and Eve. On the final exposed corner, across from a prison, the archangel Raphael stands above a scene of the Drunkenness of Noah. Taken together, the three corner sculptures present a complex theme of the relationship between divine wisdom and human frailty, God's justice and man's condition: The Venetian state, guided by the Old and New Law, exemplifies the virtues of justice (Michael), peace (Gabriel), and charity (Raphael). All three archangels appear over the Porta Media, the entrance from the Ducal Palace to the Basilica di San Marco, the doge's chapel.[47] Gabriel and Michael also have prominent places in Tintoretto's *Paradiso* (1590) on the tribune wall

---

45 On the meaning of *broglio*: Giuseppe Boerio, *Dizionario del dialetto veneziano*, p. 101. On the nature of vote seeking and political corruption, see this book, Chapter IV. 3.

46 David Rosand, "Titian's *Presentation of the Virgin in the Temple* and the Scuola della Carità," p. 78. For what follows on the iconographic program of the Ducal Palace, see S. Sinding-Larsen, *Christ in the Council Hall*.

47 Sinding-Larsen, *Christ in the Council Hall*, pp. 168–175; Otto Demus, *The Church of San Marco in Venice*, pp. 55–56.

of the Great Council. Gabriel, next to the Virgin, recalls the birth of Christ and of Venice; and Michael, at Christ's left, invokes justice. It was on the Feast of Saint Michael (September 29) that terms of office began and ended, for the archangel of justice presided over the rotation of offices and over the just distribution of power and honors.[48]

Around the walls of the Great Council were painted scenes of high points in Venetian history (the conquest of Constantinople in 1204, the victory over Genoa in 1381, the battle of Cadore in 1508), all displaying the Venetian state as dominant, its patricians as faithful servants. Overhead, the ceiling allegories depict Venice triumphant over enemies; Venice resplendent amid Peace, Honor, and Security; Venice bestowing fruits on a grateful people; Venice ruling by law and justice. Patricians leaving office commissioned paintings to commemorate their service; yet their memorials left as little room for individuality as did the grand murals of the Great Council. Magistrates are presented as servants of a political order of transcendental origin and divine inspiration: Censors and Salt Office administrators receive grace from the Holy Spirit; treasury officials sit at the feet of the Savior; Rialto tax officials are blessed by Christ.[49]

The message these votive paintings conveyed was an exposition in a minor key of the articulate and systematic scheme found in the sculpture and monumental canvases of the Ducal Palace. The state was conceived as a vessel of divine intention; the constitution, as a blessed amalgam of justice and liberty; the magistrates of government, as informed by celestial powers—an elevated scheme that implicitly transformed the nature of politics. In a conception of the body politic as a *corpus mysticum*, there was no place for self-interest, ambition, intrigue, and corruption. The iconography of the Ducal Palace, as well as the liturgy and ceremony of government, assumed the patricians of Venice to be devout, self-sacrificing, transparent, and anonymous. Such was the ideal of politics addressed to Sanuto and his peers as they walked from the *piazza del broglio* to the council chambers of the Ducal Palace.

The ideal and the reality of Venice—the Ducal Palace and the *broglio*—were potent forces both in Venetian history and in lasting conceptions of the Republic's political system. The Republic of Venice, asserted Priuli, was renowned for its riches, power, empire, and reputation.[50] Of these, only the last now survives. Modern histori-

---

48 Sinding-Larsen, *Christ in the Council Hall*, pp. 66–67.
49 Ibid., pp. 221–237; 218–219.
50 Priuli, 4:136.

ans have coined the term *the myth of Venice* to identify the cluster of notions that constitute the Republic's historical reputation.[51] The *mito di Venezia* has three principal aspects: religious, constitutional, and political. The basis of the myth was a conception of Venice's place within God's scheme for mankind: "Venice recognized itself from the first as a strange and mysterious creation—the fruit of a higher power than human ingenuity."[52] Venice was the first Christian republic, and as such it had a glory surpassing that of pagan Athens and Rome. For Venetians it was a commonplace that, "while the Athenians, Lacedemonians and Romans did not survive for more than 600 years, this Republic has lasted for more than 1,000, because it was built by Christians and inscribed with the most excellent laws in the name of Christ."[53]

The *santa repubblica*'s providential origins and destiny were popular themes for sermons in Venice, and at a Christmas service in the church of the Frari, Sanuto heard a preacher from Arezzo tell a huge crowd that Venice "was founded with the blood of martyrs during the time of the barbarous Attila, scourge of God, in order to maintain the Christian faith; and thus it will last for another 1,000 years."[54] Pietro Aretino played on the same theme in 1530 when he thanked Doge Andrea Gritti for giving him shelter from papal wrath:

> Therefore, illustrious Prince, gather up my devotion in a fold of your magnanimity, so that I may praise the nurse of all other cities and the mother chosen by God to bestow more glory upon the world, to soften our customs, to give man greater humanity, and to humble the proud, while pardoning those who err. These tasks are hers by right, as is that of opening the way to peace and putting an end to wars. No wonder the angels lead their dances and harmonize their choirs and display their splendors in the heavens above this city, so that, under the ordinance of her laws, Venice may endure far beyond the bounds ascribed by Nature.[55]

Of course, fulsome praise of this sort was expected from a professional such as Aretino, but the terms of his extravagant encomium were

51 Franco Gaeta, "Alcune considerazioni sul mito di Venezia"; Gina Fasoli, "Nascita di un mito."

52 Jacob Burckhardt, *The Civilizaton of the Renaissance in Italy*, p. 40.

53 Sanuto, 24:656; cf. 8.

54 Sanuto, 19:332; cf. 265, 286, 300, 324.

55 Pietro Aretino, *Aretino*, p. 66.

perfectly in keeping with the self-image of Venice as seen in the Ducal Palace.

In its origins the constitutional aspect of the myth arose from the religious. In an oration to Doge Gritti, the humanist Giangiorgio Trissino said that "anybody who starts considering attentively the marvelous constitution and the divine laws of this Republic, must conclude that they are not the fruit of human intellect but have been sent by God," who removed the disruptive popular element from the constitution and reconciled monarchical forces with aristocratic.[56] Inspired by God, Venetians displayed a moderate and selfless temperament manifested in a unique and well-balanced constitutional structure; this aspect of the myth was most fully elaborated by Gasparo Contarini in the early Cinquecento. Contarini, whose *De magistratibus et Republica Venetorum* did much to establish Venice's reputation in Europe, wrote that "our ancestors were concerned not with ambition and empty fame, but only with the good of their country and the common welfare. With incredible excellence of mind our ancestors founded a republic of such a sort that none like it has existed in the memory of man."[57]

Modeled on the harmonies of nature and of heaven, the Republic could not fail to endure; eternity made immortality possible. The Holy Republic thus assumed the aspect of an Aristotelian or Polybian polity, for classical models of republicanism were used to explain the workings of a constitution established with "the blood of martyrs." Humanists of the fifteenth and sixteenth centuries considered the Venetian state to be a mixture of monarchy (the doge), aristocracy (the Senate), and democracy (the Great Council), or a combination of democracy and oligarchy, or a classic aristocracy.[58] Whatever combination one chose, these ancient models served to explain the apparent immortality of Venice. With its perfect constitutional balance of powers or social groups, the Republic had arrested political decay, stepped outside of time.

The timeless equilibrium of the Republic was also seen as a consequence of the constitutional ordering of elections. As Contarini emphasized, the laws regulating electoral procedures were aimed at eliminating ambition and faction from public service. The complexity of those procedures (the way nominators and nominees were chosen,

56 Sinding-Larsen, *Christ in the Council Hall*, pp. 139–140, n. 3.
57 Gasparo Contarini, *La Republica e i Magistrati di Venezia*, pp. 10–11.
58 Felix Gilbert, "The Venetian Constitution in Florentine Political Thought," pp. 463–472.

the secret ballot and the element of hazard, the restrictions placed on
family participation) was supposed to sift special interests, whether
personal, familial, or factional, from competition for office. Rational
assessment of the civic welfare was to be the sole standard for the
distribution of honors. By its electoral regulations, Venice was thought
to have achieved constitutional immortality.[59]

Religious and constitutional aspects of the *mito di Venezia* were
explicitly held by Venetians; the political component was not so
articulated, although it was basic to Venetian self-perception. Briefly,
the political marvel of Venice, a consequence of providential guidance
and constitutional excellence, was that it had passed beyond a need for
conventional politics. A benevolent deity and constitutional ingenuity
conspired with the moderate character of patricians to create a republican order lacking the usual ingredients of political life: ambition,
faction, corruption, and violence. Self-interest, the source of grievous
sin, constitutional decay, and civic turmoil, was supposedly absent
from Venetian electoral activity and public administration. The myth
implicitly regarded the patriciate as a devoted civil service, wholly
subordinate to the needs of the state, disinterested, patriotic, and selfless. Venice's saintly and altruistic founding fathers were held up as a
model of virtue, as with Sanuto's claim that "they were not arrogant
nor did they esteem riches, although they were rich, but [only] piety
and innocence. They did not dress lavishly nor did they pursue honors,
but, satisfied and happy, they governed for the common good. There
were no disputes among them." As a result of this attitude toward
politics, Sanuto continues, Venice experienced neither sedition in the
populace nor discord within the ruling class: "All united to augment
[the Republic], so, according to wise men, it will last forever."[60] A
unique spirit of dedication and devotion meant that the Republic was
spared the violence and conflict that afflicted and ruined all other
states, thus accounting for the secret of Venice's success and the warrant for calling it *La Serenissima Repubblica*, the most serene republic:

> The city of Venice, to whoever lives here, appears to be a terrestrial
> paradise, without contentious uproar, fear of enemies . . . or turbu-
> lent spirits; this city has already maintained itself and thrived for so
> long a time, for centuries of quiet and peace, that whoever wishes to
> live in peace can find no place more serene than Venice . . . this
> city is free, without either divisions or factions . . . one can go about

59 J. G. A. Pocock, *The Machiavellian Moment*, pp. 284–285.
60 Sanuto, *Cronachetta*, p. 16.

one's affairs without offense or injury, for violence and injustice are absent . . . and for this reason the people multiply rapidly, and foreigners flock to live in this glorious city.[61]

The notion of *una terra libera* ("a free city") had powerful emotional appeal for Venetians. For Sanuto and his contemporaries, Venice was born in freedom, built by the hands of free Christians, and never subjected to an empire.[62] Others were free to seek the peace of Venice, boasts Priuli, for even during war, when Venetian forces were pushed back to the lagoon, "the city was open to foreigners, and all could come and go everywhere without any obstacle."[63] Sanuto was proud that foreigners could find objective justice in Venice, citing a case of the Forty declaring in favor of a Florentine: "The justice of Venetians is excellent, for notwithstanding some controversies with the Florentines, judgment was made against our patrician, a thing not otherwise done."[64] Although only patricians were free to vote and to make policy, the "freedom" of Venice was shared by all within the city. That was the gist of Doge Leonardo Loredan's argument in 1509 when he appealed to Venetian commoners to aid in the war: "The conservation of the Republic and of Venetian liberty touches not only the patriciate but the citizens [*cittadini*] and people [*populari*] as well, for all enjoy the benefits of the Republic. . . . and they could do as they pleased, without any tyranny or violence."[65]

Shortly before, Doge Loredan exhorted patricians to pay their taxes so Venice could prepare for war: "If we lose, we will lose a fine state; there will be no more Great Council, and we will no longer be born, as we are, in a free city."[66] A sight that astonished Philippe de Commynes in "the most triumphant city" was crowds of Venetians lined up to pay their taxes voluntarily; he noted that in other places it was difficult to collect a minimal amount, whereas in Venice the collector could not keep pace with payments.[67] Freedom to pay taxes was certainly no part of the conception of Venice as *una terra libera*; but the notion of selfless Venetians, commoners and patricians, enjoying freedom from conquest, monarchical rule, arbitrary justice, and violence

61 Priuli, 4:331.
62 Sanuto, *Cronachetta*, pp. 25–26.
63 Priuli, 4:385, cf. 62, 145, 273, 315; vol. 6, fol. 64v.
64 Sanuto, 1:496. Cf. Felix Gilbert, "Machiavelli e Venezia"; Stanley Chojnacki, "Crime, Punishment, and the Trecento Venetian State."
65 Priuli, 4:281.
66 Sanuto, 8:117.
67 Sanuto, *Spedizione di Carlo VIII*, p. 269.

was fundamental to the myth of Venice. In the context of the myth, those freedoms were only possible because politics itself had been exiled from the city, expelled from the "terrestrial paradise."

The myth of Venice was in part a product of state propaganda; officially appointed historians and panegyrists were expected to laud the Republic in its self-serving terms. But so rich a mythology did not flow solely from the needs and promptings of the state; nor did Venetians alone subscribe to significant aspects of the myth. In the fifteenth and sixteenth centuries, it attracted adherents in Italy, especially among Florentine political thinkers, and elsewhere in Europe. In the seventeenth century, the idea of Venetian constitutional excellence acquired a following among English Commonwealth writers.[68] The myth of Venice, especially its political dimension, answered a need and apparently explained a significant historical fact: that Venice had indeed enjoyed remarkable longevity and freedom from domestic turmoil.

By the sixteenth century, when the myth was fully formed, the Republic of Venice was regarded as ancient. Moreover, in contrast to other states, Venice had experienced no violent changes of power, no revolts from below, no bloody conflict within its ruling class. The myth also gained force from the anonymity of the patriciate. One need not agree that patricians selflessly devoted themselves to the state to conclude that they do not emerge from the sources as flesh-and-blood figures but remain, at all periods of Venetian history, faceless and anonymous. For whatever reason, the system triumphed over the individual. Venice was founded by flocks of refugees, achieved fortune through nameless merchants, and was ruled by an endless succession of committees. No great men, no traumatic political crisis, formed its historical memory; no legendary hero-legislator handed down the constitution to a grateful people.[69] Venice had Saint Mark, its patron; it had no Lycurgus or Pericles, Romulus or Caesar. Venetians who stood out from the patriciate usually did so by virtue of

---

68 Felix Gilbert, "Venetian Constitution"; Johannes Wild, "The Hall of the Great Council of Florence," pp. 92–93, 105, 114; Nicolai Rubinstein, "I primi anni del Consiglio Maggiore a Firenze (1494–99)," pp. 153–155; Giorgio Cadoni, "Libertà, republica e governo misto in Machiavelli"; G. Pampaloni, "Fermenti di riforme democratiche nella Firenze medicea del Quattrocento," pp. 45–50; Zera S. Fink, *The Classical Republicans*, pp. 28ff.; Nicola Matteucchi, "Machiavelli, Harrington, Montesquieu e gli 'ordini' di Venezia"; Renato Pecchioli, "Il 'mito' di Venezia e la crisi fiorentina intorno al 1500."

69 Pocock, *Machiavellian Moment*, pp. 187, 280.

running counter to their city's political ideals and were consequently regarded as villains: Doge Marino Falier, executed in 1355; Doge Francesco Foscari, deposed in 1457. What is a difficulty for the historian is, however, a matter of praise for a Venetian. Contarini asserts that Venetian anonymity is a consequence of the public spirit that pervades the ruling class:

> Our ancestors, from whom we received so flourishing a commonwealth, all united in a desire to establish, honor, and augment their country, without any regard for their own private glory or advantage. This is easy to conclude . . . for in Venice there are to be found few monuments to our ancestors, though at home and abroad they achieved many glorious things to the advantage of their homeland. There are no tombs, no statues, no naval spoils, no enemy flags, after so many great battles.[70]

Of course, not everyone regarded Venetians as god fearing, selfless, and incorruptible; and a Venetian countermyth sprang up to oppose Venice's idealization.[71] By the terms of this countermyth, Venice was considered tyrannical, imperialist, duplicitous, and cowardly. Venice's enemies found it convenient to sneer at the city's lowly origins amid mud and marsh. A common taunt was that Venetians, a pack of grubby merchants and moneylenders, would be forced back to their trade as fishers. Venetian expansion onto the mainland from the early Quattrocento gave impetus to the theme of Venetian imperialism and greed, a classic expression of which is found in the memoirs of Pope Pius II (d. 1464):

> They wish to appear Christians before the world but in reality they never think of God and, except for the state, which they regard as a deity, they hold nothing sacred, nothing holy. To a Venetian, that is just which is good for the state; that is pious which increases the empire. . . . They measure honor by the decree of the Senate, not by right reasoning. . . . you think your republic will last forever. It will not last forever nor for long. Your populace so wickedly gathered together will soon be scattered abroad. The offscourings of fishermen will be exterminated. A mad state cannot long stand.[72]

70 Contarini, *Republica*, pp. 10–11.
71 Brian Pullan, "Service to the Venetian State."
72 Pius II, *The Commentaries of Pius II*, pp. 301–304. On Venice's imperialist reputation: Nicolai Rubinstein, "Italian Reactions to Terraferma Expansion in the Fifteenth Century."

Louis Hélian, French ambassador to the Holy Roman Empire, addressing the Diet of Augsburg in 1510, conjured up a near-hysterical vision of Venice engulfing Europe: "Merchants of human blood, traitors of the Christian faith, they are secretly dividing the world with the Turks; they are thinking of flinging bridges across the Danube, Rhine, Seine, and Ebro; they wish to make Europe their province and hold it captive with their troops."[73] Francesco Vettori, a friend of Machiavelli, who himself had slight respect for Venice, attacked the patriciate:

> Regarding republics, the worst is Venice, which has lasted longer than other republics which we have noted. Is it not tyranny when three thousand patricians hold sway over one hundred thousand persons and when none of the common people can hope to become patricians? Against a patrician in civil cases, no justice can be expected; in criminal cases, the common people are wronged, patricians protected.[74]

In fact, Venetians were not so sanguine as to believe that they lived in the best of all worlds. In the early Cinquecento many of the virtues expressed in the myth of Venice were regarded as having been lost or abandoned in the recent past. Contarini wrote his influential book on the constitution at a time when many Venetians believed the Republic was in sharp decline; not surprisingly, his eulogy of the Venetian character centers on the founders of the state. Sanuto thought that his contemporaries had forsaken traditional virtues and customs, and he repeatedly castigated his fellow patricians as driven by selfishness and sunken in corruption.[75] Distraught over Venice's defeat in war, Priuli charged that the ruling class had failed the Republic, lowering its reputation and reducing it to the ruinous condition of other states. God, he believed, was punishing Venice for the ambition and corruption of its patriciate.[76] Even Pius II, who detested all things Venetian, apparently thought that Venice had only recently changed its character: "Within the memory of our fathers Venetian justice was rated very high. The state was held to be virtuous and temperate and devoted to religion. In our age all piety, all temperance, all regard for

73 Rinaldo Fulin, "Dell'attitudine di Venezia dinanzi ai grandi viaggi marittimi del secolo XV," p. 1470.

74 Francesco Vettori, *Sommario della historia d'Italia*, pp. 145–146.

75 Sanuto, *Cronachetta*, pp. 23, 30; Sanuto, 8:290–291; 11:686; 12:80.

76 Priuli, 2:31; 4:33–35; vol. 5, fol. 70r; vol. 6, fols. 128v–129v; cf. Luigi da Porto, *Lettere storiche dall'anno 1509 al 1528*, p. 26.

justice, has disappeared. In their place have come avarice, greed, ambition, envy, cruelty, lust, and all wickedness. With such a character you cannot stand. An empire built on evil foundations must crash."[77]

Clearly, the image of Venice in both its negative and positive versions was a complex affair. The enemies of Venice either turned the patriciate's supposed virtues, such as subordination to the state, back on themselves or argued that they were a thing of the past. On the other hand, Venetians praised their state extravagantly, although they tended to think of the past as a golden time, the present as one of corruption and decay. As Priuli indicates, Venice was still seen as receiving special consideration from God, but the deity had changed from a benevolent guardian to a stern taskmaster. In short, by the early Cinquecento, contrast between the myth and the reality of Venice was often perceived by patricians as a difference between past and present.

3. *The Government*

The daily government of the Republic evokes the same contrast between ideal and reality. Although often regarded as an exemplar of order and harmony, the Republic was characterized more by confusion and inefficiency. Naturally, Venetians were aware of this. Contarini confessed that when considering the complexities of his government, especially the innumerable restrictions placed on its officials, "We must often smile, for every prerogative and every authority is placed solely in the hands of councils, and no magistrate completely obtains extensive power for himself." His fond amusement at the intricacies of decision making in his city hints at the reality behind the myth of Venetian political excellence.[78]

"A Venetian law," says an early sixteenth-century proverb, "lasts but a week." Sanuto complained of his countrymen's "greediness to create offices," and Priuli thought it was in the nature of Venetians to be slow and disorderly in reaching decisions and taking actions.[79] Alberto Bolognetti, papal nuncio in Venice in the late 1570s, also concluded that long delays were intrinsic to Venetian deliberations, and his suggestion for solving the problem was nothing less than a *serrata*, a "closing" of the Great Council such as Venice experienced in 1297.

77 Pius II, *Commentaries of Pius II*, p. 304.
78 Contarini, *Republica*, p. 52.
79 On the proverb: Priuli, 4:115; cf. 2:431. On creating offices: Sanuto, 5:396. On Venetian slowness: Priuli, 2:13.

This, he calculated, would radically reduce the number of patricians who squabbled over public affairs. Doge Alvise Mocenigo told Bolognetti that he so often met resistance to his policies that he had taken to pretending the contrary of what he wanted in order to further his real purposes.[80] A generation later, Paolo Sarpi, Venice's ideologue in its battle with the papacy, noted the same combination of inertia and contention: "When an innovation is proposed, the whole Republic will certainly be opposed; but when something done ought to be undone, there will always be more in the council on the negative side than on the affirmative, and it will be said: let it go on, since it has begun." Sir Henry Wotton, Sarpi's friend and English ambassador to the Republic, observed that Venetians should have learned from their political troubles that "abundance of counsel, and curious deliberation, by which they subsist in time of peace, is as great a disadvantage in time of action." Wotton also agreed with Bolognetti that republics, which require "more hands than monarchies," are for that reason likely to encounter more difficulties.[81]

Venice's flaws were indissolubly linked to its virtues. The renowned stability and peace of Venice owed much to distrust of factionalism and to regard for the integrity of state authority. But those concerns also led to characteristics of government that made confusion and inefficiency all but inevitable: rapid rotation in office, diverse responsibilities within individual magistracies, dedication to collective decision making, a multitude of temporary commissions, overlapping competencies of councils, complex and lengthy voting procedures, and a consistent weakness of executive authority at almost all levels of government. Inefficiency, confusion, and bureaucratic conflict were prices that Venetian patricians were apparently willing to pay for maintaining their republican order. When faced with dilatoriness or unfairness in government and politics, Sanuto often said, in a tone between despair and pride, "It's the way things are done in republics," *siché le repubbliche fanno di queste.*[82] Bolognetti's criticisms were met by the boast of Marco Venier, the nuncio's greatest foe in the government,

80 Aldo Stella, *Chiesa e stato nelle relazioni dei nunzi pontifici a Venezia*, pp. 158, 165, 167, 170.
81 On Sarpi: William J. Bouwsma, *Venice and the Defense of Republican Liberty*, p. 104. On Wotton: Logan Pearsall Smith, *The Life and Letters of Sir Henry Wotton*, 2:228.
82 Sanuto, 22:172; 16:604; 24:705; 31:311; 54:622; 56:875; cf. Priuli, vol. 5, fol. 151v.

that Venetians "lived in a republic and not under an absolute prince."[83]

Venetians would have been surprised to see their government explained by tidy diagrams and orderly models. Venice's governmental structure is often neatly described as pyramidal in shape, with the Great Council as a base, the Senate in the middle tier, and the Signoria at the apex.[84] Yet such a model has little utility, at least for any time after the early Trecento. The base of the pyramid, the Great Council, was the fount of all offices and honors. It was the sovereign body of the state, but its unwieldy size meant that it could not deal with matters of government. Financial affairs and policy decisions never came before it, although proposed changes in offices and elections—matters of some moment to the patriciate—had to be approved by the assembly, and on rare occasions it sat as a court.

The Senate was the real locus of political power: "It is," wrote Sanuto, "the council which governs our state."[85] Any patrician with a claim to be one of the *Primi di la terra* had a seat in the Senate. Not everyone in the Senate can be considered a member of the governing circle, however, for the council was made up of distinct groups. Sixty regular senators were elected directly by the Great Council; the sixty of the Zonta ("addition") were nominated by the Senate and voted on by the Great Council; and the Court of the Forty (*Quarantia criminal*), elected by the Great Council, entered the Senate after sixteen months' service on two other courts of appeal. Around 140 men entered the Senate by virtue of their offices, although they could not vote and usually could only speak on matters of their own competence.[86]

The Collegio, the steering committee of the Senate, was crucial to the daily operations of the government. Wotton vividly described the Collegio as "that member of the state, where (as in the stomach) all

83 Aldo Stella, *Chiesa e stato*, p. 166. On the clash between Bolognetti and Venier in December 1579: "Memorie pubbliche della Repubblica di Venezia," fols. 62r–63v; Alvise Michiel, "Diarii, 1578–1586," MCC, MS. Cod. Sagredo, MSS. Prod. Div. 382-c, no pagination.

84 Donato Giannotti, *Libro de la Republica de Vinitiani*, p. 22; Davis, *Decline of the Venetian Nobility*, p. 21; Pullan, *Rich and Poor*, pp. 21, 24; D. S. Chambers, *The Imperial Age of Venice, 1380–1580*, p. 75, Bouwsma, *Defense of Republican Liberty*, p. 62.

85 Sanuto, *Cronachetta*, p. 104.

86 On the Senate: Enrico Besta, *Il Senato Veneziano (origine, costituzione, attribuzioni e riti)*. On the constitution: Giuseppe Maranini, *La costituzione di Venezia dopo la serrata del Maggior Consiglio*; A. Baschet, *Les archives de Venise*; Andrea da Mosto, *L'Archivio di Stato di Venezia*.

things are first digested."[87] It set the agenda of the Senate and supervised the execution of legislation. In both tasks it worked with the Signoria, thereby forming a single body known as the Full Collegio (*Pien Collegio*). The Collegio was composed of three ranks (*mani*) of *savi* or ministers: six *savi grandi* ("chief sages"), five *savi di terraferma* ("sages of the mainland"), and five *savi agli ordini* ("sages of the marine"). By the late Quattrocento, the post of *savio agli ordini* had become, in effect, a training position for younger patricians; and when the chiefs of the Ten entered the Collegio or Full Collegio, the *savi agli ordini* had to leave the meeting. The Signoria (or ducal council) fixed the agenda of the Great Council; otherwise, it only functioned by itself in a purely ceremonial role, as when it represented the Republic in welcoming foreign dignitaries. In its work with other councils, however, it entered deeply into the business of government; it presided over the Senate with the Collegio, formed part of the Full Collegio outside of the Senate, and was part of the Council of Ten. The Signoria included the doge (traditionally seen as the weakest individual in the governing circle), six ducal councillors, and the three heads of the Forty.

Finally, the Council of Ten cannot easily be placed within a pyramidal structure. In his dialogue on Venetian government, Donato Giannotti was reduced to considering the Ten an "annex" to the pyramid.[88] The Ten was made up of seventeen members: the doge, six ducal councillors (four of whom were needed for a quorum), and the ten proper. The heads of the Forty were excluded from the Signoria when the latter formed part of the Ten. Further, the Ten was often assisted in its deliberations by one or more *zonte* ("additions"), groups of from fifteen to twenty *Primi* selected by members of the Ten.

The Collegio, the Signoria, the Ten—collaboration between these councils was at the heart of Venetian government. Such a flexible system of councils merging with councils and patricians moving from council to council—the Collegio and Signoria in the Full Collegio, the Forty in the Senate, the heads of the Forty in the Signoria, the Signoria in the Ten, the Ten in the Senate, the Senate and the Forty in the Great Council—makes nonsense of the symmetrical order of the pyramidal model. Perhaps the relationship between the councils of government is better compared to the city of Venice itself, to the winding alleys and canals that always seem to bring the wanderer back

87 Smith, *Life and Letters*, 2:485.
88 Giannotti, *Libro de la Republica*, p. 22.

to a familiar *campo*, although seen from a different perspective and entered by a different approach—a maze whose order only emerges from observing the passage of others through it. A similar image of Venetian governance may have been behind Giovanni Botero's comment on Venice's serpentine waterways: "I believe that one of the main reasons for the peaceful condition of Venice is the canals which so intersect the city that its inhabitants can only meet together with difficulty and after much delay, during which their grievance is remedied."[89]

The model of a pyramid is valid for the later thirteenth century, before the formation of the patrician caste.[90] The General Assembly or *arengo*, a meeting of the people, was the sovereign body of government, called on to approve fundamental legislation and to acclaim a newly elected doge. The Great Council included about three hundred men: one hundred regular members selected by a nominating committee each year, one hundred ex officio members, the Court of the Forty, and the sixty of the Senate. The Forty was the most powerful body because it prepared legislation for the Great Council and had charge of political and financial affairs. The *Consilium Rogatorum* or *Consiglio dei Pregadi* ("Senate" was adopted under humanist influence in the fifteenth century) dealt with trade and international matters and was decidedly less important than the Forty, whose chiefs were on a par with the ducal councillors.[91]

This relatively uncomplicated structure was fundamentally altered by the most crucial event in Venetian political history, the *Serrata* ("Closing") of the Great Council in 1297.[92] By a series of legislative enactments beginning in 1297, the Great Council was transformed from an assembly of a few hundred men into a sovereign and closed corporation of over one thousand. All males over twenty-five years of age who could prove that they belonged to a family that had held a place in the Great Council in the four years before 1297 were admitted to the Great Council after being approved by twelve votes of the Forty. Within a generation, membership in the Great Council was permanent and a prerequisite for holding office. Thirty new families were admitted in 1382 as a reward for service in the War of Chioggia.

89 Quoted by J. R. Hale in the preface to *Renaissance Venice*, ed. J. R. Hale (Totowa, N.J., 1973), p. 14.

90 Lane, *Venice*, p. 96.

91 Lane, *Venice*, p. 96; da Mosto, *L'Archivio di Stato*, 1:63; Roberto Cessi, *Storia della Repubblica di Venezia*, 1:271.

92 Frederic C. Lane, "The Enlargement of the Great Council of Venice."

In 1403 a proposal to add a new commoner family to the Great Council whenever a patrician one died out was rejected. The Great Council had been changed from an elected assembly of temporary membership to an electoral assembly of hereditary membership. The patriciate had become a caste.[93]

The intention behind the *Serrata* was probably to still factional strife among patricians by giving each one with a legitimate claim a place in the Great Council. Although there were attempts to alter this settlement—most notably by Bajamonte Tiepolo in 1310 and by Doge Marino Falier in 1355—the political caste installed in the Great Council after 1297 remained the ruling class of the Republic until it voted itself out of existence, at Napoleon's behest, in 1797.

Other than the establishment of a hereditary patriciate, the most important result of the *Serrata* was to set in motion the final development of the Republic's political institutions. Between the *Serrata* and the Cinquecento, Venetian government underwent an extended accommodation to the displacement of the General Assembly by the Great Council, the most important result of which was the rise of the Senate to supremacy within the state. Early in the Trecento it became customary for the Forty to meet with the Senate, still primarily a consultative body. Gradually the Senate took over the nonjudicial responsibilities of the Forty, pushing the latter from its preeminence in government. In 1324 the Senate, which now subsumed the Forty, was declared "one body and one council."[94] The Senate assumed the functions of the pre-*Serrata* Great Council, just as the post-*Serrata* Great Council to some extent moved into the place of the General Assembly. Composition of the Senate came to be almost exactly that of the Great Council before 1297; and as late as 1403, the Signoria was still called the "collegio," a designation that soon was applied only to the *savi* of the Senate's executive committee.[95]

Venetian territorial expansion in mainland Italy in the early Quattrocento also gave impetus to the development of the Senate, for administration of the *terraferma* empire required a greater degree of internal articulation, an extensive definition of responsibilities and procedures, within the central governing assembly. By 1442 the Collegio was fully formed in the Senate, with *savi* supervising the daily

93 Lane, "Enlargement of the Great Council," pp. 241–242; cf. da Mosto, *Archivio di Stato*, 1:31.

94 da Mosto, *Archivio di Stato*, 1:63; Cessi, *Storia della Repubblica*, 1:273–274.

95 Maranini, *Costituzione di Venezia*, pp. 299, 327–328; cf. Besta, *Senato Veneziano*, pp. 43–44, 66.

business of government. The Zonta of the Senate was increased from forty to sixty members in 1450, although it was not made a permanent part of the Senate until as late as 1506. Between 1450 and 1520, ninety-six individual positions were added to the Senate from twenty-one offices, including all the important magistracies of the city.[96] These additions merely confirmed the preeminence the Senate had already attained by the mid-Quattrocento, for by that time the process set in motion by the *Serrata* was complete. In 1423 the Republic officially ceased to be called "commune" and adopted the title of "*dominio o signoria*,"[97] a change of terminology that may be seen as symbolically marking the beginning of Venice's final transition from a loosely organized medieval commune to a Renaissance bureaucratic state.

Born in 1466, Sanuto lived through a critical time in Venetian history. The constitution was fixed; it would change very little during the remaining centuries of the Republic's career. But Venetian politics, the current that gave vitality and animation to the constitutional machinery, was still in flux, still capable of altering the weight and meaning assigned by legal prescription. The peculiar genius of Venice, never more evident or more challenged than in the early Cinquecento, was the melding of a cumbersome constitution with a subtle and fluid politics to forge a stability that permitted change within an established tradition. Sanuto deplored many of the political changes of his age; but when he died in 1536, the republican order was intact and the liberties of Venice were preserved.

96 Maranini, *Constituzione di Venezia*, pp. 152–162; da Mosto, *Archivio di Stato*, 1:34–35; Besta, *Senato Veneziano*, pp. 43–44.

97 Andrea de Mosto, *I dogi di Venezia nella vita pubblica e privata*, p. xxxiii; Bouwsma, *Defense of Republican Liberty*, p. 61; Horatio Brown, *Studies in the History of Venice*, 2:45–46.

Chapter II

The Patriciate in
the Great Council

1. *The People and the Patriciate*

Creation of a patrician caste apparently sealed off the ruling class from the general populace. Whereas the General Assembly had provided a setting, however unruly and informal, for the *popolo* to express themselves on occasion, no such forum was available after the *Serrata;* and even vestiges of it were eliminated. It was traditional after a ducal election for the Signoria to present the victor to the people, announcing that "we have elected so-and-so as doge, if it pleases you." During the election of 1423, someone wondered, "If the people say 'No,' what then?" So the formula was shortened and henceforth the people were simply informed that "we have elected so-and-so as doge."[1] In his anti-Venetian polemic, Francesco Vettori asked the reasonable question, "Is it not tyranny when three thousand persons hold sway over one hundred thousand persons and when none of the common people can hope to become patricians?"[2] Some Venetians, especially the well-to-do among the commoners, must have resented their exclusion from the patriciate. No matter how wealthy they might become, how great their services to Venice, how many daughters they married to patricians, they could not hope to join the 2 percent of the population that had a right to enter the Great Council. Still, the no-

1 Marino Sanuto, "Cronica Sanuda," fol. 241r. This so-called Cronica is an accurate early seventeenth-century copy of part of Sanuto's *Vite dei dogi* and includes the period from 1423 to 1494; the Muratori edition (in *Rerum Italicarum Scriptores,* vol. 22, Milan, 1733) is very incomplete.

2 See Chapter I, n. 74.

tion of close cooperation between patriciate and people was not the self-serving fantasy of a tyrannical elite. There is every indication that the patriciate was very sensitive to the moods and needs of the *popolo*, that, to some extent, the caste relied on "the consent of the governed."[3] In fact, the very exclusivity of the patriciate, the sharp line that cut it off from the rest of the city, may have bred a certain insecurity that found expression in the government's desire to please and palliate those excluded.

Contarini claims that peace was maintained between patriciate and people because of the impartiality of justice provided by the government, because the *popolo* had their own places and institutions, and because the granaries of the city were kept well-stocked. Wotton suggested that abundant bread was most important because "the common man in this town hath no other mark of a good prince but big loaves."[4] The ambassador of King James notwithstanding, the Venetian commoner apparently had political interests that went beyond a full stomach.

Beneath the patriciate was the class of *cittadini originarii*. The *cittadini* gained full citizenship rights after twenty-five years' residence in Venice and by not engaging in manual labor. By the sixteenth century, the births of both *cittadini* and patricians were carefully recorded by the state attorneys (*avogadori di comun*), the former in a Silver Book, the latter in a Golden.[5] There was a certain amount of traffic between the books, for the children of a marriage between a male patrician and a female commoner were patrician by birth. Although the offspring of such marriages were not of high social standing within the patriciate, both families gained something from the exchange. The *cittadini* parents hoped to see their grandchildren in the ruling class, and the patrician family received a welcome infusion of money. The wealthy *cittadini* family of the Spelladi married a daughter to Carlo Zen, the great hero of the War of Chioggia, with an astonishing 40,000-ducat dowry; the Quartari married eight daughters into the patriciate with a total of 25,000 ducats in dowries.[6]

3 Frederic C. Lane, *Venice*, pp. 271–273.

4 Gasparo Contarini, *La Republica e i Magistrati de Venezia*, p. 148; Logan Pearsall Smith, *The Life and Letters of Sir Henry Wotton*, 2:277; cf. Lane, *Venice*, pp. 108–109. On Venetian justice: Stanley Chojnacki, "Crime, Punishment and the Trecento Venetian State."

5 Lane, *Venice*, pp. 151–152, 266.

6 ASV, Quarantia criminal, Grazie cento offici, 1541–1543, Reg. 255, fols. 24r–25v, 28v–30r.

Families as wealthy as the Spelladi and Quartari were among the elite of the *cittadini* class and could make the fullest use of the privileges of their class. *Cittadini* had two prerogatives: First, along with patricians, they could ship cargo on the state galleys—a substantial commercial advantage; second, and more important politically, they staffed the ducal chancellery. The influential and large secretarial order was entirely drawn from the *cittadini*. The head of the secretarial class was the grand chancellor, who was considered in a general sense to represent the *popolo*. He was elected for life by the Great Council and had a prominent place in state ceremonies. Whereas all patricians were addressed simply as "Messer," the grand chancellor, like the doge, was called "Domino."[7] As the civil service of Venice, the secretarial *cittadini* wielded influence and had access to state secrets. High-ranking secretaries, such as the four who served the Council of Ten, were the workhorses of government. They were often sent as representatives to foreign powers and as paymasters to the army. Patricians were usually in a particular office for no more than a year at a time, so secretaries provided vital continuity in administration. They knew the ins and outs of official procedure and how to lay hold of necessary files. Legislation by the Ten in 1514 stated that the secretaries were "the heart of our state." According to Bolognetti, secretaries entered affairs of government "hand in hand" with patricians.[8]

The government was solicitous of the welfare of the *cittadini*, and the lowly offices of the civil service were awarded to them as a form of poor relief. The citizen was given a sinecure that enabled him and his family, as the ritual phrase ran, "to be nourished under the shadow of our Signoria."[9] When Quartare Quartari and Bartolomeo Spelladi fell on hard times in the 1540s, both were given offices that brought in about 80 ducats a year. Alvise Ottobon was a more typical case. A bowman in the galleys, his grandfather, father, and son were all killed serving in the fleet. The Court of the Forty awarded Ottobon, at the age of 80, the income from a scribal post so that he could raise dowries for his two daughters.[10] For every patrician office elected by the

7 Felix Gilbert, "The Last Will of a Venetian Grand Chancellor," p. 506 and n. 19; Fabio Mutinelli, *Lessico Veneto*, pp. 83–84.

8 On 1514: ASV, Consiglio di Dieci, Parti Miste, Reg. 37, fol. 65v. On Bolognetti: Aldo Stella, *Chiesa e stato nelle relazioni dei nunzi pontifici a Venezia*, pp. 174–175.

9 ASV, Senato, Terra, Reg. 18, fols. 54r–54v.

10 ASV, Quarantia criminal, Grazie cento offici, 1541–1543, Reg. 255, fols. 131v–132v.

Great Council, there were perhaps three-to-five minor *cittadini* positions: notaries, scribes, guards, accountants, boatmen, licensers, messengers, brokers, measurers, porters, weighers, doormen, and supervisors.[11] The "shadow" under which *cittadini* sheltered stretched a long way. An important reason why Venetians quietly accepted patrician rule was that the government itself offered them a measure of political involvement along with a form of social security.

Cittadini made up the bulk of the membership of the six *Scuole Grandi*, philanthropic and fraternal societies, which provided them with both offices and status, always under the supervision of the Ten. Gentile Bellini's *Procession in the Piazza di San Marco* illustrates the central role the *Scuole* had in state ceremonies, while buildings such as the Scuola di San Rocco, its walls and ceilings covered with paintings by Tintoretto, testify to the wealth of the *Scuole*'s membership. About one hundred *scuole piccole* were scattered about the city, but they lacked the prestige and financial resources of the larger fraternities.[12] The *scuole piccole* were usually organized on the parish level, whereas the *Scuole Grandi* drew their membership from the city at large.

Within each of Venice's sixty parishes, congregations elected their own priest, subject to approval by the patriarch of Venice. San Nicolò de Mendicoli, the parish of fishermen, even had its own *gastaldo* or "doge," a representative elected by the community, who was received at the Ducal Palace by the Signoria.[13] Numerous occupations had their own associations, which may have provided an outlet for political energies. Artisans maintained about one hundred guilds under government supervision. The Arsenal workers (*Arsenalotti*) were especially important, and not only because their craft was vital for Venetian war fleets. They were used as guards at the Ducal Palace in time of crisis and when the Great Council was in session, as honor guards for the doge in his circuit of the piazza after election, and as pallbearers at the funeral of a doge.[14] Bakers, doctors, merchants,

11 The subject is unstudied. Cf. Antonio Stella, "Grazie, pensioni ed elemosine sotto la Repubblica veneta."

12 On the *Scuole Grandi*: Brian Pullan, *Rich and Poor in Renaissance Venice*, pp. 33–108; cf. Reinhold C. Mueller, "Charitable Institutions, the Jewish Community, and Venetian Society," pp. 44–45, 49–50. On ambition for *Scuole* offices: ASV, Provveditori di Comun, Capitolare, Reg. 1, fols. 246v–247v.

13 B. Cecchetti, "I nobili e il popolo di Venezia," p. 443; cf. ASV, Collegio, Notatorio, Reg. 14, fol. 174v.

14 On the guilds: Lane, *Venice*, pp. 318–321. On the place of the Arsenal and the workers in Venice: Frederic C. Lane, *Venetian Ships and Shipbuilders of the Renaissance*.

tavern keepers, lawyers, glassmakers, notaries, gondoliers, shipwrights, and weavers formed interest groups or corporations and made their influence felt at the Ducal Palace. Even official couriers, thirty-two men always chosen from among *Bergamaschi*, were a privileged corporation and passed on their posts to their heirs.[15]

Looked at cynically, one may conclude that all these societies and corporations are evidence of the patriciate's successful policy of dividing and ruling its subjects. The people, split into numerous and narrowly defined bodies, were fobbed off with spectacles and folk customs—and were there not some smiles at the Ducal Palace when the Nicoletti "doge" came to call? This view gains force from the government's unceasing efforts to supervise all aspects of life in the city. Yet such an interpretation is too one-sided. It fails to take into account the charity dispensed to *cittadini*, the weapons handed out to *Arsenalotti*, and the responsibility placed on the *Scuole* and guilds to provide men for the fleet. It fails to recognize the significance Venetians themselves accorded ceremonies of state; it should not be assumed that the ranks of the *Scuole* were full of men any less clever or any more gullible than the *Primi di la terra*. The desire to control was always present in the government's policies toward the city; but so too was the desire to conciliate, to give some scope to those forever barred from the ruling class.

There were occasions when the government, in particular the Ten, failed to head off vocal discontent. In 1509 galleymen (*gallioti*) from the "Pisana," recently returned from North Africa, demonstrated on the stairs of the Ducal Palace because they had not been paid. Five years later *gallioti* almost came to blows over the same issue with the guards of the Ten. In 1569, three hundred *Arsenalotti* armed with axes and mallets broke into a meeting of the Collegio and dispersed only when the doge promised to see to their complaints. In 1581 the doge was less accommodating to some angry sailors and Arsenal workers, so one Buongirolamo urged his fellows to make off with 120 bushels of flour from the warehouse near San Marco. A few days later Buongirolamo and a caulker were executed, and seven men were sentenced to the convict galleys. Buongirolamo might have benefited from the advice that Machiavelli put into the mouth of a leader of the

15 Lane, *Venice*, p. 271. On the couriers and *Bergamaschi*: Mutinelli, *Lessico Veneto*, p. 117; ASV, Collegio, Notatorio, Reg. 20, fol. 43v; Fernand Braudel, *The Mediterranean and the Mediterranean World in the Age of Philip II*, I:46, 49. On oil merchants and notaries: ASV, Senato, Terra, Reg. 18, fols. 124r–124v, 175v–176r.

Ciompi revolt in Florence: "Endeavor to have as many companions as we can [in breaking the law], for when many are at fault, few are punished." The three hundred men in the 1569 disturbance apparently escaped scot-free; but when Buongirolamo and his few comrades were punished, "the Arsenal remained quiet," and the Ten even prohibited the *Scuola della Marinari* from giving Buongirolamo a proper burial.[16]

It is significant that these demonstrations and violent outbursts involved *Arsenalotti* or *gallioti*, men used to united action, accustomed to weapons, directly employed by the government, conscious of the need for their services, and vulnerable to the least dip in commercial prosperity. Moreover, they lived together in close quarters, the workers in the *sestiere* of Castello, the galleymen often on their vessels. No other group in Venice met these conditions. Yet even the workers and galleymen very seldom turned to violence. More often they expressed their discontent passively, as when *gallioti* in Chioggia in 1510 refused to accept their pay because they wanted a raise or when some fifty *Arsenalotti* in 1513 balked at service as guards in Padua because they would suffer a loss of income.[17] In both cases the government prevailed, and peace was maintained.

Although the relationship between the ruling class and special interest groups—whether guild members, merchants, or Arsenal workers—could be documented through government legislation, the wider political world of the Venetian populace would still remain in darkness. The political connections between patricians and *popolo* will always remain elusive, in part because the notion of "the people" is amorphous, as vague as it is all-encompassing. Yet popular opinion was a part of Venetian politics and cannot be neglected. People turned out in huge crowds on some occasions and were not hesitant about making themselves heard.

In 1470 people flocked to the piazza and Ducal Palace to await word of the Turkish attack on Negroponte. Sanuto reports the fury of the people at the defeat of Venice by the Turks at Zonchio in 1499, as well as the joy of shopkeepers and artisans at the death of Leo X in 1521. In 1495 shopkeepers and artisans, furious at the duke

---

16 On 1509: ASV, Senato, Mar, Reg. 17, fol. 72r. On 1514: Michiel, fol. 106v. On 1569: Lane, *Venetian Ships*, p. 188. On 1581: "Memorie pubbliche della Repubblica di Venezia," BMV, Cod. It. Cl., VII, 810 (7298), fols. 175v–176r. On Machiavelli's advice: Nicolò Machiavelli, *The History of Florence* (New York, 1960), p. 126.

17 On 1510: ASV, Collegio, Secreta, Commissioni, 1500–1513, fols. 100r–101v. On 1513: ASV, Collegio, Notatorio, Reg. 17, fol. 79v.

of Ferrara's betrayal of Venice in favor of France, offered to pay
extra taxes to support an attack on the duchy. Anti-French feeling
was running so high that Philippe de Commynes complained to the
doge that "the people show themselves to have an evil disposition"
toward France and that even "the prisoners [at the Ducal Palace],
despising the French, stand at the windows to say awful things" as
he passes by. Crowds lined the canals in April 1499 to shriek curses at
Duke Ercole of Ferrara as he sailed to Ferrara after double-crossing
Venice in his arbitration of the Florentine-Pisan war; again, the Venetian *popolo* called for an invasion of Ferrara. When Antonio Grimani,
captain general of the fleet, returned home in the fall of 1499 from
his defeat at Zonchio, the *popolo* were in an uproar; and shop doors
throughout the city were scrawled with remarks condemning "Antonio Grimani, enemy of God and the Venetian state." His servants
were beaten up, and his sons dared not go out in public for fear of
their lives.[18]

Pietro Dolfin claims that thirty thousand people were in the piazza
a year later when news arrived of the loss of Modone in the Peloponnese; the streets and canals were full of shouts of "Marco, Marco!"
In August 1509 the marquis of Mantua, captured in a surprise raid by
Venetian forces, was taken to prison in Venice. Even at three o'clock
in the morning, his boat had to pass through canals full of people
clamoring for joy and shouting insults. For security, his cell was
guarded by nine *cittadini*, "wealthy and powerful in the city." Two
months later the *popolo* finally were granted their wish for an attack
on Ferrara; and when the fleet met disaster on the Po river in December, there was a "popular uproar" in Venice. Giambattista Malatesta,
Mantuan ambassador in Venice, was amazed by the crowds at Doge
Leonardo Loredan's funeral in June 1521: "countless persons, so that
the palace, the piazza, all the streets, windows and canals were full."
When word leaked out in June 1542 that the French ambassador had
been buying secret information from state secretaries, "the tumult of
the people" was disturbing even to the Council of Ten.[19]

---

18 On 1470: Malipiero, 1:61. On 1499 and 1521: Sanuto, 2:1335, 1377; 3:5, 688,
733; 32:207. On 1495: Marino Sanuto, *La spedizione di Carlo VIII in Italia*, pp.
485; 308–309. On Ferrara in 1499: Sanuto, 2:590, 605–606. On Grimani in 1499:
Sanuto, 2:1377.

19 On 1500: Pietro Dolfin, *Annalium Venetorum (pars quatro)*, p. 149; cf.
Sanuto, 3:688; Priuli, 2:39. On Mantua: Priuli, 4:212. On Ferrara: Priuli, vol. 5,
fols. 56v–57r; cf. Robert Finlay, "Venice, the Po Expedition, and the End of the
League of Cambrai, 1509–1510," pp. 50, 60. On 1521: ASM, b. 1454, Giambattista

Of course, it is easy enough to attract a crowd, and it takes little political sophistication to jeer at an enemy or mourn a defeat. One cannot make too much of bustling mobs and enthusiastic shouting. At the same time, Venice's crowds should not be casually dismissed, for they were probably drawn by more than spectacle and contagious excitement. The livelihood of many Venetians, foreigners and native-born, depended on the outcome of the Republic's foreign adventures. For Venice to lose part of the *stato di mar*, such as Negroponte and Modone, meant a flood of refugees entering the city (who would be given *cittadini* offices as poor relief) as well as a loss of lives, trading contacts, and property.[20] The election of an apparently friendly pope and the death of a demonstrably hostile one (Sanuto called Leo X "a captain-general of the Turk" for his alliance against Venice) promised more benefices for Venetians and perhaps a larger Venetian presence in the Romagna. The acquisition of Friuli in war with the Holy Roman Empire in 1508 opened a new area for Venice to send its officials and privileged merchants. Many Venetians, patricians and commoners, owned land in the Polesine of Rovigo, a fertile area between the Adige and the Po that Venice had seized from Ferrara in 1482. The Venetians who offered to pay extra taxes if Ferrara were attacked may have hoped to recoup their money by gathering booty from the duke's lands.[21]

The *popolo* followed the politics of the patriciate for much the same reasons that they were attentive to Venetian foreign policy. Patricians were in no way isolated from the populace. Numerous commoners had very close economic and social ties to patricians—as customers, creditors, employees, dependents, and tenants. Patricians often rented the ground floors of their homes to shops and poor families. Pandolfo and Federico Morosini rented to forty-nine families in seven parishes. Marcantonio Morosini, a procurator, had eleven tenants, with rents

Malatesta to the marquis of Mantua, June 21, 1521. On 1542: ASV, Consiglio di Dieci, Parti Secrete, Reg. 5, fols. 70r–71v, 75v, 76v.

20 On offices for refugees from Modone: Priuli, 2:363. On offices for refugees from Malvasia and Napoli di Romania in the 1540s: ASV, Maggior Consiglio, Deliberazioni, Liber Novus, Reg. 27, fol. 83r. On petitions by refugees, see for example, ASV, Collegio, Notatorio, Reg. 16, fol. 4v; Reg. 17, fol. 97v; Reg. 18, fols. 102v–103v; and ASV, Consiglio di Dieci, Parti Miste, Reg. 36, fols. 75r–75v.

21 On Venetian property in Ravenna: ASV, Collegio, Notatorio, Reg. 16, fol. 53v. On Friuli: ASV, Collegio, Notatorio, Reg. 16, fol. 35r. On Venetian property in the Polesine: ASV, Collegio, Secreta, Commissioni, 1500–1513, fols. 90r–90v. On booty in Ferrara: Finlay, "Venice, the Po Expedition," pp. 50, 52–53.

ranging from 5 to 50 ducats a year, in the parish of Santa Giustina. These included several low-ranking *cittadini* officials, an important secretary, and a boatman (*barcharuol*). Morosini also had income from eight shops at the Rialto. Francesco Molin's holdings were considerably more modest, and his tenants numbered five Arsenal workers and two boatmen. The wealthy and influential Vendramin family owned about one-fourth of the oil shops at the Rialto and San Marco.[22] Artisans, servants, and shopkeepers might find their fortunes linked with the success or failure of a particular patrician family; all found their daily lives affected by patricians establishing policies regarding salt, grain, wages, prices, galley schedules, and customs duties. Certainly the state secretaries and other *cittadini* officials must have taken a lively interest in who was likely to be running their offices for the next year. The pay and employment of *gallioti* and *Arsenalotti* were set by those who met in the Collegio and the Senate. The prosperity of everyone in the city was at the mercy of *Primi* debating war and peace in the executive councils.

It is not surprising, then, that the political doings of the patriciate and the Great Council were watched with intense interest and partisanship by so many in Venice. The *popolo* favored Filippo Tron for the dogeship in 1501 and his cousin, Antonio Tron, in 1523, only to be disappointed both times. When Doge Loredan was gravely ill in 1504, Bartolomeo Cartari, Ferrara's ambassador in Venice, predicted that Tommaso Mocenigo would be the next doge, "for it seems that his house [*casa*] is loved by all the people." Giorgio Corner was the hero of the city in July 1508 when he helped defeat imperial forces at the battle of Cadore, but exactly one year later many looked forward to his punishment for failing to oppose the French at Agnadello. Martino Merlini, a *cittadini* merchant, wrote his brother in Beirut about Andrea Gritti's prospects for the dogeship after he led Venetian forces in recapturing Padua in July 1509. In 1578 prisoners in the Ducal Palace joined their voices to those of a crowd chanting support for a candidate in a ducal election.[23]

22 On Pandolfo and Federico Morosini: ASV, Dieci Savi sopra le decime in Rialto, Condizione della città, 1537, S. Croce, Reg. 366, fols. 285v–287r. On Marcantonio Morosini: ASV, Dieci Savi sopra le decime in Rialto, Condizione della città, 1514, S. Giustina, b. 33, no. 49. On Molin: ASV, Dieci Savi sopra le decime in Rialto, Condizione della città, 1514, S. Giustina, b. 33, no. 62. On the Vendramin: ASV, Senato, Terra, Reg. 18, fols. 124r–124v.

23 On the Tron: Sanuto, 4:144; 34:128, 135, 159. On Mocenigo: ASM., b. 12, c. 58, Bartolomeo Cartari to the duke of Ferrara, May 5, 1504. On Corner: Sanuto, 7:574; 8:429–430. On Gritti: Giuseppe Dalla Santa, *La Lega di Cambrai*

Venice was not a despotism founded on terror, and it could ill afford totally to ignore the sentiments of its people. There was a constant "murmuring in the city" (*mormoratione di la terra*) that reached the ears of the *Primi*. Priuli even claims that popular opinion guided Venetian government and caused it to reach decisions aimed solely at "pleasing the mob":

> I do not wish to be silent about the many words, opinions, suggestions, whims, and nonsense which are expressed these days in Venice by patricians, citizens and people in all the piazzas, arcades, banks, churches, streets, barbershops, taverns, and at the Rialto. . . . The Fathers [of the Collegio] and senators, wishing to have the primary offices of the state, follow this popular opinion and propose such in the Senate, where it is debated and passed. Thus they aspire to become great men.[24]

Priuli cites a number of cases when the *Primi* responded to the people. In 1499 Antonio Grimani was kept imprisoned because of the anger of "the poor people" and the Great Council toward him for the defeat at Zonchio; ten years later, Grimani, now "much loved by the city," was allowed home from exile. Another defeated general, Angelo Trevisan, was thrown in jail in 1510 "to decrease the popular uproar." In order "to satisfy the people," an office was created in 1501 to investigate the malfeasance of the late doge, the much-disliked Agostino Barbarigo. In 1503 the Collegio decided not to propose new taxes "so as not to make the city [*terra*] grumble"; and when state debtors were imprisoned, the government began with patricians, not wishing to disturb or displease *cittadini* and *popolari*.[25] The Collegio did propose to appropriate interest payments of the Monte Nuovo that were going to state debtors, but "the chiefs of the Council of Ten, seeing so much grumbling in the city [about this], had the Ten revoke the decision made by the Collegio." The Ten itself aroused anger when it issued a stern edict against gambling, much of which apparently had to do with betting on elections: "Because of the great murmuring in Venice by every person of every sort about the declaration regarding gam-

---

e gli avvenimenti dell'anno 1509 descritti da un mercante veneziano contemporaneo, p. 24. On 1578: William Archer Brown, "Nicolò da Ponte," pp. 147–158.

24 Priuli, 4:246; 418; vol. 7, fol. 293v.

25 On Grimani: Priuli, 1:233, 252; 4:95. On Trevisan: Priuli, vol. 5, fols. 56v–57r, 62r–62v; Sanuto, 9:411. On Barbarigo: Priuli, 2:177. On new taxes and state debtors: Priuli, 2:13; 4:346.

bling," the Collegio prevailed on the Ten to water down the new law in such a way that the city was pacified and the Ten's reputation for rigor preserved.[26]

The notion of the Council of Ten rescinding or modifying legislation in response to popular opposition is less startling when one realizes that very often the official justification for new legislation was *mormoratione universale* or *mormoratione di la terra,* the grumbling of the city or community at some injustice or inefficiency.[27] Priuli believed that "the murmuring of the city" was the hidden force behind Venice's policy of expansion in the Romagna in the first years of the Cinquecento, for the *Primi* abandoned all prudence "to govern according to the wishes of commoners" because they sought popularity and high office in Venice. When the policy of expansion came to grief with the creation of the League of Cambrai in 1508–1509, Giorgio Emo, the man blamed for the disgrace, stayed away from the Ducal Palace "because he was in the bad graces" of the people. Priuli even claims that Venice's defeat at Agnadello in May 1509 stemmed from talk in the streets of the city: The Venetian general, Bartolomeo Alviano, attacked the French at an inopportune moment because he had heard of "common gossip on the Venetian piazzas" that the Signoria would make him duke of Milan if he were victorious. Although there is no reason to doubt that this rumor was current in Venice before the battle, even Alviano was probably not so vainglorious as to put any stock in it. The impact of gossip was rarely if ever that immediate and dramatic, although it could be troublesome. In August 1526, Francesco Maria della Rovere, the duke of Urbino and Venice's captain general, "experienced annoyance because of some gossip spread in the piazzas," most likely about who was to be in command of the Venetian-papal forces of the League of Cognac. The Ten immediately dispatched Alvise Pisani, a *savio grande,* to soothe Urbino and urge him to ignore "common gossip, which is entirely devoid of reason."[28]

26 On the Monte and debtors: Priuli, 2:407. On gambling: Priuli, 2:420–421; 408, 413; cf. ASV, Consiglio di Dieci, Parti Miste, Reg. 31, fols. 198v–199r.

27 The phrases are ubiquitous: cf. ASV, Avogaria di Comun. Deliberazioni del Maggior Consiglio, Reg. 32/14, fols. 7r, 24r, 32r, 84r, 124r; Senato, Terra, Reg. 18, fols. 50r–50v, 51v–52r; Senato, Mar, Reg. 16, fol. 62v; Collegio, Notatorio, Reg. 20, fol. 4v.

28 On the Romagna: Priuli, 2:316; cf. 312. On Emo: Sanuto, 8:431; Priuli, 4: 93. On Alviano: Priuli, 4:108; cf. 246, 343. On Urbino: ASV, Consiglio di Dieci, Parti Secrete, Reg. 1, fols. 76v–77r, 75r–75v, 78v.

Priuli complains that, with so many rumors, fantasies, and lies inundating Venice,

> one cannot determine the truth; everyone says what he pleases, dreaming up something at night and spreading it in the morning. Certainly it is a very great disgrace for the Venetian Fathers that they put up with this. There is no longer any discretion in speaking . . . as there used to be in the old days, when if one spread a rumor or spoke about the government of the state or said some unsuitable things about the Venetian Fathers or about the Republic, the chiefs of the Council of Ten would immediately summon him [and command him to silence] . . . and by such reproofs everyone kept the tongue behind the teeth because of fear. . . . Yet now no senator has enough courage to do anything because of [concern for] his own standing and so as not to displease any patrician or citizen.[29]

No doubt Priuli is exaggerating, but he is also stating a fundamental fact about Venetian politics: The political life of the patriciate was not isolated from the man in the street. What disturbed Priuli was not merely unrestrained talk, or that much of the talk was unfounded rumor, but that gossip and popular opinion reached into the Ducal Palace, affecting government policy and shaping political ambitions. The *popolo* did more than gather in crowds or grouse about a new law; they influenced the politics of the patriciate.

The connecting link between popular opinion and the patriciate was the Great Council. Indeed, the relationship between the Great Council and the city cannot be summed up in terms of command and obedience, ruler and ruled, for the Great Council retained something of the tone and function of the popular assembly it supplanted in 1297. Presiding over the sovereign assembly, the Signoria preserved its constitutional form as a municipal body by the provision that each of the six ducal councillors had to reside in a different *sestiere* of Venice, a requirement that was still rigorously enforced in the Cinquecento.[30] The Great Council performed the function within the government, wrote Contarini, of a *stato popolare*.[31] It also acted as a kind of sounding board for popular opinion. The most striking indication of this is the Venetian use of the word *terra*, which in normal usage referred to the city itself, to the community of Venetians to which both patri-

---

29 Priuli, 4:108.
30 ASV, Senato, Terra, Reg. 18, fol. 181r.
31 Contarini, *Republica,* p. 24.

cians and commoners belonged.[32] The *terra* complained of the *Primi*'s incompetence, of the paucity of meat or grain in the markets, and of an action by the Ten; it was disorganized after a fire destroyed tax records and displeased when a well-regarded person was executed; it applauded when Antonio Grimani departed for the fleet and shouted in despair when Modone was lost.[33] Doge Barbarigo's response to Commynes's complaint about displays of public hostility toward France was that, "in this city [*terra*] the people are free and freely speak."[34]

But in a narrower political context, *terra* referred to the Great Council. Doge Marco Barbarigo said to his brother, "Messer Agostino, you do everything in order to succeed to our position, but if the *terra* knew your character as well as we do, it would quickly [elect] another." Immediately after his election, Doge Agostino Barbarigo, addressing the Great Council, exhorted "the *terra* to unite"; his speech was supposed to be secret so as not to cause unrest in the city. When Paolo Trevisan opposed Doge Barbarigo on an issue, "so many in the *terra* were pleased with Trevisan's performance . . . that he was elected captain of Bergamo." Antonio Grimani was elected captain general of the fleet by the Great Council because that was "the will of the *terra*."[35] Even though the banker Alvise Pisani had offered huge sums of money to the government in time of war, "the *terra* [was] ungrateful" and did not award him an office. The *terra*'s displeasure with one patrician resulted in his defeat in a Great Council election, despite his being a member of the Council of Ten, "the rudder of the *terra*." Similarly, the *terra*'s opposition to Paolo Capello led to his defeat in an election for councillor. Doge Loredan urged patricians in the Great Council to contribute to the defense of Padua in 1513, but he did not send his sons to the siege until forced to do so by "the grumbling made by the *terra*."[36] In February 1515 legislation was before the Senate requiring the election of men from the Senate itself to staff a new office; the legislation was subsequently modified to provide that the officials would be elected not from the body of the Senate alone

32 Alberto Tenenti, "La Sérénissime République," pp. 169–170.

33 Sanuto, 8:374; 12:190; 26:503; 43:598; Michiel, fols. 86v, 97r.

34 Sanuto, *Spedizione di Carlo VIII*, p. 309; cf. Malipiero, 1:363.

35 On Marco Barbarigo: Marino Sanuto, *Vite dei dogi*, fol. 265r. On Barbarigo addressing the Great Council: Malipiero, 2:682; cf. Sanuto, *Vite dei dogi*, fols. 273v–274r. On Trevisan: Malipiero, 2:698. On Grimani: Malipiero, 1:163.

36 On Pisani: Sanuto, 22:172. On defeat for the Ten and the Ten as a rudder: Sanuto, 12:190. On Capello: Sanuto, 8:292. On Loredan: Michiel, fol. 95r.

but from "the body of our city [*città*]," that is, the Great Council. The Great Council was jealous of its right to distribute "li honori dela terra." When a state attorney asserted the Great Council's supremacy over the Senate in 1510, it was natural for him to praise the sovereign assembly as "the lord of the *terra*."[37]

Often it is not possible to tell if the word *terra* refers to the city and community of Venice or to the Great Council; some of the examples already given may refer to both simultaneously. In August 1526 the Senate was reluctant to pass certain legislation desired by the Great Council, "and about this," Sanuto notes, "it is spoken publicly in the *terra*"; finally, Doge Gritti convinced the Senate to approve the legislation "in order not to anger the Great Council." "Throughout the *terra*," writes Malipiero, "every sort of person cries out for an attack [on Ferrara]; and some seek out Constantino Priuli and Nicolò Trevisan, heads of the Ten, and made known to them that if they placed such a motion [in the Senate], they would be made procurators." The Ferrarese ambassador's warrant for saying that Tommaso Mocenigo was "loved by all the people" was that the Great Council had elected him a procurator by an overwhelming majority. Paolo Trevisan's response to Doge Barbarigo's badgering was to say, "I am a citizen of the *terra* and of this council [of the Senate] and will say what I please." Ludovico Moscolini's petition for poor relief in 1543 included the argument that his *cittadini* family "had extensively married with the patriciate of this *terra*, such that in one month alone, there were three of four marriages into the Great Council."[38]

When Sanuto or Priuli refer generally to the *mormoratione di la terra*, there is no way to tell whether it was the patriciate or the people who were restless or displeased. More often than not, the diarists probably saw no reason to differentiate between the two because in a general sense both occupied the same political world. Special interest groups lobbied at the Ducal Palace; crowds made their voices heard in the piazza; and popular opinion at the Rialto influenced elections in the hall of the Great Council. Of course, the *popolo* could not vote, and only *cittadini* could receive nonpatrician offices. It was also against the law to criticize the government, although that was a dis-

37 On the 1515 legislation: Sanuto, 19:426; ASV, Senato, Terra, Reg. 18, fols. 199v–200r. On "li honori dela terra": Priuli, 1:260. On "the lord of the terra": Sanuto, 9:539.

38 On Gritti: Sanuto, 42:401, 413–414; 417. On attacking Ferrara: Malipiero, 1:367. On Trevisan's response: Malipiero, 2:697. On Moscolini: ASV, Quarantia criminal, Grazie cento offici, 1541–1543, Reg. 255, fols. 145r–145v.

ability patricians shared with the rest of the city. In these respects the
Republic of Venice was no more liberal or free than any other state
of the time.

Yet the existence in Venice of the Great Council, occupied by a
stable, easily identifiable ruling class constantly engaged in electioneering, provided a means by which popular opinion could be registered. The harsh constitutional line that divided patrician from
commoner found no counterpart in political reality insofar as a certain
identification of the Great Council with the community brought the
popolo, in an unruly and informal way, into the political arena. While
patricians looked to the terra of Venice for support, acclaim, and
publicity, many Venetians of all conditions considered that the city
of Venice had its embodiment and political expression in the terra of
the sovereign assembly. The multiple and extensive links between
patriciate and people did much to maintain the political stability of
Venice. If the popolo had been wholly cut off from political life and
denied any outlet for their political energies, then the Ducal Palace
might have become a fortress, protecting the patrician caste from the
crowds of the city. Instead, the people had access to the Ducal Palace;
patricians lived and moved in their midst.

Venetian civic peace was a striking phenomenon in an age when
foreign invasion and domestic upheaval were common occurrences;
forms of government could change with bewildering rapidity, as happened at Florence between 1494 and 1530. Yet even in times of crisis,
such as the opening months of the War of the League of Cambrai,
when foreign observers believed that the people of Venice were ripe
for revolution,[39] the city remained at peace. In June 1509 Priuli reports:

> It is divulged by many in Venice that when the King of France
> comes with his powerful and famous army to the lagoon to besiege
> the city, he intends to have the citizens and people assume the gov-
> ernment and smash their patrician governors, for he cannot capture
> the city without creating discord and factions within it. . . . Truly,
> I doubt that any disorder and disturbance would occur if the King
> of France, following upon his recent victories, came at last to Venice.
> Venetian patricians, citizens and people would defend the city with
> heart and spirit, not unduly fearful of the whole world.

39 Cf. Antonio Bonardi, "Venezia città libera dell'Impero nell'immaginazione di
Massimiliano I d'Asburgo."

During the worst days of the war, with the enemy on the shores of the lagoon, the *popolo* remained faithful, and "Venice enjoyed such very great quiet that it seemed to be the holiest of sacristies."[40]

2. *The Great Council and the Governing Circle*

In his *Cronachetta,* Sanuto asserts that "this [Great] Council is the lord (*signor*) of the city, and it creates all the offices and magistracies of the city and all the councils." The diarist also approvingly quotes a patrician in a Senate debate as stating that "those of the Great Council are citizens, those of the Senate are patricians (*zentilhomeni*), and those of the Collegio are lords; but the Lord (*signor*) is the council [of the Senate]."[41] The question of which assembly was "lord of the city," the Great Council or the Senate, animated much of Venetian politics. The Senate had control of important business of state: finance and taxation, foreign affairs and commercial policy. Almost all legislation that came before the Great Council was first approved by the Senate, and the Great Council usually passed what was placed before it. A Senate proposal in the Great Council had the advantage that it had already been passed by the *Primi di la terra,* who could muster substantial support for their policies in the Great Council, of which they were, of course, members. Most of the motions before the Great Council were hardly important enough to warrant lobbying, however; a frequent item of business, for example, was granting a *terraferma* official a short leave to come to Venice for reason of illness or family affairs, a matter that concerned the Great Council because it touched on administration of offices. A further advantage for the Senate was that it was a relatively small and coherent body, whereas the Great Council was about five times as large and was riven with divisions based on family and social standing. The Senate was the seat of debate and decision, a congregation of the *Primi*; the Great Council was passive and generally quiescent, lacking any power of initiative. Sovereignty aside, there is no doubt that the Senate was *il signor di la terra.*

Yet the Great Council was a force to be reckoned with in politics. According to Sanuto, there were 831 posts elected by the Great Council, 550 within Venice and 281 outside. Whatever effective political power the Great Council had was derived from its right to reserve

---

40 Priuli, 4:101; 384.
41 Marino Sanuto, *Cronachetta,* p. 233; Sanuto, 30:384–385.

election of these offices to itself. The Senate had a role in many of these elections, for it made its own additional nomination by scrutiny (*scrutinio*) to the four nominees usually produced by the Great Council's nominating committees. Also, the Senate elected its own officials—about 150 in the early Cinquecento—but that was only possible by virtue of a prior delegation of authority from the Great Council.[42] When the Great Council did reject or come close to rejecting a Senate proposal, it was usually because the patriciate saw a threat to the electoral authority of the assembly. For example, in 1569, a proposal to have the captain of Brescia temporarily exercise the office of *podestà* as well passed by only 167 votes in an assembly of 1281, a victory that was probably regarded as a moral defeat for the *Primi;* and in 1539 a motion to appoint rather than elect a patrician as *podestà* of Brescia was turned down by 55 votes in a Great Council of 1,236.[43] The Great Council sometimes found it easy to defeat legislation that sapped its authority because motions to alter electoral procedures or grant petitions often required a favorable vote of two-thirds, three-fourths, or even five-sixths of the patricians present in the assembly. A small minority in the Great Council could thus stymie the moves of the *Primi.*

Primi relied for their preeminence on election by the Great Council, an assembly that adhered to the leveling principle of one man, one vote. They did not constitute a tight oligarchy within the patriciate because they were beholden to others for their power. A seventeenth-century writer emphasized that the desire of the *Primi* to enter the Senate and executive councils placed considerable power in the Great Council: *Grandi* were forced to court the favor of *piccoli.*[44] Indeed,

---

42 On Sanuto's 1493 list of Great Council offices: "Cronica di Marino Sanuto," MCC, MS. Cod. Cicogna, 969. On the number of elections in the Senate: ASV, Segretario alle voce, elezioni in Senato, Reg. 2, no. 16. Electoral procedures are described below.

43 On 1569: ASV, Maggior Consiglio, Deliberazioni, Liber Angelus, Reg. 29, fol. 23r. On 1539: Maggior Consiglio, Deliberazioni, Liber Novus, Reg. 27, fols. 65r–65v. For similar examples from the Deliberazioni for 1522 to 1624, see Liber Diana, Reg. 26, fols. 29v, 47v, 59v, 68r, 70r; Liber Novus, Reg. 27, fols. 33v, 35v–36v, 43v–44r, 44v, 90v–91r, 121v–122v, 172v, 177r–177v; Liber Rocca, Reg. 28, fols. 19r, 20r–20v, 82r–82v, 89r–89v; Liber Angelus, Reg. 29, fols. 36r, 38v, 44v, 100v, 106v–107v; Liber Frigerius, Reg. 31, fols. 42r–42v, 92v–93r; Liber Surianus, Reg. 32, fols. 17v–18r, 138r, 143r, 170v–171r; Liber Vicus, Reg. 33, fols. 9v–10r, 42r–42v, 120r–120v, 125r; Liber Antelmus, Reg. 34, fols. 49r–49v, 131v; Liber Arcangelus, Reg. 35, fols. 15r, 36v, 79v.

44 Francesco della Torre [?], "Relazione della Serenissima Repubblica di

votes were everything. Pope Clement VII complained to Gasparo Contarini in 1529 that "with you everything depends on a single ballot," a coincidental variation on Contarini's own proud statement in *De Republica* that the doge himself "only has the power of a single ballot." Francis I had high hopes for an alliance with Venice when the pro-French Andrea Gritti won the dogeship in 1523; but two months later, with a weariness born of seeing the Senate switch its allegiance to Charles V, he told the Venetian ambassador that "in a council of 300, the one with the most ballots wins."[45]

"Fear of the ballot," as Priuli calls it, held large sway in Venice. Factionalism did not turn to violence, at least in part, because, as an anonymous eighteenth-century observer of Venice wrote, "Here they fight not with blood but with ballots." That combat took many and curious forms. It was not sufficient for an important politician merely to win an election, for the size of his victory was significant as an indication of his vulnerability; too slight a margin of victory might encourage his enemies to gang up on him in a future election. A subtle expression of enmity was to nominate or elect a foe to a certain office. Sanuto was nominated to a post in the colonies by an enemy who wanted him sent far from home. An enemy also nominated Sanuto for the Ten, sure that he would be defeated and publicly humiliated, as indeed he was. In 1618 Leonardo Mocenigo's foes elected him captain general of the fleet, a "slippery employment" in which he was bound, "especially with his own inexperience in that service, so as to carry himself but that his enemies at home would not find some way to cut his throat." Mocenigo refused the post, and his enemies had to content themselves with seeing him fined 1,000 ducats and exiled for two years for his pusillanimity.[46]

Patricians in the Great Council used elections to reward or punish individuals and to make their feelings known to the *Primi*. When it seemed that Angelo Trevisan, the commander of a disastrous expedi-

---

Venezia," cc. 10–11; cf. Gaetano Cozzi, "Authority and the Law in Renaissance Venice," p. 298.

45 On Clement's statement: William J. Bouwsma, *Venice and the Defense of Republican Liberty*, p. 318. On the doge's vote: Contarini, *Republica*, p. 49. On Francis I: Sanuto, 34:378.

46 On fear of the ballot: Priuli, 4:35. On fighting with ballots: "Istoria del governo di Venezia," c. 14. On the margin of victory: della Torre, "Relazione," cc. 10–11. On Sanuto's nominations: Sanuto, 48:247, 473. On Mocenigo: Smith, *Life and Letters*, 2:127–128; cf. ASV, Maggior Consiglio, Deliberazioni, Liber Arcangelus, Reg. 35, fols. 22r–23v.

tion against Ferrara in 1509, would not be brought to trial, Sanuto sadly noted that "we are not the Venetians we were: if one does badly, he isn't punished—except by the vote." Ten years before, Trevisan was elected to the Ten for his work as a maritime commissioner at a crucial time. The Great Council hoped, says Priuli, "by elevating him to such a high honor, to make a good example for all of the conduct that should be exhibited in offices and magistracies." On the same day, the Great Council elected Vicenzo di Antonio Grimani to the Senate for the first time, both to encourage his father, the captain general, and to set an example for others. When Antonio Grimani failed to win a victory at Zonchio not long after, he did not punish the patrician commanders in his fleet for disobeying orders, "for he did not wish to displease any patrician, due to his regard for honors and votes."[47]

Antonio Loredan and Alvise Armer were elected to the Salt Office because their brothers died as heroes at Zonchio; Giacomo Polani was placed on the Zonta of the Senate because his son died at Zonchio. Girolamo Soranzo was elected to the Senate because his brother was killed by the Turks at Santa Maura. Nicolò Michiel was elected procurator for his prosecution of Antonio Grimani after Zonchio, while his two associates as state attorney were elected to the Ten. The son of Grimani's successor as captain general, Girolamo Pesaro, narrowly missed election to the Zonta in January 1501, "a sign that the *terra* wishes to elevate him for the good merits of his father"; within a month Girolamo was elected to the Senate. Francesco Bollani won election to the Zonta for having made a motion in the Senate to send Andrea Zancani, a failure as a commander in Friuli in 1499, to prison when "other senators lacked the courage to do so, for fear of offending some patricians." Two field commanders, Giovanni Paolo Gradenigo and Pietro Marcello, were defeated in the Zonta election of 1510 because they had lost the Polesine of Rovigo to the French. Luca Tron was made captain of Famagusta in Cyprus for his speech to the Senate in 1514, which led to a victory for Venetian forces in Friuli.[48]

Pietro Capello failed to win an election in the Great Council for

47 On Trevisan: Sanuto, 9:411; Priuli, 1:181. On Vicenzo and Antonio Grimani: Priuli, 1:181, 192.

48 On Loredan, Armer, and Polani: Priuli, 1:195, 202. On Soranzo: Priuli, 2: 229. On Michiel: Sanuto, 3:395–396, 595; Pietro Dolfin, *Annalium Venetorum*, p. 204. On Pesaro: Sanuto, 3:194; 1432. On Bollani: Priuli, 1:211. On Gradenigo and Marcello: Sanuto, 11:472. On Tron: Sanuto, 18:90–91.

several years because he had urged support for a Friulian noble who later betrayed Venice in the War of the League of Cambrai. Capello was also defeated in election for ducal councillor in 1511 because he was a member of the Ten when "the entire city grumbled mightily" over the execution of a popular young patrician. Antonio Condulmer was defeated in elections to the Senate for eighteen months and kept off the Zonta for two years because of his over-zealous investigation of the Loredan family after the death of Doge Leonardo. Political memories were short in Venice, for only a few years before, Giovanni Priuli was elected to the Ten as a result of the popularity gained by his brother, Alvise, who had tried to remove Lorenzo di Leonardo Loredan from his office as procurator. The Great Council had a special interest in indicating its approval of Alvise because he was upholding its right to be the final arbiter of the requirements of office holding.[49]

The Great Council had several ways of making its feelings known to the *Primi* through elections. Obviously, the rejection or elevation of one man was often an indication of the Great Council's attitude toward the governing circle's actions and policies. In September 1509, a number of Doge Loredan's relatives by marriage were defeated in the Zonta election. Priuli explains that, because the patriciate had no opportunity to vote on the doge or on his sons, who could not hold high office, it expressed its discontent by rejecting his in-laws instead. Something similar happened in the Senate in 1526, when six of Doge Gritti's in-laws were nominated for the Collegio "to annoy the doge"; they were then declared ineligible or voted down by the Senate.[50]

A more troublesome and less subtle way for the Great Council to express displeasure was for it to fail to elect anyone to a crucial office. Between 1510 and 1525, 537 elections produced no winner; the Great Council rejected all nominees to the Ten eighty-two times during the same fifteen years. In almost every Great Council meeting after Agnadello, one of the nine elections of the day had no issue. On October 4, 1517, four of the nine offices were not filled; in subsequent meetings from two to five were left vacant. Then, on March 1, 1518, "the whole *terra*," Sanuto records, "speaks of what happened yesterday in the Great Council, that of nine elections put forward, none passed. . . . The reasons that they didn't pass are many, but I don't want to

---

49 On Capello: Sanuto, 12:193; 17:578; Priuli, vol. 6, fol. 207v; vol. 7, fol. 58r. On Condulmer: Sanuto, 34:101–102. On Giovanni and Alvise Priuli: Sanuto, 31: 9, 364.

50 On Loredan: Priuli, 4:371. On Gritti: Sanuto, 43:518, 569.

waste time in writing them." The balkiness of the Great Council, then, remains something of a mystery, and there may have been more behind the failure to fill offices than stirrings of discontent with policies. Some patricians explained the phenomenon by claiming that the planets were in an unfortunate conjunction during certain Great Council meetings; others, like Sanuto, were content to say that "today the Great Council was badly disposed" or "it was a bad-tempered Council," *fo un cativo Conseio.*[51]

There was no mystery about the Great Council's motivation nor any doubt about its disposition when the Senate's nominees for the Zonta were rejected. The election of the sixty men of the Zonta could be a focus for a vote of no confidence in the *Primi* because it was the only opportunity offered to the Great Council to vote on a large body of men nominated by the Senate. Officials and council members were usually elected in the Great Council by a complex combination of nominating committees and general election. The busiest time of the year for the Great Council was August and September, when sixty Senators were elected in groups of six in ten successive meetings; the *Quarantia civile nuova*, the supreme court for civil cases, was elected in blocs of five in eight meetings; and the Ten were elected in groups of two and three over several gatherings. The election of the Zonta took place in a single Great Council session; on September 29 the Senate nominated from 145 to 165 patricians to the Zonta, and the next day the Great Council elected 60 of them as the Zonta. In general, important politicians could count on a seat in the Zonta if they were not already on an executive council, and many remained Zonta members year after year. But in years of crisis, such as 1500, 1509, 1511, 1513, and 1526—and no doubt in many other years as well— *Primi* were voted off the Zonta. As Dolfin explained when *Primi* were rejected in the Zonta election of 1500, "since the Great Council could not punish [the governing circle] in any other way, it expelled those of the Zonta in order to avenge its own, not even deeming the most outstanding [of the *Primi*] to be in the government of the Republic."[52]

The election of 1500 illustrates the uncanny precision with which the Great Council could distribute rewards and punishments, even when dealing with many people in a very heated atmosphere. During the summer of 1500, the attention of Venice was fixed on the advance

51 On the elections of the Great Council, including men nominated but not elected: Consegi, 8894–8897. On February 28 and planetary influence: Sanuto, 25: 269; 259. On bad-tempered councils: Sanuto, 28:14; 54:239.
52 Pietro Dolfin, *Annalium Venetorum*, p. 184; cf. Lane, *Venice*, pp. 264–265.

of the Turkish fleet on the city of Modone on the eastern Peloponnese. Venice was about to reap the consequences of Antonio Grimani's defeat at Zonchio a year before. Modone was considered "the eye of the Levant" because of its strategic position on the galley routes to the East. It was also closely linked to Venice, inasmuch as Venetians had founded and built it, and many still lived and traded there. A stream of requests for military aid flowed from Modone to Venice, while the Venetian fleet tried to organize itself at Zante after the death of its captain general, Marchio Trevisan. At last, the fleet attempted to relieve Modone but had to turn back before a more powerful Turkish fleet on July 24. When, on August 12, the Collegio received news of the fleet's retreat, it desperately began to collect supplies and recruit men; but it was already too late, for Modone had fallen a week before. The Senate was stunned when the news reached Venice on September 4; and although it decided to release the news piecemeal for fear of the reaction, the full extent of the loss was quickly known. "The entire city," writes Sanuto, "experiences more grief over this than it has ever had from its foundation to now." The appearance of a comet in the spring, recalls Priuli, had foretold the disaster. The Collegio was universally condemned for its failure adequately to supply Modone and for the mismanagement of the fleet. It was also blamed for weak defense of the province of Friuli. During the summer, fires set by Turkish raiders could be seen from the bell tower of San Marco.[53] In the most striking way, war had come home to Venice.

On September 20, the Great Council elected Pietro Balastro to the post of treasurer (*camerlengo*) at Cremona and Giovanni Zancani to the Ten; both had brothers who were killed at Modone. By contrast, Pietro Balbi was defeated in election for the Ten because he was currently a member of the Collegio.[54] This pattern was repeated on a larger scale on September 30 when all the *Primi* associated with the recent defeats, perhaps twenty-five men, were refused election to the Zonta "because the *terra* considered itself poorly served by them." The Ferrarese ambassador in Venice, Bartolomeo Cartari, reported to

53 On the importance of Modone: Pietro Dolfin, *Annalium Venetorum*, p. 192; Sanuto, 3:733. On the fall of Modone: Sanuto, 3:574, 582–583, 583–584, 586, 590, 598, 599–600, 602, 603, 608, 613–616, 618, 619, 620, 622, 629, 632, 637, 640, 641, 646, 652–653, 667–668, 688–692, 714, 716, 735. On reaction to the loss of Modone: Sanuto, 3:733. On the comet: Priuli, 1:321. On Friuli: Pietro Dolfin, *Annalium Venetorum*, p. 185; cf. Sanuto, 3:864; Priuli, 2:55; G. Cogo, "La guerra di Venezia contro i Turchi (1499–1501)."

54 Sanuto, 3:804.

the duke that experienced leaders were defeated by young men (*giovani*), "which indicates that this city is ill-disposed." Seven patricians were elected to the Zonta because they had relatives lost at Modone or in the fleet; the Great Council wished "to repay their merits and to give an example to our successors of such gratitude."[55]

About fifteen important patricians were elected to the Zonta, but their inclusion is further evidence that the Great Council was remarkably careful in its choices. A number of them had only recently returned to the city. Benedetto Sanuto arrived back from his post at Damascus on August 25. Paolo Capello returned on September 28 after serving as ambassador to Rome for nineteen months. Girolamo Orio was *podestà* at Bergamo until September 6. Pietro Marcello was still at his post as military commissioner in Friuli when he was elected, his reputation apparently undamaged from his connection with the Friulian raids. Marcantonio Morosini left his post as general at Cremona in January, but the Senate defeated him five times in elections to the Collegio, evidently because he had paid a suspiciously high price to acquire a strategic castle in the Cremonese. His election to the Zonta was his first victory in nine months. Marco Venier was apparently elected because he had defied the Full Collegio on September 20 when he mysteriously threatened "to tell everything" to the Great Council if his brother were forced to accept a command at Corfu.

A number of men who had been in the government in the summer of 1500 were placed on the Zonta, but their elections are the most convincing testimony of the Great Council's electoral precision. Marco Bollani and Benedetto Giustiniani were on the Collegio but won election to the Zonta because of their persistent efforts to send aid to the colonies. Both wished to refrain from attacking Milan earlier in 1499 because of Turkish advances in the Adriatic; both supported measures to strengthen the fleet, although their fears of enemy attacks near the Peloponnese were dismissed as mere fantasies. Some members of the Ten—Angelo Trevisan, Zaccaria Dolfin, Marco Molin, Francesco Tron, Antonio Bernardo, and Vitale Caotorta—were elected to the Zonta, apparently because of their attempts to aid Modone when the Collegio was slow to act. This policy was probably set by Angelo Trevisan and Zaccaria Dolfin. Trevisan was the brother of the dead

55 On the defeat of *Primi*: Sanuto, 3:853–854; Priuli, 2:58; ASMo., b. 11, c. 42, Bartolomeo Cartari to the duke of Ferrara, October 1, 1500. On rewarding relatives: Pietro Dolfin, *Annalium Venetorum*, p. 58.

captain general, Marchio, and was nominated for that post himself on July 18. Moreover, both he and Dolfin had received considerable praise for their service as maritime commissioners in 1499. In fact, their posts on the Ten were rewards for their overseeing the needs of the fleet and colonial forces. A few days after their election to the Zonta, Trevisan and Dolfin were again elected by the Senate as maritime commissioners. Three weeks later, they were made special commissioners over the Arsenal, an open slap at the regular Arsenal administrators, whose laxity in office was considered a crucial reason for the loss of Modone.[56]

The Great Council's influence on the composition of the Senate was not limited to the annual elections of August and September. The Great Council continually elected magistrates who had ex officio entrance to the Senate. Also, there were special elections to fill vacancies on the Zonta and among the sixty senators. Between 1498 and 1524, the Zonta had an annual turnover of 30 percent of its membership, and the senators had a turnover of 17 percent—a nice indication of the difference in prestige between the two groups.[57] All these elections could be used as political weapons by majorities in the Great Council. Yet although the Great Council could dispense admonitions and awards with exquisite precision, it could not enforce or shape changes in policy. The nature of the Great Council, its size and internal divisions, worked against any coherent formulation of opposition to the *Primi*. In this respect, the Great Council's power was more negative than positive, more effective in punishing than in rewarding; its careful selection and rejection of *Primi* in the short term was matched by a sluggish response on larger issues in the long term. The electoral power of the Great Council bred a politics of spite. *Primi* were wary of being chastised by the mass of the patriciate and of offending the corporate self-esteem of the sovereign assembly. Still, the governing circle and its policies remained basically unchanged. There is no evidence that the Zonta election of 1500 caused any changes in government policy. The Zonta was, after all, only one part of the Senate; and most of the men elected to the Zonta in 1500 did not differ in any crucial respect from those rejected. *Primi* remained in control. Priuli indicates that, in the Zonta election of 1509, when

56 For detailed references from Sanuto (vols. 2 and 3) on the careers of the men discussed for the two years before the Zonta election, see Robert Finlay, "The Politics of the Ruling Class in Early Cinquecento Venice," pp. 31–32.

57 These figures are based on an examination of the Consegi volumes (8892–8897) for these years.

Primi were defeated, many found their way back into the Senate by other offices "and, despite the Great Council, return[ed] to the government."[58]

Inasmuch as the Senate made all the nominations for the Zonta that were presented to the Great Council, there must have been a group within the Senate that nominated those men in 1500 who would be pleasing to the Great Council and who would be elected to the Zonta in place of the usual *Primi*. In short, some members of the Senate formed something of an opposition group within that assembly in that they followed or expressed the popular opinion held by a majority in the Great Council. The roles of occasional dissenter and general representative were filled by the Court of the Forty. Of course, the Forty in no sense formally represented the Great Council; rather, its membership was far more representative of the generality of the patriciate than were the men of the executive councils and the other members of the Senate.

Venice had three supreme appeal courts or *Quarantie*: The *civile nuova* dealt with civil cases outside the city; the *civile vecchia*, civil cases within Venice; the Forty (or *criminal*), all criminal cases. The three courts followed an order of rotation whereby the forty men elected to the *nuova* entered the *vecchia* after an eight-month term and then entered the Forty after another eight. Members of the Forty were generally younger and of a lower social and economic standing than the rest of the Senate. According to Contarini, the young and the poor of the Forty were added to the Senate to temper the views of the old and the rich. Many of the *Primi* had nothing but contempt for the Great Council, considering it a convention dominated by "babies and poor nobility"; they looked with like contempt on those elected to the Forty. Contarini preferred to regard the incorporation of the Forty in the Senate as the addition of an element of the *stato populare*, which rested in the Great Council, to the *governo de Nobili*.[59] A political function of the Forty was to bring the views and attitudes of the Great Council into the Senate.

Unlike the Zonta and the senators, members of the Forty received a salary, both because they needed it to live and because their judicial and political responsibilities added up to a full-time job. The Forty had extensive electoral authority. It had the right to elect all minor

58 Priuli, 4:369.
59 On contempt for the Great Council and the Forty: Priuli, vol. 5, fol. 85v; cf. Contarini, *Republica*, p. 105. On Contarini's view of the Forty: *Republica*, pp. 104-105.

cittadini offices, although the Collegio and Ten often (and improperly) named men to scribal and notarial posts.[60] Another significant prerogative was that of electing young, destitute patricians as galley bowmen (*ballestrarie*), posts that carried the right to ship some cargo and that were "a sort of socialized apprenticeship to trade and to the sea." The bowmen positions, writes Dolfin, were the "bread and butter" of poor patricians. Both Contarini and Priuli claim that patricians were increasingly reluctant to serve as bowmen because of desire for offices close to home. Yet competition for the posts remained strong: In 1511, four hundred young patricians presented themselves for election to less than one hundred bowmen slots. As with *cittadini* offices, the Collegio encroached on the Forty's prerogatives by nominating bowmen itself.[61]

Perhaps the Forty's most important electoral prerogative was that of electing its own three chiefs, who had the constitutional right to sit on the Signoria and to present motions to the Great Council and the Senate. The doge and the chiefs were the only officials who possessed the substantial power of being able to transfer consideration of a case from the Forty to either the Ten or the Senate.[62] Although the social standing of the men on the supreme court was low, the position of the chiefs in the Signoria and the Forty in the Senate gave the Forty a central role in the higher ranks of government. At the same time, the daily judicial and electoral business of the Forty brought it into constant contact with all groups in the city—no doubt a significant element in the Forty's reflection of popular opinion in the *terra*.

Because of the Forty's membership and responsibilities, it was the most politically unified body within the Senate. The ex officio magistrates had nothing in common with one another except the right to speak and vote only on matters of their particular competencies. Both the sixty senators and the sixty of the Zonta shared a certain

60 On the Forty's salary: Sanuto, *Cronachetta*, pp. 138–139; Sanuto, 32:426–427; della Torre, "Relazione," c. 78. On the Forty's electoral authority: Sanuto, *Cronachetta*, pp. 121–122, 124; cf. ASV, Quarantia criminal, Elezioni a cariche di ministero, Reg. 255 bis, Reg. 255 ter; Quarantia criminal, Parti, b. 22.

61 On the socialized apprenticeship: Frederic C. Lane, *Andrea Barbarigo, Merchant of Venice, 1418–1449*, p. 17. On the importance of the bowmen: Pietro Dolfin, *Annalium Venetorum*, p. 219. On reluctance to ship out: Contarini, *Republica*, p. 142; Priuli, vol. 5, fol. 263r; cf. Malipiero, 2:714–715. On competition for bowmen slots: ASV, Quarantia criminal, Parti, Reg. 22, fols. 7r–8r, 21r, 22r–22v. On the Collegio and bowmen nominations: ASV, Collegio, Notatorio, Reg. 20, fols. 194v–195r, 197r, 213v, 221r.

62 Contarini, *Republica*, pp. 71–72.

social standing, although membership in the Zonta was of slightly lower political prestige than a regular seat in the Senate. Except in extraordinary circumstances, as in 1500, the Zonta's election on the same day entailed no special distinction. The government was careful to avoid having elections for the Senate and the *Quarantia civile nuova* fall on the same day, perhaps because such a coincidence would encourage the sort of bloc voting that sometimes happened with the Zonta renewal. Not only was the Forty a socially distinctive body within the Senate; it was the only one of its size to have a legal existence and extensive responsibilities outside that assembly. The judges of the Forty met and worked together for sixteen months even before entering the Senate, and they continued to meet as a court while a part of the Senate. The Forty amounted to only slightly more than 25 percent of the Senate's voting membership; yet its social complexion and experience before entering the Senate gave the court a corporate unity lacking in other parts of the governing council.

Even though the senators, Zonta, and Forty occupied separate blocs of seats in the Senate, voting records do not distinguish among them. It is clear, however, that the Forty was a distinct force in the elections of the Senate and that it supported proposals dear to many in the Great Council, particularly ones aimed at easing the plight of poor patricians and increasing the number of state offices. The Forty had its own chambers in the Ducal Palace, so it was peculiarly fitted to be a focus for electioneering and lobbying. Although there were strict laws against such activities, and the Ten and the state attorneys looked askance at gatherings of patricians outside the council halls, it was easy, because the Forty gathered together every day, for electioneering for Senate posts to take place in its courtroom. Sanuto notes that a patrician won election to the Collegio because of intensive lobbying of the Forty. On the other hand, Sanuto claims that he failed to win because he did not sufficiently lobby the judges. In 1509 Sanuto failed to win election as a *savio agli ordini* because "the Forty did not support me," and in 1526 he considered it a good omen for his political future that the Forty was pleased with a speech he made in the Senate. In 1526 Giovanni Francesco Sagredo edged out Filippo Molin in an election for a Senate post because the Forty, which included Sagredo's son, supported him. While the three chiefs of the Forty sat on the Signoria, three "inferior" ducal councillors (or *consieri da basso*) presided over the court; these councillors took advantage of their position to curry favor with the Forty in the hopes that they would gain election to the Collegio. In 1520 the Great Council passed a law, intended to stop such lobbying, that stipulated that the "inferior" councillors could no longer accept election to the Collegio.[63]

Speeches in the Senate were sometimes aimed at winning the support of the Forty. In 1525 Zaccaria Trevisan, a *savio agli ordini*, took, in a debate on bowmen, a position designed to appeal to the incoming group of forty judges, perhaps in an attempt to win reelection to the Collegio. Ten years before, Luca Tron, a chief of the Ten, attacked the Collegio for graft and corruption, and his opponent retorted that Tron was only trying "to gratify the Forty, it being in the nature of men to listen willingly to slander of their leaders." Whether or not the charges were justified, Tron probably felt the need to please the Forty because of a rumor that he had refused to allow letters from Rome and France to be read in the Senate owing to the presence of the Forty, a rumor that had caused his defeat in an election to the Collegio. As a chief of the Ten, Tron was subsequently careful to refer matters of state to the Senate. When Paolo Trevisan asserted his right to speak in debate in 1495—"I am a citizen of this *terra* and of this council [of the Senate] and I will say what I please"—he addressed his remarks to the benches of the Forty, thereby implicitly acknowledging the latter's role as a spokesman of the *terra*.[64]

The Forty and its chiefs often supported proposals in the interests of poor patricians. The three chiefs generally required approval of the Forty before submitting a motion to the Senate or Great Council, so their actions may be taken as expressive of the court's will. Two chiefs drew up a proposal in 1492 to provide state subsidies for *poveri Zentilhomeni*. In 1520 the chiefs backed Antonio Tron's attempts to apply large amounts of tax revenue to the Monte di Pietà, a bank that specialized in loans to the poor. Two years later the chiefs proposed a motion to increase the salaries of minor officials, although the Forty was on record as opposing high salaries for the *Primi* who held ambassadorial posts. In 1523 the Forty supported a measure allowing patrician state debtors to pay in installments over two years, while retaining their offices. In 1515 the Forty opposed raising money by putting more pressure on state debtors and instead suggested an

---

63 On the Forty and elections for the Collegio: Sanuto, 33:327–328; 24:406. On 1509 and 1526: Sanuto, 9:184; 41:487. On Sagredo: Sanuto, 41:396–397. On the Forty and the councillors: Sanuto, 28:491, 507, 508, 509; cf. 29:608; Giuseppe Maranini, *La costituzione di Venezia dopo la Serrata del Maggior Consiglio*, p. 304.

64 On Zaccaria Trevisan: Sanuto, 39:210. On Tron: Michiel, fol. 151r; Sanuto, 19:335, 355, 402, 415; cf. 31:455–456. On Paolo Trevisan: Malipiero, 2:697.

elaborate plan for revamping the tax assessments of the city, a measure that probably found support among the numerous poor patricians in the Great Council who feared exclusion from office for not paying their taxes and forced loans.[65]

Poor patricians were always anxious to see the number of state offices increase, for their livelihood depended on sinecures awarded by the Great Council. Naturally, this desire for offices was voiced by the Forty. The Forty supported Pietro Tron's proposal in 1515 to create a militia of fifty young, indigent patricians, although the Collegio opposed the plan and prevented it from coming to a vote. Not only would such a militia have provided offices and salaries for needy patricians, but perhaps it would then not have been necessary to sell the forty positions on the court to young *ricchi* to raise money and men for the war. The immense problems arising from the War of the League of Cambrai prompted both Tron's proposal and the selling of offices, so it is ironic that the Forty's "greediness to create offices" may have been a partial cause of the war itself. Pope Julius II was reluctant to join the League of Cambrai, and only the intransigence of the Senate regarding his Romagnol possessions drove him into the alliance against Venice. Priuli maintains that within the Senate it was the Forty that backed the policies that led to war: "The judgment of the forty patricians of the *Quarantia criminal* in the Venetian Senate is very perilous, because they are poor, have nothing to lose, and can't pay their taxes; they heed only their own advantage and [thus] the expansion of the state in order to gain offices at home and abroad." According to Priuli, two eloquent senators, Andrea Venier and Giorgio Emo, directly appealed for support to the patricians of the Forty, "who because they are poor and desire offices, don't wish to restore the cities of the Romagna" to the pope. In short, the usually prudent *Padri* of the Collegio were swayed by the "common Venetians" of the Forty.[66]

Priuli also asserts that Venice's first move toward regaining territory lost after the battle of Agnadello, the recovery of Padua in July 1509,

65 On the proposal of 1492: Malipiero, 2:691. On 1520: Sanuto, 28:319–320; cf. Pullan, *Rich and Poor*, pp. 493, 470–471. On salaries in 1522: Sanuto, 34:34. On state debtors: Michiel, fol. 155v; Sanuto, 20:17–18; and this book, Chapter IV.1.
66 On Tron's proposal: Sanuto, 20:185; 21:147; cf. Michiel, fol. 203v. On "greediness to create offices": Sanuto, 5:396; 642. On Julius II: Federico Seneca, *Venezia e papa Giulio II*, pp. 117–122. On the Forty and Romagna: Priuli, 4:93; cf. 141; vol. 5, fol. 296v; ASV, Maggior Consiglio, Deliberazioni, Liber Stella, Reg. 24, fol. 88v.

was due to anger and emotion in the Senate, to the desire of many to recover property in the Padovano and to reconquer the mainland. The Forty's desire for offices for themselves and their relatives in the Great Council played a role in the decision to attack Padua, for the plight of poor patricians was much worse after the loss of the *terraferma* two months before. The recovery of Padua was the first step toward restoring numerous offices to the Great Council. In a debate in 1525, Sanuto argued against legislation aimed at raising the average age of those elected to the Forty, and his speech supplies valuable evidence of the Forty's influence within the Senate in the summer of 1509: "Gentlemen, permit the young to enter into government of the state, for I remember that in 1509, when Padua was recovered, it was the Forty which inspired Alvise Molin to place the proposal to take Padua. . . . and the proposal being accepted, Padua was entered on the day of Saint Marina, a victory which [signaled] the beginning of the recovery of our state."[67]

The Forty was influential in politics only insofar as it represented the interests and opinions of patricians in the Great Council. In effect, the Forty was a bridge between the majority of the patriciate and the ranks of the *Primi*, an extension of the Great Council into the governing circle. The regular round of elections and the Zonta renewal served as checks on the governing circle; but the Forty's participation in the Senate was a surer guarantee that the *Primi* would constantly be attentive to the patriciate in the Great Council.

The close identification of the Great Council with the Forty—and, perhaps, of both with the city—caused considerable embarrassment and difficulty for Nicolò da Ponte in the early months of his dogeship. When da Ponte made his inaugural speech to the Great Council on March 3, 1578, he used the occasion to attack the Forty, before which he had lost cases while serving as a state attorney. Da Ponte was an unpopular choice as doge in the city and in the Great Council; his assault on the court did not improve his poor reputation for wisdom or generosity. As one observer remarked, the new doge's speech had shown him once again to be "a man of little prudence." Da Ponte had special need of the Great Council's favor because he had convinced the Signoria to present legislation permitting his nephew (da Ponte had no son) to receive the honors due the son of a doge. After da Ponte's intemperate remarks, one councillor, Giovanni Donato, withdrew from the motion and strongly criticized the doge "for saying

---

67 Sanuto, 39:28; Priuli, 4:151.

such terrible things about the Forty." The Great Council was so visibly angry that the Signoria did not put the proposal to a vote. A subsequent apology by da Ponte to the Forty and the Great Council was of no avail; the proposal was defeated by 750 to 426 (with 109 abstentions). Nine months later, the Signoria and doge thought that the patriciate's anger had subsided enough to try again. The proposal was redrafted and the Great Council was urged to have regard for the dignity of the doge, "who represents the greatness of this Council, in which is found the majesty of our entire Republic." The flattery had no effect, and the proposal was decisively rejected once more.[68] It was not presented again. Da Ponte was, indeed, "a man of little prudence" not to know, after a lifetime in Venetian politics, that to attack the Forty was to insult the Great Council. He should have known, too, that the Great Council had a strong sense of self-esteem and that the patriciate was always ready to avenge a slight by denying an honor.

The Great Council's electoral power and the Forty's presence in the Senate both worked to secure the accommodation of many patricians to a regime in which they otherwise had slight influence. Poor and powerless patricians could feel that their votes had effect and that they had a certain representation in the Senate. To some extent, then, appearances were saved, for the official values of the Republic did not admit of distinctions of power within the ruling class. Election to the Ten or Collegio bestowed considerable, if temporary, authority on a patrician; yet he only had "the power of a single ballot." Equality within the Great Council was regarded as the guarantor of liberty in Venice. In 1523 Gabriele Moro spoke in the Senate against the domination of the government by a few men, asserting that "because I am a man born in a free city, I'll freely express my feelings." It was a commonplace of Venetian political rhetoric that "we are equal in this *terra*," and preambles to legislation often invoked that theme, as with a proposal regarding elections in 1506: "It has always been a characteristic of our state to promote equality, especially in the affairs of the Great Council." Priuli was only stating what all patricians purported to believe when he wrote that "those who wish to preserve and maintain a good republic must above all preserve and maintain equality."[69]

---

68 On da Ponte's speech: "Memorie pubbliche," fols. 2r, 3r; Alvise Michiel, "Diarii, 1578–1586," March 1578, no pagination. On da Ponte's election: William Archer Brown, "Nicolò da Ponte." On the legislation: ASV, Maggior Consiglio, Deliberazioni, Liber Frigerius, Reg. 31, fols. 41r, 55r.

69 On Moro: Sanuto, 37:296; cf. 8:117. On equality in the *terra*: Sanuto, 25:

Of course Priuli, a banker and a cynic, was aware that he was expressing an ideal. It was clear that not all were equal in the Great Council nor did all enjoy the same freedom in the city. Certainly the sort of equality resulting from voting in the Great Council did not invariably reassure a staunch republican such as Sanuto. He notes that Giovanni Emo and Bartolomeo Moro were both elected to posts by the Great Council within two days of each other, and both had previously been exiled for crimes and later absolved by the Senate: "Emo won [election to the Zonta] by lobbying and by handing out money, and today Moro won [a minor post] because he is poor, so whether one does good or ill, at the end of five years we are equal."[70]

Division between rich and poor ran through the Great Council. Priuli estimates that three-fourths of the patriciate could be classed as "poor," that is, dependent on offices for a livelihood. In 1499 a member of the Contarini clan burst in on a meeting of the Collegio to complain that he had no office and was forced to live in poverty. Patrician state debtors were legally not eligible either to enter elections or to hold office; yet whereas wealthy debtors could usually evade exclusion from office, the poor, lacking influential allies and bribe money, were not so fortunate. "There is great grumbling," says Priuli, "that the rich are able to have offices and magistracies by force of money, yet the poor, not having money, must be expelled [from office]." Priuli refers to "the senators or rich ones" (*id est Senatori over ricchi*), for (with the exception of the Forty) the governing council was an abode of the wealthy: "The first families of the Venetian nobility, the richest and most important, are almost always placed in the council of the Senate, where they deliberate with their votes according to their own benefit."[71]

In 1496, according to Malipiero, the Senate compensated rich patricians for homes burned but poor patricians were disregarded. The tax laws, also, were in favor of the rich, who opposed any reforms that might touch their income from the Rialto money market and Monte bonds. The rich also had the galley voyages of Beirut, Alexandria, and the West in their hands: "All the merchant nobles of

<hr />

357. On the 1506 preamble: ASV, Maggior Consiglio, Deliberazioni, Liber Deda, Reg. 25, fol. 28r. On preserving a republic: Priuli, vol. 5, fol. 138v.

70 Sanuto, 54:12.

71 On patrician poverty: Priuli, 4:297. On the poor Contarini: Malipiero, 1:535. On debtors: Priuli, vol. 5, fol. 95v. On "senators or rich ones": Priuli, 4:29. On the rich in the Senate: Priuli, 2:77–78.

Venice operated as one large regulated company of which the board
of directors was the Senate."[72] In part, the contempt of the *Primi* in
the Senate for the patriciate in the Great Council stemmed from a
potentially dangerous economic division within the ruling class.

Primi displayed understandable nervousness when forced to face the
political problem of indigent patricians. In 1492 two chiefs of the
Forty, Gabriele Bon and Francesco Falier, drew up a radical measure
to provide state subsidies or pensions for *"poveri Zentilhomeni"* without offices. Collecting a portion of the salaries of high officials, they
proposed to allot 100 ducats a year to every poor patrician over sixty
and 50 ducats a year to those between twenty-five and sixty. The
annual cost of the program was estimated at 70,000 ducats. The subsidies were substantial: Between 1495 and 1510, the annual average
salary for a servant was 7 ducats; for a soldier, 22; and for an important secretarial post, 88.[73] The plan, too, was on a grand scale:
Assuming that one-fourth of the 70,000 ducats went to patricians over
sixty years of age, then 175 men in the Great Council of 1,800 would
receive 100 ducats a year and 1,050 would receive 50 ducats a year.
Subsidies would go to 68 percent of the patriciate, with only 575
patricians receiving nothing. It is not surprising that Bon and Falier
ran into trouble with their project. Before they could present their
proposal to the Great Council, Antonio Boldù, a state attorney, learned
of their intentions and told the Collegio and chiefs of the Ten. When
the Collegio first learned the details it was stunned, and for a moment
nothing was said. Then the objections multiplied. Bon and Falier were
suspected of acting from motives of political ambition, perhaps to inspire the Great Council "to make them procurators"; it was forbidden,
someone pointed out, for a patrician to exalt himself by dispensing
public moneys. Moreover, it was argued, the plan would give birth to
factions in the Great Council, and eight hundred patricians in Crete
would flock to Venice to share in the largesse.

The Collegio and Ten were faced with a delicate problem: They
thought the arguments against the proposal were strong, but "on the
other hand, it was also considered that whoever opposed it would be
badly treated" in the Great Council's elections. They decided to halt

72 On 1496: Malipiero, 2:700–701. On opposition to tax reform and control of
the galleys: Malipiero, 1:406–407. On nobles as a "regulated company": Lane,
Andrea Barbarigo, p. 48.

73 On the proposal: Malipiero, 2:691; cf. Sanuto, *Vite dei dogi*, fol. 350v;
Cozzi, "Authority and the Law," p. 300. On salaries: Pierre Sardella; *Nouvelles
et spéculations à Venise au début du XVIème siècle*, p. 54.

the proposal before it reached the Great Council, so Falier, the principal figure behind the motion and "a man of great ingenuity," was called before Doge Agostino Barbarigo and instructed to carry his motion no further under pain of punishment by the Ten. Falier appeared to submit, but he secretly persuaded Bon to present the motion to the Great Council. Bon consulted with Boldù; and Boldù informed the Ten, which ordered Bon and Falier exiled for life to Nicosia "for disturbing the peace [of the city] with novelties." Two secretaries of a financial office were also exiled for helping to draw up the proposal. There was no debate on the decision, and no formal charges were leveled at the two chiefs of the Forty. The anxiety of the *Primi* that the proposal for subsidies might become public knowledge is conveyed in the orders of the Ten for dealing with Bon and Falier: "So that they would have no way of speaking with anyone, they were quickly arrested, immediately placed in chains, and sent to the castle at Zara under strict custody, in order that they can be [quickly] shipped to Cyprus."[74]

Giovanni Antonio Minio met a similar fate ten years later. Drained of funds during war with the Turks, the government presented a measure in December 1501 to cut official salaries in half. There was opposition to the proposal when it came before the Great Council from the Senate. Vitale Vitturi complained that "the rich are in the Senate," implying that wealthy men were taking advantage of the ordinary patrician in the Great Council. Gasparo Malipiero and Giovanni Antonio Minio also wished to oppose the motion, but their speaking time was cut short by the Signoria. The proposal passed the Great Council by less than 400 of 1,437 votes. A year later it came up for renewal. Doge Loredan, informed that Minio intended to speak in opposition, ordered the Great Council's chamber cleared of all but patricians in the vain hope that the city would not learn of dissension within the ruling class. Minio was a well known and eloquent lawyer (he had defended Antonio Grimani in the Great Council trial of 1500), and his intentions were probably common knowledge. Both Sanuto and Priuli charge that Minio's opposition arose from his political ambitions and that he was supported by "many poor patricians who live off their offices." (Sanuto's indignation, at least, was somewhat self-serving, for, as a member of the Collegio, he had

74 On being "badly treated": Malipiero, 2:691–692. On Falier's ingenuity: Sanuto, 10:644. On "disturbing the peace": Sanuto, *Vite dei dogi*, fols. 350v–351r. On the orders of the Ten: Malipiero, 2:692.

drafted the proposal with Costantino Priuli.)[75] In Sanuto's rendition, Minio's speech to the Great Council is an odd combination of religious philippic and crude economic analysis:

> In this war all things have gone against us because we don't show compassion to those near at hand, that is, to poor patricians who don't have the means to live. . . . This notion, put forward without compassion, displeases God . . . and by this means we seek to destroy their livelihood. . . . They are born less as inheritors of paternal goods than as successors to the benefits of this Republic; but by this motion we wish to deprive them even of these. We don't want to recognize the tribulations sent to us by God: on August 10th [1499] the captain-general, Antonio Grimani, approached with the wind astern to attack the Turkish fleet leaving Portolongo, but when he was a mile away, the wind became dead calm, and the Turks moved toward Chiarenza . . . and took Nepanto. And twice such miracles occurred, with a wind rising for an attack on the Turks, and then a dead calm. Everyone knows that this Senate [sic] has three sorts of patricians—poor, middling, and rich. Only the poor and middling pay taxes, and they are the first to be dunned, while the rich, who could give a mountain of gold, are not constrained to pay. . . . This motion takes bread from the mouth of poor patricians . . . because they will have to go to the poorhouse for lack of means to make a living; because the proposal will be renewed from year to year; and, even worse, because those who will remain in offices and administration will be in danger of being charged by the syndics for selling their judgments and for robbing the public.[76]

This was the sort of open confrontation that the *Primi* had successfully avoided in 1492: an articulation of economic divisions within the Great Council that denied the rhetoric about patrician equality. Minio's inchoate attack evoked a fierce rebuttal by Loredan in which he accused the lawyer of sins ranging from base ingratitude to conscious subversion. Loredan charged that Minio had not paid his state debts and that the Collegio had loaned him 3,000 ducats to rebuild his home after a fire. A more fundamental accusation was that Minio was

---

75 On the proposal in 1501: Sanuto, 3:918, 970, 1003, 1132; Priuli, 2:78, 80. On Vitturi: Sanuto, 3:1136. On the proposal in 1502: Priuli, 2:193; Sanuto, 4:201; cf. 3:172. On the "many poor patricians": Priuli, 2:193. On Sanuto's indignation: cf. Cozzi, "Authority and the Law," p. 301.

76 On Minio's speech: Sanuto, 4:201–202. On use of the Aristotelian division of poor, middling, and rich in Florence: Felix Gilbert, *Machiavelli and Guicciardini*, pp. 23–25.

trying "to create factions among us in this council": "It is sufficient," Loredan railed at Minio, "that you render judgment with your ballot, without coming to sow discord in this assembly." Obviously, Minio had touched a nerve within the body politic. The timing of his opposition also contributed to the uproar: Discontent with the austerity measure had increased during the past year, when so many had come to feel its effects, especially inasmuch as officials had recouped their losses by illegally exacting money from patricians and citizens who had business with them. Loredan's peroration was aimed at stilling such discontents in the name of patriotism and sacrifice:

> We want this just and blessed law to be enacted in order to provide for our great needs, to maintain the state and not to become slaves of the Turks. And—God forbid!—if it proves necessary to maintain the state, we will melt down all the chalices, crosses, and silver of the churches, including the *Palla* of San Marco, so hard would it be to see the ruin of this city. Giovanni Antonio Minio shows scant compassion for this country and state. We come with tears in our eyes to make this proposal . . . therefore, gentlemen, make the proper judgment, putting all your votes into one urn, so that, descending from the Great Council, it can be said to everyone that the law was passed by all our votes.[77]

The austerity proposal was renewed by a vote of 1,088 to 347. The next day the Ten sentenced Minio to confinement on the island of Arbe in Dalmatia. He was given no trial and was ordered to be silent on the reason for his punishment; two weeks later, he left for exile "without saying anything else." Shortly after, "a large number of patricians came to the Great Council, thinking that the condemnation made by the Council of Ten would be read out; but it was not announced, either to create more fear or so as not to make the affair public." Priuli writes that Minio's exile "was held to be a harsh condemnation, much more, in truth, than he deserved; still, initial Venetian angers are the most dangerous, and in time they are mitigated." Mitigation did not come soon enough for Bon and Minio, both of whom died in exile. Falier purchased a pardon in 1510, returned to Venice full of suggestions for improving Cyprus's income, and was elected to high office, including many terms on the Ten.[78]

---

77 On Loredan's speech: Sanuto, 4:204. On illegal exactions: Priuli, 2:78.
78 On Minio's exile: Sanuto, 4:204, 209, 210; Priuli, 2:193; cf. ASMo., b. 11, c. 3, Bartolomeo Cartari to the duke of Ferrara, January 8, 1502. On Minio's

In the seventeenth century, Alexandre Touissaint de Limojon praised Venice, albeit with some exaggeration: "The liberty of Venice permits everything, for whatever life one leads, whatever religion one professes; if one does not talk, and undertakes nothing against the state or the nobility, one can live in full security, and no one will undertake to censure one's conduct nor oppose one's personal disorder."[79] The *Primi* defined the limits of official toleration. When Bon, Falier, and Minio brought up the matter of poor patricians, they crossed the line of permissible political discourse. The subject was explosive because of the electoral power of the Great Council and because the governing circle was almost wholly composed of *ricchi*. Any action that served to point up the contradiction between official dedication to equality and economic division within the patriciate was a threat to the *Primi*.

The Ten acted irregularly and with the utmost dispatch in 1492 and 1502, not because of inherent ruthlessness, but because of fear that open recognition of inequalities in the Great Council would aid the growth of an organized faction composed of lowly patricians and led by men eager to take advantage of enmity toward the rich men of the executive councils and Senate. There is no way of telling if the accusations leveled at the three men were accurate, but apparently the government's leaders believed them to be so. The celerity shown in disposing of the dissidents indicates not alarm over a possible revolt of poor patricians, a *jacquerie* in the Ducal Palace, but rather fear of being defeated by them in the elections of the Great Council, "that plethoric and unpredictable organism."[80]

A speech by Doge Andrea Gritti provides an ironic counterpoint to Minio's humiliation. It must have been something of a shock to listen to Doge Gritti address the Great Council for the first time on May 26, 1523, one week after his election, for following the customary remarks about his intention to maintain peace and order in the Republic, he unexpectedly added that "he was ready to help the poor patricians, both publicly and privately, because in this *terra* there are rich, middling and poor, and it is very befitting that the rich aid the middling and the

---

death: Sanuto, 14:414, 423; 15:284–285. On Falier's return: Sanuto, 9:177, 185; Priuli, 4:360–361; cf. Sanuto, 10:644; 11:472, 517; 13:215; 335, 676; 19:462; 31:466.

79 Quoted by William J. Bouwsma, "Venice and the Political Education of Europe," in *Renaissance Venice*, ed. J. R. Hale (Totowa, N.J., 1973), p. 461.

80 Cozzi, "Authority and the Law," p. 301. On the development of poor patricians as a faction in the early seventeenth century: Charles J. Rose, "Marc Antonio Venier, Renier Zeno and 'the Myth of Venice.'"

middling the poor; and on this he expounded at some length." Oddly enough, Gritti's motive in making these remarks may not have been far different from Minio's: Not a popular choice as doge, he may have hoped to gain support in the Great Council by championing the cause of poor patricians.[81] In any event, one wonders what could have passed through the mind of a patrician hearing Minio's sentiments being spoken by the head of the Republic. It would not be surprising if he found in this a confirmation of Minio's accusation that a double standard ruled the patriciate, for clearly equality did not exist when a doge could speak with impunity on a subject that warranted exile for one not within the governing circle. A patrician in the Great Council was wise to "render judgment with his ballot" and to leave the expression of opinions to those in the ranks of the *Primi*. The liberty and power of the typical patrician began and ended with his ballot.

3. The Family and the Patriciate

At the heart of Venetian politics was the family.[82] Even quite distant family connections carried a political value; a patrician's honor was enhanced or diminished by the deeds of relatives, whether fellow clan members or in-laws. Doge Loredan sought revenge against Captain General Benedetto Pesaro and his secretary, Marco Rizo, for executing Marco Loredan, "who was of the doge's house [*casa*]." Ca' Loredan, Sanuto observes, never forgot or forgave a wrong. Yet while the doge and the dead man shared a common ancestor, their branches of the clan had diverged in the mid-Trecento; Marco's father was no more than a fifth cousin to Doge Loredan. In exceptional cases, hatred based on lineage was held for centuries. One of the arguments against Paolo Tiepolo's elevation to the dogeship in 1578 was that his ancestor,

81 Sanuto, 34:229. On Gritti's election, see this book, Chapter III.3.

82 Stanley Chojnacki, "In Search of the Venetian Patriciate"; idem, "Dowries and Kinsmen in Early Renaissance Venice"; and idem, "Patrician Women in Renaissance Venice"; James Cushman Davis, *A Venetian Family and Its Fortune, 1500–1900*; Margaret Leah King, "Caldiera and the Barbaros on marriage and the family"; Philip M. Giraldi, "The Zen Family, 1500–1550"; cf. Francis William Kent's *Household and Lineage in Renaissance Florence*, pp. 62, 85–91, 164; Dale Kent, *The Rise of the Medici*, pp. 37–61. "Clan" (or "house," *casa*) as used here refers to the consanguinal kin group recognizing descent from a distant ancestor and sharing a surname; "family" refers not to the nuclear kin group of parents and children but to the extended household typical of Venice; thus a "family" might be composed of four bachelor brothers (as noted by Davis, *Venetian Family*, p. 48).

Bajamonte Tiepolo, had attempted to overthrow the Republic in 1310. Family pride was equally sustaining, as Pietro Sanuto showed in a Senate debate of 1558 when he boasted that Ca' Sanuda had selected the lagoon site for "a city or republic such that the world had never seen before."[83]

Although relationships formed by marriage did not carry force for so long a time, they were of enormous significance for all aspects of patrician life. A suitor faced extended scrutiny by the prospective bride's family because he would be a political ally, a possible business associate, a caretaker of the dowry, and a guardian of one's own blood.[84] If a patrician's cousin were convicted of graft or if his nephew were elected to the Ten, his close in-laws shared in the shame or glory. Giovanni Venier was married to a daughter of Doge Loredan; hence the doge's sons aided Giovanni's brother in an election for procurator. Francesco di Alvise Foscari defended Benedetto Pesaro against charges of peculation, partly because Benedetto's nephew was wed to Foscari's daughter. Costantino Priuli sided with Francesco di Filippo Foscari in a Senate debate, and Sanuto thought it relevant that they were related: Priuli's first cousin was married to Foscari's second cousin.[85]

Sanuto wore mourning clothes in 1518 for the death of Lorenzo di Pietro Priuli, the diarist's father, and accompanied Alvise di Pietro Priuli to the Ducal Palace when the latter was elected procurator in 1524. He was proud of his connection with the wealthy and powerful Priuli brothers, who were the second cousins of his wife, dead since 1509 after three years of marriage.[86] Clearly, Sanuto considered that this brief and childless union created a relationship of lasting significance with a large part of his spouse's clan. Patrician genealogy was one of Sanuto's preoccupations, an appropriate subject for a student of Venetian politics.

A patrician's career usually depended on the wealth, size, and in-

83 On the Loredan and Pesaro incident: Priuli, 2:282; Sanuto, 4:41; ASMo., b. 12, c. 116, Bartolomeo Cartari to the duke of Ferrara, August 14, 1503; Barbaro, 8595, fols. 245v, 247v–284r; Capellari, vol. 2, fols. 235v–237v. On Tiepolo: William Archer Brown, "Nicolò da Ponte," p. 15. On Pietro Sanuto: "Memorie pubbliche," 810 (7298), no pagination.

84 Chojnacki, "Patrician Women," p. 180.

85 On Venier: Sanuto, 4:185–186. On Foscari and Pesaro: Sanuto, 6:134–135; Barbaro, 8595, fols. 129v–130r; Capellari, vol. 2, fols. 89r–90r. On Priuli and Foscari: Sanuto, 6:49; Barbaro, 8597, fols. 11r, 13v–14r, 17r; Capellari, vol. 3, fols. 248r–250v.

86 On Sanuto and the Priuli: Sanuto, 7:672; 26:54; 37:13.

fluence of his family. Belonging to a large clan did not assure success (the enormous Contarini house included many indigent and powerless men), but one's career was greatly aided by a *casa* that combined many members and financial resources. In 1527 there were about twenty-seven hundred patricians belonging to 134 clans, although it was rare if more than sixteen hundred attended the Great Council.[87] Nine clans had no males old enough to enter the Great Council, and nineteen—for example, Avonal, Balastro, Battaglia, Calergi, Celsi, Caotorta, D'Avanzago, Guoro, Lolin, Onorati, Ruzzini, Vizzamano—were close to extinction, with only one or two males of mature age. Sanuto's infrequent notes on members of these houses only serve to point up their insignificance, as when he observes in 1518 that Sigismondo di Cavalli won election to a minor post, only the second time in 138 years that the patriciate so honored his line.[88] Other clans, with as many as seventeen members—Baffo, Cocco, Civran, Da Mezzo, Manolesso, Pizzamano, Semiticolo, Viaro—seldom competed for high office. The make-up of the Signoria in the summer of 1527 reflects this, for, whereas the ducal councillors generally came from large houses (the average size of the councillors' clans was 52 men), the chiefs of the Forty were (with one exception) from small houses with names such as Lippomano (14), Bon (17), Calbo (5), and Grioni (1). Patricians of the Briani (4), Girardo (4), Zancani (11), Nadal (5), and Belegno (3) habitually were elected as supervisors of the *Fondaco dei Tedeschi* or to one of the minor courts of the Ducal Palace; their names rarely appear on lists of the Ten or Collegio.[89]

Some small and middling-sized clans—Vendramin (11), Foscari (12), Zen (19), Barbo (20), Dandolo (21), Pesaro (25), Tron (26), and Grimani (27)—were influential, usually because a member raised his clan's prestige by success in trade or by gaining rich benefices. The wealth of the Vendramin, Tron, and Grimani, gained in the Levant trade, catapulted them to the ranks of the *Primi*, as did the lucrative ecclesiastical offices held by the Barbo and the Zen. A small but wealthy clan could retain power only by allying with larger houses. For example, the Foscari wielded influence out of proportion to their number because Doge Francesco's long reign (1423–1457) gave

87 Sanuto, 45:569–572. The exact number of patricians on Sanuto's 1527 list is 2,708, which included a few patricians on Crete. All subsequent references to the number of men over twenty-five years of age in a clan derive from Sanuto's list.
88 Sanuto, 25:533; cf. 29:504.
89 On 1527: Sanuto, 45:51, 357. On officials of the *Fondaco* and minor courts: ASV, Segretario alle voci, Uffici, Reg. 10, fols. 14r, 15r, 61r.

his clan the opportunity of forging links with powerful families. Not only was Antonio Grimani from an unimportant clan; he suffered the additional social liability of a nonpatrician mother; but the fortune he amassed by dominating the Venetian pepper trade opened the way to marriage alliances with *Primi*—and eventually to the doge's cap for himself and cardinal's hats for his son and grandsons.[90]

Thirty clans, representing 59 percent of the patriciate, had over thirty members apiece, and nineteen "big houses" (*case grandi*), clans with more than forty men, made up 45 percent of the patriciate: Contarini (172), Morosini (102), Malipiero (81), Marcello (77), Venier (69), Donato (67), Michiel (67), Priuli (56), Bragadin (55), Querini (53), Loredan (52), Trevisan (50), Molin (50), Zorzi (49), Giustiniani (45), Corner (44), Pisani (44), Dolfin (42), Bembo (41).

Extremes of wealth and importance ran through the big houses, which were also dispersed in the various districts of the city.[91] Still, for all its economic and geographic diversity, the clan remained a focus for patrician identification that went beyond a nostalgia for origins. A patrician's status derived from his birth; his family introduced him to notions of political discipline and responsibility. The very nature of the patriciate as a congeries of clans invested with hereditary right to rule placed a premium on a patrician locating himself accurately in time and among his kin. Francesco Barbaro, a patrician and humanist of the early Quattrocento, wrote in his treatise on marriage that "the light of paternal glory does not permit the well-born to be mediocre; they understand that the image of their parents is more of a burden than an honor unless they prove themselves by their own virtue worthy of the dignity and greatness of their ancestors."[92]

Given the social and political traditions of the ruling class, identification with one's clan was assured. In 1364 Naufosio Morosini so identified with his clan that he died from wounds received in a fight that began when Ca' Morosini was reviled—certainly not the sort of familial pride that Barbaro had in mind. In 1450 Cardinal Pietro Morosini stipulated in his will that his library must remain in the

90 On the Foscari: Barbaro, 8595, fols. 129v–130r; Capellari, vol. 2, fols. 89r–90r. On the Grimani: Barbaro, 8595, fol. 183r; Capellari, vol. 2, fols. 184r, 185r. For more on the marriage alliances of the *Primi*, see this book, Chapter III.3.

91 Chojnacki, "Venetian Patriciate," p. 60; Giraldi, "Zen Family," pp. 73–74. The line separating middling from large houses probably lay somewhere between thirty-five and forty members; forty is a reasonable and conservative dividing line: less than 8 percent of the patriciate were in clans that numbered less than forty and more than thirty-five.

92 King, "Caldiera and the Barbaros," p. 33.

possession of his clan. In praising Cardinal Giovanni di Giorgio Corner in 1508, the Collegio declared that "his ancestors and all his house" have always served the Republic well; twenty-five years later Doge Gritti complained in the Collegio that "three houses in this city want all the bishoprics": the Corner, Pisani, and Grimani.[93] A mid-Trecento chronicler even attributed certain traits to individual clans. For example, the Dandolo were characterized as audacious and wise; the Giustiniani, as benevolent and courageous but overly proud. The seventy-five-year-old patrician of Ca' Donato who died while entertaining his favorite prostitute no doubt occasioned ribald comment about his clan's characteristics.[94]

Beyond a surname and a distant ancestor, members of a clan shared political liabilities stemming from their clan identification. Only one member of a *casa* could sit on a branch of the Procuratia or Collegio; only one could be on the Signoria or Ten; only one could serve at a time in all collegial offices, such as the Salt Office, the Grain Office, the Attorney's Office. Five men from one house could sit in the Senate, two as members of the Zonta, three as senators. No member of a clan could sit in judgment on a fellow on any council or magistracy, whether in a civil or criminal case, a stipulation that could cause difficulty: When the Ten and its *zonta* were considering pardons for a Donato, a Capello, a Foscari. a Giustiniani, and a Vendramin in 1510, a majority of the thirty-one men had to excuse themselves from voting on the issue.[95]

Several members of the same family were, however, often found simultaneously in important positions. In July 1500, five Tron, all first or second cousins, held office: Antonio as ducal councillor, Filippo on the Collegio, Francesco on the Ten, Pietro as a treasurer at the Rialto, and Luca as a government inspector (*sindico*) in Dalmatia. In July 1511 Bartolomeo Minio was elected to the Signoria at the age of eighty, when one son was a state attorney and another a member of the Collegio. Five years later Giorgio Corner was a procurator and on

93 On the Morosini: Chojnacki, "Venetian Patriciate," p. 60. On Corner in 1508: ASV, Senato, Secreta, Reg. 41, fol. 56r. On Gritti in 1533: Sanuto, 58:465; cf. Giuseppe Liberali, *Il 'Papalismo' dei Pisani 'dal Banco,'* p. 106, n. 372.

94 On clan traits: Benjamin Z. Kedar, *Merchants in Crisis*, pp. 122–123. On the patrician of Ca' Donato: ASM, b. 1454, Giambattista Malatesta to the marquis of Mantua, July 9, 1520.

95 On family members in office: Maranini, *Costituzione di Venezia*, pp. 150, 242, 332, 410; Enrico Besta, *Il Senato Veneziano (origine, costituzione, attribuzioni e riti)*, p. 79. On 1510: ASV, Consiglio di Dieci, Parti Miste, Reg. 33, fols. 8r–8v.

the Collegio, and three sons were, respectively, a ducal councillor, a senator, and a governor of Friuli. The Miani family had fewer than fourteen men, but six of them held office in 1506. The Capello had an even more striking record with twenty of twenty-four of the clan in office in 1506/1507. Sanuto thought that the positions the Capello held on the Collegio in December 1510 were unique in Venetian history, worth "noting to eternal memory": Paolo Capello was a *savio grande*; his second cousin was a *savio agli ordini*; and a distant cousin was a *savio di terraferma*. Further, his brother was a ducal councillor, and his first cousin was a chief of the Ten.[96] Obviously, the political influence of a family was increased when so many relatives occupied central positions, even if the collective action of the councils makes it almost impossible to trace that influence.

The disability that struck the average patrician most forcibly and frequently was the limitation on the number of clan members who could participate in Great Council elections. Only one member of a house was permitted to be among the thirty-six patricians charged with nominating men to office every Sunday. Such a restriction was regarded with disfavor by the large houses, which welcomed a modi-fication in the rule of 1506. In 1527 a more far-reaching proposal to alter the law met fierce opposition by the small houses, while the *case grandi* retaliated by voting down those who opposed liberalizing the electoral procedures.[97]

All clan members, moreover, had to leave the hall of the Great Council when one of their line was voted on. It was, according to Sanuto, "a remarkable event" when neither a Contarini nor a Morosini were among the nominators for the day.[98] Ordinarily, for example, Tadeo Contarini, one of the city's richest men, would find himself waiting out a vote on a Contarini, with whom he was connected by a thirteenth-century ancestor, while surrounded by other Contarini, many of whom could barely afford to keep their patrician robes in a state of repair. On no other occasion would all the Contarini in the Great Council gather together, certainly not for social events, such as weddings or feasts. Yet week after week, electoral law forced them

---

96 On the Tron: Sanuto, 3:438, 439, 542. On the Minio: Sanuto, 12:270–271, 277. On the Corner: Sanuto, 23:362. On the Miani: Marino Sanuto, "Miscellanea di Cronaca Veneta di Marino Sanuto," fol. 65r. On the Capello in 1506/1507 and 1510: Sanuto, 11:703; Sanuto, "Miscellanea," fol. 64r.

97 On 1506: Sanuto, 7:42, 147; this book, Chapter V.1. On 1527: this book, Chapter II.4.

98 Sanuto, 25:377.

to congregate and reminded them of their lineage—clan reunions that must have gone far toward maintaining a patrician's identification with his *casa* as a whole.

Perhaps a sense of grievance at being excluded from voting also played a part in reinforcing clan unity. In 1507 when a Contarini (172) was contesting a Garzoni (10) in a Great Council election, the Contarini caused "a great commotion" as they left the hall. No doubt the Contarini made considerable noise as they shuffled into the ante-chambers of the Great Council, but it appears that they were also making heard their displeasure at a fellow clan member losing so many votes to a man from a small house. Although Ca' Contarini probably would not have voted as a bloc for one of its fellows, it undoubtedly was an advantage to have many relatives, no matter how distant. A seventeenth-century commentator wrote about a branch of the Donato, one of the *case grandi*, with some exaggeration: "Since the family is numerous any of them who want the honor [of election to the Senate] can be elected, and they might be called a Seminary whose graduates are elected as soon as they reach the legal age."[99]

Complex marriage alliances maintained a family's influence, muted factional conflict, and drew the patriciate together. Some marriages were within the same large clan, bringing together branches that had grown apart. Marcantonio Zorzi of the San Severo branch of the clan married a distant cousin from another part of the city. Two daughters of Antonio Moro wedded cousins in a distant branch of the house. Giovanni Battista Morosini married a Morosini, as did his father and his grandson. Lacking male heirs, Leonardo Donato joined his two daughters to Donato brothers who were distant cousins; in his will he urged his daughters and their husbands, as well as other in-laws, to reside in his palace in Cannaregio.[100]

Of course, most marriages linked different families, although often from generation to generation. Two daughters and a niece of Andrea Vendramin married Contarini second cousins; the same Contarini family was closely connected with a branch of the Giustiniani: Giacomo Contarini's daughter wedded Marino Giustiniani, and his

99 On noises by the Contarini: Sanuto, 7:154. On the Donato: Davis, *Venetian Family*, p. 19.

100 On Zorzi: Barbaro, 8597, fol. 244v; Capellari, vol. 2, fols. 128v–129r. On Moro: Barbaro, 8596, fols. 149r, 151r; Capellari, vol. 3, fols. 137r, 140v, 141r, 142r. On Morosini: Barbaro, 8596, fols. 169v, 172r, 187v–187r; Capellari, vol. 3, fols. 127r, 129r. On Donato: Davis, *Venetian Family*, p. 7.

niece married Marino's nephew, Onfrè.[101] A daughter of Pietro Bondumier married Marco Priuli; in the next generation Pietro's nephew married Marco's first cousin; finally, the third generation saw Pietro's second cousin wedded to Marco's grandson. Similarly, two daughters and a son of Francesco Priuli wed children of Giovanni Soranzo; in the next generation two of Francesco's grandsons, as well as a Priuli from another branch of the *casa*, married Giovanni's grandchildren. Two of Giovanni Soranzo's nieces espoused sons of Pancratio Capello, and one of his grandsons married into another branch of the Capello; the connection with Pancratio's family was reaffirmed in the next generation when Giovanni's great-grandson was united with Pancratio's great-granddaughter.[102]

The extensive links between the clan of Giacomo Longo and those of Cristoforo Marcello, Andrea Dandolo, Pietro Bembo, and Pietro Bragadin illustrate the complexity of Venetian marriage strategies and the extent to which several houses could be bound together by the exchange of sons and daughters.[103] Giacomo Longo's father, Nicolò, wed a daughter of Cristoforo Marcello; Giacomo's brother, Alvise, married Cristoforo Marcello's greatniece, and Giacomo's son, Marcantonio, married into another branch of the Marcello. Finally, Giacomo's first cousins, the sons of Francesco Longo, married, respectively, a granddaughter and a great-granddaughter of Cristoforo Marcello. Giacomo himself wedded Pietro Bembo's daughter, and in the next generation his niece married Pietro's grandson, Benedetto. Giacomo's daughter married Andrea Dandolo's son, Leonardo. The Dandolo were closely linked to the Bembo, for two of Andrea's daughters espoused Pietro Bembo's sons. There were further connections among these families. Giacomo Longo married a son and a nephew to Pietro Bragadin's daughters, and Andrea Dandolo's granddaughter wed

101 On Contarini: Barbaro, 8594, fol. 282r; Capellari, vol. 1, fol. 312r. On Vendramin: Barbaro, 8597, fols. 161r–162r, 165r; Capellari, vol. 4, fols. 159v–160v. On Giustiniani: Barbaro, 8597, fols. 256v, 259v–259r; Capellari, vol. 2, fols. 145v–146r.

102 On Bondumier: Barbaro, 8594, fol. 164v; Capellari, vol. 1, fol. 178r. On Priuli: Barbaro, 8597, fols. 115v–115r, 117r; Capellari, vol. 4, fols. 96r–96v. On Capello: Barbaro, 8594, fol. 214r; Capellari, vol. 1, fols. 235v–236r.

103 On the Longo: Barbaro, 8595, fols. 234v–235v; Capellari, vol. 2, fols. 224v–225v. On the Bembo: Barbaro, 8594, fols. 114v, 116r; Capellari, vol. 1, fols. 143v–143r. On the Dandolo: Barbaro, 8595, fol. 47v; Capellari, vol. 2, fol. 13r. On the Bragadin: Barbaro, 8594, fol. 183r; Capellari, vol. 1, fol. 197r. On the Marcello: Barbaro, 8596, fol. 35v; Capellari, vol. 3, fols. 35v–35r. On the Garzoni: Barbaro, 8595, fols. 154v–155r; Capellari, vol. 2, fols. 113v–114r.

Pietro's nephew, Andrea di Nicolò. Pietro Bembo's granddaughter married Cristoforo Marcello's greatnephew. Two daughters of Vicenzo Garzoni entered the Longo and Bembo families; and two daughters of Paolo Zane married into the Bembo and Marcello, while a Zane cousin married Pietro Bragadin's brother, Nicolò.

Of twenty-three Longo marriages in three generations, twelve were into the Marcello, Dandolo, Bembo, and Bragadin; and others, such as that of Giacomo's uncle to a Garzoni, were into families close to them. The Longo *casa* was small, having only ten members in the Council in 1527, so by these marriages the Longo forged multiple links with larger clans (Longo first cousins marrying Bragadin sisters; five Longo men marrying into the Marcello) across the generations. The close and lasting nature of these connections meant that the Longo could call on the aid of many of the Marcello, Bembo, Dandolo, and Bragadin in elections and political squabbles and that the Longo would support their in-laws in similar fashion. When the Longo house and its in-laws gathered together for a wedding, a christening, or during a Great Council meeting, they must have had a sense that they were part of an interclan complex that had a call on their loyalties rivaling that of their individual houses. Tracing itself back to an eponymous ancestor, the clan coexisted with clusters of families bound by exchanges based on political and economic consideration. Much of the solidity of the ruling class derived from the weaving together of the loyalties of the *casa* with those arising from complex and continuing exchanges with other houses; alignment of the patriciate in a series of clans was paralleled by its integration in a ramifying network of marital alliances.[104] With slight exaggeration, one may say that assemblies of the Great Council amounted to the congregation of large, interlocking family complexes based on both lineage and affection, *parenti e consorti*.

In the Great Council the family had to exert its influence through a complicated electoral system expressly designed to suppress special interests, whether familial or factional. James Harrington in the seventeenth century had a character in his *Oceana* speak disparagingly of Venetian electoral procedures: "For a Council, and not a word spoken in it, is a contradiction. But there is such a pudder with their marching and counter-marching, as, tho' never a one of them draw a Sword, you would think they were training; which till I found that they did it only to entertain strangers, I came from among them as wise as I went

104 Cf. Chojnacki, "Patrician Women," p. 203.

thither."[105] This comic view is comprehensible, for a visitor to the Great Council would certainly have been bewildered, if not amused, by the highly regulated and repetitive behavior of the ruling class as it selected men to fill state offices.

There were three principal stages in the electoral process. First, patricians filed to the front of the hall where each drew a ball from an urn filled with as many balls as there were patricians present, although sixty balls were gilded and the rest were silver. If one drew a gold ball, he proceeded to the next stage of the election; but all other members of his clan returned to their seats, as did all those who drew a silver ball. Having drawn a gold ball, one went on to the second urn, containing thirty-six gold balls and twenty-four silver. Again, those who drew silver returned to the benches, while the thirty-six were divided into four nominating committees. The nine-man committees (mani) retired to separate rooms off the Great Council chamber, and the second stage of the election began.

Usually there were nine offices to be filled at every Great Council meeting. Each committee member extracted a numbered ball from an urn, the number corresponding to an election for which the individual had the right to make a nomination; if there were ten offices to be filled, the man who nominated to the first on the list also did so to the tenth. When a nomination was approved by at least six members of the committee—usually a mere formality—a secretary recorded the nominee's name; and when the list of nine nominees was completed, the nominators were dismissed from the Ducal Palace.

The third and least complicated stage of the election followed: The names of the four nominees for each office were read to the Great Council (from a master list of thirty-six) and were voted on one by one. After those belonging to a nominee's casa left the hall, about twenty ballot boys (ballottini) filed along the benches collecting ballots in urns. If the same man were nominated by two or three committees, the election proceeded as usual, so long as there were competitors in the final election. For many offices the Senate made its own nomination by scrutiny (scrutinio): Any voting member could make a nomination, and the nominee to receive the largest vote became the Senate's representative in the Great Council election.

During the early Cinquecento, two major alterations were made in the Great Council's electoral procedures. First, four nominating com-

105 Quoted by Brian Pullan, "The Significance of Venice," p. 455, n. 2. On electoral procedure: Sanuto, Cronachetta, pp. 225–231; Contarini, Republica, pp. 29–42; Maranini, Costituzione di Venezia, pp. 109–114.

mittees were substituted for two in most elections, a change designed to create more competition and to decrease the influence of lobbying in contesting elections. Second, in 1527 two members of each clan were permitted to enter the nominating committees.[106]

According to Contarini, the electoral system had several virtues. It insured that all the members of the Great Council, not merely a few powerful groups or families, shared in the honors and offices of the Republic: Everyone could participate in the government and "have equal power with the highest citizens." Yet equal power was exercised only by hearkening to the voice of the majority in the final stage of election, for in the earlier stages, everyone was subject to the laws of chance. Rejecting both democracy and oligarchy, the electoral system aimed at an equality of "virtue and civic obligation" by combining hazard in the selection of nominators with consideration in the committees and final election. Contarini notes that the element of consideration was strengthened by "the fifth order," that is, by the addition of the Senate's nominee to the competition in the Great Council.[107]

A seventeenth-century commentator disagreed, asserting that "Fortune more than prudence dispenses the honors" of the Republic.[108] One's chances of entering a nominating committee and drawing the office desired were slight: one-fourth of 1 percent in an assembly of sixteen hundred patricians. In short, a patrician needed many supporters to be both nominated and elected. Sanuto claims that he once had five hundred supporters in the Great Council who would nominate him for state attorney, but only ten passed the first urn and none drew the nominating authority for the office. A more cogent reason than poor luck for Sanuto's persistent lack of nominations and victories was that he came from a small and unimportant family. In thirty-two of fifty-four elections in which he nominated or was nominated, a member of his family or a relative by marriage was a party to the nomination; in the remaining cases, either friends were involved or he traded nominating authority with someone in the committee, an illegal but widespread practice. Family relationships, then, were the foundation of the Great Council's nominating procedure and decisively influenced the choice of victor. A contemporary of Contarini complained that "in the elections of the Great Council, the voters are

106 On the increase in committees, see the 1515 revisions (given in the notes of the edition) to Sanuto's 1493 *Cronachetta*. On 1527, see this book, Chapter II.4.

107 Contarini, *Republica*, pp. 42–43.

108 della Torre, "Relazione," c. 17.

sworn to elect the best and most capable of the city; notwithstanding this, all vote for their fathers, brothers, relatives, and friends, judging that they will more surely repay [the favor]."[109]

It is no surprise that most nominations for offices were made within the family, but what is less expected is that a number of clans closely cooperated with one another over a long period of time in order to dominate a select group of offices. The *Longhi* ("Long") clans (or the *case vecchie*, "the old houses"), the twenty-four houses credited with having founded Venice before A.D. 800, organized themselves in the Great Council and manipulated the nominating procedures. An anonymous document of the late seventeenth century records that sixteen *Curti* ("Short") clans (or the *case nuove*, "the new houses"), some of the houses that supposedly achieved distinction after A.D. 800, made a pact in 1450 to exclude the *Longhi* from the dogeship, a conspiracy that was successful until the election of Doge Marcantonio Memmo in 1612.[110]

The author also claims that Memmo's triumph paradoxically resulted in the political ruin of the *Longhi*. Before 1612 they were a unified group by virtue of their exclusion from the dogeship by the *Curti*, inasmuch as they had to cooperate with one another to obtain other offices in the Great Council. The *Longhi* voted as a bloc, displaying a unity lacking in the more numerous *Curti* clans. An elderly member of the Soranzo, an old house, "speaking with tears in his eyes," told the anonymous reporter that such cooperation was dead after 1612, even though "in their own interests there would have been greater success if the old houses [*i Vecchi*] had not relaxed their ancient discipline after attaining the dogeship."[111]

Certainly the *Longhi* had their share of offices. On April 15, 1510,

109 On Sanuto's supporters for state attorney: Sanuto, 25:355; cf. 27:320. On Sanuto's elections: Sanuto, 5:89; 6:145, 327, 348, 355; 13:388; 18:305; 22:157–158, 399–400, 538; 24:666, 668, 677; 25:12, 377, 594; 26:40, 52; 27:672, 684; 28:405–406, 493; 29:8, 96, 504, 641; 31:311; 32:254; 36:527, 595; 38:289, 328; 52:326; 54:112, 541. On the quotation: Francesco Longo, "Diarii, 1537–1540," fol. 42v.

110 "Distinzioni Segrete che corrono tra le Case Nobili di Venezia," fol. 4v. The *Longhi* houses: Badoer, Barozzi, Basegi, Bembo, Bragadin, Contarini, Corner, Dandolo, Dolfin, Falier, Giustiniani, Gradenigo, Memmo, Michiel, Morosini, Polani, Querini, Salamon, Sanuto, Soranzo, Tiepolo, Zane, Zen, Zorzi. The sixteen *Curti* houses: Barbarigo, Donato, Foscari, Grimani, Gritti, Lando, Loredan, Malipiero, Marcello, Mocenigo, Moro, Priuli, Trevisan, Tron, Vendramin, Venier (cf. Emmanuel A. Cicogna, *Delle iscrizione veneziane*, 4:495–496). For discussion of these clans and the dogeship, see this book, Chapter III.3.

111 "Distinzione Segrete," fols. 6v–7r.

Maximilian I of the Holy Roman Empire wrote to the "ancient nobility" of Venice, calling on them to throw off the yoke of the "new nobility," who had led the Republic away from respect for imperial prerogatives. He grandly promised the *Longhi* control of the government, as well as the status of a free city of the Empire for Venice.[112] Although Maximilian's knowledge of Venice was limited, he was probably aware that *Longhi* and *Curti* had been at loggerheads in the ducal election of 1486; his pious hope of defeating Venice without striking a blow may have inspired him to convert clan animosities into an incipient civil war. The emperor's ignorance is clear from the number of important offices held by the *Longhi* at the time he wrote his appeal. In 1527 *Longhi* clans included 944 members (or 35 percent) of the twenty-seven hundred man patriciate. Naturally, this does not necessarily mean that they represented the same percentage in the Great Council, which never exceeded two thousand in one assembly, although absenteeism was probably evenly spread among the clans. In March 1510 *Longhi* had one-third of the key positions on the executive councils; five of six ducal councillors were from the old houses, as were all three state attorneys.[113] Maximilian's notion that the old families were ready to revolt must have seemed ill-informed indeed.

The twenty-four *Longhi* clans and the sixteen *Curti* known as the *ducali* ("ducal") together comprised all but two of the nineteen *case grandi*, those houses exceeding forty members of Great Council age in 1527. Ten of the *Longhi* were big houses (with 670 men), as were seven of the *ducali* (with 452); the Molin (50) and Pisani (44) completed the roster. Of the thirty clans that had at least thirty members apiece and included 59 percent of the patriciate, fourteen were *Longhi* (with 811); ten were of the *ducali* group of the *Curti* (with 555); and six (with 235) belonged to the remaining ninety-four *Curti* clans. In other words, although the *Longhi* made up only 35 percent of the patriciate, they represented half of the houses with more than thirty members and 55 percent of the *case grandi*. This heavy representation among the big houses gave *Longhi* clans an advantage in the Great Council out of proportion to their number; they were in a unique position both to enter the nominating committees and to vote as a bloc in elections.

It is suggestive that the *Longhi* and the sixteen *Curti* should so closely coincide with the big houses. If a conspiracy to exclude the

112 Bonardi, "Venezia città libera"; cf. Sanuto, 10:346–349.
113 Sanuto, 10:69–70; cf. Bonardi, "Venezia città libera," pp. 134–135.

old houses from the dogeship occurred in the Quattrocento, as seems likely, perhaps the division along the lines of *Longhi* and *Curti* was associated with a battle for dominance between the largest and most powerful clans of the city, with the majority of the smaller *Curti* clans at least tacitly cooperating with the *ducali*. Sanuto concludes his account of the ducal election of 1486 by lamenting the animosity between *Longhi* and *Curti* and by quoting the opinion of some sages that "it was necessary to reduce the big houses, and with time, marriage and kinship things should calm down."[114] This is no more than a hint. In all likelihood, the alleged conspiracy—surely a crucial event in Venetian political history—will remain mysterious, not least because officials concerned with state security "in every time have labored to suppress or at least to conceal it."[115]

Official suppression and covert organization insured that the conspiracy was hidden from historical view. At the same time, the Great Council's elections provided a means for *Longhi* clans to organize themselves secretly and to obtain offices that might otherwise have been denied them. Although *Longhi* were only 35 percent of the patriciate, they usually held from one-third to one-half of the thirty-six nominations in a given meeting. Moreover, in virtually every meeting of the Great Council from 1507 to 1527 (or in 15 percent of the elections of that period), they were in contests in which they had three-fourths or more of the nominations. In short, *Longhi* houses concentrated their forces on a few of the nine elections in every assembly.[116] For example, on November 28, 1518, they had eleven of the thirty-three nominations for the day, and eight of their nominees were in competition for three of nine offices; on October 10, 1519, they held 44 percent of the nominations, with 80 percent of their nominees in 33 percent of the elections.[117] This pattern was maintained in 405 elections between 1507 and 1527 and appears only in competition for 147 offices of the approximately 800 elected by the Great Council: sixty-two posts within the city, forty-nine in mainland administration, thirty in colonial administration, and six naval positions. The *Longhi* won 73 percent of these elections.

At least for posts in Venice, *Longhi* houses showed special interest in a small group of offices. Sixty-two offices were at stake in 296

114 Sanuto, *Vite dei dogi*, fol. 273v.

115 "Distinzione Segrete," fols. 6v–7r.

116 These remarks are based on examination of the Consegi (8894–8898) lists from March 1507 to March 1527, encompassing about 350 meetings and three thousand elections.

117 Consegi, 8896, fols. 179r, 245r.

elections, but 67 percent of the latter were to only twenty-one offices or posts: middle-level judicial magistracies, the courts of the Ducal Palace, the Loan Office (*camera degl'imprestiti*), the Senate, the Zonta, and the Ten.[118] A further indication of the deliberate nature of these electoral patterns is that *Longhi* did not concentrate their forces on a few offices in elections for *terraferma* and colonial posts, even though they did so within Venice. Nor were the old houses apparently interested in positions on the *Quarantie*. When the forty seats on the *Quarantia civile nuova* came up for renewal, roughly one-half of the Great Council's elections would be devoted to them, with five men elected in eight successive meetings. On such days the pattern of nominations for *Longhi* was uneven. For example, on December 23, 1520, they had nine of the sixteen nominations for the four regular offices up for election; but in the *Quarantia civile nuova* elections, they had only six of seventeen. In other words, *Longhi* received 39 percent of the nominations for the nine positions; yet in the regular elections they had 56 percent and in the *Quarantia*, only 35 percent. In the *Quarantia* elections from February 13 to March 13, 1519, the same patterns prevailed. *Longhi* clans had a large number of the regular nominations (from 50 to 58 percent) and a significantly smaller percentage (20 to 32) of the nominations to the judicial council.[119]

On some days, *Longhi* clans won many of the offices, so their tactic of packing elections was successful. For example, in the nine Great Council meetings of January and February 1522, they won an average of 40 percent of the elections, even though their record of wins and losses was uneven: On the first meeting of each month, they failed to win any elections, but they won five of nine on January 25 and six of eight on February 23. Their maneuvers apparently provoked opposition on occasion, a possible explanation of why 12 percent of the elections dominated by the *Longhi* failed to produce a winner. The Great Council was unable to elect anyone to the Loan Office in four successive meetings in 1518 when in each election three-fourths of the nominees were from the old houses; and the same proved true in 1519 when three assemblies failed to elect a lord of the Arsenal.[120]

Clearly, the *Longhi* houses were highly united in the Great Council. A minority within the ruling class, they won about 40 percent of the Great Council's elections from 1507 to 1527 by virtue of considerable secret organization, for which they were peculiarly fitted. They repre-

118 For more detail, see Finlay, "Politics of the Ruling Class," p. 89, n. 2.
119 Consegi, 8896, fols. 139r, 193r, 194r, 195r, 197r, 198r.
120 On 1522: Consegi, 8897, fols. 60r–68r. On 1518 and 1519: Consegi, 8896, fols. 163r, 167r–169r; 235r, 236r, 237r.

sented 55 percent of the *case grandi*, which gave them an advantage in the Great Council. At the same time, 71 percent of the *Longhi* were members of big houses. In other words, slightly more than one-half of the *case grandi* members were *Longhi*, while almost three-fourths of the *Longhi* patricians themselves belonged to one of the *case grandi*. This meant that most patricians of the *Longhi* had a better chance than others to enter a nominating committee, as well as better opportunity for united action than the far more numerous and relatively smaller *Curti* clans. The nature of covert *Longhi* organization is, however, wholly obscure, although some patricians must have supervised the distribution of nominations and the dispositions of votes. Officials charged with insuring honest and faction-free elections would have been inclined to look the other way rather than expose a rift within the ruling class—and, of course, many of those officials were also members of *Longhi* clans. If official sources fail the historian, so too does Sanuto, who, as a member and partisan of the *Longhi*, was hardly likely to record the illegal activity that gave the old houses a significant share of the Republic's offices.

It was best, perhaps, to avoid the touchy issue altogether, especially inasmuch as animosities between *Longhi* and *Curti* were peacefully channeled into the Great Council, only surfacing at rare intervals in ducal elections. There is, in fact, no echo of the clan division within the Senate or executive councils, no sign that it touched the field of programs and policies. Energies were directed instead toward striving for office in the Great Council. One of the strengths of the Venetian political system was the role of the Great Council in reconciling potentially dangerous splits within the patriciate. The rich and the poor, the old houses and the new, worked out their frustrations and ambitions within the constitution because every patrician had a seat in the sovereign assembly and a part to play in the electoral process. The Great Council was politically important less for the power it wielded or the issues it considered than for the functions it performed: as sounding board for the populace, restraint on the governing circle, and defuser of discontent within the ruling class. Politically as well as constitutionally, the Republic was founded on and drew its strength from the Great Council.

4. *Politics in the Great Council: July 1527*

In the spring of 1527, years of diplomatic blundering by Italian states and invasions by foreign armies culminated in the terrible sack of Rome. Early in May imperial troops broke into the city, where they murdered and looted for more than a month. Pope Clement VII Medici took refuge in Castel Sant'Angelo, while in Florence, Medici supporters fled and a republic was reestablished. News of the Roman horrors and the plight of its ally reached Venice on May 11, stunning the city; fresh accounts of devastation and brutality by the emperor Charles V's lansquenets were received almost daily as late as early July. Venetian-papal forces of the League of Cognac dithered near Milan and Tuscany, unable or unwilling to act against imperial troops. Charles V had Italy at his mercy.[121]

While Venice tried to absorb the news from Rome and reinvigorate the league, northern Italy was struck by torrential rain, which continued into late June. The Piazza di San Marco was repeatedly flooded, and there was so much fresh water in the canals—"a fearful event," says Sanuto—that frogs could be heard at night. The Polesine was wholly inundated; the Po, Brenta, Adige, and Fiume rivers broke their banks. Flooding wiped out grain crops just before harvest time; eight thousand mills in the Veneto stood idle, unable to grind because they were broken or under water. The price of grain rose from 8 lire a bushel in May to more than 16 lire in mid-June, the highest in fifty-one years, according to a chief of the Forty. The flour warehouses at San Marco and the Rialto closed in mid-June, amid a crush of people eager to buy the last bushel. Danger from disease, moving north from Rome along with refugees and soldiers, added to that of famine. The Health Office (*Sanità*) began supervising entry to Venice in mid-June, but soon Sanuto reported, "Many are sick from fever in the city and many die; and there is a very great and unbearable heat." The stage was set for the epidemic and starvation of the next year: "The poor die of hunger, which is pitiful, and nothing is done; the Piazza di San Marco seems like a purgatory, and also the streets, the Mercerie, the churches, everywhere."[122]

On June 15 a Florentine preacher, Benedetto da Foiana, spoke on the Apocalypse for four hours in the church of the Incurabili, attacking Clement VII and praising the emperor. Luca Tron, a *savio grande*

---

121 On the sack: Sanuto, 45:77, 86, 87–88, 90–92, 167–168, 469–470. On Florence: Sanuto, 45:137–141, 205. On Charles V's power: ASV, Consiglio di Dieci, Parti Secrete, Reg. 2, fols. 11v–12v.

122 On the rain: Sanuto, 45:283, 292. On the flooding and crops: Sanuto, 45: 292, 296, 304, 320. On grain prices: Sanuto, 45:177, 424, 491. On disease: Sanuto, 45:321, 388, 401, 609. On the consequences of disease and famine: Sanuto, 46:609; cf. Brian Pullan, "The Famine in Venice and the New Poor Law, 1527–29."

echoed this radical sentiment in a Senate debate on June 25, "saying 'It is the will of God that the emperor prospers.'" A week later a man was arrested by the Ten for suggesting that "soon the standard of the emperor will fly in the Piazza di San Marco." The piazza on June 20 witnessed "a very melancholy" Corpus Christi procession. For the first time since Agnadello, the piazza was cordoned off, because of rumors that "the doge and patricians would be killed, especially given the many foreigners in the city," a scene that caused Sanuto great distress and evoked complaints among the people about Doge Gritti's cowardice.[123]

Within the councils the atmosphere was no more harmonious. Eight of Gritti's relatives were nominated as *savi grandi* so that the Senate could have the pleasure of voting them down. There was such anger and bitterness over the duke of Urbino, Venice's captain general, for not opposing the imperial army that his wife and son were put under virtual house arrest in Murano. The Ten argued about everything and divided over forwarding affairs to the Senate and sending instructions to the army and to the ambassador in Istanbul. Poor patricians in the Great Council complained publicly about the Signoria's raising money by selling offices. In this atmosphere of crisis and acrimony, it is little wonder that, when the crown on a statue of Justice on the doge's state ship was knocked into the water during the annual Wedding of the Sea (*Sposalizio del Mare*), the accident was seen as a bad omen, foretelling more evils to accompany those already gathered upon Venice.[124]

Amid these political and natural calamities—defeat, pillage, flood, famine, disease, dissension—the Great Council and all the important committees of government were preoccupied with legislation designed to alter the voting procedures of the sovereign assembly. Nothing better testifies both to the enduring insularity of the patriciate and to the vitality of Venetian electoral politics and parliamentary procedures than this preoccupation at such a moment. At the same time, conflict over the legislation took place within the context of events at home and abroad.

During most of July, the patriciate was caught up in a controversy

123 On Benedetto: Sanuto, 45:322. On Tron: Sanuto, 45:387. On the emperor's standard: Sanuto, 45:437. On the procession: Sanuto, 45:355–356.

124 On Gritti's relatives: Sanuto, 45:450; cf. 43:518, 569. On Urbino: Sanuto, 45:410–411; ASV, Consiglio di Dieci, Parti Secrete, Reg. 2, fol. 17r. On division in the Ten: ASV, Consiglio di Dieci, Parti Secreti, Reg. 2, fols. 14r, 14v–15r, 17v. On complaints of poor patricians: ASM, b. 1461, Giambattista Malatesta to the marquis of Mantua, June 17, 1527. On the crown: Sanuto, 45:223; cf. 483.

over a proposal to change the rules restricting the number of a clan allowed to enter the nominating committees of the Great Council.[125] Sometime in early July, four ducal councillors—Bendetto Dolfin, Antonio Gradenigo, Francesco Marcello, and Alvise Michiel—drew up their proposal, the preamble to which stated:

> According to necessities, various provisions were made from time to time by our wise and just founders, all toward the end that our patricians, with universal satisfaction, may participate in honors and public benefits. Yet at present one sees a great increase in the number of patricians, such that great inequality arises regarding drawing from the urn in the Great Council, for when only one [member of a clan] goes into an election [that is, into a nominating committee], the rest of his house are prohibited from going to the urn, even if not linked [to the man who enters the committee] by blood or close affinity.[126]

Of course, the law that only one member of a clan could become one of the thirty-six nominators worked against the *case grandi* because they had more members to be excluded than did the smaller houses. The four councillors, all men from big houses, showed their proposal to Doge Gritti but kept it secret from the Ten and the Collegio, only spreading word of their intention immediately before the Great Council convened on July 14. Because it was an exceptionally hot day, only eight hundred patricians attended the assembly, but many came "from the big houses who usually don't attend . . . to give their support to the proposal which benefited them." The Great Council was informed that the councillors' motion would exclude only close blood relatives from the nominating committees and otherwise permit entrance to any number of men from the same clan. After the proposal (to be voted on at the next meeting) was announced, the Great Council went on with its usual business of elections.[127]

Opposition to the councillors quickly developed. On July 16, the Ten and its *zonta* of fifteen men met with the Collegio and the procurators of San Marco. The meeting was convened by a chief of the Ten, Francesco di Filippo Foscari, called *il Grando*, eighty-four years old, gout ridden, and one of the city's most important and experienced politicians. He considered that the proposal was "of the very greatest importance, because it splits the city into two parts, the small and

125 The following account is based on Sanuto, 45:483–567.
126 Sanuto, 45:562–563.
127 Sanuto, 45:483.

the big houses." The Foscari had only twelve members eligible to enter the Great Council in 1527, whereas the four councillors came from clans that had from thirty-nine to seventy-seven. Furthermore, five members of the Ten other than Foscari were from houses that had an average of twenty-three men, and one of the remaining four— Giorgio Corner, a prominent member of a large house—was absent, so Foscari had a majority of his council behind him. Although not present at the meeting, Doge Gritti supported the councillors. His clan numbered only thirty, but his in-laws were almost all from the *case grandi*—Donato, Pisani, Malipiero, Loredan, and Giustiniani. Indeed, it is likely that Gritti was the dominant figure behind the proposal and its presentation.[128]

Foscari argued that the councillors were to blame for not having consulted the Ten before presenting their proposal, which required "mature and rigorous consideration." When he began his attack on the councillors, two of them left the meeting. At least four councillors were necessary for the Ten to have a quorum; and when another, Francesco Marcello, started to leave, Foscari vehemently insisted that he stay. Finally, the Ten voted to suspend consideration of the motion until further discussion had taken place. As usual when the Ten were sharply divided, an oath of secrecy about the council's business was taken by everyone at the meeting. Immediately afterward, however, Foscari led the two other chiefs of the Ten into the Signoria, where he protested than the councillors were acting "against the peace and quiet of the state."[129]

Negotiations and private meetings apparently took place on the seventeenth, and on the following day the Collegio met with the Signoria and the heads of the Ten. The Collegio never took an official position regarding the councillors' proposal, but the council was probably as divided as the Ten. The presence of such combative personalities as the *savi grandi* Luca Tron and Leonardo Emo, both from *case piccole*, explains the reluctance of the four councillors to present their motion to the Collegio for approval. At any rate, no progress was made in this meeting; although, later in the day, two chiefs of the Ten, Giacomo Badoer (with thirty-six men in his clan) and Andrea Molin (with fifty), met with the Collegio and presented a compromise that

128 On Foscari: Sanuto, 45:428, 501. On Gritti's relations: Barbaro, 8595, fols. 196v–197r; Capellari, vol. 2, fols. 191v–192r. On Gritti's involvement in government, see the discussion on the censors in this book, Chapter IV.3.

129 Sanuto, 45:501; ASV, Consiglio di Dieci, Parti Secrete, Reg. 2, fols. 19v–20r.

would allow two members of a house to enter the nominating committees. The four councillors appeared in the Ten on July 20, a Saturday, with their own compromise: Rather than permitting any number of one clan who were not close relatives into the committees, they now proposed that only four be allowed in, one in each committee. This did not satisfy Foscari and his supporters, although Doge Gritti spoke in favor of it.[130]

Attendance at the Great Council on Sunday jumped to 1,357 because of agitation over the proposal and because elections for the Senate were beginning. All those not members of the assembly, excluding the secretaries, were evicted from the chamber, a usual procedure when dissension was expected. After the councillors' modified proposal was read to the patriciate, two chiefs of the Forty, Francesco Calbo (with five clan members) and Nicolò Grioni (with one), stated their intention of presenting a contrary motion. As members of the Signoria, they had the right to make proposals; but the councillors claimed that a regulation of the Ten prohibited Calbo and Grioni from doing so in the absence of their colleague, Marino Pisani, a member of a large house, who was probably staying away to avoid siding with the four councillors against Calbo and Grioni. This obstacle was overcome when Pietro Bragadin, a councillor not in agreement with his colleagues, even though he came from a *casa grande*, volunteered to support the motion of the chiefs of the Forty. Another limitation on the chiefs had been overcome earlier, for sometime in the previous week the Forty had approved their proposal, a necessary preliminary to the chiefs' making a motion in the Great Council. The proposal they submitted was the modification of the councillors' motion suggested by the Ten three days earlier, that is, to permit only two per house to enter the committees rather than four. However, the murmuring of the Great Council, probably accompanied by catcalls and stamping of feet, made it clear that the *case grandi* were displeased, so Bragadin announced that he was withdrawing his support from the motion. Because the councillors continued to dispute the two chiefs' authority to make a motion, Calbo and Grioni were stymied again. Gritti temporarily resolved the impasse by ordering the grand chancellor to postpone the matter until the next Great Council session.[131]

When the Great Council met again on July 22, Bragadin and Daniele Moro, the sixth councillor (and from a *casa* of thirty-four), agreed to support Calbo and Grioni, apparently on condition that no

130 Sanuto, 45:503, 512.
131 Sanuto, 45:521.

other alterations be permitted in the voting procedures. Both Foscari and Marino Pisani registered silent protests against the proceedings by boycotting the assembly, although the former opposed the *case grandi* motion and the latter supported it. Foscari had the backing of a majority of the Ten, but the two other chiefs of the council, Giacomo Badoer and Andrea Molin, wanted to modify the voting procedures to favor the big houses. Inasmuch as at least two chiefs of the Ten had to be in accord to take an action, Foscari was reduced to an impotent boycott when he could not sway his colleagues.

Both motions were read to the Great Council and the ceremonial call for requests had been issued twice when Gritti once more blocked Calbo and Grioni. He called the state attorneys and chiefs of the Ten before the tribune of the Signoria and pointed out to them that the motion by the chiefs of the Forty to allow only two members of a clan into the committees included a clause that stipulated that it could not be altered or revoked without the consent of four councillors and two chiefs of the Forty. Gritti asserted that the regulations of the Ten prohibited such a stipulation. Although Bragadin and Moro argued that Calbo and Grioni were not exceeding their authority, the vote was put off once again; and the weary Great Council—the third to hear the motions read—was adjourned while the law was consulted.[132]

Gritti refused to convoke the Great Council on Tuesday, the twenty-third, perhaps hoping that a compromise could be hammered out in the executive committees. In the morning the Signoria was enlivened by a hot dispute between the four councillors and their dissenting colleagues, Bragadin and Moro, while the chiefs of the Ten argued out their differences in a meeting of the Collegio. After midday the Full Collegio assembled to hear Calbo and Grioni adduce proof that the disputed clause in their motion was legal. They also heard the mercurial Bragadin announce that he was abandoning the chiefs of the Forty once more and joining with the other councillors; Moro, however, continued to support Calbo and Grioni. During a meeting of the Ten and its *zonta* on the afternoon of the twenty-fourth, a state attorney, Angelo Gabriel, who was from a *casa* of seven members, placed fresh obstacles before the councillors when he demanded, as the official guardian of the law and constitutional procedures, that they submit the proposal to him for approval. When the councillors refused, Gabriel angrily threatened to begin legal proceedings against them. In all likelihood, Gabriel was in league with Calbo

132 Sanuto, 45:521, 524.

and Grioni; and if he pressed charges against the councillors, the case
would be heard by the court of the Forty, which had already approved the actions of its chiefs.[133]

An air of excitement and anticipation must have permeated the
Great Council when it met again on Thursday, July 25. Among the
1,332 patricians were "many partisans of the *case grandi*, who usually
don't attend." Excitement was heightened by the contrast between the
two proposals, for Calbo, Grioni, and Moro had abandoned their
earlier compromise that allowed two per house into the committees,
as they now proposed that the nominating procedures remain unchanged. The bickering of the last few days had apparently destroyed
chances for a compromise, and the Great Council was therefore faced
with a clearer choice than before. Immediately after the proposals
were read, Gabriel went before the Signoria at the head of the hall
and informed Gritti that his councillors were under legal charges and,
being suspended from office, could not submit motions to the assembly. Not surprisingly, an argument erupted between Gabriel and the
five councillors, a battle that the chiefs of the Ten joined when Gritti
called them forward to restore order. Finally, Badoer and Molin decided that Gabriel lacked the authority for his injunction and ordered
that the motions be put to the vote.[134]

After the call for comments had been given three times, Michiel
Trevisan, a member of a large house, went to the *renga*, a pulpitlike
affair from which speeches were made, and opposed the councillors,
insisting "that peace and unity have made the Republic great." The
chiefs of the Ten cut Trevisan short because he was not addressing
himself specifically to the motion as the rules of the Great Council
required. Benedetto Dolfin, a councillor, replied to Trevisan, declaring
"that he and his companions presented [the motion] to create equality
and justice for all"; but, according to Sanuto, Dolfin "has a slight
voice and was little heard." The Great Council was finally permitted
to vote: 17 abstained; 62 opposed both motions, and the councillors
defeated their opponents by 672 to 589—a total of 1,340 votes or 7
more than there were patricians present in the Great Council. The
case grandi immediately benefited from their victory: Four Contarini
and two each of the Corner and Donato entered the nominating committees of the day.[135]

Peace was not yet to be. At the regular Great Council meeting on

133 Sanuto, 45:529, 533.
134 Sanuto, 45:534, 535.
135 Sanuto, 45:535–536.

Sunday, July 28, the results of the voting were challenged. The state attorneys, Angelo Gabriel and Giovanni Alvise Navagero (whose clan had nine members), told the Signoria that they were enjoining the motion passed on Thursday because of the extra ballots cast. A motion required one-half of all the votes of the Great Council to pass, and the *case grandi* proposal had won by only four votes, that is, by less than the number illegally cast. The state attorneys wanted the Great Council to vote on the validity of Thursday's vote, a procedure opposed by the councillors and by Doge Gritti, who dismissed the assembly to forestall it. Many members of the large clans, thinking that the controversy was over, had not come to the Great Council, and Gritti wanted to give them time to assemble their forces once more. Many patricians must have regretted the reopening of the conflict, and Sanuto was not alone in fearing the growing division and bitterness within the ruling class: "One hopes for good fortune in this affair, which is of the greatest importance for these times, that this division has come between the large and small houses, and that it is spoken about openly."[136]

Patricians of the *case grandi* were out in force for the special Great Council meeting on Tuesday, the thirtieth. Gabriel spoke once again about the disorder in the voting on Thursday, whereas Dolfin presented the councillors' viewpoint that the vote was valid. Marcantonio Contarini, the third state attorney, defended the councillors against the attacks of his own colleagues, but according to Sanuto few took him seriously because he belonged to the largest clan in Venice. Gabriel and Navagero submitted a motion to annul the vote of the twenty-sixth, and it passed by 832 to 757, with 3 abstentions. The two groups of opponents immediately presented their proposals again. Sanuto went to the *renga* to speak against the councillor's proposition. He asserted that

> our saintly ancestors had wished for thirty-six houses to be in the elections, nominating forty houses for the court of the Forty and not only nine, as could happen [with the councillors' proposal]. In any case, in-laws and cousins from other houses may be nominated: one father has three sons, one will have six, while others don't marry—yet they all remain equal. Thus it is with republics, so that all may participate. . . . I praised the motion of the councillor [Moro] and the two chiefs of the Forty, to continue as usual and not make innovations.

136 Sanuto, 45:548.

He also pointed out two irregularities in the councillors' proposal: A motion to alter procedures of the Great Council required a two-thirds vote, and the ducal election could only be discussed when the dogeship was vacant. "I was brief," he boasts, "made an excellent speech, and was lauded by those with objectivity." His objection that a two-thirds vote was necessary was ignored by the Signoria, while his latter point may fairly be described as nitpicking: The *case grandi* proposal only stipulated that its provisions were *not* to apply to the ducal election.[137]

Sanuto was the only speaker on either side of the controversy, so the vote followed immediately: 7 abstained; 9 voted against both proposals; 788 supported the councillors; 788, their opponents. A Great Council meeting of 1,593 patricians had split precisely down the middle. Another vote was taken: 9 abstentions, 795 for the *case grandi*, 791 for the *case picole*. Neither side received one-half the ballots, and the number of voters had mysteriously risen by 3. Fearing that the *case grandi* proposal would again be passed by illegal ballots—thus necessitating another vote to annul the victory—some patricians wanted the Great Council to recess; but the law required voting to continue for fifteen ballots or until midnight. A third vote proceeded: 5 abstentions; 797 for the councillors; 792 for Moro, Calbo, and Grioni; with the total vote growing by yet another ballot, even though secretaries were dispatched around the chamber to supervise the passing of the voting urns. A fourth vote returned to the proper total but produced another deadlock: 3 abstentions, 796 for the alteration, 796 for the status quo. Francesco Foscari, the chief of the Ten, announced that the Great Council had to disband because it was past midnight. Because three councillors ended their terms of office on Wednesday, July 31, the Signoria determined that the Great Council would meet the next day. "I pray to God," writes Sanuto, "for the good of our Republic, we make an end to this."[138]

Advantage seemed to lie with the big houses, who were still recruiting men who had failed to attend the Ducal Palace on Tuesday. There is a hint of desperation in Foscari's attempt to put off a meeting on the thirty-first by arguing that the by-laws of the Ten required it to assemble on Wednesday, after which there would not be time for the Great Council to convene. With his councillors insisting on a Great Council meeting, Gritti promised Foscari to dismiss the assembly by

137 Sanuto, 45:557–558.
138 Ibid.

vespers so that the Ten could go about its business. The *case picole* had run out of room to maneuver.

The *case grandi* were determined to let nothing postpone the Great Council. Giorgio Corner, 74 years old and patriarch of his large clan, received last rites on July 27, a victim of the fever that entered Venice in June. Brother of the ex-queen of Cyprus and fabulously wealthy, he was a dominant *Primi* for three decades, missing election to the dogeship in 1521. He died on the afternoon of the thirty-first, and official mourning would usually have brought most government business to a halt. But his sons-in-law, all men from large houses—Trevisan, Malipiero, Loredan, and Contarini—kept his death secret: "His in-laws and cousins came to the Great Council, saying that he was in a bad way, in order to vote on the motion. . . . yet all knew that he was dead."[139]

Naturally, all Venice knew about the division within the patriciate. Clearing the hall of the Great Council of bystanders before debate and voting could hardly keep the controversy secret and tongues still. It was an especially dangerous time for the patriciate to be so divided— and for those divisions to be widely known, inside the city as well as abroad. Part of the emperor's army was straggling up the peninsula from Rome, alarming towns along the way; in Rome, Florence, and Venice, speculation was rife about how Charles V would deal with Italy. Lacking grain and meat, endangered by disease, Venetians faced exceptionally hard times. A patrician expressed a common sentiment in mid-July when he said, "Everything is gloomy for us." The reputation and popularity of the *Primi* had not improved since the dismal Corpus Christi procession a month before. The spectacle of the entire patriciate, as well as the executive councils of government, embroiled in a seemingly endless and bitter quarrel, could not inspire confidence among Venice's allies or populace.[140]

Perhaps because of these considerations, and perhaps from fear that deadlock between the clans might develop into something more serious, the *Primi* closed ranks. On the afternoon of the thirty-first, shortly before the Great Council assembled, the councillors modified their motion for the second time, adopting the proposal abandoned by their opponents six days before, which allowed only two members of a house into the nominating committees.

---

139 Sanuto, 45:559.
140 On the patrician's sentiment: ASMo., b. 57, c. 91r, Giacomo Tebaldi to the duke of Ferrara, July 18, 1527. On reports of the controversy, cf. ASMo., b. 57, c. 98r, Giacomo Tebaldi to the duke of Ferrara, July 30, 1527.

Seventeen days and six Great Council meetings after the councillors first announced their proposal, seventeen hundred patricians filed into the Ducal Palace. The councillor Francesco Marcello was there, even though he was ill; Marino Pisani, the chief of the Forty, attended for the first time since the controversy began. Sanuto notes that all the patricians in Venice were present, and he lists the names of forty-six men who had not been in the hall of the Great Council for twenty years, including fifteen Contarini and eight Morosini. It was, perhaps, the largest assembly of the Great Council ever gathered simply to vote on a piece of legislation. After the new proposal of the councillors was read, the three chiefs of the Forty announced their support for it, a maneuver that prevented opposition from the floor, for debate was permitted only for contrasting motions. Sanuto and others were prepared to speak against any alteration in the voting procedures, but the chiefs of the Forty were happy to have forced the councillors to accept the compromise they themselves had so recently supported. As for the councillors, they had to be content with a measure that favored the *case grandi,* even if not to the extent that their original (and then modified) proposal envisaged. Finally, the motion was approved by a vote of 914 to 789, with 3 abstentions and only 4 illegal ballots.[141]

Bitterness between the houses of the patriciate did not end with passage of the compromise proposal. On August 25 Sanuto won nomination to the Senate but the Great Council rejected him by 707 to 389. "I was badly treated," he complains, "because of the speech I made [on July 30]. Ca' Contarini and Ca' Morosini treated me poorly and didn't want to elect me. And Ca' Michiel, Ca' Dolfin, and other big houses as well, because I spoke against them. Yet God is just!"[142] The men of the *case grandi* were taking their revenge in the manner appropriate to Venetian patricians—"not with blood but with ballots." As Sanuto knew only too well, it was a difficult system in which to make one's way. Given the complicated procedures of the Great Council and the relentless desire of its members for offices, an able and ambitious patrician might despair of advancement. After one particularly disappointing defeat, Sanuto wearily exclaims that "one can't rail against heaven," a sentiment also echoed in the Venetian adage that "offices and wives come from heaven." The same fatalistic tone sounds in Priuli's lament about the injustice of the sovereign assembly: "It is

141 Sanuto, 45:560–561, 567.
142 Sanuto, 45:665–666.

useless to appeal against the judgment and balloting of the Great Council." Often spiteful, unfair, and unpredictable, the value of the Great Council for republicans such as Sanuto lay in the possibility it held out for all to participate in government and the means it provided to force a measure of equality on the *Primi* who ruled the *terra*. Thus the faults of the Great Council could be justified: "It's the way things are done in republics."[143]

---

143 On railing against heaven: Sanuto, 25:353. On "offices and wives": Sanuto, 22:66; cf. 40:665. On Priuli's lament: Priuli, vol. 5, fol. 151v. On the way of republics: Sanuto, 22:172; cf. 16:604; 24:705; 21:331; 54:622; 56:875.

Chapter III

Ducal Politics and the Patriciate

1. *The Doge*

On the morning of November 21, 1505, a placard was found posted on the church of San Giacomo di Rialto. It depicted three figures, the Virgin, Saint Mark, and Doge Leonardo Loredan, gathered around the city of Venice. The Virgin angrily laments to Saint Mark that Venice is saddled with such a monstrous doge, while Loredan smugly announces, "I don't care [about anything] so long as I can fatten myself and my son Lorenzo." A day later, another placard on the Ducal Palace predicted that Loredan would end as did Doge Marino Falier: by beheading, as was appropriate for a "tyrant." After describing the first placard, Priuli goes on to discuss the office of doge:

> It is commonly said that a Venetian prince is a mere tavern sign and that he can't do a thing without the consent of his councillors, the Collegio, or the councils. But I wish to assert that a Venetian prince may do as he pleases. Everybody desires his goodwill and to be agreeable [to him], and if sometimes there is a councillor or somebody who wishes to oppose him, it is necessary to proceed with discretion, otherwise he will meet with a severe rebuff and embarrassment. It is true that if a doge does anything against the Republic, he won't be tolerated; but in everything else, even in minor matters, he does as he pleases, so long as he doesn't offend the honor and dignity of the state.[1]

---

1 Priuli, 2:394; cf. Sanuto, 6:258–259; Mario Brunetti, "Il doge non è 'segno di taverna.'"

Priuli's resounding assertion of ducal power contrasts strongly with modern estimations that consider the doge "the figurehead of the republic, the point of least weight and greatest splendor, the brilliant apex to the pyramid of the Venetian constitution,"[2] who, as a glorious symbol of state and a passive instrument of the patriciate, "did little but preside over great receptions and council meetings."[3] There is considerable evidence to back up such judgments. Doges who tried to assert themselves (Falier in the Trecento and Foscari in the Quattrocento) were not successful, and their very attempts led to the placing of more efficient and burdensome controls on the office. The oath that a doge took on his election underwent continual revision, and as it became always more elaborate, it also became more petty. Each subsequent oath dropped outmoded rules and added new ones, but the impetus to control and impede him never faltered. By the end of the Quattrocento, according to the oath, the doge could not open his own mail and his verbal and written communications were closely supervised. He could not reply to a question on policy without instructions from his councillors; he could not receive foreign visitors in private nor accept gifts from them; he could not display his coat of arms outside the Ducal Palace. His sons were not permitted to hold office; his use of public money was carefully scrutinized and controlled; and he could neither leave the city nor move about it without permission. Dozens of regulations circumscribed his speech, movements, influence, and independence.[4]

The ducal oath was concerned with more than restricting the doge, however. The time when the dogeship was vacant, usually no more than a week, presented an opportunity for governmental reform, for streamlining judicial procedures, improving secretarial efficiency, tightening up administration of the basilica and of charitable foundations. Incorporating such concerns, the oath's provisions often added to the doge's authority and prestige. In 1521 public audiences by the doge were restricted to afternoons—but only so that the doge would have his mornings free for important business. In 1539 he was charged

2 Horatio Brown, *Studies in the History of Venice*, 1:306–307.
3 James Cushman Davis, *The Decline of the Venetian Nobility as a Ruling Class*, p. 21. For similar judgments, see Giuseppe Maranini, *La costituzione di Venezia dopo la serrata del Maggior Consiglio*, p. 273; Roberto Cessi, *Storia della Repubblica di Venezia*, 2:3; J. H. Plumb, "Venice: The Golden Years," p. 231; cf. B. Cecchetti, *Il doge di Venezia*, p. 269; D. S. Chambers, *The Imperial Age of Venice, 1380–1580*, pp. 86–93; Frederic C. Lane, *Venice*, p. 267.
4 On the ducal oath: E. Musatti, *Storia della promissione ducale*.

with insuring that the *Ospedali delle incurabili* was properly run. The oath of 1577 required the doge to review both secretarial account books and court procedures; eight years later his authority was extended to overseeing judicial offices at the Rialto, and he was to lead the Signoria in revamping court administration.[5]

Even the restrictive clauses in the oath of office indicate the importance of the dogeship, for it is doubtful if Venetians would have been concerned to hamstring a thoroughly subdued and purely ceremonial figure. Of course, they may have been frightened by the frequency with which republican governments elsewhere in Italy had been subverted by tyranny; actions of men such as Francesco Sforza of Milan and Lorenzo de' Medici of Florence may have provoked Venice into greater awareness of its republican ideals. Care was taken that the doge did not emulate the excesses of other Italian rulers. Doge Nicolò Tron (1471–1473) had his portrait put on a coin, but after his death the practice was forbidden as more appropriate to tyrants than to heads of republics. Also, Doge Nicolò's son, Filippo, was elected to the Ten and then forced to relinquish the office.[6] Still, Venetians probably acted so suspiciously toward the doge less because of alarm over foreign example than because of potential danger. The oath itself indicates that the doge wielded an amount of power that alarmed the patriciate, that his office had built into it a degree of authority that required careful surveillance. That surveillance, however, was rather after the fact. The forthright and detailed provisions of the oath had the greatest force—indeed, perhaps fulfilled their most essential function as cautionary reminders—during ducal vacancies, those brief periods when no one was in the office to bend (and sometimes break) the promises made at election. The high tide of antiducal sentiment always crested at the death of a doge and was channeled into the oath; election of a new doge returned affairs to normal: acceptance of *il Serenissimo*'s authority on almost all matters, deference to a prince who "may do as he pleases."

Doge Agostino Barbarigo, a handsome man with a long white beard and dignified air, held an elaborate court, requiring brides and newly elected men to present themselves before him. Priuli records that, after Barbarigo's death,

5 ASV, Maggior Consiglio, Deliberazioni, Liber Deda, Reg. 25, fols. 182r, 183r; Liber Novus, Reg. 27, fols. 50r, 50v; Liber Frigerius, Reg. 31, fols. 14v–15r, 130r, 132v–133r.

6 N. P. Aldobrandini, *Le monete di Venezia*, p. 19; Marino Sanuto, "Cronica Sanuda," fol. 399v.

It was charged that he was very imperious, because he did everything that he wished; with his arrogance, he placed all his friends
and dependents in offices as they fell vacant, without any consultation. Nobody dared to oppose him as he did what he pleased with
offices and benefices. It was charged that he allowed some to kiss his
hand. The greatest accusation was regarding his taking gifts from
everyone—an unbelievable thing! This diminished and tainted his
reputation, because otherwise he would have been the most worthy
prince the Venetian Republic ever had.

These excesses, as well as his misuse of public funds, account for
the uproar that followed Barbarigo's death and for several new provisions in the ducal oath. Moreover, a new office, the Investigators
of the Dead Doge, was created to ferret out wrongdoing in ducal
administration.[7]

Doge Leonardo Loredan's abuse of power was not as grand nor his
temperament as imperious as Barbarigo's. Yet Loredan, like Tron a
generation earlier, used his influence to get his son Lorenzo elected as
procurator; and when the Investigators checked the book of the
chancellery for the laws on the matter, they found them unaccount-
ably altered in Lorenzo's favor. The 1521 ducal oath again stipulated
that the doge must only speak generally when replying to foreign
representatives—clearly a response to Loredan's disregard for the provision. On September 21, 1519, Loredan expressed his own opinion to
Giambattista Malatesta, the Mantuan ambassador, regarding a debt
owed by the marquis to Venice: "But then, at the same instant, Andrea
Gritti, Alvise Molin, and Francesco Bragadin stood up, saying to the
doge that he shouldn't respond so resolutely without consulting them."
The doge remained incorrigible; Malatesta, when before the *savi* on
October 5, relates that Loredan "took me by the hand, in public, as
soon as I entered the Collegio; he took me by the hand and would not
let go until I departed. Whispering in my ear, he said [and Malatesta
wrote the rest in cipher] 'Be certain that I and my following will do
all we can for the marquis!' "[8]

That Gritti's chastisement of Loredan on September 15 stemmed
from carefully orchestrated opposition to him rather than from out-

---

7 On Barbarigo: Priuli, 2:176, 178; cf. Michelangelo Muraro, "La Scala senza
Giganti."
8 On Lorenzo Loredan: Sanuto, 21:364, 383. On the 1521 oath: ASV, Maggior
Consiglio, Deliberazioni, Liber Deda, Reg. 25, fol. 181v. On September 21 and
October 5: ASM, b. 1454, Giambattista Malatesta to the marquis of Mantua.

rage at abuse of power is clear from Gritti's actions as doge. On Gritti's death, the oath of 1539 forbade relatives of the doge from petitioning the Signoria in his presence; it insisted that the doge's relatives could not receive ecclesiastical offices from the Signoria and that certain secretarial offices must be legally conferred by the doge, and once again, the doge was forbidden to go beyond the mandate of the Signoria in dealing with ambassadors. Sanuto records at least one instance in 1526 when Doge Gritti conferred alone with a foreign representative—a flagrant and apparently widely known violation of the oath of office. Gritti was even more a supporter of Federico II, marquis of Mantua, than was Loredan; and Malatesta wrote to Mantua on July 29, 1527, that, "yesterday I could not find *il Serenissimo* alone and therefore could not give him your message"; however, the message was secretly delivered the next day. In September 1528 when the Ten learned that the French ambassador, Jean Langeac, planned a private meeting with Gritti, they considered sending a secretary to inform the ambassador, "I have reported to the doge what your excellency committed to me, that is, your wish to speak with His Serenity alone and not with others; he replied that according to the laws of this most excellent Republic, he could not say anything by himself—and that your excellency certainly knows this. . . . Your most prudent excellency will have to be content with the presence of four councillors attending His Serenity, as our procedures require."[9] This stern language was rejected in favor of a more diplomatic reply. That was just as well, for surely the ambassador (and the Ten) knew that the formalities were not always observed.

The restrictive clauses in the oath were, then, somewhat in the nature of campaign promises, even if made after the election; they should not be confused with political reality and are inadequate evidence for assessing ducal power. The dominance of official ideology meant that the exercise of ducal influence was usually covert and subtle; it did not and could not display itself as despotic authority but had to move within a complicated constitutional system. The doge and his council entered into all other councils of government. The Signoria was an integral part of the Ten, which needed a quorum of four councillors to assemble, and as a member of the Collegio, the

9 On the oath of 1539: ASV, Maggior Consiglio, Deliberazioni, Liber Novus, Reg. 27, fols. 48v–50v. On 1526: Sanuto, 43:377–378. On July 29, 1527: ASM, b. 1461, Giambattista Malatesta to the marquis of Mantua. On September 1528: ASV, Consiglio di Dieci, Parti Secrete, Reg. 2. fols. 78r–78v.

doge helped to run the Senate; with the Signoria, he presided over the Great Council.

In addition, the doge was responsible for overseeing judicial offices and for insuring honesty and competence in government. Doge Marco Barbarigo extended that responsibility to include weekly audiences in which he heard complaints against officials. According to the Ferrarese ambassador, Doge Loredan's pursuit of justice in his weekly rounds of palace offices instilled fear in the hearts of magistrates. When certain officials were deadlocked on a civil case, the doge could cast the deciding vote, a prerogative that Loredan at least once exercised illegally on a criminal case. Doge Gritti displayed a special passion for the dispensation of justice, and Sanuto records that his maiden speech in the Great Council laid unusual emphasis on the duty of officials to be honest and fair, warning that those who failed in this would be punished. Gritti's admittedly selective concern for probity in government was probably the decisive element in the reestablishment in 1524 of the censors (*censori*), magistrates commissioned to uproot corruption in elections. In 1529, after hearing rumors of maladministration in an office, Gritti dispatched the state attorneys to seize its records and investigate the matter. Three years before, he rousted the state attorneys out of church to investigate a complaint by a prostitute that a patrician had assaulted her; he personally convened a meeting of the Forty to secure an indictment against the man.[10]

As a sort of ombudsman, the doge's authority extended to all offices; but he had a more direct role in the supervision and administration of the chancellery. Even more than patricians, the *cittadini* secretaries were anxious to please the doge, on whom promotions and appointments often effectively depended. As always, whoever controls access to records and the flow of paperwork in a government is in a position of considerable authority. The doge and the grand chancellor, both called "Domino," were in office for life; and cooperation between them undoubtedly redounded to the benefit of both. The grand chancellor considered himself directly responsible to the doge, and the latter resisted sporadic attempts to restrict his authority over

10 On Barbarigo: Malipiero, 2:680. On Loredan: ASMo., b. 11, c. 96, Bartolomeo Cartari to the duke of Ferrara, October 10, 1502; Sanuto, 39:181–182, 184. On Gritti: Sanuto, 34:229; 41:84; 50:417. On the censors and Gritti, see this book, Chapter IV.3.

the chancellery. In 1532 when objection was made in the Collegio to his having removed a chancellery official without a hearing, Gritti asserted that the chancellery was under his orders alone and that he could appoint and remove officials as he saw fit.[11]

To the extent that a principle of opposition was built into the Venetian constitution, with overlapping functions insuring confusion and competition among offices, the doge's ability to move through all levels of the government and his duty to maintain orderly administration made his position both vital and arduous. Sanuto states that the doge "has a remarkable jurisdiction, but also many burdens, as does our most serene prince at present, who does not stint in toil for the good of the Republic: in the morning, the Collegio, then dinner and the Ten, the Senate or a public audience; on holidays, the Great Council. Thus days of rest are rare during the year." Given his central responsibilities and busy schedule, the doge was badly needed in the councils.[12]

Doge Barbarigo's illness in June 1495, when Venice was preparing to battle France, was considered "a serious hindrance to affairs of the city . . . both for advising about and executing decisions; and everyone prays for his health." Sanuto adds that, "the city lamented his absence from the Collegio [in times when] the needs of the Republic are so great. . . . And this illness arose from great exhaustion, since he never ceased to work; . . . he never had an hour's repose and wished to do everything."[13] When Barbarigo entered his last illness in July 1501, he was at first determined to continue attending the councils. Finally he called his councillors and *savi* to his bedside and told them "that he recognized how essential it was for the Republic to have a leader at the government," therefore, "for the health and welfare of the Venetian state, seeing that he could no longer exercise his office, he wished to renounce the dogeship." Judging that Barbarigo had but a short time to live, the Full Collegio graciously refused his resignation. Although the doge's death was shortly after greeted with joy, Priuli admired Barbarigo's last gesture: "He showed exceptional charity toward the country, for, seeing that he was too weak to fulfill his office, he did not wish the Republic to suffer; truly, the Venetian

---

11 Sanuto, 57:775; cf. 789, 843–844.

12 On principle of opposition: Maranini, *Costituzione di Venezia*, p. 99. On Sanuto's statement: Marino Sanuto, *Cronachetta*, p. 78.

13 On Barbarigo's illness: Malipiero, 2:695; Marino Sanuto, *La spedizione di Carlo VIII in Italia*, p. 408.

Republic without a prince, that is, a revered leader, is like a headless fly—everything falls into disorder."[14]

Confusion reigned in the Senate in April 1511 when Doge Loredan's illness prevented his attendance. The Senate adjourned in tumult after the entire assembly became embroiled in an argument between a councillor and a chief of the Ten. Priuli stresses that the reason for the unseemly behavior was the absence of the doge, whose authority would have brought the commotion to a speedy end. This function of the doge was recognized in the oath of 1567, which stated that the doge's presence in the Great Council "obviates many disorders and inconveniences arising every day in the voting."[15]

Doge Grimani's absence from the councils during his last months led to predictable squabbles among *Primi* and to a certain lack of focus in governmental activity. When it was clear that Grimani would not be able to resume his duties, the Full Collegio urged the sickly doge to abdicate, in return for which he was offered 1,000 ducats a year as a pension and the honors accorded a doge at his death. The offer was rejected, apparently because the doge's grandsons did not want to give up the income of the office and their own billets in the Ducal Palace.[16]

Fortunately for the *Primi*, Grimani died within a week after he refused to resign; his continuance in office might have led to a repetition of the Foscari deposition of 1457, a central event in Venetian history that should be reevaluated in the light of the necessity for a working doge. According to the traditional view, the Loredan clan, using the Council of Ten as their instrument of revenge, forced Foscari out of the Ducal Palace, thereby ending a thirty-year vendetta against the doge; the excuse given for Foscari's removal was his absence for some months from the councils, but the true reason was the desire of the doge's enemies to humiliate and defeat him.[17] There is a kernel of truth in this account, for there is no doubt that the Loredan hated

14 On Barbarigo's attempted resignation: Priuli, 2:173. On refusing the resignation: Sanuto, 4:111–112; cf. Priuli, 2:173. On reaction to Barbarigo's death: Sanuto, 4:113; Priuli, 2:176. On Priuli's admiration: Priuli, 2:173.

15 On 1511: Priuli, vol. 6, fol. 167v. On 1567: ASV, Maggior Consiglio, Deliberazioni, Liber Angelus, Reg. 29, fol. 29v.

16 Sanuto, 34:116; cf. da Mosto, *I dogi di Venezia nella vita pubblica e privati*, pp. 284, 286.

17 On the deposition: Giorgio Dolfin, "Cronaca Veneta dalle origini al 1458," fols. 447v–450r. Sanuto, "Cronica Sanuda," fol. 316r. On the traditional view of the deposition: Cessi, *Storia della Repubblica*, 1:399–401; H. R. Trevor-Roper, "Doge Francesco Foscari"; F. Berlan, *I due Foscari*; E. Vecchiato, *I Foscari ed i Loredano*.

Foscari and took advantage of events to act against him. But the Ten, led by Giacomo Loredan, needed the backing of the Signoria, the Collegio, and a special *zonta* of twenty-five *Primi*—a total of fifty-two men—to force Foscari out of office. There is no indication that the Loredan could expect such broad support for an act of personal vengeance. Indeed, it would have been highly dangerous for them to move against the doge for such a motive. Moreover, in return for his resignation, Foscari was offered a pension of 2,000 ducats a year, continued right of entrance to councils, and the burial rights of a doge—terms that are almost identical to those proferred the highly respected, albeit ailing, Grimani.[18] Nor was Foscari's illness a fiction of his enemies. His death within a week after vacating the Ducal Palace probably was not due to uncontrollable rage at hearing the bells announcing his sucessor's election but was, rather, the natural end to the illness that, along with other personal difficulties, had kept him from affairs of state. In short, Foscari's removal was essentially due to the reason advanced by the Ten—his incapacity or unwillingness to exercise his office—instead of to more dramatic causes. He was simply not doing his job. Far from signaling the final end of ducal power, the Foscari deposition testifies to the continued authority resident in the dogeship and to the importance of maintaining an able and energetic individual in the key office of the government.

Burdened with responsibilites, deeply involved in the daily business of government, the doge moved across the range of councils and magistracies. In addition, his life tenure in office added to his importance and authority. Except for the procurators of San Marco, other officials were elected for six months to a year. Councillors and *savi* might come and go, but the doge remained, exerting continual pressure on decision making and policy formation. Furthermore, the doge was almost invariably elected from among the nine procurators, who, acting as treasurers of the government and as fiduciaries for private individuals, enjoyed a prestige second only to that of the doge. Wotton described the Procuratia as "commonly the seminary of their princes." In fact, procurators even wore ducal garments, without, of course, the specific insignia of the doge.[19] The procurators could and commonly did use their office to garner support for a future ducal election. While a

18 ASV, Consiglio di Dieci, Parti Miste, Reg. 15, fols. 139v–142r.
19 On the procurators: Reinhold C. Mueller, "The Procuratori of San Marco in the Thirteenth and Fourteenth Centuries." On the "seminary of their princes": Logan Pearsall Smith, *The Life and Letters of Sir Henry Wotton*, 2:134. On the procurators' dress: "Le vesti e maniche ducali."

procurator, Francesco Foscari dispensed more than 30,000 ducats to poor patricians to provide dowries for their daughters, generosity that created supporters for him in the Great Council. Similarly, Nicolò Marcello was elected doge in 1473 because of his philanthropic activity while a procurator. Unlike the doge, procurators were elected by the usual procedures of the Great Council, so they entered office (and competed for the dogeship) with substantial support within the patriciate.[20] The man who became doge was usually experienced, adept, and relatively popular—in all, a formidable figure, ready to profit from the opportunities offered by his new, permanent position.

Clearly, the doge did more than "preside over great receptions and council meetings." Yet even at these occasions, his role was by no means passive. During the *case grandi* controversy of 1527, Gritti controlled the timing of the legislative battle, proroguing and convening the Great Council to suit the aims of the large clans. Loredan's fiery reply to Minio in 1502 led to the exile of the latter, as well as to the easy passage of unpopular austerity legislation. More often than not, ducal intervention in debate was decisive; few cared to oppose the head of state. In December 1526 Gritti made an impassioned speech in the Senate against a motion by the *savi di terraferma*: "with [ducal] cap in hand, he prayed God to inspire the best deliberations," while condemning those who disagreed with him. The proposal was modified to please the doge and passed by two hundred votes to thirteen. When the doge opposed a measure, it was usually defeated; and if he failed to get his way, as happened with Barbarigo in 1496, "everything proceeds very slowly [in executing the policy] because the doge opposes the decision." In other words, the doge could to some extent rescue victory from defeat by delaying the Collegio's execution of the Senate's decisions.[21]

Councillors, *savi*, and patricians in general were attentive to the desires and moods of *il Serenissimo*. When Gritti was feeling poorly, an official reporting to the Collegio was praised "with few words" and denied the traditional approbation for a job well done. A magistrate who had performed improperly faced public humiliation when he presented himself before the doge. A patrician's political capital was increased by an invitation to dine at the Ducal Palace, by the doge's

20 On Foscari: Sanuto, "Cronica Sanuda," fol. 241r. On Marcello: Malipiero, 2:662–663. On the procurators' support and experience: Lane, *Venice*, p. 267. On ducal electoral procedures, see this book, Chapter III.3.

21 On Gritti in 1526: Sanuto, 43:420–421; cf. 60–61. On Barbarigo in 1496: Malipiero, 1:480–481.

praise in the Collegio, and by his attentiveness in the Senate or Great Council. Even Sanuto, no friend or supporter of Gritti, was overwhelmed in 1526 when the doge deigned to reply to him during debate, for "very rarely does the most serene prince respond to a private citizen in the Great Council, so that even if I didn't defeat the motion, I don't care, since I gained the very greatest honor."[22] To be sure, the Ducal Palace was no Versailles, where a monarch's frown or smile could determine a career, but the patricians of Venice did well to court the doge's favor and seek his commendation. Patricians thus eagerly flocked to receptions and meetings, stages upon which ducal power, attended by compliance and deference, was most evident.

Ducal political capital lay in the immense prestige of the office, a resource that could be squandered. Thus the principal complaint against Loredan was that he did not measure up to the dogeship, that he failed to exert the full authority of his high office because of concern for his family. Priuli stresses that Loredan was a man of abundant goodwill and sanctity but with an excessively timid and weak character. People complained about Loredan, confirms Sanuto, "for not giving his opinion." The defeat at Agnadello left him "half dead" and incapable of action. Trembling between two patricians during the Corpus Christi procession of June 1509, Loredan was a poor example of courage for beleaguered Venice. The doge even feared for his safety in the Ducal Palace, calling up one hundred armed men from the Arsenal to guard him every night. In June 1510 he exhorted the patriciate to contribute men and money to the defense of Padua, but members of the Collegio lacked the courage to suggest he send his own sons. When the subject was finally broached, Loredan ingenuously replied that his four sons were in poor health, an answer that caused resentment among those urged to make sacrifices. October 2, 1513, the twelfth anniversary of Loredan's election, was marked by the burning of Mestre by enemy forces. At this time, Michiel wrote that "many virtually hate the doge due to our abundant bad fortune—and because of this grumbling, he threw a guard of eighty men around the Ducal Palace." The doge still refused to make the all-important gesture of sending his sons to war. Earlier Loredan's pusillanimity was contrasted with Doge Foscari's heartening the city by wearing a splendid golden robe when Venice was defeated.[23] The doge inevitably set the

22 On the officials before the Collegio: Sanuto, 41:273; 43:211. On Sanuto and Gritti: Sanuto, 43:205.

23 On Loredan's character: Priuli, 4:92. On not "giving his opinion": Sanuto,

tone of the city. Loredan's failure to provide leadership in crisis partially explains the extended depression that settled on Venice during the War of the League of Cambrai.

Loredan's tendency "to put his head between his legs" in time of trouble appeared when the welfare of his family was at stake. When representatives of mainland cities complained to the Signoria about the corruption and petty tyranny of Venetian officials, Loredan's sons defended the officials, striving to gain supporters among the patriciate against the death of their father, an event always expected momentarily. Not wishing to harm his family's future political success, Loredan went along with his sons "because of fear of the ballot." Priuli claims that the doge's eldest son, Lorenzo, was a "sagacious, very astute, and wicked man, who for reasons of intriguing for office has done every evil . . . his father being the doge, he holds large sway, and he has a great name and reputation in the city more from fear than from love." Lorenzo prevailed on his father to back his election as procurator and apparently he arranged for the books of the chancellery to be altered in order to obscure the illegality of his election. He was the power behind the scenes because of, as Priuli puts it, "always having the ear of his father."[24]

The anonymous placard of 1505 recognized this fact early in Doge Loredan's reign: "I don't care [about anything]," the doge is made to say, "so long as I can fatten myself and my son Lorenzo." Complaint is not about ducal power itself, which seems to be taken for granted, but at its misuse, its subordination to familial interests. Priuli's precise and accurate evaluation of ducal authority may have been concerned both with Loredan's effective abdication of power and with Lorenzo's covert manipulation of his father's office. The diarist seems to disdain the good but weak Loredan while reluctantly prizing the deplorable yet strong Barbarigo, "who would have been the most worthy prince" Venice ever had if not for his greed. By not rising to the demands of his office, Loredan may have brought more trouble

---

8:18. On Loredan and Agnadello: Sanuto, 8:247–248, 266, 390. On Loredan in the procession: Sanuto, 8:373; 252–253. On Loredan's guards: Priuli, 4:384. On defending Padua: Priuli, vol. 5, fol. 152v; cf. Sanuto, 10:649. On Michiel's statement: Michiel, fol. 89v; cf. Sanuto, 17:108, 109, 113, 118, 120. On the contrast with Foscari: Sanuto, 8:252–253.

24 On his "head between his legs": Priuli, vol. 5, fol. 58v; Sanuto, 8:252–253. On "fear of the ballot": Priuli, 4:35. On Lorenzo's character and on having his father's ear: Priuli, 4:92.

and anxiety on Venice than Barbarigo ever did with his imperious manner and courtly innovation.

Fittingly, the doge was shown on the placard with the Virgin and Saint Mark, holy companions traditionally depicted with the head of the Republic in paintings, sculptures, coins, and state ceremonies. The placard thereby cleverly parodied a fundamental theme of Venetian political religiosity: the sacred aura that enveloped the doge and was another manifestation and source of his authority. Of course, the office, not the man, was glorified; but in practice the two were to some extent conflated. The doge as the living symbol of the state made a powerful impact on foreigners and Venetians alike. His death meant the closing of the Ducal Palace and the cessation of governmental activity (only in 1521 was the oath revised to permit the essential needs of the state to be met during the ducal vacancy). Three groups of fifty *Arsenalotti* established themselves about the Piazza di San Marco and the courtyard of the Ducal Palace, while all the bells of the city rang. The Signoria did not leave the Ducal Palace, where the body of the doge was laid out, attended night and day by twenty-eight patricians dressed in scarlet "as a sign that the Signoria still lives, though the doge is dead." After three days, an enormous file of patricians and *Scuole* members accompanied the body out of the Ducal Palace, pausing at the last stair before the courtyard for the Signoria to give permission to proceed. Only in death could the doge leave the palace without his councillors. Arsenal workers carried the body on a circuit of the piazza, repeating the movement that had begun the reign, and at the door of the basilica, lifted it to the sky nine times. The funeral mass ended official ceremonies, and the family took the body for burial.[25]

In the brief time between announcement of his election and coronation, the doge-elect received minor ecclesiastical orders in the basilica, so that he could administer benediction. Ducal *laudes* emphasized the sacral dimensions of his office, sometimes using texts derived from Byzantine imperial ceremonies. The doge's robes and cap, the ring that he wore, the umbrella carried above him in processions, the sword

25 On the doge's sacred aura: Chambers, *Imperial Age of Venice*, pp. 187–188. On the ducal vacancy: Sanuto, *Cronachetta*, pp. 70, 80; idem, 30:421–422. On "the Signoria still lives": Sanuto, *Cronachetta*, p. 80. On the funeral ceremony: ASM, b. 1454, Giambattista Malatesta to the marquis of Mantua, June 27, 1521; cf. Bianca Tamassia Mazzarotto, *Le feste veneziane*, pp. 224–228; Edward Muir, "The Doge as *Primus Inter Pares*: Interregnum Rites in Early Sixteenth-Century Venice."

that followed him, all trailed religious associations, a melange of pious folklore and political faith. The doge alone united the Ducal Palace, center of state administration, and the basilica, martyrium and sanctuary. Although the doge was crowned on the stairs of the palace (in a ceremony that stressed the religious aspects of government), it was in the church that he was first presented to the *popolo* and took custody of the standard of Saint Mark. Although by law the doge could not be depicted as a sovereign in the mosaics of the basilica, he is represented there as the chief guardian of the relics, and he had the responsibility for nominating the chief ecclesiastic of the church.[26]

Finally, the doge played the central role in pageants throughout the year: the Wedding of the Sea; the processions of Corpus Christi, Ascension, and San Marco; visits to San Zaccaria, San Rocco, and San Giorgio. A master of ceremonies at the basilica in the early seventeenth century described a ceremony instituted a century earlier:

> The doge goes to [the church of] Saint Marina in triumphal procession where he hears low mass, then he returns to San Marco, where a solemn mass is sung and the procession files past, after which he returns to the Ducal Palace. This observance is because on this day [July 17] in 1509 the city of Padua was recovered for the Venetians by Andrea Gritti (who later became doge), at which time affairs began to prosper against the League of Cambrai, [an alliance] made against these patricians by all the major powers of Europe and Christendom, which was so bad [for Venice].[27]

The triumphal procession to Saint Marina was a relatively minor occasion in Venetian devotional rounds; yet it served the same functions as the better known and more sumptuous displays: With the doge as centerpiece, it commemorated Venice within the context of a provi-

---

26 On the religious character of the ducal office: Gina Fasoli, "Liturgia e ceremoniale ducale," *Venezia e il Levante fino al Secolo XV*, 2 vols. (Venice, 1971), 1:261–296; idem, "Nascita di un mito," pp. 456, 459–460; Otto Demus, *The Church of San Marco in Venice*, pp. 44–45, 55–56, 59; Michelangelo Muraro, "Ideologia e iconografia dei dogi di Venezia." On the ducal *laudes*: F. Alberto Gallo, "Musiche veneziane nel ms. 2216 della Biblioteca Universitaria di Bologna," 108ff.

27 Giovanni Stringa, *La Chiesa di San Marco*, p. 75. On other ceremonies: Mazzarotto, *Feste veneziane*, pp. 155–205, 270–288. On the political significance of processions and other ceremonies: Edward Muir, "Images of Power: Art and Pageantry in Renaissance Venice."

dential design and, with custom and ceremony, ventured to renew innocence and virtue.

A living icon of the state, the doge was raised above his fellow patricians, a position that could have direct political benefit insofar as an attack on him always ran the danger of being branded as lack of respect or even sedition. In 1511 Loredan informed Luca Tron, a chief of the Ten and a bitter enemy, that "the doge is head of this state" and Tron, "a private citizen." There was some murmuring in the Great Council over this arrogant assertion, but the mantle of *il Serenissimo* easily shielded Loredan from disciplinary action. In the ducal oath of 1577, future councillors were instructed not to correct or chastise the doge in the presence of foreign representatives, for that would be contrary to ducal dignity and, hence, to the reputation of *la Serenissima Repubblica.*[28]

The doge's ceremonial and symbolic importance cannot be separated from the more mundane, less glamorous, aspects of his office—his busy routine and prominent participation in councils, his life tenure, his supervision of the chancellery and judicial offices—for his manifold responsibilities made him an essential and hardworking head of state, the linchpin of government, while his exalted status extended his effective authority to the most minor matters. Venetians were never entirely happy with this unique combination, but they wanted an altogether exceptional person as their doge. On the one hand, the doge was supposedly merely first among equals, paying taxes, so Sanuto claims, "like any other Venetian citizen," and, according to Contarini, having only "the power of a single ballot."[29] On the other, he was given a place in government which made him an influential and vital figure indeed.

Representing the Republic, moving amid religious and political panoply, he was forbidden to voice an opinion without permission of his councillors. Expected to lead the city in crisis, with moral suasion and heroic example, he was also to be bland and accommodating. The ducal oath expressed these contradictions, with new responsibilities given to the doge at the same time he was presumably hedged about with more restrictions. Frustration was the natural outcome of this

28 On 1511: Sanuto, 13:478–479. On 1577: ASV, Maggior Consiglio, Deliberazioni, Liber Frigerius, Reg. 31, fols. 12v–13r.

29 Sanuto, *Cronachetta*, p. 78; Gasparo Contarini, *La Republica e i Magistrati di Venezia*, p. 49.

process, no less for patricians who saw the doge elude surveillance and control than for the doge himself, never allowed quite the leadership his position implied and his experience demanded. Barbarigo and Gritti, for example, died disappointed men, worn out by constant struggle with a political system not amenable to dictates and domineering personalities. Barbarigo grumbled in 1495 "that everyone persecuted him, that he has been made old and can no longer bear the weight of the dogeship."[30] Loredan chose not to struggle, thereby provoking discontent by his failure to wield the authority bestowed on him. A delicate balance of temperament and ability was required of doges, and it is unsurprising that so few proved to be paragons who could simultaneously please the *terra* and satisfy their own ambitions.

In fact, all unwittingly, and perhaps despite themselves, Venetians went some way toward solving a problem that had bedeviled and destroyed so many city-states, that is, how to provide strong executive authority while preserving republican govenment. To a certain extent, the dogeship did, as Contarini suggests, provide the advantage of a monarchy without its disadvantages, although this was not accomplished by the ideal means that Contarini generally saw at work in the Venetian constitution.[31] As with much else in Venetian politics, the office of doge was the product of compromise in which official ideals diverged sharply from political reality, yet in such a fashion that stability was reinforced and the ideals made to seem effective. The doge was never transformed into a thoroughgoing executive, with a corps of bureaucrats ready to translate commands into action. For Venetians the doge was sufficiently powerful already. It was enough to have in the Ducal Palace a prince who "does as he pleases, so long as he doesn't offend the honor and dignity of the state": that was a compromise that both respected the realities of power and preserved the integrity of republican institutions.

2. *The Governing Circle: A Gerontocracy*

Sanuto noted in 1518 that he had come across a prophecy in an ancient volume: "When caps dance on heads, when gold rises, and when the young rule, the world will either advance or fall asunder.' " He thought that signs pointed to the prophecy being fulfilled in his own time:

30 Malipiero, 2:173.
31 Cf. Lane, *Venice*, p. 267.

First, caps in the French mode bounce on the head when one hurries
. . . ; gold has grown in value, so that the ducat is worth more than
ever. And the young reign: the pope is young; the king of France,
the king of Spain, the king of England, and the king of Hungary are
very young; Selim, emperor of the Turks, is about 42 years of age.
There are two old ones, Emperor Maximilian and our doge of
Venice.[32]

Whatever one may think of Sanuto's interpretation of the first two
conditions of the prophecy, he required no fanciful exegesis for the
third. Europe's princes were indeed a youthful group. Pope Leo X was
43 years old; Francis I, 24; Henry VIII, 27; Charles I of Spain, 18; and
Lewis II of Hungary, 12. Maximilian I was 59 years old, and Doge
Loredan was 82. When Maximilian died within a year, Charles succeeded him as Holy Roman emperor; and with the exception of
Venice's, the thrones of Europe were occupied by men under the age
of 44. Excluding Loredan, the average age of Europe's princes in 1518
was 33, a low figure partly because Leo was elected at 38, an unusually
young age for a pope. During the Renaissance, popes were elected
at an average age of 54 and died at an average age of 64. It was, in contrast, rare for doges to be elected before the age at which most popes
were already dead. Between 1400 and 1600, the average age of the doge
at election was 72, an average of 18 years older at election than the
pope, the only other political figure of the period who assumed office
at an advanced age.

Renaissance notions of man's longevity make the age of the doge
look even more remarkable, for in that epoch "old age" was conceived
of as commencing at 40. By contrast, modern times thinks of old age
as beginning at 65—a clear reflection of the different life expectancies
of the two periods.[33] Henry VIII died at 56; yet he outlived all but
one of the eleven English monarchs of the fifteenth and sixteenth centuries. Popes have died at an average age of 79 since 1800, whereas only
three Renaissance popes reached the age of 70. Erasmus and Michelangelo were not speaking rhetorically when they referred to themselves as "old" at 40, although the former died at the age of 70 and the
latter at 89. In each case, their old age was especially melancholy, for
they had outlived virtually all their contemporaries, as well as the

32 Sanuto, 26:210.
33 For what follows, see Creighton Gilbert, "When Did a Man in the Renaissance Grow Old?"; cf. David Herlihy, "The Generation in Medieval History."
On age differences and generations in general: Julián Marías, *Generations*.

cultural milieu in which they came to maturity. Of course it is possible that their melancholy was somewhat relieved because of the respect accorded their many years, inasmuch as in most societies a natural consequence of low life expectancy is the placing of great value on the presumed wisdom of the elderly.

As the advanced years of the doge indicate, old age had enormous prestige in the patrician republic. The sculpture of an elderly and prudent Solomon was placed near the entrance of the Ducal Palace, representing not only the justice of the Old Law but the wisdom of years—no doubt a comforting sight to the elderly *Primi* who strolled past it. The governing circle of Venice constituted a gerontocracy, which probably emerged in the second half of the Trecento, when the ruling class had crystallized and the government was no longer as loosely organized as in the previous century. Given great respect for age, the existence of a patrician caste founded on a monopoly of office holding was the essential precondition for the emergence of the gerontocracy. It is likely that the well-to-do patricians who formed the governing circle enjoyed a longer average life expectancy than the rest of the population. They could expect to occupy high office as long as they were able, willing, and acceptable to their peers. Veneration for old age found institutional expression in the Great Council, where patricians deferred to and elected their elders, the senior members of the clans that composed the ruling class.

Venice was governed by the old men (*vecchi*) of the hereditary patrician caste. By custom, high office was generally closed to those considered "young men" (*giovani*). Patricians entered the Great Council at the age of 25. They were eligible for election to the Senate at 32 (after 1431), although it was unusual for a patrician to become a senator before he had passed 50. A patrician could legally enter the Ten at 40; but, again, it was rare for election to occur before 50. Election as a ducal councillor could occur at the age of 25, although in practice, as Sanuto says, only "the oldest and most important of the city" gained that post.[34] In short, deference to the elderly pushed the age of de facto eligibility to councils some ten to twenty years beyond the legal requirement.

This exclusion from power rankled among the "young." Priuli criticized the doge and the *Primi* in 1509 because "they valued their own

---

34 Sanuto, *Cronachetta*, p. 305; Enrico Besta, *Il Senato Veneziano (origine, costituzione, attribuzioni e riti)*, pp. 81–85; Maranini, *Costituzione di Venezia*, p. 305.

lives as though they would live forever, yet they had no certainty of living even one year longer, not to mention five—and all on account of their advanced years." Contarini asserts that the only outstanding distinction within the patrician caste was that of age. Although he considered that generational differences imparted a healthful tension to the constitution, he followed Aristotle in stating that the role of the young is to obey, that of the old to command. Nevertheless, the *giovani* were given a place in the Senate. Because there was little prestige attached to serving on the supreme court, the judges of the Forty were usually younger than senators; hence *giovani* entered the central council by means of this constitutional back door. In this way, according to Contarini, "the natural coldness of the old comes to be moderated by the heat of the young. Still, these youths are not equal in number to the elderly but just sufficient so that in the Senate's judgments there may be, or appear to be, some sign of heat."[35]

In 1525, about the time that Contarini was writing his treatise, Sanuto successfully opposed legislation that would have made it more difficult for young men to gain election to the Forty. The proposal called for the judges of the Forty to serve first on the Court of the Forty (rather than sixteen months on the two other supreme courts and then on the Forty), thereby raising the prestige of the Forty and, hence, the average age of the men willing to serve on it—a devious piece of legislation that indicates the powerful assumptions regarding age and offices that permeated Venetian politics. Addressing the Great Council, Sanuto drew a parallel between the generations necessary to the councils and a painting on the Senate's wall of three trees of varying sizes. He argued that to approve the legislation would be contrary to the intentions of Venice's ancestors, who wished that the young, the middle-aged, and the old be in the Senate, "as cold, tepid and hot blood mingles and makes an excellent composite, greatly benefiting our Republic." To the charge that the *giovani* introduced an unseemly wrangling over proposed legislation, he replied that "one wishes to have persons about who oppose motions because truth is found by arguing about matters." Finally, he asserted that to exclude the young from the Senate would deprive them of the chance of learning how to govern the state.[36]

It hardly needed another participant in the debate to warn that the

35 On Priuli's criticism: 4:24. On the distinction of age: Contarini, *Republica*, p. 32. On the Forty: Contarini, *Republica*, pp. 107, 73.
36 Sanuto, 38:377–378; 39:24–29.

legislation might "bring the old to blows with the young," for some
hostility between the generations was common within the councils.
In 1500 Antonio Grimani wanted his trial for incompetence as captain
general of the fleet removed from the Great Council, "seeing the
youngsters badly disposed toward him and wishing to be judged by
the elders in the Senate, where he hoped to be absolved." Similarly,
the relatives of Angelo Trevisan opposed having him tried in the Great
Council in 1510 because they did not want him subject to an assembly
dominated by "babies," where he would be "placed in danger of the
judgment of juveniles and of a great medley of persons who won't be
content to listen to reason and who will judge by emotion."[37]

Some historians have cast this hostility between the generations into
ideological terms, contrasting a reformist, expansionist, and antipapal
giovani party with a conservative, oligarchic, and propapal *vecchi*
party.[38] But there is no indication that the *giovani* as a group shared
anything but relative youth, restlessness, and exclusion from office.
Nor did the *vecchi* share anything other than advanced years, suspi-
cion of the young, and monopoly of power. On specific issues and for
brief periods, the adventuresome spirits of the *giovani* did lead some of
them to a measure of united action. At various times some *giovani*
supported an attack on Ferrara, subsidies for the Pisan rebellion against
Florence, a Great Council trial for Grimani, and expansion into the
Romagna.[39] Yet neither the young nor the old had a common program
or political philosophy; neither had a common policy toward church,
government, or foreign affairs. Hostility between young and old arose
over place and position and had no ideological dimension. Conflict was
inherent both in the structure of government, which admitted all
patricians to the Great Council yet left authority in the hands of relatively few, and in the Venetian reverence for age, which placed
powerful offices in the hands of those with the greatest experience and
maturity. As Priuli complains, "spirited youth" were left to look on

37 Priuli, 1:327; 279; vol. 5, fols. 85v–86r.
38 Federico Seneca, *Venezia e papa Giulio II*, pp. 36–38, 134–135; idem, *Il doge
Leonardo Donà*; Aldo Stella, *Chiesa e stato nelle relazioni dei nunzi pontifici a
Venezia*, pp. 3–6, 8, 11; William J. Bouwsma, *Venice and the Defense of Repub-
lican Liberty*, pp. 162–293; Gaetano Cozzi, *Il doge Nicolò Contarini*; but see also
M. J. C. Lowry, "The Reform of the Council of Ten, 1582–3; William Archer
Brown, "Nicolò da Ponte."
39 On Ferrara: ASMo, b. 8, c. 61, Aldobrandino Guidoni to the duke of
Ferrara, September 1, 1496. On Pisa: Malipiero, 2:512. On Grimani: Pietro Dolfin,
Annalium Venetorum (pars quatro), p. 87; Priuli, 1:327. On the Romagna:
Sanuto, 5:617.

while the "hoary and old Fathers" of the Republic dictated affairs. James Howell more eloquently described the same phenomenon a century later: "gray heads sway, and green heads obey."[40]

This was not the case in states where the dynastic principle and monarchial institutions precluded any political expression of deference to the elderly. For example, in 1434 Cosimo de' Medici began his rule of Florence at the age of 45; he was succeeded by Piero di Cosimo at 48, Lorenzo di Piero ("the Magnificent") at 21, and Piero di Lorenzo at 21. The Medici gave important offices to and were influenced by men who were close in age to themselves.[41] In their thirties Bernardo Rucellai and Piero Capponi were major oligarchs and close to Lorenzo "the Magnificent"; in their mid-forties they helped in 1494 to overthrow his incompetent son and restore the Republic. In 1502 their families supported an attempt to give an aristocratic turn to the Republic with the creation of a Florentine "doge," the *Gonfaloniere* for life, an office to which the 50-year-old Piero Soderini was elected. (Significantly, Savonarola, an admirer of the Venetian constitution, had opposed the creation of the office as too dangerous for Florence.) At the age of 37, Cardinal Giovanni de' Medici restored his family's rule in 1512, six months before his election as Pope Leo X; and he later dispatched his 24-year-old nephew to attend to Florence. In the last Republic of 1527–1530, the man in charge of the city much of the time was the *Gonfaloniere*, 54-year-old Nicolò di Piero Capponi. The restoration of Medicean rule meant the domination of Florence by Pope Clement VII, aged 52, acting through Duke Alessandro, aged 20. Seven years later, 17-year-old Duke Cosimo I had slight difficulty setting aside his leading mentors, 54-year-old Francesco Guicciardini and 63-year-old Francesco Vettori, in order to rule in his own name.[42]

All these Florentines assumed power or wielded influence at an age that was *troppo zovene* in Venetian political terms; most died before

40 On Priuli: 4:141. On Howells: Brian Pullan, "The Significance of Venice," p. 452.

41 This statement is based on information drawn from Francis William Kent's *Household and Lineage in Renaissance Florence*, pp. 164–226, 306–308; cf. Lauro Martines, *The Social World of the Florentine Humanists, 1390–1460*, pp. 145–198.

42 On Rucellai and Capponi: Kent, *Household and Lineage*, pp. 80, 84, 86, 174–175, 199. On the *Gonfaloniere*: Nicolai Rubinstein, "Politics and Constitution in Florence at the End of the Fifteenth Century," p. 181; Sergio Bertelli, "Pier Soderini 'Vexillifer Perpetuus Reipublicae Florentinae' 1502–1512." On Savonarola: Donald Weinstein, *Savonarola and Florence*, p. 247. On Nicolò Capponi: Kent, *Household and Lineage*, p. 223. On Duke Cosimo: Eric Cochrane, *Florence in the Forgotten Centuries, 1527–1800*, pp. 39–40.

they would have been politically eligible for high office in Venice. For example, Lorenzo "the Magnificent" (1449–1492) ruled for twenty-three years and died at 43, an age in Venice that would have marked the onset of a long apprenticeship in state service prior to gaining a position of power. The gap between Florence and Venice in the matter of age in politics may be measured by the statement of a Florentine humanist, Alamanno Rinuccini, who wrote a dialogue in 1479, when Lorenzo was 30, complaining that in his city everyone is "driven round and round by the lusts of a young man."[43]

In Venice the conflict of generations was perennial because of the significance of age differences in the political system. In brief, the Venetian political definition of old age was identical with modern conventional notions that assign the advent of old age to the mid-sixties. Outside a Venetian political context, premodern standards came into play, and a man of 40 was thought to be entering the winter of his years. Thus Sanuto classed 59-year-old Maximilian with 82-year-old Loredan as one of Europe's *vecchi*; but at 59, a Venetian would have been considered "too young" (*troppo zovene*) to be politically eligible for the dogeship. Sanuto expressed concern at 50 that his great age might prevent him continuing his diary; yet at that age he was not old enough to be a serious contender for state attorney, an office for which he yearned. Pietro Bembo lamented in 1529, when he was 60, that he was too old to assume the post of official historian; however, he was still twelve years short of the average span at which Renaissance doges were elected.[44]

Clearly, with an average age at election of 72 years, the doge was extraordinarily old for his time. But the advanced age of the doge was by no means exceptional in Venetian politics, and what made the Venetian Republic a gerontocracy was the extent to which government was in the control of old men. Three men were separately elected as ambassadors to Constantinople in their early seventies. Pietro Lando, a future doge (1538–1545), was elected *podestà* of Padua at the age of 73. Cristoforo Moro in 1517 was elected *podestà* of Verona at the same age, and he died while serving as a councillor two years later. Francesco Falier was 79 in 1509 when he refused a post in the overseas colonies; but at 80, three years before his death, he was a chief of the Ten. Francesco di Filippo Foscari was a chief of the Ten

---

43 On Rinuccini's statement: Martines, *Florentine Humanists*, pp. 299–300.

44 On Sanuto: 21:485. On Bembo: Carlo Lagomaggiore, "*L'Istoria Viniziana di M. Pietro Bembo,*" 8:15.

at 84, and Francesco Bragadin held the same position at 72. In August 1514 all three of the chiefs were over 80 years of age. Both Alvise Priuli and Sebastiano Giustiniani were members of the Collegio at 74; Marcantonio Barbaro died while serving on the Collegio at 77. Marcantonio Morosini was 89 when he sat on the Collegio in 1506. Marco Bollani was 86 and the oldest patrician in Venice when he was elected to a special commission of the Ten in 1517. Paolo Capello was 82 when he served on the same commission in 1532.[45]

Military commands, with all their physical difficulties, were not reserved for younger men. Sanuto pointedly notes that the enemy commander of Spanish forces in 1514 was only 32 years old; the opposing Venetian generals at the same time were 59 and 64. Domenico Malipiero, the diarist, died at 85 while commanding forces at Treviso. Doge Gritti persuaded 75-year-old Domenico Contarini to accept election as general in 1526. Antonio Grimani was captain general of the fleet in 1499 when he was 60 years old, as was Marchio Trevisan at 67. The latter was succeeded by Benedetto Pesaro, whom Priuli considered "exceptionally libidinous" for "always wanting a woman" at the age of 72. Angelo Trevisan was 70 when he led his fleet to destruction on the Po river; he fled to Venice, where he was prosecuted for neglect of duty by the state attorney, 78-year-old Bernardo Bembo, the father of Pietro. Antonio Tron was elected to replace Trevisan, but he refused the dubious honor because of his lack of experience in maritime affairs and not because of his 71 years. The election of such elderly men to arduous commands may partially explain Venice's frequent misfortune in wartime. Priuli notes with some exasperation that common sense alone should dictate the selection of younger men, who could better bear the fatigue and danger of war.[46]

45 On the three elections for ambassador: Sanuto, 23:126–127, 295–296. On Lando: Barbaro, 8595, fol. 209r; Capellari, vol. 2, fols. 204v–205r. On Moro: Sanuto, 23:531; 25:238. On Falier: Priuli, 4:361; Sanuto, 25:473; 27:5; 33:466. On Foscari: Sanuto, 45:556. On Bragadin: Sanuto, 53:223, 467. On the chiefs of the Ten: Sanuto, 18:410. On Alvise Priuli: Sanuto, 43:658. On Giustiniani: Sanuto, 57:410, 582. On Barbaro: Charles Yriarte, *La vie d'un patricien de Venise au XVIème siècle*, pp. 337–338. On Morosini: Sanuto, 56:845; 57:62, 144.

46 On the Spanish commander: Sanuto, 19:51. On Malipiero: Sanuto, 17:268, 269; Malipiero, 1:xix–xx. On Contarini: Sanuto, 43:332, 326. On Grimani: Frederic C. Lane, "Naval Actions and Fleet Organization, 1499–1502"; Ester Zille, "Il processo Grimani." On Marchio Trevisan: Sanuto, 2:1305; Barbaro, 8595, fols. 138r, 141r–141v; Capellari, vol. 4, fols. 133v–134r. On Pesaro: Priuli, 2:287; Capellari, vol. 3, fols. 209v–210r. On Angelo Trevisan: Sanuto, 27:324–325; 28:26; Robert Finlay, "Venice, the Po Expedition, and the End of the League of

With men of such advanced age still active in state service, one could be *giovane* in politics and yet be considered *vecchio* by conventional standards. Francesco Bollani was declared "exceedingly young" in his mid-forties to gain election to the Senate, even though he was more than a decade older than the minimal age required to enter that council. When Paolo Trevisan died at 53, Sanuto mourned that Venice should lose so able a man, and perhaps a future doge, at so "very young" an age. Another man regarded as a potential doge, Francesco di Alvise Foscari, died at what was considered the premature age of 58. Francesco Donato, who won the dogeship in 1545 at 78, was elected councillor at the noteworthy age of 51 in 1518; and perhaps his youth was even more evident on the Ten in the next year when his fellow chiefs were 80 and 76, respectively.[47]

It was highly unusual for Marino Morosini to win election in 1509 as a state attorney at the precocious age of 46. Alvise Pisani was elected to the Ten at the same age in 1514, and Sanuto notes that such an event "never before has happened." Pisani's political career, which began with such promise, was cut untimely short in 1529 when he died of a fever at the age of 60 while commanding Venetian forces near Naples. Vicenzo Capello was made a fleet commander by the Senate in 1511 when he was "zovene di anni 43." Four years later, Girolamo Pesaro, son of the venerable captain general, was elected captain of Padua, "even though he is not yet 44"; and he was soon after the youngest patrician in the annual procession of the government on the feast day of Saint Mark.[48]

Because Pesaro came from an illustrious family, it is not surprising that he began his political career not many years before his signal success. The assumption that a politician was still young in his mid-forties influenced the age at which one entered politics. It was common for patricians to begin seeking offices only in their late thirties. Sanuto was not, therefore, a late starter at 32, nor Contarini at 36 or

---

Cambrai, (1509–1510)." On Tron: Sanuto, 9:417; 24:128; Priuli, vol. 5, fol. 57r. On selecting younger men: Priuli, vol. 5, fol. 36v.

47 On Bollani: Malipiero, 1:185; Barbaro, 8594, fol. 105r; Capellari, vol. 1, fol. 167v. On Paolo Trevisan: Malipiero, 2:697; Sanuto, 6:243; Barbaro, 8597, fol. 35r; Capellari, vol. 4, fol. 137r. On Foscari: Sanuto, 25:351. On Donato: Sanuto, 26: 65; 27:5.

48 On Morosini: Sanuto, 8:422. On Pisani: Sanuto, 18:73, 250; 48:207, 223, 232, 234, 237. On Capello: Sanuto, 13:25. On Pesaro: Sanuto, 18:452; 20:328, 514; 56: 192; Capellari, vol. 3, fol. 207r.

Malipiero at 37.[49] For a man to begin office hunting at 25 when he entered the Great Council was probably a sign that he lacked the status and resources necessary to advance far in politics. In all likelihood, his career would not go much beyond the posts he gained in his youth. Conversely, to enter politics at a late age—the ideal time was perhaps in the early fifties, on retirement from business—was an indication of a patrician's stature and confidence.

Ducal politics was the preserve of the *Primi*, the veterans of government. Between 1400 and 1500, the average age of the doge at election was 69; 1500–1600, 75; 1600–1700, 72; 1700–1797, 67. One doge, Francesco Foscari in 1423, was elevated at the age of 49; fourteen doges were elected between the ages of 60 and 66; thirty-three between 67 and 77; and nine between 78 and 88.[50] In general, a politician was not thought of as a likely prospect for the dogeship until in his mid-sixties. Tommaso Mocenigo at 65 was regarded as a strong candidate in 1501, but Antonio Tron was "too young at 60." Giorgio Corner was a "youngster of 48" in 1503 when elected *podestà* of Padua; his age of 66 in 1521 helped make him one of the important contenders for the dogeship. Domenico Trevisan was "too young at 58" as a ducal aspirant in 1504, yet a favorite in the election of 1523 at the age of 77. In the election of 1578, Giacomo Soranzo was judged to have insufficient gray hair at 61, whereas Paolo Tiepolo was a stripling of 55, "which made his aspiration seem a little presumptuous." The victor was 87-year-old Nicolò da Ponte, whose great age helped him overcome his undistinguished family background—as one elector sneered, he "did not want to make a doge of someone from a shithouse (*cha merda*)." Finally, in the hotly contested election of 1618, Agostino Nani was the youngest competitor at the age of 63. Wotton reports that Nani tried to overcome the twin handicaps of youth and good health in the week before the election: Nani "was noted by some vacant searching wits to tread softly, to walk stoopingly, and to raise himself from benches where he sat, with laborious and painful gesture, as arguments of no lasting man. Such a counterfeiting thing sometimes is ambition."[51]

---

49 On Sanuto: Berchet's preface to Sanuto 1:45. On Contarini: James Bruce Ross, "The Emergence of Gasparo Contarini," p. 34 and n. 90. On Malipiero: Sagredo's preface to Malipiero, 1:xix.

50 This information is drawn from da Mosto's *Dogi di Venezia*.

51 On Mocenigo and Tron: ASMo., b. 11, c. 121, Bartolomeo Cartari to the

Because the political definition of old age effectively limited competition for the dogeship to very elderly patricians, it necessarily involved consideration of the contenders' male heirs as well. To be "without sons" (*senza fioli*) when competing for the dogeship was a distinct advantage. If a patrician had sons, they would have reached a conventional old age by the time he was elderly enough to be politically eligible for the ducal office. The sons might then exercise power by virtue of their influence on their father. Priuli states that "Venice's ancestors didn't wish that the doge should have sons, because they recognized that the doge would not be able to maintain proper judgment [in public affairs] when influenced by them."[52] One of Agostino Barbarigo's advantages in the election of 1486 was that he lacked male heirs; in contrast, his principal opponent, 78-year-old Bernardo Giustiniani, had a son who was a participant in the election. The favorite after the death of Barbarigo was Filippo Tron, who was *senza fioli*. Leonardo Loredan overcame the liability of a large family (four daughters and four sons) by the happy chance of Tron's death just before the election and by his own delicate health, which seemed to betoken a short tenure in office. To everyone's amazement, Loredan lived for twenty more years; and to no one's surprise, his oldest son emerged as a power behind the scenes while in his mid-forties. In 1521 Giorgio Corner's three sons told against him, and in 1523 Domenico Trevisan's six sons were a decisive drawback to his ambitions.[53]

In short, ducal electors were faced with the task of selecting a doge who was neither sickly and senile nor over-endowed with "youth" and sons. The electors of 1423 were faced with candidates most of whom suffered from one of these liabilities. Marino Caravello and Francesco Bembo were "too old and too weak"; Leonardo Mocenigo's brother was the late doge; Pietro Loredan was needed to command

---

duke of Ferrara, September 27, 1501. On Corner: ASMo., b. 15, c. 51, Giacomo Tebaldi to the duke of Ferrara, June 22, 1521. On Trevisan: ASMo., b. 12, c. 54, Bartolomeo Cartari to the duke of Ferrara, April 29, 1504; Sanuto, 24:128. On the 1578 election: "Naratione delle eletione d'M. Nicolò da Ponte al principato di Venetia, 1578," cc. 180–203, discussed by William Archer Brown, "Nicolò da Ponte," pp. 126–142. On the 1618 election: Smith, *Life and Letters*, 2:136.

52 Priuli, 4:40–41.

53 On Barbarigo: Sanuto, *Vite dei dogi*, fols. 270v–271r. On Giustiniani: Sanuto, *Vite dei dogi*, fol. 269v. On Tron: Sanuto, 4:144. On Loredan: Barbaro, 8595, fols. 247v–248r; Capellari, vol. 2, fols. 235v–237v; Priuli, 2:40, 394; 4:92. On Corner: Sanuto, 30:458. On the 1523 election: this book, Chapter III.3.

the fleet; Antonio Contarini had too many sons, daughters, and in-laws; and Francesco Foscari at 49 was too young, and being married for the second time, the expectation was that "his wife will bring forth a son every year." Four of Foscari's five sons died young; but the fifth, Giacomo, confirmed the accusation made in the election when, twenty-two years later, he was exiled to Greece for accepting gifts from the duke of Milan. He was caught up in more trouble and exiled again in 1450 and 1456.[54]

Patricians never forgot Foscari's long and turbulent reign, and they avoided placing such a youngster in the ducal palace again. Yet three doges were regarded as having barely entered their political maturity at the time of their elections: Barbarigo was elected at 66, Loredan at 65, and Gritti at 66. Omitting the reign of Grimani (elected at 88, he served for one year and ten months), the average term of the doges between 1486 and 1538 was seventeen years. By contrast, the average ducal reign in 1400–1486 and 1538–1600 was six years; the six doges before Barbarigo held office for an average of only two and one-half years. Venetians, both patrician and commoner, resented a doge who remained in office for a long time. The celebration when Barbarigo died was in part due to his lengthy stay in office. Only eight years after Loredan's election, Priuli comments that "a doge who remains in office for a long time tends to bore the city and will be hated by everybody." The death of Gritti was greeted with joy after his more than fifteen years' tenure.[55] Apparently one of the anticipated advantages of electing elderly men was that one would not have to put up with them for long.

A disadvantage of electing elderly men was that their infirmities sometimes kept them from their duties. Sanuto complains that "it is bad to elect these old ones," because they cannot always attend to the affairs of the city. Although Priuli thought that Venice benefited from government by the old, he adds that some "doddering and decrepit" vecchi could not bear the burdens of state service. The regulation allowing men over 70 to leave the Senate when debate was in progress —a provision that must sometimes have occasioned a noticeable exo-

54 Sanuto, "Cronica Sanuda," fols. 244r; 241r, 297v–298r, 300r, 305r; Cessi, Storia della Repubblica, 1:399.
55 On Barbarigo: Priuli, 2:174. On Loredan: Priuli, 4:372; Sanuto, 34:128. On Gritti: ASMo., b. 20, c. 3, Giacomo Tebaldi to the duke of Ferrara, January 7, 1539.

dus—is a hint that the elderly were not always equal to the tasks given them.[56]

But the Venetian Republic was not led by dotards. The needs of government were obviously too crucial for the Great Council to elect senile men to office, even when those offices generally involved brief terms. Further, the Signoria willingly accepted illness or extreme old age as an excuse for declining an office, as when Antonio Tron refused election to the Collegio in 1524 because he was 84 years old. Having life tenure in office, the doge presented special problems, and not all had the qualities that John Chamberlain admired in Leonardo Donato in 1611:

> This duke is esteemed one of the most sufficient men of his age, and indeed yt is very rare and almost miraculous to see a man of his yeares (drawing toward fowrescore) of that dexteritie and pregnancie of wit and memorie, and withall of such rediness of tongue and elocution, and I doubt whether theyre whole Senate (yf he were gon) could afford them such another.

Unfortunately, Antonio Grimani's capacities did not outlast much more than one year of his reign, and when the 90-year-old doge died, the event was applauded as much as if he had inflicted on Venice a reign as lengthy as those of his two predecessors. "Because of his senility," notes Sanuto, "he died with a bad reputation."[57]

Leaders of the *giovani* were young only by a Venetian political yardstick. Filippo Tron, principal proponent of aid to the Pisan rebellion, was 61 years old in 1498; Nicolò Michiel, reputed "head of the young men" agitating for Grimani's trial by the Great Council, was about 50 in 1500; and Giorgio Emo was 59 when he was spokesman for the bellicose youngsters who wanted Venetian expansion in the Romagna in 1509.[58] No doubt most of the *giovani* were young, that is, less than 40 years old; and many occupied their time serving

56 Sanuto, 3:87; Priuli, 2:52–53. On men over 70 in the Senate: Maranini, *Costituzione di Venezia*, p. 247.

57 On Tron: Sanuto, 35:314. On Donato: Norman Egbert McClure, ed., *The Letters of John Chamberlain*, 1:302. On Grimani: Sanuto, 34:128; 116.

58 On Tron: Barbaro, 8597, fol. 143v; Capellari, vol. 4, fol. 139v. On Michiel: Pietro Dolfin, *Annalium Venetorum*, p. 87; Barbaro, 8596, fols. 87v, 89v; Capellari, vol. 3, fol. 82v. On Emo: Marino Sanuto, "Miscellanea di Cronica Veneta di Marino Sanuto," fol. 74r; Barbaro, 8595, fols. 99v–100r; Capellari, vol. 3, fols. 53v–54r; Seneca, *Venezia e papa Giulio II*, pp. 19, 26, 38–39, 51.

in the lesser magistracies of the city, collecting taxes and duties, patrolling the canals, issuing licenses, sitting on minor courts. Certainly they often evinced a desire for more excitement than that afforded by the staid councils of Venice. But many of the so-called young were men already into their fifties; in conventional terms, the most influential *giovani* were decidedly *vecchi*. Both those patricians within the governing circle and those awaiting their turn to enter it were old men. Still, the two groups were separated by more than a number of years: *Vecchi* monopolized the high offices of government, whereas *giovani* could only chafe at their impotence and listen to counsels to bide their time, as their fathers had done before them. In this regard the ruling class of Venice was similar to that of the Roman Republic, where "influence was in the hands of careful old men, who enjoyed deference, understood caution, and expected of the younger generation only that it might in the course of fifty years or so produce its own crop of careful old men."[59]

The remarkable concord that existed within the governing circle, as well as within the ruling class as a whole, owed much to the shared experience of the *vecchi*, who spent decades together in political activity, voting on and negotiating with one another, moving from office to office, shaping policy, quelling squabbles, arranging marriages, surviving scandals. A crucial by-product of electing the senior members of the clans to office was that a high degree of consensus was thereby maintained within the patriciate. This consensus was never seriously threatened by conflict between the generations, in part because the "young men" were given numerous minor offices, as well as a voice in the Senate, mixing the "hot" with the "cold." Moreover, time was on the side of the *giovani*; the advanced age of those in power meant that there was a fairly rapid turnover of leadership at the very top.[60]

Most important of all, by the time a patrician gained access to power, he had a formidable commitment to a political system that had put him through an apprenticeship of fifteen to twenty years after he had reached the beginning of a conventional old age. Acceptance of such an apprenticeship by men of mature years required them to subordinate themselves—their personalities, ambitions, and resources—to making their way in service to the Republic. In a letter of 1355, Petrarch enjoined future doges and, by implication, all patricians to consider themselves "leaders not lords, nay not even leaders, but

59 Ramsay MacMullen, *Enemies of the Roman Order*, p. 6.
60 Cf. Sanuto, 7:156–157.

honored servants of the State."[61] That was not always easy to do. Some highly successful and powerful merchants, such as Giorgio Corner, Antonio Grimani, and Andrea Gritti, began their political careers only in their late forties or early fifties. Entering a new world, far removed from the independent and forceful milieu of business, they became timeservers. Influential, experienced, and assured, they had to learn to insinuate their ambitions in a political system that deplored arrogance, ostentation, and personal power. They had to find their way through the interstices of a complicated constitutional structure in which accommodation and conciliation were necessary to accomplish the slightest task. Too, they had continually to submit themselves to the electoral judgment of the patriciate in the Great Council in order to retain the offices that gave them power and prestige.

Domenico Morosini, called "the Wise" by his contemporaries, was a model of success in Venetian politics. He entered public life in 1472 at the age of 55, apparently after a career as a merchant in the Levant. For the next thirty-seven years, he was almost continually a member of the Collegio and the Ten. His strength as a politician evidently lay in his amiable and conciliatory character. In fact, Doge Barbarigo sponsored legislation in 1496 designed to permit Morosini's entrance to the Collegio in place of another patrician who "wished to dispute everything." Morosini apparently blended perfectly into the governing circle, only attracting attention by virtue of his loquacity (his intervention in debate, Sanuto records, was lengthy) and his learning. In 1497 he began work on his *De bene instituta re publica*, a prolix and confusing analysis of constitutional structure, with particular emphasis on Venice. Ten years later, he became, at 89, the city's oldest patrician. He attended the Senate up to the day of his death, in 1509, at the age of 91, just as the War of the League of Cambrai broke upon Venice.[62]

Morosini's study of constitutions, which he never completed, is an unimaginative and anodyne work. It is appropriate, then, that one of the few strongly expressed opinions in *De bene instituta re publica* should deviate from Venetian constitutional provisions only insofar as it is a distillation of four decades of experience by a Venetian geronto-

---

61 Lane, *Venice*, p. 180.

62 On the character, career, and offices of Morosini, see Claudio Finzi's introduction to his edition of *De bene instituta re publica*, pp. 1–70. On the 1496 legislation: Malipiero, 1:437–438. On Morosini in debate: Sanuto, 3:660; 6:164–165. On Morosini's death: Sanuto, 8:27.

crat. In a republic, Morosini argues, the council of elders (*consilio seniorum*) should be completely separate from the popular, that is, youthful, assembly (*consilio iuniorum*). Also, election to the *consilio seniorum*, which rules the republic, should be for life and should be permitted only to men of at least 40 years of age. Unlike Contarini, Morosini could see no value in drawing relatively young men into the governing council. According to Morosini, the young, who lack judgment because of the shallowness of their experience, bring disorder and risk to affairs of state. The elders of the Republic are moderate, cautious, and agreeable; having seen so much and lived so long, they make the wisest and safest governors.[63]

The psychological qualities fostered by the Venetian political system were those that favored patience, conformism, and compromise. Patricians pursued their ambitions through an exceedingly lengthy *cursus honorum*. From the age of 25 to about 45, a patrician found high offices closed to him, although a host of minor positions, in the city and abroad, introduced him to government. From 45 to about 55, he slowly entered the outer edges of the governing circle, gaining elections to governorships, the fleet, ambassadorial posts, middle-level financial and judicial magistracies. From about his mid-fifties, he was an increasingly important colleague of the *Primi*, routinely gaining entrance to the Ten, the Collegio, the Signoria, and the Senate, although his access to the dogeship could not be taken for granted until into his mid-sixties. By his mid-sixties, a successful patrician was clearly a political *vecchio*, one of the veterans of government who kept an eye on younger men as they accumulated years and experience. Of course, at any stage in this process of advancement, a politician's progress might be halted, especially if his personality or opinions proved uncongenial to the *vecchi* whom he aspired to join. That happened to Sanuto, who was a political failure primarily because of his persistent and undiplomatic criticism of the governing circle, as when he won acclaim in 1524 for opposing a motion passed by the Senate: "The Great Council wished to do me honor, especially the *giovani*; however, the *vecchi* did not want me [elected] because I oppose them."[64]

---

63 On young and old in government: Domenico Morosini, *De bene instituta re publica*, pp. 118–119; 107, 123–124, 155–156, 197–198. On Morosini's book: Gaetano Cozzi, "Domenico Morosini e il 'De bene instituta re publica.'"

64 Sanuto, 36:149–150. On Sanuto's career: Chapter V.2.

A patrician's concern for his political future throughout his long apprenticeship, as well as for the political welfare of his heirs when they reached maturity, led him to moderate his opinions and seek agreement with his opponents.[65] A highly conservative temperament was thus shaped, one that may be described by appropriating Alexis de Tocqueville's analysis of the conservative mentality formed in the new American republic:

> All men are at last constrained, whatever may be their standard, to pass the same ordeal; all are indiscriminately subjected to a multitude of petty preliminary exercises, in which their youth is wasted and their imagination quenched, so that they despair of ever fully attaining what is held out to them; and when at length they are in a condition to perform any extraordinary acts, the taste for such things has forsaken them.

Under the impact of such pressures, ambition would lose its greatness, and the passions of men would abate.[66] Venice may be said to have achieved this condition by the commitment of its ruling caste to a political system that was a republic in form and a gerontocracy in fact. At the end of his apprenticeship, a patrician was bound to favor the status quo, to honor a process that had brought its reward in due time. Having played it safe for so long, he was hardly likely to change after becoming one of the Republic's senior citizens. Stability and harmony were virtues to be placed before the uncertain attractions of novelty and contention.

An important part of the myth of Venice was a conception of Venetian patricians as discreet and temperate managers, subtle and prudent diplomats, self-sacrificing and anonymous administrators— men so dedicated to the state, so subordinate to it, that their personalities faded into dim reflections of its imperatives. The reality that gave birth to this conception was a political system that bent patricians toward compromise, accommodation, and self-effacement by demanding such modes of political behavior from the men who would be *Primi di la terra*. In effect, the myth proclaimed what the political system promoted: It was wise for a patrician to be deferential, conventional, and anonymous. Enjoying a justified reputation for being temperate, prudent, and unimaginative, the careful old men of Venice

---

65 Priuli, 4:35; vol. 5, fols. 168r–168v.
66 Alexis de Tocqueville, *Democracy in America*, 2:259; 261.

PLATE 1. *Venice as Justice*. Late fifteenth-century work by Bartolomeo Bon; above the Porta della Carta on the facade of the Ducal Palace, Venice. See p. 28. *Photo Böhm*

PLATE 2. *A Meeting of the Collegio*. Late seventeenth-century illustration by an unknown artist; in the Museo Civico Correr, Venice. See pp. 39–40. *Photo Böhm*

PLATE 3. *Doge Francesco Foscari Kneeling before the Lion of Saint Mark.* Copy made in 1885 by L. Ferrari of an original work of the later fifteenth century by Bartolomeo Bon; above the Porta della Carta on the facade of the Ducal Palace, Venice. See pp. 116–117. *Photo Böhm*

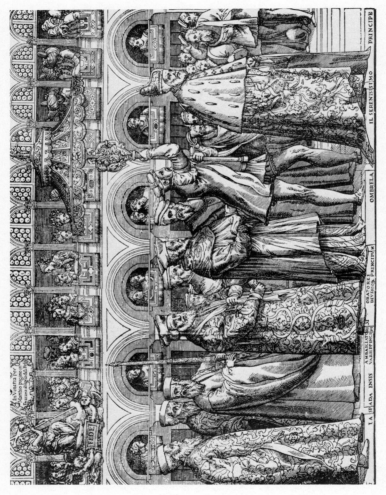

PLATE 4. *Procession of the Doge on Palm Sunday.* Detail from a mid-sixteenth-century woodcut by Matteo Pagano; in the Museo Civico Correr, Venice. See pp. 121–122. *Photo Böhm*

PLATE 5. *Doge Antonio Grimani Adoring Faith and Saint Mark in Glory.* Begun about 1555 by Titian; in the Room of the Four Doors, Ducal Palace, Venice. See p. 147. *Photo Böhm*

PLATE 6. *Doge Andrea Gritti with Saint Mark Adoring the* Virgin, *with Saint Bernardino, Saint Alvise, and Saint Marina.* Late sixteenth-century painting by Tintoretto, after an earlier work by Titian; in the Hall of the Collegio, Ducal Palace, Venice. See p. 158. *Photo Böhm*

PLATE 7. *Allegory of the War of the League of Cambrai.* Late sixteenth-century painting by Jacopo Palma il Giovane; in the Senate chamber of the Ducal Palace, Venice. See p. 163. *Photo Böhm*

PLATE 8. Funeral monument of Doge Nicolò Tron. Detail of the work by Antonio Rizzo, begun in 1476; in the church of Santa Maria dei Frari, Venice. See p. 232. *Photo Böhm*

insured the survival of essentially the same political order from the Era of the Commune to the Age of Napoleon. The older generation governed, while the younger, for century after century, produced its own crop of careful old men. It is most appropriate, and surely no coincidence, that this most long-lived of republics was also history's most successful gerontocracy.

3. Ducal Politics, 1486–1523

Intrigue to gain the dogeship was a constant of political life and a focus for the incessant, if muted, hostility running through the patriciate. It was a consideration behind proposed legislation, positions on foreign policy, numerous elections, and perhaps even tactics on the battlefield. At first glance, however, it is difficult to see how a politician could aim at the office, considering how the almost perverse complexity of ducal electoral procedure appears to defy such ambition. Wotton called the method of electing the doge "one of the most intricate and curious forms in the world"; and, expressing both his monarchical and Protestant prejudices, he slyly suggested that it was "a monk's invention of the Benedictine order," whose "whole mysterious frame therein doth much savour of the cloister." At the other extreme, a participant in the election of 1578 thought that the electoral process gave rise to an "inferno of deviltry."[67]

The ducal election lasted five days, with two stages of the process allotted to each day. Thirty members of the Great Council, exclusive of patricians under thirty years of age, were selected by lot. Retiring to a separate chamber, this group of thirty reduced themselves by lot to nine, who then elected forty men by a majority of at least seven votes each. After electing the forty, the nine returned to the hall of the Great Council with their list of nominees, "without looking at, speaking or making a sign to anyone."[68] These nominees were announced to the chamber and checked to insure that no clan had more than one representative, a precaution followed at every stage of the election. The group of forty assembled in a separate room and reduced their number by sortition to the twelve men who were to elect the

---

67 On the electoral process: Sanuto, *Cronachetta*, pp. 70–74. On the twelfth-century origins of the process: da Mosto, *Dogi di Venezia*, pp. xv–xvi; cf. Maranini, *Costituzione di Venezia*, p. 291. On Wotton: Smith, *Life and Letters*, 2:136–137. On 1578: William Archer Brown, "Nicolò da Ponte," p. 138.

68 Sanuto, *Cronachetta*, p. 71.

next group of twenty-five by at least seven votes apiece; although
forbidden to nominate themselves, the twelve could elect a member of
the previous group of forty. The twenty-five were reduced by lot to
nine, who elected forty-five patricians by the usual majority of seven
votes. The forty-five drew lots to select eleven of their number, and
the Eleven (the *Undici*) elected the Forty-one (the *Quarantuno*) that
then elected the doge by at least twenty-five votes.

During its deliberations, the Forty-one was closeted in the chambers
of the Senate and could communicate only with the Signoria. Each
elector made a nomination on a slip of paper and put it into an urn;
nominations were individually drawn and voted on until a nominee
received the requisite twenty-five votes. If a nominee were present, he
had to leave the room while his merits and faults were discussed; permitted to return in order to defend himself, he had to leave again
when voted on. To insure freedom of expression in these deliberations,
the business of the Forty-one was not to be revealed for fifteen years.
Yet nothing was confidential once the electors were released from
their task, if secrecy was indeed maintained that long. In a 1615 election, lasting twenty-four days and 104 ballots, members of the Forty-
one climbed out of windows of the Ducal Palace to collect their
bribes of money and gifts. More usually, illicit communication with
the outside world was apparently through the servants who waited
on the electors.[69]

Although complex and lengthy, the ducal electoral system was not
designed to eliminate ambition altogether. The stages of sortition
meant that political interests would not have total sway, but the element of chance was also constrained. It would have been abhorrent to
the *Primi* to think of leaving the election of the head of state in the
hands of an arbitrarily selected group of patricians from the Great
Council; nor would they have wanted the dogeship to fall to one
outside their number. Ambition was channeled by the electoral process: By the third step in the procedure—the election of the forty by
the nine—the election was safely out of the hands of the Republic's
sovereign assembly and in the grasp of the *Primi*. There was nothing
inevitable in this, but the web of patronage and family connection
that formed the matrix of the patriciate almost certainly insured the
dominance of the rich and powerful once the election was in motion.

In fact, a leading role for the *Primi* was considered an integral part

69 da Mosto, *Dogi di Venezia*, p. 416; Sanuto, 30:485.

of the election. Equality reigned only in the first selection of thirty men by lot from the Great Council,[70] and although it could hardly be legislated, it was presumed that the nine selected by lot from the thirty would then elect forty important politicians. The groups charged with electing the twenty-five and the forty-five were also to install *Primi*, and the Eleven were to elect a group of forty-one of "the most experienced, worthy, and important of the city."[71] In short, nine arbitrarily selected and relatively undistinguished patricians were charged with electing forty men of political significance, who would then maintain others of like position in subsequent stages of the election.

Hard bargaining for votes was inherent in the ducal election. It is no accident that the last two stages of the process excluded any element of hazard. Election of patricians by the Eleven (who, Sanuto remarks, "almost elect the doge") and the election of a doge by the Forty-one were matters of choice and consideration.[72] The social and familial connections within the patriciate meant that the election would generally be controlled by the *Primi*; but the electoral process also accounted for the danger that a group of influential men might try to manipulate the election. So while politically significant men emerged as dominant electors, they had to face the obstacle of three stages of sortition after the election of the forty by the nine. No individual could be certain of remaining in the electoral colleges, and no competitor was sure of retaining his supporters throughout the election. It was necessary, then, to marshal support prior to the election, but the crucial element of chance meant that no one was assured of victory. One had to run for election without being sure of completing the course.

This combination of sortition and election was an ingenious attempt to find a middle ground between an election by the Great Council and one by a simple conclave of the governing circle. For Venetians, it was an essential compromise if the ducal office was not to be dominated by an unruly lower nobility or controlled by an authoritative politician backed by a powerful clique. The dogeship was too important and too powerful to permit election to it to be either too open or too closed. Hence a means was provided by which the election could be placed in the hands of *Primi* while limiting the ability of any

70 Contarini, *Republica*, p. 65.
71 Sanuto, *Cronachetta*, p. 72.
72 Sanuto, *Cronachetta*, p. 72.

group to impose its will without an overwhelming majority or substantial good luck.

Not everyone was happy with the method of electing the doge, and there was occasional agitation to change it. Reporting the election of Pietro Mocenigo in 1475, Malipiero states,

> Some of the greatest senators of the city were left out of his Forty-one. . . . There was grumbling, and also some consideration was given to how such an inconvenience could be prevented in the future. Some agreed that the council of the Senate should elect two groups of forty-one [electors], which, meeting separately, will elect two doges; and if both elect the same man, he is to be considered elected; and if two are elected, they will be voted on in the Great Council, and the one with the most votes wins.

In 1521 a number of patricians wanted to reform the electoral system by having the Great Council elect the Forty-one directly. Two years later there were rumors that the reformers of the ducal oath would propose that the Eleven elect one hundred men to be presented to the Great Council, which would name forty-one of them to elect the doge.[73]

A reform was finally introduced during the election of Pietro Lando in 1539. When the Eleven was taking an especially long time to produce a college of forty-one, and with discord in the group so great that there was doubt whether they could complete their task, the Great Council accepted from the Ten a proposal requiring the nominees to the Forty-one to be put before the Great Council for a vote. A majority was necessary for an individual to take his place in the Forty-one; and if a nominee were rejected by the Great Council, the Eleven had to propose an alternate. In its exertion of some control over the Eleven and in drawing more patricians into the electoral process, the reform of 1539 had the same aim as previous proposals. It was also typically Venetian to solve a difficulty arising from a complex and competitive procedure by a further complication and additional balloting. In any case, the reform had little effect. The Great Council rarely rejected a nominee of the Eleven, and intense competition in the final stages of the ducal election continued through the sixteenth and into the seventeenth century.[74]

---

73 On 1475: Malipiero, 2:664-665. On 1521: Sanuto, 30:458. On 1523: Sanuto, 34:139.

74 On 1539: ASV, Maggior Consiglio, Deliberazioni, Liber Novus, Reg. 27,

In the late Quattrocento, after the thirty-four-year reign of Francesco Foscari, doge followed doge fairly rapidly, and apparently only the election of Pietro Mocenigo in 1475 and that of Andrea Vendramin in 1476 caused even minimal controversy. The election of August 1486 was another matter, for it was characterized by an intense struggle for the dogeship between the *Longhi* and *Curti* clans. One leading contender was Agostino Barbarigo, the younger brother of the immediately deceased Doge Marco, who at the age of seventy-two had only survived in office for nine months; his popularity and short reign made many patricians sympathetic to placing another Barbarigo in the Ducal Palace. In all likelihood, Agostino needed every advantage because he was not a popular figure and his principal opponent was the highly regarded and learned Bernardo Giustiniani.[75]

Giustiniani, however, was from one of the largest *Longhi* clans, and his strong position in the late stages of the election alarmed the *Curti*. Aided by his son's lobbying in the Eleven, Giustiniani came very close to victory. Malipiero reports that "in the Eleven which elect the Forty-one of the doge, there were five of the old houses; and it is known throughout the city that they wished to place many of their own in the Forty-one in order to make Bernardo Giustiniani the doge. And they went about with wicked arguments, such that it was time to remove the dogeship from the hands of the *Curti* and give it to the *Longhi*." Twice Giustiniani received twenty-three votes in the Forty-one, and he was advised by relatives that if he stood firm in the electoral bargaining, he would win; yet he spurned this counsel and cast his support to Barbarigo, perhaps because he valued the unity of the patriciate more than his own triumph.[76]

Giustiniani's graceful surrender did not end the matter, for a vendetta against his *Longhi* supporters broke out. According to Sanuto, a member of the *Longhi*, the *Curti*

> could not tolerate their [that is, the *Longhi*] wishing to return to the dogeship from which they had been deprived from 138– [*sic*] to now; they began to defeat those of the ancient houses who were

---

fols. 49v–50r.; cf. ASMo., b. 20, c. 7, Giacomo Tebaldi to the duke of Ferrara, January 15, 1539. On competition in the final stages: cf. da Mosto, *Dogi di Venezia*, pp. xxxii, 378, 387, 416, 438, 444, 452, 473.

75 On Giustiniani: Patricia Labalme, *Bernardo Giustiniani*; idem, "The Last Will of a Venetian Patrician (1489)."

76 Sanuto, *Vite dei dogi*, fols. 269v–270v.

nominated in the Great Council, especially in elections for the
Senate and Council of Ten. . . . While it lasted it was a very dangerous affair, and the city spoke of nothing else than this most important of events, that is, the splitting of the city [*terra*] into two
parts.[77]

Five *Longhi* in the Eleven had managed to install sixteen of their
number in the Forty-one, enough to delay *Curti* gaining the dogeship
but not sufficient to win it for themselves—a nice indication of how
the electoral procedure favored minority groups and fostered bargaining. Not surprisingly, the *Longhi* who had voted in the Eleven were
especially blamed for Giustiniani's near-victory, and very shortly after
the election four of them were defeated in contests for the Senate. In
the Zonta election at the end of September, only seven patricians from
Longhi clans were placed in the Senate, while many who could usually
count on a seat were defeated. "And nothing else," Sanuto laments,
"is spoken of in the city . . . and if God does not favor us, a very
great division will follow in the state."[78]

Duke Ludovico Sforza of Milan sought out the Venetian ambassador, Marcantonio Morosini, and questioned him about the quarrel between the clans in Venice. Sforza suggested that the rulers of Italy
might have second thoughts about their policies toward Venice after
having witnessed such dissension. Morosini's report of this warning
alarmed the Ten, which urged the doge to address the Great Council.
Accordingly, on October 8, Barbarigo had the chamber cleared of all
but patricians and, urging unity and harmony for the good of the
Republic, emotionally asserted that equality reigned within the ruling
class. The doge's speech reportedly made a powerful impression on
the Great Council, but in the elections that immediately followed,
only one *Longhi* member won office, although that may have been
because *Longhi* clans boycotted the elections.[79] Moreover, soon after
the speech, some patricians of the Capello clan gave Andrea Barbaro
a list of the twenty-four *Longhi* houses, with instructions that no
member of those clans was to receive votes in the Great Council.
Barbaro showed the list to his relative, Biagio Michiel, who promptly
wrote to his friend, Doge Barbarigo, urging him to take action to save
the Republic from discord, perhaps also reminding him of his recent

77 Sanuto, *Vite dei dogi*, fols. 271r–271v.
78 Sanuto, *Vite dei dogi*, fols. 273r; 270r–270v; cf. Malipiero, 2:681.
79 Malipiero, 2:682; Sanuto, *Vite dei dogi*, fols. 273v–274r.

exhortation to the Great Council. Michiel unwisely compared official inaction in this vital matter to the negligence that would permit water to invade salt beds; even more unwisely, he chose to attack the Capello, to whom Barbarigo was related by marriage. The doge's family instincts proved stronger than his friendship with Michiel. He turned the vitriolic letter over to the Ten, which accused Michiel of slandering the head of state and exiled him to Treviso for five years. No action was taken against the Capello for circulating the blacklist. Nor were the culprits caught who posted anonymous placards on the Ducal Palace in November with a list of *Longhi* clans and an injunction to refuse them election to office.[80] Months after Barbarigo's election, resentment still simmered between the old and new houses, an inauspicious beginning to a ducal term that was to be characterized by hostility and conflict.

By 1499 Barbarigo had been in office for thirteen years and was in ill health at the age of seventy-nine. One consequence of the doge's advanced age was that speculation over a successor never ceased and virtually dominated political activity among the *Primi*. In 1499 that speculation centered on Antonio Grimani, who on April 14 was elected captain general of the fleet as Venice turned its attention to the Turkish threat in the Adriatic. Grimani graciously accepted the post and offered to put up 16,000 ducats to outfit the fleet, a generous proposal intended to aid him in achieving the dogeship. He was the acknowledged leader of Venetian commerce and could afford to purchase a cardinalate for his son at the cost of 30,000 ducats. Although his mother was a commoner, he had marriage connections with the most powerful families of the city. Priuli, a great admirer of Grimani, states that "from poverty he became very rich in the shortest time, and for wealth he is held to be first in Venice . . . a good part of Venetian merchants are governed by him: what he sells, they sell, and what he buys, they buy—because in all his affairs he is exceptionally fortunate." A presumed portrait of Grimani (now in the Correr Museum) shows a strong, jowly face, with a determined mouth and hooked nose. Everyone expected him to be the next doge; his loan to the government and his acceptance of the captain general's standard were seen as penultimate steps toward the Ducal Palace.[81]

When Grimani sailed from Venice in the summer of 1499, his reputation was at its height. It was destroyed at Zonchio on August 12.

80 Malipiero, 2:682–683; Sanuto, *Vite dei dogi*, fols. 274r, 275r; cf. 299v.
81 Priuli, 1:220–221; Malipiero, 1:163; cf. 188; Sanuto, 2:619–620.

Three years before, while commanding the fleet in Apulia, he had displayed exemplary valor, landing his galley beneath the walls of Monopoli and directing the attack on the city under fire. This heroism won him a procuratorship. Unfortunately, at Zonchio, Grimani was faced with peculiar military and personal difficulties. At the last moment before the battle, with the Venetian and Turkish fleet lined up against each other, Andrea Loredan, the commander at Corfu, arrived with a number of galleys. He had not received permission to leave Corfu, but his action in hurrying to the battle was consonant with his reputation for courage and for being "a man who made the whole Levant tremble." It was not the first time he had disobeyed Grimani. In 1494 Captain General Grimani had complained to the Collegio that Loredan had refused to follow commands and had opposed him on crucial matters. At Zonchio, either harried by circumstances or disgruntled at Loredan's heroic arrival, Grimani told his captain to seek action where he pleased. Taking Grimani at his word, Loredan sailed his ship, the *Pandora*, toward a large Turkish vessel. While both fleets looked on, the two combatants grappled, caught fire, and were destroyed. Loredan and another commander who went to his aid were killed. The Venetian fleet did not stir.[82]

Nor did Grimani punish the fleet commanders for not obeying his previous orders to attack. When, at Zonchio, Malipiero urged Grimani, "Punish those who disobeyed!" the captain general replied, "If I had your freedom, I would." The restraint felt by Grimani was political in nature, for his officers were elected by the Great Council and he could only make himself enemies by levying charges against them. Further political considerations were discerned in the battle itself: Rumors circulated in Venice that Grimani "did not wish to aid Andrea Loredan because if a victory were gained all the glory would be his, hence he let him perish." The event is likened by Malipiero to one in 1463 when one aspirant to the dogeship refused to help another reduce a castle, fearing that added glory for his rival would result in electoral victory for him back home.[83]

Whatever Grimani's motives in the battle or afterward, his political career was in ruins. His failure to win a victory and to discipline his

---

82 On Grimani in 1494: Malipiero, 1:373–374; Sanuto, *Spedizione di Carlo VIII*, pp. 492–495. On Zonchio: Lane, "Naval Actions and Fleet Organization." On Andrea Loredan: Priuli, 1:183; cf. 134, 165; Malipiero, 2:694.

83 On Malipiero and Grimani: Pietro Dolfin, *Annalium Venetorum*, p. 67; cf. Priuli, 1:326. On rumors in Venice: Malipiero, 1:185.

commanders gave an opportunity to his enemies at home, foremost of whom was Filippo Tron, the son of Doge Nicolò. There is no doubt that Tron used Grimani's misfortunes to remove his principal rival for the dogeship. Enmity between the two men was intense. In 1497 Tron opposed the entire Collegio, which was following Barbarigo's lead, in trying to block Grimani from acquiring the patriarchate of Aquileia for his son. A year later Grimani opposed Tron's support for Venetian involvement in the Pisan rebellion against Florence because he feared that the backing Tron received for his policy from younger patricians would catapult him to the dogeship. Four days after Grimani gave 16,000 ducats for the fleet, Tron made a mock offer of 10,000 to Barbarigo in the Collegio, a taunt the doge chose to ignore. Zonchio, then, put a formidable weapon in Tron's hands. After receiving news of the indecisive encounter, he presented a motion in the Senate to recall Grimani and elect a new captain general in his stead. On September 15, 1499, Marchio Trevisan, Tron's ally, was elected captain general by the Great Council. He was given a wide commission to investigate Grimani's management of the fleet, as well as instructions from the Collegio to Grimani to report to Venice for trial.[84]

Grimani was ordered to return home on a swift warship and not on his own splendid galley, the prerogative of the new captain general. According to Malipiero, an eyewitness, when Grimani learned of the humiliation arranged for him, he exploded, "That pig Filippo Tron . . . shall not have such great pleasure, nor that ravenous beast, Marchio Trevisan, to have me displaced from my galley!" Yet he only played further into his enemies' hands, for Tron then won passage of a proposal that Grimani must be placed in chains and, if he landed in Venice on his own galley, be instantly beheaded. Grimani's sons pleaded on their knees before Tron not to send such a draconian order, but in the end they had to intercept their father's galley, transfer him to a warship, and chain him before reaching Venice. On November 2, Grimani was put in prison immediately after landing near the Ducal Palace, and Malipiero laments that "it was very pitiful to see one in such extremity who shortly before had been so blessed, destined to be doge, and to see his son [Cardinal Domenico], who might be pope, in such low fortunes."[85]

84 On 1497: Sanuto, 1:747. On Pisa: Malipiero, 1:512. On Tron's mock offer: Malipiero, 1:163. On Tron's Senate motion: Sanuto, 2:1296; Priuli, 1:192–193.
85 On Grimani's statement: Pietro Dolfin, *Annalium Venetorum*, p. 68; cf.

Ducal politics continued to play a central role in Grimani's subsequent fate. The principal state attorney in charge of prosecuting him was Nicolò Michiel, an ambitious man who was rumored to see the conviction of Grimani as a route to the dogeship. In conflict over the venue of the trial, Doge Barbarigo, a Grimani ally, supported a hearing in the Senate, where the defendant could expect some sympathy; but Michiel, defying Barbarigo and the Signoria, insisted that the trial be held in the Great Council and even denied the pathetic pleas of Grimani's sons as they knelt before him in the piazza. Michiel, claims Priuli, was approached by those of "Ca' Grimani and their relatives, who have the greatest power in the city, and promised money and benefits if he would not bring charges in the Great Council." After a battle between Barbarigo and Michiel lasting from November 1499 to March 1500, it was decided to hold the trial in the Great Council—a clear defeat for the *Primi*, who were in ill repute because of wartime setbacks. During this conflict, the Great Council showed its appreciation to Michiel for his championship of its sovereignty by nominating him as duke of Crete; and after Grimani's conviction, Michiel was awarded the exile's seat on the Procuratia, a crucial step toward the dogeship.[86]

Amid the political in-fighting, little was heard of Leonardo Loredan, but certainly he and his large clan did their best to insure Grimani's removal from the scene. Aided by Barbarigo, Ca' Grimani tried to have Ca' Loredan expelled from the Great Council during consideration of Antonio's case, "since the Loredan hate the Grimani for the death of Andrea." Also, Leonardo had his own ambitions for the dogeship, which would most likely never have been fulfilled if not for Grimani's misadventure at Zonchio and Tron's subsequent actions. When the Great Council in June 1509 voted to allow Grimani home (he had fled exile and was living with his son in Rome), Sanuto notes that Grimani "is a great enemy of our doge, and he was his rival; if not for his exile, this doge would never have been elected."[87]

Sanuto, 3:173; Priuli, 1:220. On Grimani's return: Malipiero, 1:188; 181–182; Sanuto, 3:35.

86 On Michiel's motivation: Pietro Dolfin, *Annalium Venetorum*, pp. 8, 68. On Barbarigo and the trial: Sanuto, 3:121; Pietro Dolfin, *Annalium Venetorum*, pp. 59–60. On pleas and bribes by the Grimani: Priuli, 1:326; Sanuto, 3:106, 69, 101, 103, 108, 118–119, 121, 143. On Michiel's election: Sanuto, 3:115, 395–396; Pietro Dolfin, *Annalium Venetorum*, p. 204. On Grimani's trial: Zille, "Processo Grimani."

87 On hatred between the Loredan and the Grimani: Pietro Dolfin, *Annalium*

Even so, Loredan's election in October 1501 was a near thing. "When Doge Barbarigo died," Sanuto says, "the whole city shouted that Filippo Tron would be elected." But Tron died in the week before the election, a coincidence that led some to murmur of poisoning, although cooler heads concluded he had died from obesity. Another rival for the dogeship, Captain General Benedetto Pesaro, had foreclosed his chances when he executed two patricians (one of them a Loredan) for disobedience, thereby arousing the ire of many in the Great Council. With Grimani, Tron, and Pesaro out of competition, Loredan's way was clear. To be sure, his four sons were an obstacle, but the Loredan clan (fifty-two men in 1527) and its connections were assets. His relative youth at sixty-five would have told against him but for his uncertain health. A portrait by Giovanni Bellini (in the National Gallery, London) shows him with slight, delicate features, with perhaps a hint of the high-strung temperament one associates with a chronically weak constitution. Certainly patricians were willing to consider so "young" a man as doge, following the fifteen-year term of Barbarigo, only because he was not expected to survive long.[88]

Loredan's strength in the Great Council was translated into seven supporters in the Eleven, which led to a three-day delay in the election, as nine votes were needed to approve nominations to the Forty-one. His main competitors at this stage were Marino Leone and Nicolò Mocenigo, whom luck had favored in the earlier drawings; by dint of hard bargaining, they put a number of their own supporters in the final electoral college and almost denied Loredan his expected victory. Leone came within three votes of the dogeship on October 2, and some thought he would be elected the next day. But during the night Loredan managed to split his opposition, and on the third he won a thirty-one vote victory.[89]

For the next twenty years, intensity of electioneering for the dogeship fluctuated with Loredan's health. For example, in May 1504 when Loredan seemed mortally ill, Tommaso Mocenigo was elected to the Procuratia by more than thirteen hundred of fourteen hundred votes,

---

Venetorum, p. 71; cf. Sanuto, 3:312–313. On Grimani's return from exile: Sanuto, 8:412; cf. 556, 558.

88 On Tron's prospects and his death: Sanuto, 4:144. On Pesaro's prospects: ASMo., b. 11, c. 121, Bartolomeo Cartari to the duke of Ferrara, September 27, 1501; cf. Sanuto, 4:231; 6:133–134; Priuli, 2:34. On the strength of the Loredan: cf. Sanuto, 32:214. On Loredan's assets: Sanuto, 4:144. On Loredan's delicate appearance: Sanuto, 28:309.

89 ASMo., b. 11, c. 121, Bartolomeo Cartari to the duke of Ferrara, September 29, 1501; Sanuto, 4:131.

and crowds flocked to his home to acclaim him the next doge. Marcantonio Morosini was also mentioned as a likely successor, "since he is
an attractive gentleman, rich, without sons, and beloved by patricians."
Loredan outlived them both by more than a decade—indeed, he survived all but a handful of the forty-one men who had elected him.
Would-be doges disappeared from the scenes with some regularity,
although the passage of years kept hopes undimmed that Loredan's
next illness might be his last. In March 1520 furious electioneering
broke out when the doge seemed, finally, beyond recovery. His return
to the Senate on March 23, after nearly a month in his sickbed,
stunned even those who thought they had become accustomed to such
virtual resurrections, not least of whom was Antonio Grimani, whose
hypocritical congratulations sparked laughter in the assembly and even
a smile from the convalescent.[90]

Grimani's substantial following in the patriciate, as well as his very
advanced years, made him the leading contender to succeed Loredan.
Others were also frequently mentioned: Marco Donato, "who has no
sons but is a great miser"; Domenico Trevisan, "who will lose the
dogeship for having six sons"; Andrea Gritti, "who has no sons, but
few want him"; and Antonio Tron, much liked by the people and
"without sons." As it happened, when Loredan died on June 21, 1521,
Grimani's most serious competitor was Giorgio Corner, who, with an
annual income of more than 25,000 ducats, was the city's wealthiest
man. His family owned vast estates on Cyprus (a legacy of his sister's
rule there as queen) and on the *terraferma*. The Corner palace at San
Maurizio, purchased and refurbished for 30,000 ducats, was the most
magnificent in the city; its destruction by fire in 1532 was considered
by Sanuto (who went to see the blaze with his friend, Gasparo Contarini) a major disaster for Venice. Merchant, landholder, and politician, Corner had also served as a general, most prominently in 1508
when he and Bartolomeo Alviano led Venetian forces to victory
against Maximilian at the battle of Cadore.[91]

Corner's liabilities as a ducal candidate were his three sons, his age of
sixty-six, his great eminence in Venice, which provoked envy and

90 On Mocenigo and Morosini: ASMo., b. 12, c. 52, 58, Bartolomeo Cartari to
the duke of Ferrara, April 25 and May 5, 1504. On the survival of Loredan's
Forty-one: Sanuto, 7:156–157; 27:324–325; Sanuto, "Miscellanea di Cronica
Veneta," fol. 32r. On Loredan in March 1520: Sanuto, 28:371; 146, 293, 309, 326,
332, 338, 353, 359, 491.

91 On those mentioned for the dogeship: Sanuto, 28:309; ASM, b. 1454, Giam-

hostility—and his membership in a *Longhi* clan. The election of 1521 turned into another struggle between the old and new houses, with Corner dispensing largesse to overcome opposition to a *Longhi* as doge. On June 21, the Ferrarese ambassador reported that Corner was "spending and spending a great deal of money, and because of this many think he will win." A week later the Mantuan ambassador observed that others were still being touted: "The young men of the city say, 'Age, Madness, Wisdom, Arrogance or Power will be doge,'" which one may take to refer respectively to Grimani, Tron, Trevisan, Gritti, and Corner. Within a few days, however, only Grimani and Corner were talked about. Their sons, Cardinal Domenico Grimani and Cardinal Marco Corner, transferring their bitter rivalry from Rome to Venice, engaged in "the very greatest lobbying by night and day," visiting palace after palace, sending secret messages and gifts to garner support in the Great Council. Both claimed the lead in patrician (and popular) opinion, but the Mantuan ambassador thought that Grimani had the edge, "though there is no doubt that if Corner wished to back somebody else, especially Antonio Tron, he would bury Grimani."[92]

From the point of view of the *Primi*, the election began very badly. Thirty men were drawn from the Great Council, and the nine who survived from that group included no supporters of the principal ducal competitors; moreover the nine comprised a number of men from small houses (Calergi, Zancharuol, Vitturi, Cavalli, and Zulian) that were of no political account. When the names of the forty elected by the nine were read to the Great Council, "the entire council was stupified, seeing the character of those who were nominated; and there was great grumbling that *li Primi di la terra* were not named." The state attorneys informed the Signoria that the election of the forty should be annulled because the nine, by excluding *Primi*, had not followed electoral procedures; but the councillors ruled that the prior selection of the nine by the thirty was the only stage of the election that could be so enjoined.[93] *Primi* emerged as the dominant electors in

---

battista Malatesta to the marquis of Mantua, March 4, 1520. On Corner's wealth: Priuli, 4:107, 174; Sanuto, 56:751–754, 953, 975–976; cf. Deborah Howard, *Jacopo Sansovino*, pp. 132–140; Giuseppe Liberali, *Le 'dinastie ecclesiastiche' nei Cornaro della Chà Granda*, pp. 7–27.

92 ASMo., b. 15, c. 51, Giacomo Tebaldi to the duke of Ferrara, June 22, 1521; ASM, b. 1454, Giambattista Malatesta to the marquis of Mantua, June 27, 1521.

93 Sanuto, 30:434–435.

the later stage of the election, but perhaps the unusual complexion of the initial electors gave Corner a slight advantage insofar as the smallest houses of the patriciate apparently were outside the struggle between the *Longhi* and *Curti*.

As in the 1501 election, a long delay ensued after the formation of the Eleven. Giovanni di Giorgio Corner was a member of the Eleven, as were two Corner in-laws, "for which reason," wrote the Mantuan ambassador, "it is held almost for certain that Giorgio Corner will be doge." As the election dragged on, opposition to the elevation of a *Longhi* mounted. Sanuto reports that

> it is known that the closeted Eleven are not in condition to hurry, for they are hard set against one another. It is said that they have requested cards and dice, which is a sign that they will be a long time. Hence, secret meetings have begun in the city, [with] talk about this desire for change, about this Corner who wishes to be elected doge, which [it is said] is not to be tolerated; and we will punish those who give him support; this man goes about procuring followers and would gain the dogeship with money; he is the father of a cardinal and a very rich man; and for . . . [*sic*] years there has not been a doge from the old houses, and he wishes to be elected; and he has three sons, and each will want to hold separate courts, so that it won't be possible to put up with them.

What was said in the Eleven and later in the Forty-one is unknown but may have been similar to that in the election of 1578, when the *Longhi* and *Curti* fought once again and when the victor, Nicolò da Ponte, had a commoner for a mother: "The sum of the individual discussions [wrote a participant in the Forty-one] was talk of ducal houses, excluded houses, and of Jews, gentlemen and peasants. On every side many things were said in this regard."[94]

Passions must have been running high in the Forty-one because Corner was never able to obtain more than fifteen votes and Grimani easily won election, the oldest man ever to ascend the ducal throne. As in 1486, revenge was planned against those who supported the *Longhi* candidate. *Curti* intended to expel Marco Dandolo, Corner's brother-in-law, from the Zonta for having helped install *Longhi* in the Eleven; other *Longhi* were to be defeated in elections for the Ten,

---

94 On Corner's chances: ASM, b. 1454, Giambattista Malatesta to the marquis of Mantua, July 2, 1521. On Sanuto's statement: 30:458. On the election of 1578: William Archer Brown, "Nicolò da Ponte," pp. 127–142.

the Senate, and the Forty. *Longhi* were blamed not only for backing the wrong ducal candidate but for having bypassed *Primi*, such as the three heads of the Ten, in their attempt to place colleagues in the Forty-one. Rewards were also to be distributed: As a member of the Eleven, Bernardo Marcello, a chief of the Ten, had been instrumental in opposing *Longhi* nominations to the final electoral college; his reward (which he never received) was to be a procuratorship.[95]

Despite these vindicative plans, it was the Corner who enjoyed the sweetest revenge. At the end of 1521, Pope Leo X died, and there was a fair chance that Cardinal Domenico Grimani might gain the papacy. The possibility of a Grimani on both the ducal and papal thrones was shattered by Cardinal Marco Corner, who threw his support (and considerable funds) behind Domenico's opponents. When Francesco di Giorgio Corner returned to Venice from Rome, he was greeted by an enraged Doge Grimani, who charged that Cardinal Marco "almost ruined this state" by denying the papacy to his son.[96] Antonio Grimani had waited twenty-two years for the dogeship after being sent into exile by his enemies, only finally to achieve his ambition at the cost of one he desired even more.

It was during Grimani's early years of exile that Andrea Gritti entered the political arena. He had spent his early career as a grain merchant in Istanbul and was fluent in Greek and Turkish. Mixing business with service to Venice, he was both a diplomatic agent and a spy, probably helping to initiate an end to the Turco-Venetian war (1499–1503) from a prison cell where he languished after the discovery of incriminating letters. He returned to Venice in 1502, leaving behind several illegitimate sons, who continued in trade and took service with the sultan. Diarists describe him at this time as exceedingly handsome, eloquent, and forceful—characteristics evident in Titian's memorable later portrait (now in the National Gallery of Art, Washington). His career became distinguished from that of other successful merchants who entered politics when he took command of Venetian forces during the War of the League of Cambrai and recaptured Padua from Maximilian in July 1509; from that moment he began to be mentioned as a future doge. In 1511, when he was only fifty-six, a renewed illness of Doge Loredan prompted Gritti to the ploy of having relatives on the Ten write him a letter of fulsome praise, commending his conduct

95 On defeating *Longhi*: Sanuto, 30:458, 474; cf. 31:210.
96 On the papal election: Sanuto, 32:433; cf. 207, 208, 215, 384–385.

in the army "in such a way that he might aspire to the dogeship."[97]

Such machinations may not have been entirely necessary, for the Signoria genuinely valued Gritti's services, though less for his military acumen, which was slight, than for his popularity with the mercenary troops. The latter lamented his capture by the French at Brescia in 1512 because he was the only commander who combined the influence needed to pry money from the government with a desire to keep his mercenaries' payments up to date. Imprisonment, in fact, saved him from the embarrassment of explaining how his forces were destroyed and gave him the opportunity for friendship with the French king; once again, he helped negotiate peace terms while in confinement. His later commitment to a Venetian-French alliance, which was to play a part in the 1523 election, may stem from his stay in France.[98]

In 1517 Gritti presided at the occasion that ended the war, the return of Verona to Venetian custody. Amid the jubilation at his later triumphal entry, there must have been many who thought he would be the next doge. His achievements, abilities, and presence all spoke in his favor; and he could, when he wished, be quite charming. But apparently his charm was more in evidence when dealing with sultans and kings than with fellow patricians, who considered him arrogant, domineering, and self-righteous. The day before Loredan died, Gritti told Giambattista Malatesta, the Mantuan ambassador, that he was not likely to win the election "because of the great envy I arouse in this city"; others, Malatesta noted earlier, "say that he is imperious."[99]

Gritti was not a favorite for doge when Grimani died in May 1523. Instead, it was assumed that Antonio Tron would be elected. He was perhaps the most unusual politician of his day, enjoying wide popularity among the *popolo* for his humanitarian concerns and evoking uneasiness among the *Primi* for his criticisms of the government. In

97 On Gritti in Istanbul: James Cushman Davis, "Shipping and Spying in the Early Career of a Venetian Doge, 1496–1502," pp. 97, 108. On Gritti's most successful illegitimate son, Alvise: Francesca Lucchetta, "L'Affare Zen' in Levante nel primo Cinquecento," pp. 113–115; Tibor Kardos, "Dramma satirico carnevalesco su Alvise Gritti governatore dell'Ungheria, 1532." On Gritti in 1502: Sanuto, 4:244, 254; Priuli, 2:198–199. On Gritti and Padua: Giuseppe Dalla Santa, *La Lega di Cambrai e gli avvenimenti dell'anno 1509 descritti da un mercante veneziano contemporaneo*, p. 24. On 1511: Priuli, vol. 6, fol. 480r; cf. ASV, Consiglio di Dieci, Parti Miste, Reg. 34, fols. 74r; 76v.

98 Priuli, vol. 5, fols. 278v–279r; vol. 7, fols. 222v, 296v.

99 ASM, b. 1454, Giambattista Malatesta to the marquis of Mantua, June 20, 1521, and March 4, 1520, cf. Sanuto, 34:41; 157, 158, 159; Priuli, vol. 5, fols. 278v–279r.

1521 his was the "Madness" which young men said might be doge, surely a slighting reference to his predilection for going against the grain of Venetian politics. This characteristic was dramatically evident in the days before the 1523 election, when he not only refused to seek support but publicly declared that he "did not want to be [doge] and would refuse [the office] if elected."[100] Tron's remarkable disclaimer gave a critical boost to Gritti's chances, as did Corner's decision not to try for the dogeship again but to throw his support to Domenico Trevisan, who, however, had no fewer sons than two years before. Lorenzo Loredan, also mentioned as a candidate, had made too many enemies during his father's reign.

By the middle stages of the election, Tron had no backers in the electoral colleges, which were dominated by Gritti. The latter had eighteen supporters in the group of forty-five, while his closest competitor, Leonardo Mocenigo, had only ten. In the next crucial lot, Gritti's dominance was translated into six backers in the Eleven, with the other electors divided among three contenders. In short, Gritti's victory was virtually certain; it only remained to come to terms with those who could veto his nominations to the Forty-one.

Bargaining began in the Eleven, and by the end of the first day, only twelve had been approved. Gritti's efforts to place his supporters in the Forty-one were evidently hampered by Venice's international political situation during the election, and in particular by his own very pro-French views. Shortly before the election, France had requested Venetian aid against Milan and Charles V. Gritti was notorious for being "all for the French" and a proponent of an anti-imperial alliance. While the Eleven was meeting, news arrived from Milan of an incident that reflects the attention paid to ducal politics in Europe: An effigy representing Gritti had been erected in Milan, with a fish in one hand and a frog in the other—in other words, a Gritti election would mean French dominance of Venice. No doubt those in Venice opposing a French alliance were also against raising Gritti to the dogeship.[101]

Finally, Gritti was able to place twenty-two of his supporters in the Forty-one, only three short of certain victory. According to Malatesta, Gritti's opponents tried to form a united front against him

---

[100] For discussion of Tron, see Chapter V.1. On Tron's statement: Sanuto, 34:133.

[101] On the election: Sanuto, 34:141–147, 148. On Gritti being pro-French: Sanuto, 34:113, 150, 353; cf. Erwin Panofsky, *Problems in Titian*, pp. 179–182.

but could not agree on a candidate who could overcome his lead. Nevertheless, Gritti had great difficulty rounding up the necessary votes and in the end had to call on the support of Alvise Pisani, to whom he was linked by a close marriage alliance. By vespers on May 20, the Forty-one elected Gritti by twenty-five votes.[102]

There was no doubt in Venice that Pisani was responsible for Gritti's victory. Indeed, in 1531, two years after Pisani's death, Sanuto viewed a painting by Titian that was interpreted by many as an allegory of the doge's election:

> I saw a new painting in the Collegio, which included the likeness of the doge, kneeling before Our Lady with Babe in arms, and with St. Mark presenting him. Behind Our Lady are three saints, Bernardino, Alvise and Marina. The explanation circulating is that they have argued as to which of them elected the doge. St. Bernardino says, 'He was elected on my day.' St. Marina says, 'He was elected for having recaptured Padua on my day, July 17.' And St. Alvise says, 'I have the name of the procurator, Alvise Pisani, his in-law, who was in the Forty-one and who was the cause of his election as doge.' So St. Mark, seeing this argument among the three saints, decided to present them to Our Lady and the Son to determine which of them was behind the election of His Serenity to the dogeship.[103]

The alliance between Gritti and Pisani brought both to the pinnacle of their power in Venice. Pisani was one of the most feared politicians in the city; his wealth and financial acumen gave him substantial influence behind the scenes well before 1523. Priuli claims that "the honor and reputation of Venice" rested upon the Pisani bank, the only large bank to survive the panic of 1499 and to liquidate with full payments to creditors the next year. A new bank, much aided by political connections, spread its influence even wider, becoming essential to the government for transferring funds and raising money. It dominated Venetian finance from 1513 to 1521, and in 1516 a state loan was repaid by credits drawn on it; three years later the government owed Pisani 150,000 ducats.[104]

Election to the Ten at the age of forty-six was testimony that Pisani

---

102 ASM, b. 1454, Giambattista Malatesta to the marquis of Mantua, May 21, 1521; cf. Sanuto, 34:149, 164.

103 Sanuto, 55:19; cf. J. A. Crowe and G. B. Cavalcaselle, *Titian*, 1:344–345, 356–357; Michelangelo Muraro and David Rosand, eds., *Tiziano e la silografia veneziana del Cinquecento*, pp. 135–136.

104 On Priuli's claim: Frederic C. Lane, *Venice*, p. 328. On Pisani's finances: idem, "Venetian Bankers, 1496–1533," pp. 71, 82–83; idem, *Venice*, p. 328.

enjoyed "the greatest power in the land." In 1516 at forty-eight he was elected a procurator for a loan to the government of 10,000 ducats. The day before this election Pisani gave a 10,000-ducat dowry, far in excess of what the law allowed, for the marriage of a daughter to a son of Giorgio Corner; his "new relative aided him greatly" in winning the procuratorship. Pisani purchased a cardinal's hat in 1517 for his son Francesco and a procuratorship for another, Giovanni, in 1527. He gave each of his five daughters at least 8,000 ducats as a dowry, and between dowries and marriage costs he spent on them the astounding sum of more than 40,000 ducats. Many daughters, few sons, and much money were a happy combination in Venetian politics. Two daughters entered the wealthiest and politically most important branch of the Priuli clan; another married a grandson of Doge Grimani; and the fifth wed Giovanni di Pietro Capello, son of an important politician and member of a family with close ties to the Corner and the Priuli.[105]

In November 1520 Pisani married Giovanni to Andrea Gritti's granddaughter, a match, observed Malatesta, "which suits Messer Andrea very well." Within two years he was able to elevate his kinsman to the dogeship while he himself was sitting in the Forty-one. During the election, the Piazza di San Marco was cluttered with venders for the celebration of Ascension week, which would prevent the new doge from making his traditional circuit. After dinner on May 19, Pisani turned to a companion in the Forty-one and said, "Start dismantling the Ascension shops in the Piazza, for we will certainly have a doge by morning." His prediction was only slightly premature—Gritti did not win until the evening of the twentieth—but his optimism was well founded. Pisani called up the necessary votes to elect Gritti, the final one being cast by Pietro Capello, whose daughter-in-law was Paula di Alvise Pisani.[106]

In March 1523 Sanuto cryptically referred to those in high places in Venice who were promoting a "monarchy in the city." He may have been thinking of Alvise Pisani and of the remarkable series of marriages he had witnessed in recent years, bringing together under the aegis of the powerful financier the largest fortunes and the greatest

---

105 On elevation to the Ten: Sanuto, 18:250; cf. 17:73. On the marriage and the procuratorship: Sanuto, 22:223; 220, 225. On expenses for his sons and daughters: Sanuto, 24:460; 36:410. On the Pisani family: Barbaro, 8596, fols. 256r–256v, 258r; Capellari, vol. 4, fols. 226r–227v.

106 On November 1520: ASM, b. 1454, Giambattista Malatesta to the marquis of Mantua, November 17, 1520. On May 19 and 20: Sanuto, 34:155–157.

powers in Venice: the Gritti, Grimani, Corner, and Pisani families. If so, Sanuto had abundant reason to endorse the astrologers who warned of dire omens on the day Gritti was crowned. The diarist expresses disapproval of Gritti's laxness in making a circuit of the piazza and of his not immediately distributing the customary money to the mob; he notes that the first law passed under the new doge was for more taxes, and he may even have found a certain significance in Gritti's ducal cap slipping off because it was too small for his head.[107] Nor was he alone in his discontent. Young men made an effigy of Antonio Tron, "short and with a beard," dressed as a doge, and ran a mock circuit of the piazza, chanting his name. Few people cheered Gritti when he was carried about later, and when Tron, as the oldest patrician in the Forty-one, announced the results of the election in the basilica, he was again repeatedly acclaimed and the new doge ignored. Even Gritti's dispensation of grain at below market prices did not please the people: "All complained about his election."[108]

Immediately after the election, Gritti approached Alvise di Giovanni Priuli to chastise him for his vehement opposition during the past week. Alvise Priuli insisted on giving his reply publicly: "It is true what I have said, that I never supported you and I never will, because I don't want to make the doge a tyrant." Significantly, Alvise Priuli was also a bitter foe of Pisani, and his alarm over the outcome of the election clearly arose from his recognition that Gritti's triumph was Pisani's as well. Four years before, Alvise Priuli accused Pisani of being a danger to the Republic and forced him to renounce his son's claim to a benefice. Now, less than a month after the ducal election, Gritti overrode prerogatives of the Senate and used his influence to acquire more benefices for Cardinal Pisani because "Alvise Pisani, the procurator . . . has his granddaughter in his house, and he made him doge." Alvise Priuli's premonitions were shared by others, including the individuals who scrawled insults to bankers on a wall at the Rialto in October 1523. The one aimed at Gritti's presumed *éminence grise* read, "Alvise Pisani, traitor, under this doge you will steal the Ducal Palace!"[109]

<hr />

107 On Sanuto's fear of monarchy: 34:5–6. On Sanuto's complaints: 34:157, 159, 185, 187, 188.

108 Sanuto, 34:157, 159, 201.

109 On Alvise Priuli and Gritti: Sanuto, 34:158. On Alvise Priuli and Pisani: Sanuto, 27:522, 526–528; 28:124, 126, 130, 137. On Gritti and the benefice: Sanuto, 34:245. On the insult to Pisani: Sanuto, 35:140, 148.

Of course, one cannot know if Sanuto's unnamed subverters of the republican order were Pisani and Gritti, but their alliance was in 1523 the most potent and recent, making them the most likely candidates for his highly colored insinuation. But he need not have worried, for Venice's republican fabric was too strong even for so forceful and autocratic a character as Andrea Gritti. His projects, such as an alliance with France and elimination of political corruption, were continually frustrated. Perhaps the conditions of his victory continued to bedevil him, inasmuch as few wanted him as doge and many feared him. Given his unbending character, so at odds with the Venetian milieu, he was never able to surmount that initial obstacle and build up a following within the patriciate that would give him scope to accomplish his ends. Five years after his election he was complaining about being "surrounded on all sides by hatred."[110]

A fundamental strength of the Venetian constitution was that the dogeship was elective. Patricians never lost their fear that the ducal office might turn into a monarchy; hence their concern for a doge "without sons." Familial bonds, although at the heart of Venetian politics, were also perceived as a threat to republican liberty. In the 1470s, two Mocenigo brothers held the dogeship, their reigns separated by only three years. The Barbarigo brothers did succeed each other, and likewise the Priuli brothers in the mid-Cinquecento. Doge Tron's son, Filippo, was the ducal favorite in 1501; his nephew, Antonio, in 1523. Lorenzo Loredan was a feared aspirant to the Ducal Palace after his father's death. Gritti's strongest competitor in 1523 turned out to be Leonardo Mocenigo, whose father and uncle had been doges. True, these cases remained exceptional, and more typical was the popular and temperate Domenico Trevisan, kept from the dogeship by his many sons, one of whom, Marcantonio, won the dogeship in 1553 partly because he was *senza fioli*.

Venetian concern for dynastic tendencies in the Ducal Palace may have been excessive, but the power inherent in the dogeship, as well as the fate of other republics, warned against overconfidence. Theoretically only first among equals, the doge was the most formidable single figure in Venice. It need not always have been so, for the political importance of the office depended on the ability and desire of an individual to exert his influence and on his talent for maintaining a following. Such considerations were more effective in restraining ducal power than elaborate oaths and complex electoral procedures. A strong

110 ASV, Consiglio di Dieci, Patri Secrete, Reg. 2, fols. 84r–84v.

man could slip through the electoral maze and pay only lip service to the most carefully constructed promises. The effective restraints on the dogeship, like the office itself, were political rather than constitutional in nature. Ducal power was blunted and diffused by the same conditions that molded competition for the dogeship: constant maneuvering for advantage, the rise and fall of reputation, shifting alliances and lasting vendettas, the web of lineage and dependence, daily electioneering in the Great Council and the Senate, the volatile allegiance of patriciate and people, a host of compromises and hesitations. More than anything else, these hedged in both the *Primi* who competed for the Ducal Palace and the man lucky enough to enter it. But whatever the efficacy of either formal or informal restraints, both were responses to the problem created by the Venetian constitution itself, that at the very center of government, in the visible symbol and embodiment of the Republic, there stood a politician.

Chapter IV

Patriciate and Constitution
in the Italian Wars

1. *War and Finance, 1509–1517*

A late sixteenth-century painting by Jacopo Palma il Giovane in the Senate chamber of the Ducal Palace illustrates how the War of the League of Cambrai was perceived through the myth of Venice. An allegory of the war, the painting depicts Doge Leonardo Loredan loosing the fearsome lion of Venice on a timorous Europe, who is mounted on the legendary bull and cowering behind a shield with the arms of the league: Spain, France, the Empire, the papacy, Hungary, Mantua, and Ferrara. But Venice's achievement in the long, dreary war lay in mere survival, not in military heroics. In 1517 Venice celebrated the reacquisition of the key city of Verona, obtained by paying 100,000 ducats to Emperor Maximilian, who gave the city to France, which then bestowed it on Venice. In a speech to the Senate at that time, Loredan put the best face on this end to the war: "Now this state will enjoy a great reputation, for the entire world has seen how we have prevailed with so many leagued against us; this state has achieved greater fame [than before], not only within Italy but outside as well."[1] As it happened, Loredan proved correct about Venetian fame, although Venetians were keenly aware they owed their survival and recovery more to the protection of the lagoon and the power of money than to military or republican excellence.

---

1 Sanuto, 24:79.

That awareness was articulated in October 1517 when a Turkish ambassador, Ali Mohammed, was taken by Venetian officials to the top of the San Marco bell tower to view the city and its surroundings, a courtesy usually extended only at high tide when visitors could not see the layout of the lagoon's channels. The ambassador, whom Sanuto calls "an intelligent and wicked man performing the office of spy for his master," asked a series of undiplomatic questions about the defenses of the city: How far is it to the mainland? Can an army attack by way of Chioggia? Which direction is Friuli? What is the best approach for an enemy fleet? The best area in which to place artillery? He concluded that it would be an easy task for the sultan's army to throw a bridge from the mainland and conquer Venice. Nettled, a patrician replied to this unseemly boast: "My lord ambassador, be advised that in our late cruel war, when all the kings of the world were against the Signoria, not one man in this city was killed. All was accomplished with money and the deaths of foreign soldiers. The city was crowded with people, as full as an egg, but it could not be taken."[2]

Money and the deaths of foreign soldiers: Venice had expended large amounts of both in the recent past. The War of Ferrara (1482–1483) was costly, stirring discontent among patricians because taxes were raised and government salaries cut. Support for the Pisan rebellion against Florence between 1496 and 1499 seriously depleted the treasury and strained relations between rich and poor patricians. War against Milan in 1499, against the Turks from 1499 to 1503, and in the Romagna in the early years of the Cinquecento were further drains on Venetian resources. The government was forced to cut salaries in 1501 and 1502, a measure that prompted Minio's protest in the name of poor patricians. In the spring of 1508, Venice soundly defeated Maximilian and acquired Gorizia and Trieste in Friuli, "which later were that repast, that bad morsel, that poisonous food that has spoiled St. Mark's stomach" because the emperor was thereby impelled to join France in the League of Cambrai.[3]

On May 14, 1509, French forces representing the league defeated Venice at the battle of Agnadello, and within a month Venice lost

---

2 Sanuto, 25:73; cf. 39:479.

3 On the War of Ferrara: Malipiero, 1:289–290. On the Pisan rebellion: Priuli, 1:65, 90, 94, 96–97, 103, 113, 114, 120; Malipiero, 1:482, 512. On Venetian policy in the early Cinquecento: P. Pieri, *Intorno alla politica di Venezia al principio del Cinquecento*. On the quotation: Nicolò Machiavelli, *Second Decennale*, in *Machiavelli*, 3:1461.

almost all the mainland empire it had acquired since the early Quattrocento. France conquered Venetian Lombardy; Maximilian, the Veneto; and Pope Julius II, the cities of the Romagna. Spain evicted Venice from the ports of Apulia, while Ferrara and Mantua recovered territory previously lost. It was an unprecedented disasater for Venice and an ill omen for Italy. "What will happen to the others," Machiavelli wondered, "if this one burned and froze in a few days only?"[4] What made this war different for Venice, however, was not merely the scale of the defeat but the length and intensity of the conflict that followed, lasting eight years and placing enormous strains on Venetian resources and, eventually, on the Republic's political system itself.

Loss of the *terraferma* empire meant the end of substantial revenues for Venice. Tax money ceased flowing toward Venice, and customs duties from the mainland were effectively wiped out. For example, the Salt Office, which usually brought in thousands of ducats a year, failed to collect much revenue as late as 1515; in 1510 the magistracy was reduced from six to four offices and did not recover its former size until 1516. Venice began regaining lost territory as early as July 1509, when Padua was retaken, but it was to be years before the mainland assumed its previous place in state finances. Priuli claims that the mainland consumed the riches Venice reaped from the *stato di mar*, although this view was clearly shaped by his moral judgment that possession of mainland property had led to the decline of the Republic, to Venetian patricians turning from the hardy life of mariners to become languorous country gentlemen. In fact, revenue from the mainland made up about 27 percent of the government's income in 1469, a percentage that considerably increased later in the century. In 1518 income from Padua, Vicenza, Verona, Brescia, and Bergamo totaled 553,454 ducats, of which less than 150,000 were earmarked for military expenditure and mainland defense, while the remainder went into Venetian coffers.[5]

---

4 On the battle of Agnadello: Francesco Guicciardini, *Storia di Italia*, 2:745–749. On the League: Federico Chabod, "Venezia nella politica italiana ed europea del Cinquecento"; F. Cipollini, "La Lega di Cambrai"; Francesco Ercole, *Da Carlo VIII a Carlo V*, pp. 99–105; Alessandro Luzio, "I preliminari della Lega di Cambrai"; G. Occion-Bonafons, "Intorno alle cagioni della Lega di Cambrai"; Federico Seneca, *Venezia e papa Giulio II*; Robert Finlay, "Venice, the Po Expedition, and the End of the League of Cambrai." On the quotation: Machiavelli, *Second Decennale*, in *Machiavelli*, 3:1460.

5 On loss of revenue from the mainland: Priuli, 4:209. On the Salt Office: Marino Sanuto, *Cronachetta*, p. 124, n. 2; ASV, Maggior Consiglio, Deliberazioni,

Nor would Priuli have found many of his fellow citizens agreeing with him that it was best to abandon the *terraferma* to its own decadent inhabitants. He calculated in 1509 that Venetian property on the mainland was worth more than 3 million ducats. In 1522 the Senate had difficulty constituting a commission to review custom taxes because only fifteen senators met the requirement of not owning property in Padua or Treviso. The 1518 tax register for land held by patricians and *cittadini* in the Padovano includes 1,523 individuals, families, and institutions with holdings ranging from patches of ground to vast tracts. The monastery of San Giovanni at Torcello had 465 *campi* (with a *campo* at slightly more than one-third of a hectare). Alvise Pisani registered over 10,000 *campi*, while Gasparo Contarini owned 445 and Alvise Saraxin, a *cittadino*, 10. Alvise di Pietro Priuli, the diarist's uncle, possessed about 250 *campi*, though he stipulated that he could not vouch for the accuracy of his inventory "because for more than ten years I have not been outside" Venice.[6] Because of the war, patricians lost income from their mainland property for years. During the siege of Padua in the autumn of 1509, more than 400,000 ducats worth of property was destroyed. The three Barozzi brothers usually realized 118 ducats a year in produce from their land in the Padovano, but from 1509 to 1514, they barely scraped 20 ducats from it. The Barbarigo family did not regain control of its estates in the Veronese until 1516.[7]

Loss of state and private income was accompanied by decline in revenue from trade. Enemy domination of the mainland cut off Venice from its principal customers in Germany, and the city suffered as enemy troops devoured the grain and wine of the captured lands.

Liber Deda, Reg. 25, fols. 53r, 119v; cf. Gasparo Contarini, *La Republica*, p. 118. On Priuli's claims: 4:45–47, 50–51, 65, 67–68, 133; cf. 1:196. On revenue in 1469: Gino Luzzatto, "L'economia veneziana nei secoli '400 e '500," pp. 62–63. On the budget in 1500: Frederic C. Lane, *Venice*, p. 237. On income in 1518: ASV, Senato, Terra, Reg. 20, fols. 152r–153r.

6 On the worth of mainland property: Priuli, 4:50. On the 1522 tax commission: Sanuto, 33:45–46; cf. ASV, Senato, Terra, Reg. 22, fols. 66v, 87r. On the 1518 tax register: ASV, Dieci Savi sopra le decime, Condizione de' nobili e cittadini veneti per beni in Padova e territorio, 1518–1523, Reg. 418, in which see, on the monastery, no. 231; on Pisani, no. 1148; on Contarini, no. 957; on Saraxin, no. 159; on Priuli, no. 998; cf. no. 1233, no. 1351.

7 On the siege: Priuli, 4:412. On the Barozzi: ASV, Dieci Savi sopra le decime in Rialto, Condizione della città, 1514, S. Geremia, b. 34, no. 34; cf. Collegio, Notatorio, Reg. 20, fol. 15r. On the Barbarigo: Frederic C. Lane, *Andrea Barbarigo*, p. 38.

Galley voyages to the West were discontinued from 1509 to 1517, while trade with the Levant declined as the Venetian role as middleman was thus eliminated. Trade fell not only because of Venetian difficulties at home but because of turmoil in the Levant prior to the extension of Turkish authority to that area in 1516. Martino Merlini, merchant of Venice, wrote to his brother in Beirut in 1512, "When your letters arrive, I tremble to the heart with fear that more bad news is coming."[8] Commerce also suffered because Venice's distraction by the war made it possible for the Turks to consolidate their position in the Aegean and southern Adriatic without hindrance. Foreign merchants in Venice went without business, and the *Fondaco dei Tedeschi* was shut because of war with the Empire. For much of the war, trade—"the foundation of our city," the Senate declared in 1524, "as necessary as air to the body"—was at a standstill.[9]

With income from mainland property and trade seriously diminished, patricians had a third source eliminated when the goverment suspended interest payments on the state bond issues of the Monte Nuovo. The Monte Nuovo was created in 1482 to finance the War of Ferrara. Patricians and citizens were forced to make loans to the state, based on a percentage of the value of their property; and interest was paid on the so-called bonds (*imprestiti*), which were actually entries in the ledgers of the Loan Office.[10] Interest payments of 5 percent were made each year and by 1509 amounted to 150,000 ducats. Before the war the Monte Nuovo was a popular, even preferred, investment. Priuli and his father, for example, held 20,000 ducats worth of bonds, receiving an annual income of 1,000 ducats. But after Agnadello, the government could not keep faith with bondholders, and in October 1509 the Senate decided to redeem the bonds at the current market price, not at their original purchase value—a severe financial blow to

8 On enemy domination of the mainland: Sanuto, 13:61–62. On the galley voyages: Sanuto, 23:583; Michiel, fol. 279v; cf. Frederic C. Lane, "Venetian Shipping during the Commercial Revolution," p. 15. On trouble in the Levant: Sanuto, 20:411; 23:110; 106–110; cf. Michiel, fols. 271r–271v, 274v, 275v. On Merlini: Giuseppe Dalla Santa, *La Lega di Cambrai e gli avvenimenti dell'anno 1509 descritti da un mercante veneziano contemporaneo*, pp. 3–4.

9 On Turkish consolidation: cf. Andrew C. Hess, "The Evolution of the Ottoman Seaborne Empire in the Age of the Oceanic Discoveries, 1453–1525," pp. 1,903–1,906. On closing the *Fondaco*: Priuli, vol. 5, fol. 161v. On 1524: ASV, Senato, Terra, Reg. 23, fol. 61r.

10 Frederic C. Lane, "Public Debt and Private Wealth, Particularly in Sixteenth-century Venice"; idem, *Venice*, pp. 238, 324–325.

the already hard-pressed patriciate. Bondholders discovered, as Priuli puts it, their "hands full of flies," their investments mere "paper and ink." "Many say," the banker records, "that when the Monte Nuovo was ruined, so too was the city of Venice." A new series of bonds, the Monte Novissimo, was created in 1509 to finance the war; hence patricians were subject to new loan demands at the same time they lost interest payments from the old exactions. With financial stability called into question, Venetian money declined in value, while foreign and counterfeit currencies flooded the city's markets.[11]

Customs revenue that trickled into Venice was applied to the expenses of war, which consumed "a mountain of gold." Between 1509 and 1510, Venetian land forces increased from 7,000 to 15,785 men, the latter army requiring 60,000 ducats a month in 1510 and a record sum of 84,000 in June 1512. The cash for these mammoth expenditures was hard to find. In June 1510 the treasury was exhausted when only 1,700 ducats were sent to the army. In October 1511, with Treviso and the fortress of Osoppo in Friuli under siege, and with the enemy burning the Lido, there was no money for the army; and when Marghera was destroyed two years later, money again was not to be found.[12]

Venetian wartime financing was on a day-to-day, emergency basis. There was provision for future expenditure, and usually something remained in the coffers of the Ten for cases of extreme urgency; but the financial system that maintained Venetian defenses was as uncertain and shortsighted as that of all other contemporary states.[13] For example, an unexpected retreat from the Polesine in May 1510 found the government unprepared to pay for more troops; the only source of funds was a loan of 7,000 ducats from Alvise Pisani. This short-term financing insured poor performance by the troops and thereby

---

11 On the Priuli investments: Priuli, 4:411. On Priuli's reaction to suspension of payments: 4:17, 411. On foreign and counterfeit currency: Sanuto, 19:411; cf. ASV, Consiglio di Dieci, Parti Miste, Reg. 37, fol. 109r; Reg. 38, fol. 39r; N. Papadopoli, "Una tariffa con disegni di monete stampata a Venezia nel 1517."

12 On customs revenue for war: Sanuto, *Cronachetta*, p. 148, n. 2; cf. Priuli, vol. 5, fol. 399r. On a "mountain of gold": Priuli, vol. 5, fol. 346r. On army increases and expenses: Priuli, 4:195; Sanuto, 10:589–591; 11:594; 14:484. On June 1510, October 1511, and 1513: Sanuto, 10:491–492; 13:10; 12, 13, 18, 39, 40, 48, 49, 50–51, 55; 17:109, 119.

13 On the reaction of Florence to financial crisis: Anthony Molho, *Florentine Public Finance in the Early Renaissance, 1400–1433*; L. F. Marks, "La crisi finanziaria a Firenze dal 1494 al 1502."

prolonged the crisis. The mercenaries were relentless in their demands for money; Priuli thought them "beastly men, without reason or discretion," who "stood about scratching their bellies," prompt to blackmail their employers at the approach of an ememy. In March 1511, Albanian cavalry threatened to desert if not paid immediately, and about one thousand mercenaries began decamping when a French attack was imminent. Priuli was in the Senate when this news arrived, and he reports that the *Primi*, including his father and uncle, were "in a frenzy to find money," keeping the treasury open all night and finally dispatching funds by early morning.[14]

Lacking its usual resources, the government resorted to abrupt and petty measures to raise money. In 1514 alone, licenses for eighty oil shops in the city were auctioned; the sixty notaries servicing the Rialto and the Ducal Palace each had to pay a special 200-ducat tax; the right to sell malmsey (*malvasia*) was auctioned, infringing the rights of many shopkeepers. Such measures, no matter how numerous, could not go far toward meeting the needs of the state, so larger sums were raised in other ways. Between 1508 and 1515, eighty-four general taxes of varying amounts were levied on the city, compared to only thirty between 1500 and 1508. The Jewish community could always be counted on for substantial forced loans, with little recourse but to pay. Estates confiscated from those considered disloyal to the Republic were put up for sale, notably that of Caterina Corner at Asolo, whose sale required a special commission of *Primi*; Alvise Pisani and Tadeo Contarini negotiated with the government to purchase Conegliano for about 25,000 ducats. In January 1514 the Senate approved a proposal to increase the tax on grain entering the city to provide funds to pay the interest due on the Monte Novissimo, a measure that some councillors, Luca Tron, Alvise di Giovanni Priuli, and Marino Morosini, opposed because it was hard on the poor, who would think that the *ricchi* were paying for the war at their expense.[15]

---

14 On the Polesine and Pisani: Sanuto, 10:334. On the mercenaries: Priuli, vol. 6, fol. 483r; Gaetano Cozzi, "Authority and the Law in Renaissance Venice," p. 310. On March 1511: Priuli, vol. 6, fols. 111v–112r; cf. Sanuto, 12:12, 22, 36.

15 On the 1514 measures: Michiel, fols. 114v, 118r, 130v–131r; Sanuto, 18:147, 186, 265; ASV, Senato, Terra, Reg. 18, fols. 105v, 124v, 128v. On the taxes: Sanuto, 20:7–15; cf. ASV, Senato, Terra, Reg. 19, fols. 1r–6v; Felix Gilbert, "Venice in the Crisis of the League of Cambrai," p. 284. On the Jews: Brian Pullan, *Rich and Poor in Renaissance Venice*, pp. 467–482; cf. ASV, Senato, Terra, Reg. 18, fol. 23v–24r; Priuli, 4:408; Sanuto, 9:245. On Asolo and Conegliano: Sanuto, 27:594; 20:446. On 1514: Michiel, fol. 103r; Sanuto, 18:441, 443, 444.

Many of these measures were unpopular, but the Ten's policy of absolving lawbreakers and exiles for payment caused special discontent. Those banished for crimes of violence and corruption were permitted to return to the city for payment of sums ranging from 100 to more than 1,000 ducats. They made Venice a dangerous place, and there was a notable increase in murder and gang warfare. The Lords of the Night (*Signori di notte*), a police magistracy, was enlarged in 1514 because of the many thugs "going about doing great damage and killing people." A year before, the Ten had executed five men for robbery, and Michiel claims that they were not given pardons for cash as usual "because the *terra* was disgusted" with their violence. But in general, when the price was right, the Ten was willing to accommodate criminals to raise money. For example, in 1513 Antonio Priuli was absolved of the murder of Giorgio Loredan for 1,000 ducats and a subsidy for troops at Padua. In 1512 Gabriele Trevisan was cleared of murdering a *cittadino* because his relatives paid to have his victim inscribed in the list of those banished by a police magistracy. Priuli argues that to call the murdered man an outlaw was "a calumny done by force of money, for this patrician is very influential, with money, relatives and support in the city. . . . There was great grumbling in the city over this absolution . . . the populace and Venetian citizens complain mightily of like injustices but must of necessity exercise patience."[16]

Increased taxes and absolution of criminals won little favor among Venetians, but the problem of state debtors in office struck particularly hard at the patriciate. If unable or unwilling to pay taxes or forced loans, a patrician would be inscribed in the Signoria's debtor book and by law would be ineligible to enter a nominating committee or an office. The book was placed on the tribune in the Great Council, and the Signoria was supposed to check it during elections to insure that debtors were excluded from the proceedings. In practice the Signoria was lax about excluding debtors, precisely because rich patricians were often debtors and could marshal support against exclusion. However, as the war approached, the goverment determined to collect the approximately 300,000 ducats owed to it: barely two weeks before Agnadello, the Collegio proposed to the Senate that

---

16 On pardons for money: cf. ASV, Consigli di Dieci, Parti Miste, Reg. 33, fol. 8v; Reg. 34, fols. 41r–41v. On the *terra*'s disgust: Michiel, fol. 97r. On Antonio Priuli: Michiel, fol. 97r. On Trevisan: Priuli, vol. 8, fols. 168r–168v; cf. vol. 6, fols. 64v, 94r, 261v–262r.

debtors pay within eight days or be deprived of offices. When Pietro Contarini of the Zonta objected that this would harm poor patricians, Doge Loredan "threatened Contarini not to speak in such a manner," and the motion easily passed. The next day it was approved by the Great Council, and Sanuto notes that "I was very anxious to oppose it but let it pass so as not to entangle myself in such things."[17] Was Minio's fate seven years before on his mind?

By July 8, only 45,000 ducats had been raised despite numerous appeals. Loredan told the Great Council that, "there are many rich men who didn't wish to pay . . . all these powers are leagued against us for our arrogance, because we are overweening: all spend money, all wear linings [in their cloaks]. . . . and all wear clothes in the ducal manner [with ermine and gold]." A drastic measure to collect money was proposed a month later: On August 5 a Senate motion to confiscate and sell the goods of debtors came before the Great Council, where it was defeated by 700 to 650. Loredan made another emotional appeal to the Great Council (Sanuto records that "some did not wish to hear it and were admonished to listen to the doge") and it passed by 864 to 650.[18] Priuli attributes the large negative vote to

> the great multitude of poor patricians there has always been in this Great Council who don't wish to pay taxes, and even less to sell goods liable to taxation, because they are poor; and they also don't want to see those goods fall into the hands of the rich. They want the rich to support the war and to defend the poor and the Republic, even though it is necessary, if one wants to preserve the Venetian Republic, that there be rich, middling and poor, as well as patricians, citizens and people, and that all give support, little or great, according to their powers and possessions.[19]

Clearly, many patricians thought the war should be paid for by the *Primi,* possibly because they were held responsible for Venice's misfortunes. In fact, some rich patricians, such as Alvise Pisani, were generous with their wealth, although most were not. The Grimani brothers, whom Sanuto calls "very rich," were typical: When Loredan made an appeal for loans a year after Agnadello, Marino advanced 13 ducats; Francesco, 10. The Ten declared that the avarice of wealthy

17 On the money owed: Priuli, vol. 6, fol. 563r; cf. ASV, Senato, Secreto, Reg. 43, fol. 26r. On the legislation: Sanuto, 8:140-141, 143.
18 On July 8 and August 5: Sanuto, 8:497; 9:30.
19 On Priuli's statement: 4:201-202.

patricians indicated "slight affection and charity toward their country," and Sanuto wrote in August 1509 that "there are many rich men in the city but few wish to give money and aid the state because they have the example of the principal ones doing nothing."[20]

The widespread feeling that "the rich don't love their country and don't want to pay," the official commitment to equality within the patriciate, and above all, need for more money, compelled the government to take action against an open scandal, especially because wealthy patricians continued to slide into offices, sometimes bribing secretaries to list them as fully paid. In February 1511 another resolution to expel debtors from office passed the Great Council, but this time there was a pretence of acting against the *Primi*. Forty men, including such notables as Andrea Gritti, Tadeo Contarini, Paolo Capello, and Giorgio Emo, were presumably expelled from the Senate, although in fact they probably paid a nominal portion of their debt and remained in the assembly. Although Marino Morosini and Domenico Malipiero were among twenty-five members of the Senate named as debtors in August 1512, they still held their seats shortly after; Luca Zen, a procurator, appeared on expulsion lists no less than four times. The reading of debtors lists in the councils eventually became tiresome, and perhaps a bit embarrassing, so in November 1512 the government decided that patricians could not attend unless they had a certificate issued by various financial offices attesting that they had paid their debts to the state. This procedure most likely eased rich patricians around the law, because the secretaries charged with issuing certificates were always eager to please important men.[21]

Complaints about debtors in office continued, as did threats to expel them. A ruling that all who held office without paying their debt would be liable to a 500-ducat penalty only insured that office-holding debtors would simply ignore an increased debt. When the Rialto fire of January 1514 destroyed tax records, Sanuto lamented that "it was very damaging to the Republic, for the debtors were a well of gold."[22] In truth, that well provided scant relief. The attempts of the govern-

---

20 On the Grimani: Sanuto, 10:384. On the Ten: ASV, Consiglio di Dieci, Parti Miste, Reg. 33, fols. 23r; cf. fol. 45v. On August 1509: Sanuto, 9:14–15; cf. Michiel, fol. 451r.

21 On "the rich don't love their country": Sanuto, 10:322. On the supposed expulsions: Sanuto, 11:754, 788–789; 14:639, 640; 15:125, 158, 330. On the certificate: Sanuto, 15:330, 335. On the secretaries: cf. Priuli, 4:409.

22 On the penalty: Sanuto, 14:65–66. On the "well of gold": Sanuto, 17:464.

ment to extract money owed it by *ricchi* foundered on the fundamental obstacle that those in charge of collecting debts were indistinguishable as a group from rich debtors. It was in the self-interest of the men on the executive councils not to hound the rich for payment, for not only were they usually friends and relatives, they might soon be seated on the Collegio or the Ten, ready to extend similar leniency and consideration to colleagues temporarily out of office.

In 1515 Sanuto notes that, "the debtors do not pay. Those on the Council of Ten will sell anything in order to get money. These are tight times, money doesn't flow—yet it is necessary to send it to the field . . . thus everything is done for money." Finally, the government was driven to the desperate and humiliating expedient of raising money by auctioning its own offices for low-interest loans. The state became an object of commerce. Such a measure was fundamentally repugnant to Venetian political values, which regarded government office as a sacred and selfless responsibility, distant from family loyalties, personal ambition, and financial gain. No doubt because of this, the outright sale of patrician offices never took place, and some competition was retained in elections, not only between those offering money but between the latter and those not wealthy enough to afford loans. In some respects, the "office loans" (*imprestiti di onori*) were an ideal means of raising money, for they loosened the purse strings of wealthy patricians and could be resorted to on a continuing basis as well as when special needs arose. For instance on May 7, 1516, the Signoria determined that expenses for the immediate future would require between 80,000 and 100,000 ducats. The doge convened the Senate, which decided to create procurators for advancement of loans. Within two weeks, 20,000 ducats had been raised with the elections of Alvise Pisani and Giorgio Emo and dispatched to Venetian forces, which regained Brescia a few days later.[23]

It is testimony to the self-confidence of patricians that they should so avidly seek offices in their bankrupt and defeated state. Perhaps it is also evidence of their need and cupidity. Although salaries for many offices were eliminated in April 1509, holding a post still offered numerous opportunities for a patrician to exact money from those in need of his services. In addition, many places in government, such as

23 On debtors not paying: Sanuto, 20:446. On the sale of nonpatrician offices: R. Mousnier, "Le trafic des offices à Venise"; cf. Antonio Stella, "Grazie, pensioni ed elemosine sotto la Repubblica veneta." On 1516: Sanuto, 22:214, 215, 223, 229, 241, 248–250.

seats in the Senate, were desirable because of their prestige, influence, and access to affairs of state.

There was a tremendous demand for offices during the War of the League of Cambrai, partly because the conflict itself eliminated or diminished alternative sources of income. The four sons of Andrea Barbarigo made a living from office holding when the war disrupted their mainland properties and bond payments. Also, about 120 mainland officials of all ranks from *podestà* to castle keeper fled to Venice as the armies of the league entered Lombardy and the Veneto. They were a substantial addition to the number of men in the Great Council whose entire livelihood lay in state service and whose plight was captured in doggerel verse in June 1509: "Today the Council, tomorrow the Senate: but offices no more they create." True, the *terraferma* offices were gone, but positions in Venice and the overseas colonies remained, the latter more than ever sought after because they offered a relatively inexpensive life and opportunities for trade.[24]

Competition for office was made more intense by the size of the patriciate assembling in the Great Council. Based on the number of patricians present during elections for procurator, the Great Council was larger in the early Cinquecento than at any other time in its history. By these calculations, the largest assemblies in the 1480s numbered about one thousand; in the first decades of the sixteenth century, about sixteen hundred; by mid-century they were down to fourteen hundred; by 1600 the average was twelve hundred; and by the 1620s the level of the 1480s had been reached once again. In 1488 the chiefs of the Forty argued that the rising number of patricians warranted the creation of a new office, treasurer at Ravenna. The late 1480s also saw the appearance of the first *Calza* ("Stocking") company, fraternal orders of young patricians meeting for parties and social activities; most of these societies were formed between 1507 and 1533. In short, the ruling class was in the midst of its greatest expansion at precisely the time that war was forcing more patricians into office seeking. Young men who would otherwise have gone on galley voyages or entered business in the city or abroad instead entered the Great Council to gain a sinecure. Moreover, in July 1514 the Ten began a policy of admitting men of less than twenty-five years of age into the Great Council in return for 100 ducats each. In all, somewhat more than

---

24 On the Barbarigo: Lane, *Andrea Barbarigo*, p. 39. On the mainland officials: Sanuto, 8:469–472; cf. 13:58–59; Priuli, 4:92. On the doggerel: Sanuto, 8:445–446. On overseas posts: Priuli, 4:200–201.

three hundred underage patricians bought their way into the assembly during the war, increasing the number in the chamber so much that an additional bench was required. It was, however, quickly removed when patricians disdained to sit at what was evidently regarded as a spot for the youngsters.[25]

Loss of the *terraferma*, decline of trade, suspension of Monte payments, increase in taxation, and growth of the Great Council all worked to create a patriciate hungry for office. Even so, the office loans did not dominate the Great Council until the late summer of 1515, when Venice needed funds to aid Francis I's invasion of Italy. Movement toward office loans was halting and confused, although the notion of advancing money for offices appeared early in the war. In March 1510 the Ten and its *zonta* declared that they would admit ten men above the age of thirty to the Senate for 2,000 ducats each. After promising the required sum, the patrician was admitted to the Senate if he gained at least one-half the vote of the Ten and its *zonta*. By the middle of April, seven patricians had bought their way into the Senate, and the government was 14,000 ducats richer. Men entered the Senate in this fashion throughout the war, although the Ten did not assume authority to elect all offices in return for money. Sometimes the Ten and its *zonta* would show appreciation for a loan by co-opting the lender. For example, in February 1512 Francesco di Filippo Foscari and Alvise Pisani loaned 1,000 ducats, and shortly after they were voted onto the *zonta* to reward their generosity. Similarly, a month before, Alvise Capello and Girolamo Basadona were elected to high office in the Great Council because they loaned money to the state. In these cases, patricians were rewarded for their contributions, but they had not placed bids for the places they won.[26]

For a long time, service in Venice's defense was a principal means

---

25 Giannantonio Muazzo, "Del Governo Antico della repubblica veneta, delle alterazioni, e regolazioni d'esso, e delle cause, e tempi, che sono successe fino ai nostri giorni," cc. 90–91. On the size of the patriciate: James Cushman Davis, *The Decline of the Venetian Nobility as a Ruling Class*, pp. 54–56. On the Ravenna post: ASV, Maggior Consiglio, Deliberazioni, Liber Stella, Reg. 24, fols. 88v; cf. fols. 125r–125v. On the *Calze* companies: Lionello Venturi, "Le Compagnie della Calza (sec. XV–XVI)." On admitting young men: Sanuto, 18:335–336, 349, 363, 366–367, 377, 387–388, 417, 457, 460; 19:22, 68–70; 20:95, 287, 370; 21:349; ASV, Consiglio di Dieci, Parti Miste, Reg. 37, fols. 44v, 97r. On the bench: Sanuto, 19:419; 20:53, 136; cf. Michiel, fol. 151r.

26 Sanuto, 10:44, 150; 13:415, 461; 14:417; cf. ASV, Consiglio di Dieci, Parti Miste, Reg. 33, fol. 137v; Felix Gilbert, "Venice in the Crisis," p. 285.

of obtaining office, a notion that first appeared in August 1511 when the Senate passed a proposal giving a state debtor entrance to the *Quarantie* in return for two months' service of the debtor and of five men paid by him. The Great Council passed the motion by 465 to 355, indicating substantial discontent over the measure, probably because the assembly's electoral prerogatives were being usurped. The *Quarantie* had already been affected by the war, for in August 1509 the *civile nuova*, the supreme appeals court for cases outside the city, was suspended because the mainland was lost. Poor patricians thereby lost forty positions that brought in a meager income. The August 1511 proposal meant that more seats on the courts would be taken by those who could afford the approximately 200 ducats it cost to subsidize a troop of five men for two months. Many patricians also feared that especially young and inexperienced men would enter the *Quarantie* and eventually, when they entered the Forty, the Senate. Whatever the opposition, ninety-three patricians wanted to serve—most at Treviso for greater safety—and thirty-six were elected by the Great Council. In November these men entered the *Quarantia civile vecchia*; but eight months later when they moved on to the Forty and the Senate, the Signoria tried to exclude them from the latter on the grounds that they were debtors, an argument the ducal council lost because a condition of the judges' service was that debtorship would not be a disqualification for office.[27]

The Signoria's ingratitude was of a piece with the Great Council's resentment toward those wealthy enough to serve Venice with men and money. Patricians who had served at Padua and Treviso during the dangerous summer of 1513 were not elected to the Zonta. In August of that year some were nominated for the *civile vecchia* but failed to win election. Sanuto believed that such defeats would discourage those able to serve the Republic. He had served at Padua in the autumn of 1513, paying for five men and a horse, but in December he was defeated in election by Giovanni Ferro, a rich patrician who had loaned nothing. "Such is the justice of this city," he says, "that he who does more is crazy. And many are displeased with this wrong done to me." From December, men who had served at Padua or Treviso, even those with substantial outlays for troops of twenty-to-sixty men, had an increasingly difficult time winning election. A year later the Signoria called for patricians to serve at Padua and few volunteered.

27 Sanuto, 9:69; 12:345, 350, 350–352, 381–384; 13:193; 14:518; Priuli, vol. 6, fols. 345r, 345v–346r.

Sanuto mentions, with some satisfaction, that "men of account" could not be found to serve.[28]

In October 1513 Alvise di Pietro Priuli, a *savio di terraferma*, suggested that those who intended to serve at Padua should be voted into an office and then enter the army; he evidently combined this with recommendation that the doge instruct each administrative bureau of the city to dispatch one of their officials for twenty days or pay a substitute to serve. The idea was not taken up, although Priuli presented it again in December after the electoral defeat of returned volunteers, this time warning that, if it were not acted on, "rich men will be able to take all the offices, including the Senate and *zonta* [of the Ten]." His proposal was rejected again, although the Senate passed another that provided for the election of fifteen patricians to serve at Padua for ten ducats a month.[29]

A far more radical notion was put forth by Pietro Tron, a *savio di terraferma*, in May 1515. Tron wanted the government to establish a patrician militia, composed of fifty to one hundred young men under thirty years of age, elected by the Senate, and receiving a salary of 10 ducats a month. It was to be a permanent institution, maintained in peace as well as war, giving young patricians the sort of experience in land warfare that the galleys had always provided for the sea. Moreover, Tron argued, the militia would inculcate that military *virtù* without which republics could not survive and expand. In all, a solution to Venice's problems with which Machiavelli would have been in full accord. Tron was supported by the chiefs of the Forty and by Captain General Bartolomeo Alviano; but his fellow *savi*, conjuring up the specter of Julius Caesar subverting the Roman Republic, argued that Venice's founders had wisely refrained from turning patricians into warriors. As with many divisive proposals, Tron's was not permitted to come to a vote. The *Primi* decided to stay with the status quo, with all its known defects, rather than venture into unknown and possibly dangerous territory.[30]

---

28 On the Zonta and *civile vecchia* elections: Michiel, fol. 89v; Sanuto, 16: 604; cf. 492. On Sanuto's statement: 17:357; 25–27; 19:239. On December and after: Sanuto, 17:372, 398, 483; 18:437–438; 19:75, 360; 20:219. On the Signoria's appeal: Sanuto, 19:239.

29 Sanuto, 17:208; 212, 220, 228, 240, 384–385.

30 On the Ten's proposal: Sanuto, 20:185, 190–191; Michiel, fol. 167r; Priuli, vol. 5, fol. 94r. On Machiavelli's criticism of Venetian military organization: Nicolò Machiavelli, *Il Principe*, chap. 12; idem, *Discorsi*, in *Machiavelli*, 2:30; 3:31.

Patricians who could not win election in the Great Council continued to enter the Senate by giving money to the Ten; about forty
patricians a year were involved in these transactions. The number
willing to advance money or service for a seat on the supreme courts
declined when election did not follow the sacrifice. Spirits were low
and purses tight when Doge Loredan appealed to the men of the
Senate for general loans on August 2, 1515. Giorgio Corner gave 400
ducats and Alvise Pisani, 300; but many rich men gave nothing, while
some did not even attend the assembly when they heard rumors of the
new appeal. Sanuto thought it shameful that the wealthy Luca Vendramin advanced nothing and that the bankers Antonio and Silvano
Capello loaned a mere 100 ducats. The doge's appeal netted only
4,102 ducats.[31]

It was a crucial moment for Venice to run short of money. The
army under Alviano was dangerously isolated in Vicenza, awaiting the
arrival of France's army from across the Alps to attack Milan and aid
Venice. Alviano warned on July 3 that, if money were not sent, his
army would dissolve before the French arrived. On the sixteenth, a
letter arrived from Francis I promising to restore the Venetian state
within six months, and on August 11 word came that he had passed
the mountains and was in Italy. In this atmosphere of crisis, the loans
for office began on August 12 on the basis of legislation passed in the
previous two weeks. In little more than a week, Alviano received the
needed money and moved his forces toward Milan, which France
captured on September 1. On September 15, French and Venetian
forces decisively defeated the Swiss, allies of Spain and Leo X, at the
battle of Marignano. Alviano was killed in the battle, and Francis I
credited him and Venice with the great victory. Venice's need for
money remained pressing, but the end of the war was at last in sight.[32]

Loans for office threw the Great Council into disarray. Age, reputation, and service to the state meant nothing in the elections. Only
those who gave loans obtained office; and unlike the previous general
loans, these were conditional on receiving election to a particular posi-

31 On patricians in the Senate: cf. ASV, Consiglio di Dieci, Parti Miste, Reg.
33, fols. 137v–139r. On Loredan's appeal: Sanuto, 20:451; ASV, Senato, Terra,
Reg. 19, fols. 36r–36v.

32 On Alviano and the French: Sanuto, 20:216, 248, 312, 321, 354, 364-365, 388,
400, 454, 491, 493, 500. On August 12: Sanuto, 20:498; cf. Consegi, 8895, fols.
229r–235r; Cozzi, "Authority and the Law," p. 314. On Marignano: Sanuto, 20:
112, 116–117; cf. Emil Usteri, *Marignano*.

tion. Many *vecchi*, long accustomed to sitting in the executive councils, found themselves ignored because they did not advance money. Sebastiano Foscarini, a well-known student of philosophy, failed to win entrance to the Senate, "and the Great Council laughed uproariously, as if to say that not philosophy but money is necessary." Bernardo Tagliapietra had spent more than two years in French prison, and normally the Great Council would have acknowledged his suffering with the award of an office; but he too was rejected for not offering a loan. Giacomo Soranzo objected to the auctioning of offices, so the Great Council defeated his son, who had presented 600 ducats to enter the Senate. According to Michiel, the chamber of the Great Council was a scene of bedlam on August 24, the very day on which money was hurriedly dispatched to Alviano:

> By the end of the day 47,000 ducats had been raised, though with the greatest shame and disrepute for the Great Council. When the nominators were sequestered, those who knew or thought that they would be chosen [by them] immediately ran to the tribunal [of the Signoria] to offer money; and when their competitors outbid them, they would turn back to add on more by yelling, as is done at auctions. Those in the Great Council crowded in front [of the hall] to see and hear better, so that there wasn't a bit of order. Also, those on the bench [of the Signoria] received information from the nominators, and learning of some rich man who would be nominated, they sent for him to come to the Great Council in order to have him make an offer and be elected.

Turmoil in the Great Council was almost matched by that at the Rialto as patricians rushed to raise money for office loans by selling their Monte Novissimo bonds, although so many were put on the market at once that their value rapidly fell.[33]

Two problems soon arose with the office loans: It proved difficult to collect the money promised, and the Great Council's resentment over the innovation led to electoral defeats for lenders after the excitement of August and September had died away. Patricians loaning money were supposed to pay the amount promised within three days of election, but many lenders evaded the regulation. By September 1, 78,000 ducats were pledged, and only 20,000 had been collected, despite grumbling in the Great Council and threats by the Signoria.

---

[33] On those defeated: Sanuto, 20:520–521. On August 24: Michiel, fol. 189r; Sanuto, 20:554; cf. 575. On the bonds: Michiel, fol. 189r; cf. Sanuto, 21:26.

On October 24, the Ten declared that anyone holding an office without having paid would be expelled from it if satisfaction were not made in three days; however when that limit expired, a new one of twenty-five days was set. On December 15 the deadline was eight days; then a ruling of the twenty-second set eight days for one-half of the outstanding debt and eight additional days for the rest.[34] Threats kept pace with new deadlines, and once more the government found itself caught on a treadmill, excoriating patricians for not paying debts while shunning actions necessary to collect them. In general, though, the office loans were successful in raising money, even if they also did much to swell the Signoria's book of state debtors.

Within a month after the beginning of the office loans, many patricians were boycotting the Great Council because those offering money were failing to win election, a development that threatened to dry up the new source of funds entirely. Office loans were disliked for a number of reasons. Patricians whose only source of influence was a vote in the Great Council disliked seeing its electorial authority circumvented by the combination of auction and election; their cooperation with the new procedures thus proved to be short-lived. A more qualified discontent was felt by those who disapproved of such important positions as the state attorneys and Salt Office going to the highest bidder. Naturally, wealthy patricians benefited most from the new procedure, while the numerous *poveri* in the sovereign assembly apparently retaliated by denying them their electoral bids. Youth was another characteristic of those who especially profited from the office loans, so some patricians were rejected by those who believed that *giovani* should not take a shortcut to positions of authority and prestige. Finally, lenders were rejected simply because they offered too little. For example, Lorenzo Capello was elected to the Senate without a loan because his opponents pledged only 100 ducats each; this was the Great Council's way of saying that seats in the governing council should not go cheaply.[35]

Still, despite defaulting officeholders and an obstinate patriciate, office loans brought in much-needed revenue. By June 1516 more than 300,000 ducats had been collected, with the most lucrative sales being for the post of procurator. The first vacancy in the Procuratia after

34 Sanuto, 21:25–26, 62, 70, 257, 387, 412, 493, 521–522; cf. ASV, Consiglio di Dieci, Parti Miste, Reg. 39, fols. 32v, 37r, 56r, 58r.
35 Sanuto, 20:554; 21:58–59; 22:27, 581; 23:245, 269, 317; Michiel, fols. 193r, 207r.

office loans began opened when Luca Zen died in April 1516; two thousand patricians crowded the Great Council hall and voted in Zaccaria Gabriel for a pledge of 8,000 ducats. Soon a proposal to elect more procurators without waiting for vacancies passed the Senate; seven procurators were duly elected and the state was 75,000 ducats richer.[36]

Although office loans permitted a patrician to declare ambition for positions and to offer payment for election, the government never went so far as to eliminate competition or to circumvent entirely the nominating procedures. In September 1516 Alvise Barbaro, a chief of the Forty, presented a proposal in the Senate aimed at expediting the election of lenders to office. He proposed replacing the Senate's *scrutinio* nomination to the Great Council with nomination of the individual who offered the largest loan. Sanuto successfully opposed the motion on the grounds that it wholly abandoned the principle of electing the best man to office and that it destroyed the possibility of those without money gaining victory.[37] In defeating this and like proposals, the *Primi* stopped short, in the name of traditional values, of outright sale of offices. The mingling of auction and election was inefficient and clumsy, but it had the virtues of preventing rich men from completely dominating elections and of preserving some of the Great Council's electoral power.

Nonetheless, the adoption of loans for office led to far more than grousing about the power of money and affronts to tradition. It had an unintended, indeed unforeseeable, effect on Venetian politics, reshaping relationships between the key councils of state, as well as the patriciate's perception of the constitution. Long after the consequences of Agnadello were seemingly overcome, the emergency measures of war continued silently to condition modes of political behavior. In the end, it proved easier to reconstitute the mainland empire than to erase the imprint left on the Republic's politics by the means used to rescue the state.

2. *Offices and Power, 1509–1517*

In 1493 Sanuto confidently stated that the Senate is "the council which governs our state," but in the midst of the War of the League

---

36 On the amount collected: Sanuto, 22:277–278. On the procurators: Sanuto, 22:166, 169–171, 172, 198, 214, 215, 220, 227–228, 237, 277–278.
37 Sanuto, 22:562.

of Cambrai, he asserted that the Council of Ten "governs our state in these times because all affairs of state are dealt with in that council." Writing around 1524, Contarini also considered that the extension of the Ten's authority was a significant development of recent years.[38] The origins of this shift of power are to be found in the loans for office because the entrance of patricians "by force of money" into the Great Council and Senate altered the balance of the councils, draining authority and influence from the larger and more representative assemblies into smaller, more exclusive executive committees.

Tensions that existed between the principal councils were increased when *giovani*—"born and bred," Priuli accuses, "in the shadow of so opulent a state"—entered the Great Council and Senate. According to the *Primi*, underage patricians brought considerable disorder and electoral corruption to the sovereign assembly. Priuli refers to "the power of the youngsters" in the Great Council; Sanuto complains that, when young men are admitted, "The law is broken, and everything goes topsy-turvy." When two hundred *giovani* were allowed into the Great Council in the late seventeenth century, an observer lamented that bringing them "from the schoolroom to the Great Council" to vote for the Ten and the Senate had broken Venice into three parts: "youth without discretion, nobles without quality, and a nation in degeneracy." More than a century earlier, the reaction was similar. For example, Sanuto refers to "the great confusion" in the voting of the Great Council as *giovani* unjustly defeated good men. One wealthy youth, Giovanni di Giorgio Emo, won the post of treasurer by having two hundred patricians lobby for him in August 1515; a year later he had to flee the city when it was reavealed that he was using official funds to buy votes. Two months later Giacomo di Giorgio Corner aroused the ire of the doge and state attorneys because of the multitude of youngsters following him about and creating disturbance in the Great Council. In both the Great Council and the Senate, young men showed a certain amount of unity, voting for their contemporaries and rejecting hitherto revered elders. But as in the streets of the city, violence, too, sometimes flared up in the hall of the Great Council; the Ten had to issue new laws against carrying weapons into the Ducal Palace.[39]

---

38 Sanuto, *Cronachetta*, p. 102, n. 1; Contarini, *Republica*, p. 89.

39 On the "opulent" state: Priuli, 4:141. On the "power of the youngsters": Priuli, vol. 5, fol. 86v. On "the law is broken": Sanuto, 19:323. On the late seventeenth century: Francesco della Torre, "Relazione della Serenissima Repub-

Appalled by the disorder they saw and resentful of the power of the *giovani*, *Primi* were always ready with an excuse to withdraw the right of electing certain offices into the Senate and the Ten, a tactic made easier by the war because commanders in the field were empowered to appoint administrators to the areas they recaptured, although this was a prerogative that worked against the electoral authority of the Senate as well as against that of the Great Council. As a result, in September 1510, the Senate passed a resolution reiterating laws of 1497 and 1505 that declared that all appointments made by the Collegio, the Signoria and the field commanders were annulled and that the Great Council alone could elect *terraferma* offices. In June 1514 some *savi* who consistently defended the rights of the Great Council—Luca Tron, Giovanni Trevisan, Antonio Condulmer, and Gasparo Malipiero—narrowly succeeded in winning Senate approval for a motion that suspended all *scrutinio* nominations by the Senate to the Great Council, except for the posts of captain general, fleet commander, and councillor. This was a significant measure because the Great Council's constitutional monopoly of elections had much greater practical effect once the Senate ceased having a voice in nominations to a whole range of offices. Yet a series of exemptions to the law in subsequent years proved that the Great Council could never relax its vigilance against the encroachments of the Senate, as when a Senate motion of October 1529 called for a *scrutinio* election for an important post in Dalmatia. But the Great Council, although occasionally willing to make exceptions to its own laws, refused to let the Senate have a free hand, even during the height of the office loans. In November 1516 the Signoria proferred a motion to the Great Council in which, pleading urgent need for money and time lost in elections, it suggested that the Senate temporarily be allowed to make all necessary elections; the Great Council rejected the proposal, evidently preferring to reserve to itself the right of auctioning government positions.[40]

---

blica di Venezia," c. 27. On "the great confusion": Sanuto, 20:126. On Emo: Sanuto, 20:469; 23:87. On Corner: Sanuto, 21:215; cf. Michiel, fol. 202v. On rejecting elders: Sanuto, 18:328, 385, 417, 418, 453, 469; Priuli, vol. 7, fol. 110r. On weapons: Sanuto, 19:396; cf. 354, 380; 20:219, 361.

40 On appointments by commanders: ASV, Consiglio di Dieci, Parti Miste, Reg. 39, fols. 18v–19r; Maggior Consiglio, Deliberazioni, Liber Deda, Reg. 25, fols. 55r, 58v; cf. Sanuto, 9:405. On June 1514: Sanuto, 18:291, 305; cf. Malipiero, 2:706; ASV, Maggior Consiglio, Deliberazioni, Liber Deda, Reg. 25, fols. 96r; Chapter IV.3 of this book. On November 1516: Sanuto, 23:146. On Collegio usurpation of Senate appointments: ASV, Senato, Terra, Reg. 19, fols. 120r–120v.

Offices that properly belonged to the Great Council were also filled by the Ten. The post of galley commander was sold by the Ten for 1,500 ducats, a controversial measure that, however, brought in more than 60,000 ducats.[41] Still, the Ten's major contribution to diminishing the Great Council's electoral authority was its policy of allowing entrance to the Senate for money, a practice begun very early in the war. The crucial nexus between the Great Council and the Senate was severely strained by every patrician who paid to enter the latter, whether as a regular senator or as a member of the Zonta or Forty; every man sitting for payment lowered the prestige and influence of the Great Council by making it likely that the Senate would be less representative of and responsive to the patriciate as a whole. Thus, admitting men to the supreme courts for service or payment meant the substitution of rich for poor, contributing to a more homogeneous Senate at the expense of one somewhat attentive to the needs and wishes of indigent patricians. Placing rich men in the Forty had the effect of demolishing the bridge between Great Council and Senate.

Whereas the Great Council could retaliate against the Senate's threat to its power by periodically reasserting its electoral authority, the Senate was· usually reduced to impotency when the Ten or the Collegio declined to bring state business before it, a policy whose roots lay in men entering the Senate for money. Since 1510 patricians had been entering the Senate by advancing loans or serving in the army, and from that time the executive councils began pushing the hitherto governing council from the center of crucial affairs. In part, that policy was due to need for close consultation and rapid decision during Venice's crisis; prolonged debate among more than one hundred men was not the way to run a war. But Venice had been at war before with the Senate holding center stage. For the *Primi* the new consideration was the danger of sharing decisions and state secrets with those they considered immature, unreliable, inexperienced, and dissolute— traits expected in those who must purchase their way to power rather than earn it by lengthy, disciplined service.

Ironically, expenditure for a place in the Senate resulted in a decrease in the value of its acquisition insofar as it led to a withdrawal of significant business from that assembly. On December 6, 1512, Vittore Morosini objected to the Collegio ordering troop movements without consulting the Senate, an aspect of Sanuto's complaint that

---

41 Priuli, vol. 5, fols. 93r–94v; Sanuto, 10:23; Michiel, fol. 105v.

"there is little discussion in the Senate now." Morosini's protest evidently had some effect because the subject was discussed in the Senate five days later, in a debate that ended with the Collegio's proposal being turned down.[42] On the same day, the Ten did not risk discussing a treaty with France in the Senate owing to "the great multitude" in attendance there.

When the Ten allowed another patrician into the Senate on October 18, 1513, Sanuto thought it appropriate to remark that "in every regard few things of importance are dealt with in the Senate." Four days later Sanuto indicates that there were also policy differences between the executive councils and the Senate. The latter was excluded from considering Leo X's request that Venice concede Verona to Maximilian:

> Nothing is done in the Senate; all is dealt with in the Ten. Every morning the chiefs of the Ten gather with the Collegio. . . ; it is said that they deal with the matter of peace [urged] by Rome. The Collegio does not wish to come to the Senate with [a proposal for] writing to Rome because the Senate wishes to get out of the war and abandon Verona to the emperor in order to avoid something worse.

The pope most likely did not long remain ignorant of the support for his position; it was generally said that everything done in the Senate was immediately known to the papal ambassador in Venice because "there is now such a very great number in the Senate." A letter to Rome in January 1514 was composed in the secrecy of the Ten, because "at present the Senate does nothing of significance: everything is dealt with in the Ten, [working] with its *zonta*." All matters regarding France and Rome were treated in the chambers of the Ten "where they can be held secret, because everyone soon learns what the Senate does."[43]

Opening wide the gates of the Senate with the inauguration of straightforward office loans in August 1515 confirmed and reinforced the executive councils in their policy of secrecy and exclusion. An immediate result of office loans in the autumn of 1515 was an unprecedented turnover of membership in the Senate. Forty-six new

42 On December 1512: Sanuto, 15:374, 391.
43 On October 1513: Sanuto, 17:217; 228. On the "great number" in the Senate: Sanuto, 17:262; 265. On January 1514: Sanuto, 17:440; 228. On France and Rome: Sanuto, 20:228.

men, most of them relatively young and inexperienced, entered as
senators, while twenty-four were elected to the Zonta; of course, the
Forty already had its share of such patricians, for the court had been
opened for payment for some time. Usually the Senate had a maximum
of 150 patricians in attendance, but 230 came on September 29, many
to vote their friends onto the Collegio, which, however, continued to
be composed of veterans like Alvise Pisani, Pietro Capello, and
Cristoforo Moro. Not only did the *giovani* elect their favorites to
the Collegio, they placed their own in offices previously closed to
them, such as treasurer in Venice and lord of the Arsenal. In the
latter case, the Collegio and Ten created their own post of commissioner of the Arsenal, who became the effective head of the shipworks
during the war, leaving the young lord of the Arsenal with a fancy
title and little authority.[44]

Complain as they might, *li antiqui senatori* were outnumbered in
the Senate, which was partly their own fault because they disdained
to compete with and offer loans against the *giovani*. Unless they had
access to meetings of the Ten, the veterans of government were frozen
out of vital matters as the Senate was reduced to "doings of little importance, some lobbying, taxes, and listening to letters which produce
melancholy." "Those of the Senate," says Sanuto, "who don't enter
the Council of Ten, complain greatly that the government of this city
has been reduced to a few, only to those thirty-three who now vote
[on the Ten and its *zonta*], an exceedingly dismal affair and one unusual in this Republic."[45] The rare occasion when the Collegio or Ten
was forced to present matters to the Senate, as with the debate over
troop movements in 1512, often resulted in humiliating defeats for the
executive councils, thereby further confirming their intention of keeping important business from an increasingly resentful and antagonistic
assembly.

The changed composition of the Senate made the Collegio and the
Ten natural allies; the *Primi* in both executive committees were old,
experienced, and contemptuous of the youngsters crowding the Senate.
Not only did the daily business of the two committees during the war
give them common concerns; the Collegio needed the Ten to protect
its growing autonomy because it was, after all, constitutionally a

44 On new men in the Senate: Sanuto, 21:157, 158–159, 191, 192–193, 198. On
September 29: Sanuto, 21:156–157. On the Arsenal: Sanuto, *Cronachetta*, p. 120,
n. 2; cf. 15:484; 17:389.
45 Sanuto, 19:23; 315; cf. 30:229; Malipiero, 1:492.

creature of the Senate. Once the Collegio began referring matters to the Ten, the latter could assert that state security precluded the Senate's interference with its own steering committee. Usually collaboration between the Collegio and the Ten was out of public view, with the chiefs of the Ten spending hours closeted with the *savi grandi* or *savi di terraferma*; but sometimes the alliance and its implications were driven home to the Senate. For example, in November 1516 a motion was proposed in the Senate to annul all appointments and salaries established by the Collegio without the assent of the Senate. This was essentially a repetition of one passed in September 1510 in which the Great Council's right to elect *terraferma* officials was reaffirmed, clear evidence that the Collegio was negligent of laws restricting its authority. The first vote was inconclusive, and before a second could be taken, the chiefs of the Ten stepped in and prohibited further action on the ground that, because the Ten had participated in the Collegio's actions, the Senate had no authority to reverse its own elected officials.[46]

Special commissions or *zonte* facilitated the hold of the Collegio and the Ten over state policy. The *Primi* often had recourse to such commissions on especially important decisions, such as the execution of Falier in 1355 and the deposition of Foscari in 1457. Indeed, until the early Quattrocento, the Senate itself was merely an elaborate group of *zonte* meeting with the Forty and designated magistrates. In general, the patriciate looked with disfavor on the use of *zonte* because they were essentially constitutional shortcuts, a means of spreading responsibility and insuring continuity of control without the restrictions attaching to magistracies. Because the *zonte* were not properly offices, their members could be elected or appointed without having to undergo a period of *contumacia*, a length of time, usually equal in length to the term of office, in which reelection to an office was prohibited. Hence, whereas a member of the Ten had to wait a year before being eligible to that council again, a patrician on the Ten's *zonta* could stay on it indefinitely. Until 1529 the *zonta* of the Ten was simply co-opted, a procedure making it easy for that council to enlist *Primi* who were temporarily out of high office.[47]

46 Sanuto, 23:179; 250–252.

47 Sanuto, *Cronachetta*, p. 162; Giuseppe Maranini, *La costituzione di Venezia dopo la serrata del Maggior Consiglio*, pp. 139–142; cf. Giovanni Antonio Venier, "Storia delle Rivoluzioni Seguite nel Governo della Republica di Venezia e della Istituzione dell'Eccelso Consiglio di X sino alla sua Regolazione," c. 46.

The Collegio's *zonta* depended on the pleasure of the Senate, so it was an occasional instrument, normally involving no more than three or four men who served for three months (one-half the term of regular *savi*) at a time. The Collegio generally had recourse to *savi di zonta* when the Senate failed to elect *savi grandi*, a not infrequent occurrence during the war, when relations between Senate and Collegio were tense. *Savi di zonta* were elected for the first time on December 28, 1509, one week after a military defeat for which the Collegio was held partially responsible. After the Senate twice failed to elect three *savi grandi*, the Collegio proposed the creation of three special *savi*; those subsequently elected were just finishing terms as *savi grandi*. It seems likely that the Senate was willing to elect the same men it held responsible for errors because of a desire to maintain continuity of leadership in a time of crisis, hoping at the same time to keep the Collegio on a tighter leash by electing men to terms of office one-half the usual length. The Collegio's *zonta* was put under even more stringent controls in May 1515, when the Senate voted to impose a *contumacia* of three months on the *savi di zonta*. This set up a system of rotation in which *Primi* would serve three months as *savi di zonta*, followed by a break of three months or, more likely, election to the Signoria, the Ten, or the *zonta* of the Ten.[48]

Although *savi* were almost invariably elected from the membership of the Senate, legally any patrician was eligible. Perhaps because of this, it was decided in 1528 that the creation of extraordinary *savi* required prior approval by the Great Council. But when the Signoria proposed the election of *savi di zonta* in March 1529, Bartolomeo Pisani argued that such positions worked to place some *Primi* "in the Collegio perpetually," and the proposal was rejected.[49] No less than in the Senate, occasional majorities in the Great Council thus expressed their suspicions regarding the possibilities inherent in the *zonta* for the creation of a permanent corps of men exercising executive power.

According to Sanuto, the Ten and its *zonta* ruled Venice during the War of the League of Cambrai. Indeed, it became very rare for the Ten to meet without its *zonta*, which was always drawn from among the *Primi*. Politicians who failed to win a place on the Collegio or the

---

48 On December 1509: Sanuto, 9:422. On the defeat: Finlay, "Venice, the Po Expedition." On May 1515: ASV, Senato, Terra, Reg. 19, fols. 17r–17v. On rotation: cf. ASV, Segretario alle voci, elezioni in Senato, Reg. 2, no. 16.

49 Sanuto, 50:89; 92, 247; cf. ASV, Senato, Terra, Reg. 25, fols. 49r, 121v, 130v; 131r, 158v; cf. Cozzi, "Authority and the Law," p. 333.

Ten could have access to power through the constitutional back door of the special commission. Election to the Collegio while a member of the Ten's *zonta* entailed no disqualification for either post, so the two executive councils were further welded together by overlapping memberships. Besides the regular *zonta* of the Ten, there was also a fifteen-man *zonta di danari* for financial matters, similarly co-opted by the Ten. From October 1511 the Ten only selected patricians from the Senate for the financial *zonta*, a policy that broke precedent and displeased some members of the Great Council, although the Ten's motive was probably to incorporate in the structure of the Ten any *Primi* left stranded in the Senate after the autumnal elections for the Collegio, the Signoria, and the Ten.[50]

The Ten and the Collegio assumed almost complete control over the government out of a desire for secrecy and a fear of *giovani* interference with policy. They were not motivated by a despotic spirit but by a traditional and powerful respect for age and order, values fundamental to the Venetian system and shared by the entire ruling class. According to the *Primi*, loans for office changed the very nature of the Senate, so they closed ranks about the select executive councils, co-opted patricians of like background and sentiment, and froze the Senate out of important matters. The executive councils possessed no corporate personality or institutional biases that impelled them to dominate the more representative councils, for such could hardly co-exist with the rapid rotation in office that characterized them. Members of the Ten were elected in August and September for one year; the three chiefs of the councils were selected by the Ten from among their number to serve as executives for one month at a time. Ducal councillors served for eight months and were elected in groups of two or three at various times of year, while the *savi* had six-month terms, with half of them being replaced every three months. The three chiefs of the Forty were in office for two months; and their close colleagues, the three state attorneys, were elected singly for sixteen-month terms at different times of year.

There were thirty-eight positions among the Ten, Collegio, Signoria, and state attorneys, but in any given month between forty-seven and fifty-seven individuals occupied those positions (a more precise estimate is not possible because it was common for a patrician to move from one position to another). Thus a *savio di terraferma* could stay

---

50 On the Ten ruling Venice: Sanuto, *Cronachetta*, p. 120, n. 1. On the *zonta di danari*: Sanuto, 13:11.

within the governing circle by winning election to the Signoria or the Ten or by appointment to the *zonta* of the latter. This lateral mobility was combined with a high turnover in the executive councils: Between 1501 and 1525, 25-to-30 percent of those elected to the Ten and the Signoria failed to complete their terms of office, mainly because of election to other positions or because the law regarding numbers of a clan on a council required resignation. In 1515/1516 the *zonta* of the Ten experienced a 46 percent turnover of its membership, with patricians leaving to take up positions as ambassadors or councillors. In the later Cinquecento, between forty and fifty men moved through the twenty-five places on the Ten (excluding the Signoria) and its *zonta* in the course of a year.[51] In short, a constant stream of patricians—always chosen from among the *Primi*—coursed through the executive councils, meeting one another coming and going, assuming various and overlapping responsibilities.

It would be inaccurate simply to say that the Council of Ten came to dominate Venice during the war; rather, the *Primi* as a group instinctively took refuge from a newly tumultuous Senate behind that executive council whose wide definition of competence made it virtually immune to scrutiny and censure. It may appear that the Collegio, which developed a more autonomous existence during the war, used the Ten more than it was used; but again, the Collegio was merely a device of the governing circle, drawn into the shadow of the Ten so that the *Primi* could more comfortably and privately gather together. The use of *zonte* by executive councils indicates that neither a small clique of men nor an ambitious committee had seized power, for the addition of special commissions to the Ten and the Collegio diffused authority more broadly within the governing circle, while still keeping it removed from the Senate and unaccountable to the Great Council.

It was in the nature of Venetian politics to abhor divisiveness and value consensus—a consideration that explains an otherwise odd phenomenon that occurred in the Council of Ten during and after the war. As the Ten extended its purview and, in a manner of speaking, drew power to itself, its meetings grew in size, with right of entrance to the council being given to the fifteen of the *zonta*, six *savi grandi*, five *savi di terraferma*, twenty-two procurators, three state attorneys,

---

51 On turnover between 1501 and 1525: Consegi, 8893-8897. On 1515/1516: ASV, Consiglio di Dieci, Parti Miste, Reg. 39, fols. 21r–21v; Reg. 40, fols. 116r–116v. On the later Cinquecento: M. J. C. Lowry, "The Reform of the Council of Ten, 1582–3," p. 287.

and three special *savi* for financial affairs. In 1523 some councillors suggested "returning the Council of Ten to that veneration it had before, since now it has grown to so great a number that seventy-one [patricians] enter the council."[52] The Ten, then, had become the congregation of trustworthy and prestigious politicians that the Senate was no longer seen to be; its total membership was exactly one-half the usual attendance of the Senate. In all likelihood, however, seventy-one patricians rarely if ever gathered together in the chambers of the Ten. Instead, the Ten acted as a sort of shuttle, moving back and forth among the *Primi*, weaving them into its deliberations as the occasion demanded and good politics suggested.

Given the nature and role of the Ten, no person or clique could manipulate it for personal advantage except in relatively trivial fashion. Of course, sometimes the aims of a faction coincided with those of the *Primi* as a whole, as when a Loredan on the Ten helped push through Foscari's deposition. More typical, however, was an episode in August 1501 when the Ten was seeking "a new means to rescue some who did not want to serve as ambassadors." The solution was found in an administrative shuffle whereby an office was created by the Ten, appointment to which allowed one to refuse other offices without a fine. Giorgio Emo, lately a member of the Ten, benefited from this arrangement by entering the new post and regretfully refusing election as ambassador to France. In 1511 relatives and friends of Andrea Gritti on the Ten were equally solicitous of his political well-being, writing him a letter extolling his service as general in order to boost his reputation and chances for high office. A more serious case of favoritism occurred in the same year when the Ten levied exceptionally lenient sentences on those friends and relatives of Alvise Soranzo who had helped Soranzo escape prison. Soranzo's father-in-law was Paolo Capello, "of important lineage and authority, not only in the city but in the Senate" and with close connections to many on the Ten. Such influence peddling was by no means peculiar to the Ten, but a seat on that council was no doubt a better place than most from which to dispense favors. Special favors, however, could be as easily withdrawn by the next group of men to enter the Ten, as outgoing members discovered in 1524 and 1567 when their successors revoked a series of grants made to importunate petitioners.[53]

52 Sanuto, 35:33; 35, 36.
53 On Emo: Sanuto, 4:90–91. On Gritti: Priuli, vol. 6, fol. 480r. On Soranzo: Priuli, vol. 6, fols. 64r–64v; 93r–94r. On 1524: ASV, Consiglio di Dieci, Parti

Michiel records a striking instance of an attempt to use the power of the Ten against political opponents. In July 1516, the Ten issued a declaration condemning the practice of sodomy among certain elderly Venetian patricians, which was posted at the Rialto, "with tremendous complaint by many, who said this is not a subject to publicize; there was great laughter, especially among foreigners." Sanuto confirms that the notice provoked consternation and hilarity, with foreigners "saying 'These old ones go at it!'—hence this news will travel to the whole world." If Michiel is right, however, the intention behind the Ten's action was hardly a matter for comedy:

> It is known for certain that this ill-considered declaration was produced for a special purpose: to punish or to damage the reputation of some important men because of the rivalry which exists among the members of the Ten and Collegio. These [men] are said to have this vice but otherwise are honest, very liberal in debate, and freely attack others, who, since they cannot find anything else against them, conceived this means to ruin them.

By any reckoning, this was a clumsy attempt at vengeance, relying more on the force of public embarrassment for the unnamed deviants than on actual entrapment. Not surprisingly, the elaborate snare only netted a judge of the Forty, who was duly tortured and eventually exiled for five years.[54] Oblique thrusts at enemies, political advertisement for friends, favors for well-wishers, perhaps some petty graft—these were the opportunities for personal aggrandizement offered by a place on the Ten, and only if one could obtain the agreement of a majority of the thirty other members on the council and *zonta*.

Collective action by the Ten and its *zonta* made opportunities for individual abuse of authority rare. The chiefs were in charge of the Ten's guards in the Ducal Palace, and they convened and set the agenda of the council. These responsibilities gave them a transitory precedence over their colleagues but no real chance for establishing policy or acting without approval of the council. In 1531 Giacomo di Giorgio Corner, a chief of the Ten, on his own authority released a man imprisoned in the Ducal Palace. Pietro Tron, another chief, and Doge Gritti were intent on punishment but did not want Corner to

---

Miste, Reg. 46, fols. 199r–200r. On 1567: ASV, Consiglio di Dieci, Parti Comune, Reg. 28, fol. 44r.

54 Michiel, fols. 255r; 256v; Sanuto, 22:386–387; 425, 430, 431, 445, 446; 23:338.

undergo formal trial for abuse of authority; Gasparo Contarini, assuming Corner's position as chief, argued strongly against punishment. Finally, the Ten fined Corner 1,500 ducats and deprived him of election to the Ten for two years, a sentence suggested by Corner's friends. The *Primi* looked after their own. Tron was praised by the *terra* for his perseverance in the matter; Corner was rejected for the Zonta by the Great Council three days after his deposition; and Gritti succeeded in removing an opponent from the key executive council.[55] Corner's removal, in fact, probably had more to do with political in-fighting among *Primi* than with abuse of power per se.

In 1505 when removal of another chief of the Ten was contemplated (and finally carried through), a patrician vigorously argued that "one who is among the seventeen pillars of this city" should not be so humiliated. In fact, the Ten was highly regarded as a defender of republican liberties and as a guardian against subversion and foreign threats. Contarini asserts that the office was modeled on such ancient magistracies as the ephors of Sparta, the sort of extraordinary officials all republics need in order to survive. In 1511 when the Ten suspended three state attorneys, the city disapproved, but for Sanuto the action was justified "because it is necessary to enforce that which is passed by the Ten, which is the rudder of the city." (Significantly, by 1520 he also considered the post of *savio grande* "the rudder of the state.") He clearly disapproved of the Ten's 1516 declaration against sodomy; yet he also comments—and almost certainly without sarcasm—that "since it is done by the most excellent Council of Ten, it is necessary to obey and praise it."[56]

High regard for the Ten clearly lessened as the council grew in size and influence, when it ceased being merely "seventeen pillars" and became instead an umbrella shielding seventy-one *Primi* as they decided in secret the affairs previously debated in the Senate. Priuli records that many came to regard the Ten as "the ruin of the Venetian Republic" because of its poor decisions, more often the product of lobbying than of careful, disinterested judgment. In 1515, the Ten, complaining that its reputation had been lowered by constant disputes

55 Sanuto, 54:616–617. On enmity between Gritti and Corner: cf. ASV, Consiglio di Dieci, Parti Secrete, Reg. 3, fols. 1r–1v.
56 On 1505: Sanuto, 6:113; cf. Domenico Morosini, *De bene istituta re publica*, p. 98; Cozzi, "Authority and Law," pp. 306–307. On Contarini: *Republica*, pp. 86–87. On 1511: Sanuto, 12:190. On the *savi grandi*: Sanuto, 28:508. On 1516: Sanuto, 22:386–387.

and confusions about its decisions, decided that all petitions to the council would require approval by two-thirds of the Ten and its *zonta*; if there ensued further confusion over the outcome of that vote, another vote, requiring a four-vote margin of victory, would be taken to determine the result of the first. Six months later this procedure was revoked for cases in which the Ten was collecting money owed the government. Having pushed the Senate from preeminence in the state, the Ten was suffering the consequences that inevitably attended the council at the center of Venetian government.[57]

The executive councils did not retreat from their new position of power in 1517 when the crisis came to an end. During the war the governing circle came to prefer its less troublesome mode of doing business; it was therefore reluctant to return significant power to the Senate. This attitude is related to the development during the war of a more united governing circle, socially homogeneous in character and institutionally gathered in autonomous executive councils.[58] Before the war the Senate had been, in effect, the meeting ground of the *Primi* and the forces of the Great Council. The composition of the Forty, constant electioneering for Senate seats, and the electoral significance of the Zonta made the Senate the irreplaceable forum for confrontation and negotiation between the governing circle and the mass of the patriciate. Loans for offices, while they left the constitution unaltered, transformed the political dynamics that had made the councils of state work together. The Great Council thereafter had less political impact on the Senate; the Senate's prerogatives of decision making and debate drained away as *giovani* entered the assembly; the Collegio and the Ten formed an alliance that became the effective governing council of the city and the rallying point for *Primi*, who no longer had to deal as much with those not their social and political equals. These changes were rooted in the government's policy of using offices as a source of revenue, and when that policy was abandoned, the changes themselves were not eradicated; the end of the war did not result in the recovery of the pre-Cambrai political milieu of Venice.

On January 15, 1517, Spanish forces left Verona as the French marched in; the imperial commissioner gave the keys of the city to

---

57 On the "ruin of the Venetian Republic": Priuli, vol. 6, fol. 208r. On 1515: ASV, Consiglio di Dieci, Parti Miste, Reg. 39, fols. 22r–22v, 87r; cf. Reg. 38, fols. 71r–71v.

58 On the new social exclusivity of the governing circle: cf. Gilbert, "Venice in the Crisis," p. 290; Cozzi, "Authority and the Law," pp. 334–335.

Lautrec, the French marshal, carefully watched by Andrea Gritti, who would later receive the tokens in his turn. The next day the Senate voted to end loans for office, a measure the Great Council overwhelmingly approved a few days later. After eight years of struggle and upheaval, says Sanuto, "for the good of everyone, the city began to breathe again." A spirit of release and celebration swept Venice, with constant parties and a bevy of marriages that had been postponed because of hard times. Plans were made to send off the Flanders galleys, and the market value of Monte bonds shot up. In the following months, the government rescinded special legislation enacted during the war, such as that admitting underage patricians to the Great Council and that suspending the *contumacia* period for many offices. *Vecchi* began winning elections in the Great Council, while those who had loaned money met with almost universal defeat, "especially those who loaned to enter the Senate." Debate revived in the Senate, although the executive councils retained their grasp on policy.[59]

In the years after 1517, Venice was caught between France and the Spanish-Habsburg empire, the latter ruled by Charles V, who, Sanuto told the Senate in 1521, "is not a Maximilian, who was a naked babe, but an Emperor." Rivalry between the two powers drew Italy into a new war and involved Venice in enormous expenses for its own forces and subsidies for its allies. The Ten started allowing "many young patricians" into the Senate for payment in October 1521; the next month eighteen-year-olds began buying their way into the Great Council. In March 1522 the office of procurator was put up for loans and soon 200,000 ducats were collected, revenue that apparently satisfied the government for the time being, for nothing came of a suggestion to auction all offices three months later. On July 8 the Senate narrowly passed a motion to reinstitute office loans, but it was never presented to the Great Council owing to substantial opposition there.[60]

Thus the pattern of the War of the League of Cambrai reappeared, persistent and seemingly inevitable: a costly military establishment, pressing need for money, exceptional taxes, threatening of state

59 On the city breathing: Sanuto, 23:506. On defeat for lenders: Sanuto, 25: 83–84; cf. 24:551, 618. On the other developments: Sanuto, 23:506, 540, 545–546, 550, 558, 583, 593, 598; 24:140, 450, 469.

60 On international politics in 1521: Cozzi, "Authority and the Law," pp. 327–328. On Sanuto in 1521: Sanuto, 31:145. On offices and money: Sanuto, 32: 43; 34, 38–39, 65–66, 75, 81, 96, 105–106, 111–112, 122, 126–131; 33:46, 254, 263, 274, 282, 285, 294, 295, 300, 323, 347, 357, 370–372, 379, 448, 481–482, 634–638. On procurator loans: ASV, Senato, Terra, Reg. 22, fols. 80r–80v, 82r.

debtors, futile appeals to rich patricians, Great Council and Senate entrance for money. Lenders were denied access to the Senate only from January 1517 to October 1521. Again there was great reluctance to resort to auctioning offices, especially given the experience of a few years before; but the temptation was too great, the source of revenue too handy. Loans for office began in August 1526, even though need for money was not as desperate as in 1515. In a speech to the Senate, Sanuto unsuccessfully opposed the reintroduction of loans, telling the assembly that "our forefathers did not make war by selling offices and magistracies, but now we will sell the government of the state."[61] Thus also was the contraction of power in the government maintained and even reinforced: *Giovani* entered the Great Council and Senate in droves, bringing what *Primi* perceived as disorder and confusion in their wake. The Senate and the Ten encroached on the electoral prerogatives of the Great Council in an attempt to lessen the influence of that unruly assembly. The Collegio, more independent than ever, kept business from the Senate, while its links with the Ten insured the continued dominance of the latter in vital state affairs.

Nothing, in short, was new—and yet everything was. Loans for office, and the reaction of the government to them, were originally temporary, emergency measures of war; after fifteen years they had established new modes of politics in Venice, reaffirming and widening the gap between rich and poor patricians, between exclusive and representative assemblies. The clock, then, was not turned back to the days before Agnadello, which came increasingly (and unrealistically) to be seen by patricians as a golden time, when Venice was powerful, the ruling class united, and the political system an arena in which republican values were realized and respected.

3. Politics and Corruption, 1494–1533

According to Priuli, Agnadello and its aftermath gave rise to a new proverb: "Laws were defeated along with Venetian forces." When the *terraferma* empire was lost, he elaborates, electoral corruption was retained. Indeed its role in Venetian political life expanded as patri-

---

61 On development toward office loans: Sanuto, 43:32, 39, 90, 105, 107, 205; 44:321–322, 563–565; ASV, Senato, Terra, Reg. 24, fols. 106r–106v. On Sanuto's statement: 43:318.

cians sought in the Ducal Palace the honors and income they had abandoned to the armies of the League of Cambrai.[62]

Priuli was aware, of course, that electoral corruption did not commence in 1509; his diary is replete with condemnations of it well before Agnadello, all bearing hallmarks of the idealism and naïveté usually characterizing Venetian notions of the proper relationship between public service and personal ambition. Venetians would have agreed with Thomas Jefferson's contention that, "whenever a man has cast a longing eye on offices, a rottenness begins in his conduct." In Venice even the most harmless manifestations of ambition for office were prohibited, and "corruption" was a broadly inclusive juridical term embracing a range of activities from soliciting votes to outright fraud. State service was supposed to be ideally distant from any personal considerations of advantage or prestige. Yet, more than anything else, office seeking dominated and shaped Venetian political life. Given the large number of offices available (more than eight hundred), the frequent rotation in office combined with rapid turnover in membership, and the necessity for sometimes holding multiple elections for one post, the search for place and position took up an enormous amount of time and energy in the Venetian political system.

Venetian politicians were fond of saying that "offices and wives come from heaven," but there is a fatalism in the proverb at odds with the relentless place seeking of the patriciate. Lobbying for office was probably the dominant political preoccupation of the typical patrician, who wanted a place in government for personal income, social prestige, and political influence. As a job market and a permanent convention, the Great Council was the natural focus for this activity. The Venetian term *broglio*, from the area on the piazzetta where patricians sauntered and made their deals before entering the councils, meant, in its widest usage, political intrigue or corruption in general.[63] *Imbroglio* most likely stems from the Venetian term—an apt derivation, inasmuch as confusion or entanglement are fair descriptions for office seeking in Venice. The image of patricians lining up to form nominating committees and dropping ballots into urns must be combined with

---

62 Priuli, 4:16; 108–109, 179.

63 On the proverb: Sanuto, 22:66. On *broglio*: Antonio Pilot, "La teoria del Broglie nella Republica Veneta," pp. 176–189, a summary of an anonymous document of the late seventeenth century, "Discorsetto in propositione de' Broglio," no pagination.

one of aspirants and supporters, both patrician and commoner, crowding the courtyard of the Ducal Palace, clustering on the stairs leading to the Great Council and the Senate, applauding their favorites, booing their enemies, and respectfully giving way before one of the city's *Primi*.

There were times when a claque's support was inappropriate, for a patrician might lobby to lose an election. Certain posts were considered dangerous, inconvenient, arduous, expensive, or undignified; moreover, refusal of important offices often entailed a heavy fine. Thus a patrician might be congratulated for a defeat and receive condolences for a victory. Both kinds of actions were considered unseemly; and in 1526 a measure was proposed (drawing on others of the Quattrocento) designed to pull up "the pernicious roots of ambition" by forbidding patricians to shake hands, embrace, and offer either congratulations or condolences after an election. Patricians in the Great Council laughed when the motion was presented, and Sanuto argued against it, but it still passed—testimony, perhaps, to the patriciate's ambiguous commitment to the principle of wholly honest elections. In any case, the law was neither obeyed nor enforced, and in 1533 it was modified as follows: "It is forbidden to those of the Senate and of our Great Council . . . to say to anyone elected or defeated for any magistracy, office or council: 'I favored you' or 'I honored you.' . . . it is only permitted to say: 'I am happy' or 'I am sorry.' "[64]

Much lobbying went on in the Ducal Palace for election to ecclesiastical and secretarial positions. According to a secretary of the Ten, *broglio* was essential for advancement in the chancellery. Competition for the influential and lucrative post of grand chancellor was especially intense, with state secretaries, "all with hats in hand, lobbying extensively at San Marco and the Rialto, and many patricians lobby with them. . . ." The fury of this electioneering is revealed in a 1581 treatise by Antonio Milledonne, an important secretary: After a humiliating rejection by the Great Council for the chancellorship, he went into hiding and wrote a dialogue that somewhat hysterically asserted that defeat was good for one's soul.[65]

---

64 On avoiding office: Donald E. Queller, "The Civic Irresponsibility of the Venetian Nobility." On the law: Sanuto, 58:154; cf. 55:316; ASV, Senato, Terra, Reg. 24, fols. 64r–64v.

65 On ecclesiastical posts: Sanuto, 6:528–529; 7:633; 27:632, 648; 50:437, 438–439; Priuli, 4:38. On the necessity for *broglio*: Antonio Milledonne, "Dialogo de Antonio Milledonne con uno amico suo," fol. 58v. On competition for grand

There was a plethora of illegal methods for enlisting supporters, gaining nominations, and winning elections. At one extreme these included soliciting support from friends and relatives and at the other, purchasing votes and cheating during the nominating procedures and elections. A seventeenth-century commentator called the method of solicitation *broglio honesto*, or "honest electioneering," because it was so mild a form of corruption and so widespread within the ruling class. In *broglio honesto* an individual expressed his ambition for an office to friends and relatives, and they in turn lobbied for him among their own connections.[66] Another aspect of *broglio honesto* was the exchange of nominating power within a nominating committee. The nine men in each Great Council committee freely traded their rights to nominate offices in order to obtain nominating power to a post desired by a friend or relative; although not illegal, it was considered improper in the early Cinquecento to nominate oneself. This intra-committee cooperation explains why the vote of approval for a nomination was a formality: Most of the nine men broke the law by switching nominations, so a spirit of accommodation insured that the six votes necessary for approval could easily be garnered.[67]

Patricians kept strict account of their nominations and expected payment in kind, even after a long time. In November 1529 Nicolò Paruta named Sanuto to an office, and the latter returned the favor in March 1530. Sanuto nominated Lorenzo Contarini to the Senate because "nine years before he named me for state attorney." It took Alvise Mocenigo fifteen years to pay back Sanuto for a 1506 nomination, and Sanuto reimbursed Marco Zancani after no less than thirty-two. To some extent, debts were to the family rather than simply to the individual: Sanuto records that he was nominated to the Zonta by Alberto Contarini because, seventeen years before, the latter had received nomination to the Forty from Sanuto's brother, Leonardo.[68] If every Great Council meeting involved such exchanges, an extra-

---

chancellor: Sanuto, 23:523; 489, 528, 530; Michiel, fols. 278r–278v; cf. Sanuto, 12: 76; 34:362, 376–377; 36:464, 470; Priuli, 4:119–120, 126. On Milledonne: "Dialogo de Antonio Milledonne."

66 "Discorsetto," no pagination.

67 On exchanging nominations: cf. Sanuto, 28:405–406; 29:8; 45:488; 52:326. On not getting approval: Sanuto, 54:163; cf. 27:649–650.

68 On Paruta: Sanuto, 52:310; 53:13. On Lorenzo Contarini: Sanuto, 36:595. On Mocenigo: Sanuto, 32:254. On Zancani: Sanuto, 57:235. On Alberto Contarini: Sanuto, 25:12.

ordinary network of electoral obligations must have spread through the ruling class. The details of these exchanges—such as the relative value of nominations and the limits of repayment to kin—must remain a mystery. Yet because debts were paid after many years and because thirty-six men were nominated every election day, it is reasonable to assume that some sort of political account books were used to keep track of outstanding obligations.

A far more disreputable form of *broglio* was the selling of votes, although it is a short, if significant, step from trading nominations to trading money for nominations. In 1524 Giovanni Emo, recently returned from exile for using official funds to buy votes, created a scandal by distributing pistachios and marzipan in the Great Council. Emo was no doubt merely trying to cultivate good will, for nominations and votes cost several ducats, and even poor patricians could not be bought by sweets. In 1508 Giovanni Vendramin, grandson of a doge, was exiled for two years, deprived of offices for five, and fined 200 ducats for "giving money to corrupt patricians because they aided him in the Great Council." Such bargains were a staple of Venetian politics, and although the law prescribed severe punishment for those who were caught, patricians wealthy enough to purchase votes had sufficient funds to buy their way out of trouble. Vendramin, for example, was allowed home from exile after less than ten months by purchasing a pardon from the Council of Ten.[69]

With great demand for offices, and with rich men willing to pay for them, some poor patricians organized themselves into groups to sell their votes in blocs. In 1491 Paolo Barbo, a leading politician, was warned that one hundred votes would be cast against him in every election and he would be "defeated for every position" unless he paid a large bribe. In all likelihood, such practices only became highly sophisticated and played a significant role in the Great Council with the extraordinary demand for offices caused by the War of the League of Cambrai, a development that provides some warrant for Priuli's contention that *broglio* worsened after Agnadello. Sanuto mentions the existence of groups known as "the Switzers" (*sguizari*)—called so in reference to the mercenary soldiers of the Swiss cantons—for the first time in September 1515, a month after office loans began. The Switzers were poor patricians who collected money from men nominated in the Senate's *scrutinii* in return for votes in the Great Council

69 On Emo: Sanuto, 36:625. On Vendramin: Sanuto, 7:602; 603, 608, 609–610; 8:387; cf. 7:612, 620.

and from men who wanted committee nominations; they were highly organized, with their own record keepers and "councillors." Their so-called captains made a deal with the highest bidder prior to the elections and signaled their followers on the Great Council's benches "whom they wanted to win by tipping their hats, whom they wanted to defeat by tugging their beards." A patrician willing to advance hundred of ducats in loans to the government for an office was not liable to balk, scruples aside, at spending a little more to insure nomination and election, especially when the Great Council proved reluctant to elevate lenders. Switzers thus wielded considerable influence, and Sanuto lamented that a victory was hardly possible without catering to them: "Nowadays, because of money, whom they wish to elect is elected."[70]

Lobbying and cheating dogged elections at every stage. As patricians lined up to draw from the urns, they continued to importune one another. Laws regulating comportment in the Great Council included prohibitions against standing when not necessary, changing seats, linking arms, and breaking the queues—all actions that gave opportunities for electioneering or the appearance of it. Even the physical layout of the Great Council chamber was designed to counter *broglio*. Instead of facing the tribune of the Signoria, as in a theater or classroom, patricians sat on benches at right angles to the front of the hall. Thus those supervising voting could better monitor the movements of those filing to the tribune to draw balls from urns, as well as movement from bench to bench and the progress of *ballottini* among patricians with the final voting urns.

Indeed, careful scrutiny was necessary at every moment: to make sure that a counterfeit gilded ball was not already in a patrician's hand before he dipped it into an urn; to prevent the thirty-six nominators from collaborating on their intentions before they were separated into committees; to keep the nominators from talking or exchanging signals with those still on the benches; to stop notaries from carrying messages, last-minute pleas, or bribes to the thirty-six lucky men; to seal off the rooms where the committees retired; to prohibit patricians either from leaving the hall once the electoral procedures were set in motion or from lounging on the Signoria's tribune.[71] The five men—

70 On Barbo: Malipiero, 2:688–689. On the Switzers: Sanuto, 21:70; cf. 26:316–317; 28:65, 663; 54:8; Cozzi, "Authority and the Law," pp. 312–313.
71 Cf. ASV, Magistrato Censori, Capitolare, Reg. 1, fols. 18r–18v, 25v–29r; Consiglio di Dieci, Parti Miste, Reg. 39, fols. 70r–71v.

three chiefs of the Ten and two censors—appointed to supervise over one thousand patricians had an impossible task.

Fraudulent techniques centering around the voting urns made the final vote especially difficult to control. The urns (*bossoli*) were designed by Antonio Tron in 1492, when he was a chief of the Ten, and remained in use until 1797. Previously, two urns or ballot boxes were carried around the Great Council, one for and one against the candidate. Three were used for votes on propositions: affirmative, negative, and abstention (*non sincere*). Tron divided the urn into three vertical parts, so that it could be used for either kind of vote, and placed a cover on it with two lateral wooden cuffs to prevent anyone seeing in which compartment the ballot was put. He conceived this *bellissima fantasia*, as Sanuto calls it, to permit a secret ballot and thus help prevent lobbying. A ballot made of cloth was used so that the sound of it dropping would give no clue as to how one voted. The urn was not, however, impervious to fraud. Patricians would take it from the hands of the *ballottino* in charge of carrying it around the benches and tip it to move ballots from one compartment to another. There was also no way to prevent extra ballots being cast, a trick frequently employed by the Switzers. The Ten offered 2,000 ducats in 1519 for information on the culprits inserting "fistfulls of ballots" into the urns.[72]

Ballottini were also a problem in maintaining honest elections. Originally, men from the supreme court were entrusted with circulating the urns, but because they displayed an unjudicial partiality toward their friends, the task was given in 1467 to nonpatrician youths of less than fifteen years of age. Apparently the innocence of youth did not long survive acquaintance with the patriciate in pursuit of office, for in 1492 secretaries, beginning long apprenticeships in the chancellery, were put in charge. Predictably, this too failed to eliminate abuses. Four years later, Giovanni Foscarini, recently elected to the Senate, was accosted by two *ballottini*, who informed him they were responsible for his victory because they had shifted negative ballots into the other side of the urn. They wanted payment for this kindness, but Foscarini turned them in to the Ten, not because of outrage at the deed, according to Malipiero, but from fear that the fraud and his complicity in it might be revealed. Subsequent investigation exposed

---

72 On the urn: Marino Sanuto, *Vite dei dogi*, fol. 341r; idem, *Cronachetta*, p. 230. On the ballot: Contarini, *Republica*, p. 36. On tipping and stuffing the urn: Sanuto, 52:153; 28:65; 67, 82, 94.

another *ballottino* who headed a group that collected money for fixing elections. In 1579, the Ten uncovered a cabal of three *ballottini* and fifteen patricians fixing elections by using counterfeit ballots. *Ballottini* could also earn money, and with far less risk, simply by providing information on the progress of an election or by carrying messages from bench to bench as they passed the urns around.[73] In short, a certain amount of cheating was virtually inevitable so long as a secret ballot was used and a large number of people were in contact with the urns.

One of the laws aimed at preventing electoral corruption prohibited competitors for office from visiting one another in their homes after the Great Council adjourned. This was part of an attempt to eliminate the social foundations of *broglio*, the assembling of patricians outside councils and churches. One reason why patricians lobbied openly in the Ducal Palace was that it was generally illegal for numbers of them to congregate elsewhere. The Senate's nominees to the Great Council's elections were forbidden to come near the Ducal Palace until one hour after its doors were closed for elections; to insure honesty further, patricians were forbidden to leave the Great Council chamber once elections began. When Giorgio Corner tried for the dogeship in 1521, he had to organize secret meetings throughout the city to drum up support. It was forbidden in 1505 for a patrician to stand as a godfather for another's child because christenings had turned into boisterous political gatherings where money and gifts were exchanged that had little to do with the religious occasion. The Court of the Forty was a powerful and united lobbying force precisely because it had its own chambers in the Ducal Palace, to which office seekers flocked at all hours of the day and night.[74]

The government paid special attention to the phenomenon of dinner parties, which performed the same function in Venice as did town taverns in colonial Massachussetts and coffeehouses in Augustan England: They were mediating mechanisms that helped make the political system work by bringing together politicians outside the formal assemblies. Giorgio Corner could afford such political entertainment on

73 On 1467 and 1492: Malipiero, 2:656; 689. On Foscarini: Malipiero, 2:701; cf. Sanuto, 1:323–324. On 1579: Alvise Michiel, "Diarii, 1578–1586" no pagination. On legislation regarding *ballottini*: ASV, Magistrato Censori, Capitolare, Reg. 1, fols. 25v–29r, 31r–32r.

74 Sanuto, 6:215; 30:458; 40:656–657; 56:889, 912–913; Priuli, 2:385–386; Michiel, fol. 151r.

a lavish scale. According to Malipiero, when Corner's daughter was married in 1496, "He banqueted a hundred and more patricians at a time, for with such guile ambition is exercised, and the guests are more easily bent to his desires and to attend to his requests." A year later, the Ten, led by Antonio Tron, issued a new series of regulations governing entertainment: It was forbidden to give dinners to gain nominations or votes; wedding parties were limited to forty persons; and dinner parties had to end by eight o'clock between September and March and by eleven o'clock the rest of the year. In 1506 these rules were reissued, with the added proviso that patricians were not to combine their wedding parties with entertainment after electoral victories, and only ten patricians were allowed to partake of the latter. A law of 1531 went even further by forbidding more than eight patricians from meeting in a private home, one indication perhaps of how recourse to dinner parties kept pace with increased demand for offices during and after the war.[75]

Members of the Signoria and the Collegio, who were forbidden to attend weddings, often were dined by the doge, and apparently they found it expedient to conduct political business in these select and informal gatherings. The Forty was also a focus for electioneering; a patrician's chances for a seat on the Collegio or for one of the Senate's offices were enhanced if he dined the court. A lighter expense, and another way to win the Forty's goodwill, was to provide the judges with wine for after-dinner get-togethers. In 1532 the censors tried to limit the conviviality in the Forty's chambers by forbidding giving dinners there on the days in which the Zonta was nominated and elected. Those days, in fact, were the height of the season for political entertainment, for "some patricians who wish to be elected or to elect someone to the Zonta banquet twenty-five, thirty and more patricians in various places."[76]

Clearly, *broglio* was at the center of Venetian political and social life, a position into which it moved from about the mid-Quattrocento. The Senate expanded its membership by almost one hundred separate positions between 1450 and 1520, multiplying the opportunities for

75 On Corner: Malipiero, 2:704. On 1497 and 1506: Malipiero, 2:644; Sanuto, 1:838. On sumptuary legislation: G. Bistort, *Il magistrato alla pompe nella Republica di Venezia*. On 1531: Sanuto, 56:371.

76 On the Signoria and the Collegio: Sanuto, 3:125; 25:398, 462; 29:492; ASV, Maggior Consiglio, Deliberazioni, Liber Diana, Reg. 26, fol. 54v. On dining the Forty: Sanuto, 24:406; 56:954. On Zonta dinners: Sanuto, 56:954.

intrigue that would be rewarded with a seat in the governing council. From the late 1440s, the Senate took an increasingly important part in the Great Council's elections; the Senate's creation of *scrutinii* nominations was, according to Sanuto, a significant element in the increase of electoral corruption. Also, from the late Quattrocento, most Great Council nominees were chosen by four rather than two nominating committees, a reform intended to combat corruption but that had the opposite effect because it extended opportunities for vote trading and canvassing. As was often the case in Venetian politics, a complication of the political machinery, originally intended to overcome the corruption of an earlier, simpler system, only made more room in which *broglio* could expand. Finally, from the mid-Quattrocento the number of patricians increased at the same time that mercantile and maritime sources of income were decreasing. More and more, patricians came to the Ducal Palace to compete for a livelihood, hoping for a sinecure that would offer a decent salary, as well as for a chance to profit from office in numerous other ways, mostly illicit.[77]

In a long perspective, then, the years after 1509 saw a continuation of the rising curve of electoral corruption, even if the speed of ascent was steeper, more explosive, than before. Sanuto and Priuli were not exaggerating when they complained that post-Agnadello Venice witnessed electoral corruption at its height, *broglio in culmine*, an unprecedented growth of lobbying and ambition. The appearance in those years of both the Switzers and their (supposed) opponents, the censors, is evidence that the diarists were not merely myopic. "Laws were defeated," says Priuli, "along with Venetian forces." In fact, many of the laws against lobbying were temporarily suspended, although the grosser forms of electoral corruption, such as selling votes and cheating, remained illegal. It would have been contradictory to punish mere expressions of ambition when the Ten was selling seats in the Senate and bids were accepted for offices in the Great Council. Ambition, however, was only supposed to be expressed to the Signoria.[78]

Electioneering was more open and intense than ever before. The custom of having patricians swear an oath that they had not lobbied

77 On *scrutinio* and increase in corruption: Sanuto, 24:657. On the increase in nominating committees: Sanuto, *Cronachetta*, passim. On increase in corruption in the late Quattrocento: Cozzi, "Authority and the Law," p. 299.
78 On increase in *broglio*: Sanuto, 11:614; 16:565; Priuli, 4:98, 194–195, 302; vol. 5, fols. 58v, 191v. On suspension of laws: Sanuto, 24:657.

for office was abandoned in July 1509 because too many souls were being placed in jeopardy. When Mestre was burned by imperial troops on September 29, 1513, Sanuto was alarmed by the *Primi*'s preoccupation with elections: "Nothing is done! . . . and many complain that *savi* are voted on with such things [going on], with the bell for the Great Council heard [by all] this morning and tomorrow as well." On September 30, with the flames of Mestre still visible, Michiel writes that "while in Venice the election of these magistracies [of the Zonta] is attended to, the enemy ravage the entire countryside with the greatest damage not only to private incomes but to [the Republic's] reputation." In 1515 a patrician lamented that ambition for office was so great that when a magistrate died his post was filled before his body was carried home. According to Priuli, lobbying went on for months before an office fell vacant; dinner parties and secret meetings never ceased. Loans for office gave rise to new sorts of pacts; in November 1515, the Ten took action against a "pernicious and detestable corruption" whereby a few patricians arranged among themselves which of them was to make a loan to the Signoria, a stratagem that both restricted the Great Council's choices and limited revenue received by the government.[79]

Lobbying was especially intense in the Senate, where the entrance of *giovani* meant that representatives of a generation traditionally excluded from important positions were in direct competition with *vecchi* for *scrutinii* nominations and for some posts on the Collegio. Nomination of forty-four men, rather than the prewar average of twenty, to become the Senate's nominee for state attorney in May 1512 reflects this competition, as do similar contests for ambassadorial and financial posts. *Giovani* incursions on Collegio posts were limited to the *savi agli ordini*, the officials with responsibility for maritime affairs. The *savi agli ordini* were the lowest ranking officials of the Collegio, and their importance lessened after the end of the Turkish war in 1503. But they were far from negligible in significance in the opening decade of the Cinquecento; nor were they always much younger than other *savi* (Giovanni Antonio Minio held the post at sixty-four in 1502 and Sanuto, at forty-four in 1510). Relegation of the office to a mere training spot for patricians of "downy beards," as

79 On the oath: Priuli, 4:174; cf. Sanuto, 20:408. On Mestre: Sanuto, 17:103; 105; Michiel, fol. 88v. On filling a post at death: Sanuto, 20:406. On lobbying for months: Priuli, 4:33. On November 1515: ASV, Consiglio di Dieci, Parti Miste, Reg. 39, fol. 42v.

Contarini calls them, only took place when underage men (that is, men less than thirty) began paying 200 ducats for nominations to the Collegio in 1513.[80]

Although the entrance of *giovani* to the Senate exacerbated lobbying, the *scrutinio* procedure had already insured that assembly a prominent role in Venetian *broglio*. The Senate's nominee to the elections of the Great Council had a twofold advantage over his four competitors from the nominating committees: First, he had the backing of a majority in the Senate, which meant a good deal in terms of prestige and votes in the final election; second, he was often chosen at least one day before the election, giving him valuable time in which to round up support, whereas the Great Council's nominees were voted on immediately after nomination. The *scrutinio* nominee was selected by majority vote after the senators, Zonta members, and judges of the Forty made their nominations. Intense lobbying attended both the initial nominations and the final vote, all of which were carried out secretly. The Senate's nomination supposedly exemplified the considered wisdom of the *Primi di la terra*; in reality it was more susceptible to *broglio* than were the nominations of the Great Council, which involved a substantial element of chance. According to Priuli, there was an even simpler reason why lobbying was worse in the Senate than in the sovereign assembly: The former was far smaller and more homogeneous, therefore more conducive to reaching accord with one's colleagues, than was the crowded and tumultuous Great Council.[81]

There were various attempts made to restrain electioneering in the Senate, culminating in the law of 1514 in which *scrutinii* for all but a handful of posts were abolished. In 1497 the Collegio won approval of a measure to do away with them for more than fifty offices "because of the great lobbying [*pregierie*] which is carried on, so that senators cannot deal with public business." More than twenty-five additional posts were put on the list in 1505, although in subsequent years *scrutinii* for many of them reappeared in the Senate. The opinion after 1509 that "the Senate does nothing but lobby [*pratiche*], and this has ruined and will continue to ruin this city" was central to the 1514

80 On lobbying in the Senate: Sanuto, 11:614; 12:92; cf. Priuli, 4:33. On nominations for state attorney: Sanuto, 14:182; cf. 13:468; cf. 15:78. On *savi agli ordini*: Sanuto, 4:201; 9:184; 10:55–56; 12:92; Contarini, *Republica*, p. 80. On sales of *savi agli ordini*: cf. ASV, Consiglio di Dieci, Parti Miste, Reg. 34, fol. 93r.

81 On lobbying for the *scrutinio*: cf. ASV, Maggior Consiglio, Deliberazioni, Liber Deda, Reg. 25, fol. 98r. On Priuli's statement: vol. 5, fol. 191v.

attack on the Senate's nominating authority. On May 12, 1514, Antonio Condulmer, a *savio di terraferma*, proposed that the posts of lords of the Arsenal be nominated by the Great Council alone because "so great was the lobbying of those in the Senate, and so many were nominated that it was remarkable to behold." This measure was the precursor of one sponsored by Condulmer, Luca Tron, and others a month later that annulled *scrutinii* for all offices but captain general, fleet commander, and councillor.[82]

The political influence of men in the Senate meant that *scrutinii* were slowly reinstated, as they were after 1497 and 1505; but the 1514 law nonetheless was a blow against lobbying and, perforce, brought about an increase in the influence of the Great Council. Thus the most radical attack on the Senate's electoral authority sprang from essentially the same motive as did the assault on its deliberative prerogatives by the Ten and the Collegio. Opposition to the *giovani* in the Senate led to its power being drained off simultaneously by the most representative assembly and the most exclusive councils. Having lost its power over policy, the Senate was not even to lead the *terra* in corruption.

A further indication that *broglio* was considered an especially serious problem in the Senate is that when the censors were created in 1517 their task was to combat lobbying in that council alone. The task of fighting electoral corruption properly belonged to the state attorneys, so their decline in power was a necessary prelude to the rise of the censors. The state attorneys once ranked among the most important officials, with extensive and vital responsibilities as "the civic conscience of the governing aristocracy."[83] They stood with the doge and the Ten as guardians of the law. Along with the doge, with whom they worked closely, they could enter all councils and inspect the accounts of any office; in state ceremonies they were equal in dignity to the chiefs of the Ten. As Sanuto wrote in 1493, "They have the very greatest authority and are among the principal members or offices of this Republic." By that time, however, the state attorneys were already on the decline. From the 1470s, legislation was passed restricting

---

82 On 1497 and 1505: Sanuto, 1:713–714; 6:251, 254. On the Senate lobbying: Sanuto, 13:172. On 1514: Sanuto, 18:188; 291, 305; Michiel, fol. 115v, cf. Sanuto, 18:418, 422–423; Michiel, fol. 122r; Donato Giannotti, *Libro de la Republica de Vinitiani*, pp. 94–95.

83 Cozzi, "Authority and the Law," p. 307.

their judicial authority, and Doge Agostino Barbarigo's manipulation of the office so reduced its prestige that investigation of abuses of authority after his death had to be entrusted to a new magistracy.[84]

It was the War of the League of Cambrai that spelled the definitive decline of the office. The Ten's method of raising money and the Collegio's acerbic dealings with the Senate were direct affronts to the state attorneys' responsibility for upholding the law; allowing exiles absolution for payment was a unilateral abrogation of penalties the state attorneys had obtained and were responsible for enforcing. Loans for office left them impotent to enforce laws against electoral corruption. Not surprisingly, Contarini states in 1524 that the authority of the state attorneys had waned as that of the Ten had grown. Insofar as the former "represented the law as a function of equality [whereas] the Council of Ten represented it as a function of authority," the shift in power between the two magistracies was yet another aspect of the more authoritarian state that emerged from the war.[85]

The decline of the state attorneys made the position less sought after by the *Primi* or by those concerned to enforce the law, and when the post was opened to office loans, the election of incompetents further diminished its prestige and force. In fact, even the state attorneys' most dramatic victory probably contributed to their losing political influence in the long run. In 1510, following precedents established by the trial of Antonio Grimani in 1500, they defied the Signoria and the Senate and won transfer of Captain General Angelo Trevisan's trial to the Great Council. This championship of the Great Council's sovereignty was seen by the *Primi* as an alliance with a juvenile mob against the prudent "old ones of the Senate," who no doubt subsequently were pleased to restrain the authority of an office that could be so used against them. An indication of how much the state attorneys' influence declined during the war is their failure in

84 On Sanuto in 1493: Sanuto, *Cronachetta*, p. 98. On the legislation of the 1470s: Cozzi, "Authority and the Law," p. 307. On Barbarigo: Sanuto, 4:118; Agostino Rossi, "Gl'Inquisitori sopra il doge defunto nella Repubblica di Venezia." On legislation restricting the state attorneys: Sanuto, 4:177; 5:30, 345; 6:142, 350, 583; 7:81; 8:399, 411; 9:368; 10:443, 450; 11:590; 12:187, 188, 189; 20: 425; 22:79, 84–85, 380, 382–383; 23:317; ASV, Senato, Terra, Reg. 19, fols. 35r–35v; Maggior Consiglio, Deliberazioni, Liber Deda, Reg. 25, fols. 103v–104v, 123r–123v, 134v, 169r–169v.

85 On Contarini: *Republica*, p. 94. On the quotation: Cozzi, "Authority and the Law," p. 306; cf. pp. 308–309.

1532 to win transfer of a trial from the Forty to the Great Council, despite the precedents of their substantial victories in 1500 and 1510.[86]

Thus, when the government began to set its house in order after 1517, it was thought that the state attorneys were not sufficient to deal with the problem of electioneering; moreover, a magistracy was clearly needed that could devote itself entirely to the issue—unlike the Ten, which was distracted by numerous other responsibilities. *Broglio* by no means lessened with the end of the war. Rather, it increased as *vecchi* tried to regain their customary precedence in all important offices; as *giovani* fought to retain their posts without the aid of payments; and as those not wealthy enough to afford loans saw offices opening up to them again. Many Great Council elections after January failed to produce a winner, perhaps owing to furious competition for positions.[87]

On September 12, 1517, in the midst of the bustling autumnal electoral season, Marco Foscari, a *savio grande*, proposed the creation of two censors to restrain "the lobbying for *scrutinii*," which evidently had been substantially reintroduced to the Senate since the law of 1514. He was opposed by Bernardo Donato, a chief of the Forty, and by Luca Tron, a *savio grande*, who wanted the state attorneys to retain responsibility over electioneering. Foscari's motion passed the Senate; and when it was sent to the Great Council the next day, Sanuto supported it at length, asserting that, after recovery from the war, "a disease damaging to this most excellent Republic has stirred up, that is, ambition." The Great Council voted to institute the censors, and soon Marco Foscari and Gasparo Malipiero were elected to the office, with one-year terms and salaries of 120 ducats. They were commissioned to fight electioneering in the Senate and to administer oaths of rectitude to *scrutinii* competitors. In pursuit of these aims, they were empowered to summon up to twenty patricians to their chambers in the course of an investigation and to levy penalties of up to three years' exclusion from councils for conviction of lobbying. As testimony to the censors' high status, they immediately succeeded the state attorneys and chiefs of the Ten in ceremonial dignity and were given the honor of dressing in scarlet robes.[88]

---

86 On 1510: Finlay, "Venice, the Po Expedition," pp. 61–62. On 1532: Sanuto, 55:211, 306, 308, 310, 315, 316.

87 Sanuto, 25:259, 269; 27:299; 28:14, 201, 338.

88 On Sanuto's speech: 24:657; 667–668. On creation of the censors: Sanuto,

Foscari and Malipiero started the new office in impressive fashion, imprisoning a senator whom they caught soliciting votes on October 1, although the Ten released him after only four days. Three weeks later the scope of their office was vastly increased when its competence was extended to the Great Council, where they were "to proceed with the authority and means of the state attorneys." On December 17, the Ten upheld a sentence of the censors calling for a ten-year exile for a patrician selling his vote. In elections for *savi agli ordini* four days later, twenty-one men were nominated but none elected because the censors prevented lobbying. This novel situation prompted Foscari and Malipiero to propose a new mode of election in the Senate. They suggested that aspiring patricians give their names to the grand chancellor, who would read them to the assembly; nominees were also to be permitted to inform no more than five senators of this act before the voting. The Senate approved the proposal, which stipulated that the new procedure applied only to its own elections and not to *scrutinii*.[89] This was a significant change in voting procedures, in effect a limited legitimation of *broglio honesto*, and it was to receive wider application when the censors were revived in 1524.

In general, patricians serving as censors did not live up to the standards of diligence and initiative set by Foscari and Malipiero; by October 1521 the failure of the office to fulfill its functions was apparent. Most censors were less interested in enforcing the law than were the first occupants of the office. Sanuto records that by December 1518 the censors, Vittore Michiel (the diarist's father) and Moisè Venier, were not applying the new election procedures and that "more lobbying than ever is done." In the Senate, *broglio* returned in force to the elections for *savi*, and in the Great Council no action was taken against the Switzers.[90]

The censors were, however, actively concerned with where they sat in the Great Council, a consideration of some significance because a position from which electoral activity could be scrutinized was necessary for performance of their duties. Questions of personal honor and

---

24:660–661; 25:296, 299; ASV, Senato, Terra, Reg. 20, fols. 71r, 82r; Maggior Consiglio, Deliberazioni, Liber Deda, Reg. 25, fols. 143v–145v.

89 On imprisoning the senator: Sanuto, 25:8. On the extension to the Great Council: ASV, Maggior Consiglio, Deliberazioni, Liber Deda, Reg. 25, fol. 146r. On December 17: Sanuto, 25:137. On *savi* elections: Sanuto, 25:170. On the new procedure: Sanuto, 25:293, 295; ASV, Senato, Terra, Reg. 20, fol. 114r.

90 Sanuto, 26:291; 38, 316–317; 28:65.

bureaucratic precedence soon overwhelmed this practical matter. In November 1518 Michiel and Venier proposed moving their seats at the head of the Great Council hall closer to the entrance of the Forty's chamber, where the nominating committees were sequestered, a move that apparently placed them closer to the tribune than were the state attorneys. The latter vehemently objected that the proposal was "against their honor"; the censors rejoined that lobbying was carried on with impunity in front of the state attorneys. The Signoria upheld the censors' right to present their motion to the Great Council, a decision reversed a few days later when new councillors entered office. The censors stayed put.[91]

The Ten also took actions that diminished the authority of the censors. They relieved the censors of responsibility for administering the electoral oath, a blow to their prestige rather than a loss of power, and they sometimes countermanded their sentences against malefactors. The censors faced a further obstacle, for although their competence had been extended to the Great Council, it fell short of the Ten and its *zonta*, which elected many officials. In March 1518 the Ten and its *zonta* made a preliminary nomination of twenty-six men to a financial post, and Sanuto reports that before the final election "many patricians lobbied with great fury because the laws of the censors and those against lobbying do not extend to the Ten."[92] The censors could not effectively act against *broglio*, even assuming such an ambition, so long as the Ten provided a refuge from the law.

Suggestions for abolition of the censors came first from patricians whose opposition to electioneering was unquestionable. In March 1520 Sanuto induced Giovanni Antonio Memmo, a chief of the Forty, to propose eliminating the censors' salary as a gesture of protest against the ineffectuality of the office. Antonio Tron, a *savio grande*, wanted the office itself abolished, while the Signoria wanted to preserve both salary and office. Memmo's motion received sixty-three votes in the Senate; Tron's, forty-nine; and the councillors', ninety. A second vote gave victory to the councillors. In January 1521 the issue arose again when the Senate was debating administration of the electoral oath. Sanuto suggested abolishing the censors, as lobbying was worse than ever; but when this idea was put to a motion by a chief of the Forty, it failed to pass by a vote of 106 to 92. Sanuto contends that the office

---

91 Sanuto, 26:216, 229–230, 240, 241; 27:265.

92 On administering the oath and countermanding sentences: Sanuto, 28:56, 665; cf. 29:17. On March 1518: Sanuto, 25:309; cf. 311–312; 26:398, 401, 480, 486.

was retained because some patricians wanted the salary, prestige, and little work. Finally, in October 1521, the Signoria and the Collegio proposed abolishing the censors, perhaps because of the great *broglio* that had gone unchecked during the autumn elections, perhaps because it was clear that the Senate was moving toward ending the office in any event. As Sanuto notes, the censors had borne "little fruit" after four years of existence.[93]

Three years later, a motion to reestablish the censors—"because of the very great lobbying going on, so that nothing else is attended to"—was approved by the Senate and the Great Council. Memories of the censors' ineffectuality had faded, and the autumn electioneering in 1524 was, as usual, very intense. In the election for the Zonta, many *vecchi* were defeated; in contests for the Procuratia (for loans), patricians bargained with one another in front of the state attorneys.[94] Almost certainly, the figure behind the revival of the censors was Andrea Gritti, elected to. the dogeship sixteen months before. The day after the Zonta election, Gritti complained of the lobbying in progress for appointments to the Ten's *zonta*. On the same day, Marino Zorzi, a councillor and a Gritti supporter in the ducal conclave, announced that he intended to revive the censors. A week later, a Collegio proposal to that effect passed the Senate and then was narrowly approved by the Great Council at 795 to 623. "The reason for so many negative votes," claims Sanuto, "was because the mob wished to be able to lobby. Nothing else is done at present. No one can enter the Senate without electioneering."[95]

This state of affairs did not change greatly with the recreation of the censors, although if Gritti had had his way, they would have made more effective use of their authority. The first censors in 1524 were Marino Morosini, Gritti's strongest supporter in his fight for a French alliance and an indefatigable state attorney when he held that office, and Gasparo Malipiero, Gritti's first cousin (as was Marco Foscari, Malipiero's colleague as censor in 1517) and political ally. The doge was solicitous of their prestige, making room for them on the dais of the Signoria, next to the state attorneys and chiefs of the Ten. Morosini and Malipiero were diligent in keeping *scrutinii* votes confidential,

---

93 On March 1520: Sanuto, 28:363, 390, 391. On January 1521: Sanuto, 29:559, 571–572. On October 1521: Sanuto, 32:37, 42; 30:158; ASV, Senato, Terra, Reg. 22, fol. 67r.

94 Sanuto, 37:7; 1, 11; 36:624.

95 Sanuto, 37:51–52; 7, 11, 18, 56–57.

administering oaths, proposing electoral reforms, and punishing of-
fenders. However, they suffered from a serious liability: Unlike the
state attorneys and chiefs of the Ten, the censors required proof of
wrongdoing to levy charges and could not take action on accusation
alone. Thus when Malipiero and Morosini charged a patrician with
cheating on September 15, 1525, they were forced to release him, with
"little honor" to their office, because they had no proof of violation.
Gritti was absent from the Great Council when the Signoria declared
that the censors had exceeded their authority, but when the latter
appealed to Gritti the next day, he said he would take action; before
the day was over, the Ten gave the censors authority to press charges
by virtue of their office alone.[96] In short, Gritti's backing of the
censors gave them the same freedom of prosecution as that already
possessed by their foremost rivals.

Morosini and Malipiero proposed two electoral innovations, which
were accepted by the Ten. First, in order to combat Switzers, the
votes of those discovered lobbying were to be cast against the patrician
for whom they were lobbying. Second, inasmuch as there were "many
ambitious men" in the Great Council, those who desired a nomination
were permitted to give their names to the grand chancellor, who then
made up four master lists of the aspirants for the committees—an extension of the procedure conceived by Foscari and Malipiero in 1517
for elections in the Senate.[97]

Again, however, the high standards of the original censors were not
followed by their successors, although after October 1526 they were
severely hampered by reintroduction of loans for office. Once more,
censors paid more attention to seating arrangements than to limiting
electoral corruption. Gritti was frequently impatient with them for
doing nothing; and when, during the Zonta election of 1529, he saw
patricians lobbying for votes in front of the censors, he instructed
them to take action. Nothing was done, although the doge furiously
insisted that the law had been broken. Five months later, he had the
laws against *broglio* read to the impatient Great Council, "after which
il Serenissimo rose and exhorted all not to tolerate such disorders, both
those who give money for magistracies and those who take it. . . . so

96 On Morosini: Sanuto, 24:240, 295, 309, 311, 315, 353, 384; cf. Finlay, "Venice,
the Po Expedition," p. 61. On Gritti's support: Sanuto, 37:86. On the censors'
diligence: Sanuto, 37:71, 79, 216, 267, 280–281, 457. On accusation by the censors:
Sanuto, 39:428, 431, 434, 439; cf. 37:216.
97 Sanuto, 37:449, 507–508.

he spoke, admonishing, almost protesting, that these irregularities no longer be committed." When the nominating committees finished their business, Gritti took custody of their lists and only released the names for voting one by one. Unabashed, patricians continued to lobby. Indeed, on the fourth anniversary of Gritti's election, ten of his relatives were nominated for censor in the Senate and then soundly defeated: The doge was being taunted for his concern with *broglio*.[98]

Gritti had a hand in one major electoral reform during his reign, the 1529 alteration in the procedure for selecting the *zonta* of the Ten. When the Ten co-opted the fifteen members of its special commission, there was always considerable lobbying over which the censors had no control. In September 1529, the Ten, evidently led by Gritti and Francesco di Filippo Foscari, decided to have the Great Council's committees make thirty-six nominations to the *zonta;* after the assembly elected fifteen of them, the Ten and its outgoing *zonta* approved their selection with a two-thirds vote.[99] This procedure had the virtue of taking selection of the *zonta* out of a closed, self-perpetuating group and the defect of allowing the influence of lobbying at three stages in the election. But, as with the 1514 law against *scrutinii*, a measure that increased the Great Council's electoral authority was put through to decrease the effect of *broglio*.

Except for the 1526 law against shaking hands and extending congratulations, every measure by the censors for combating *broglio* was put forward when Marino Morosini was in office. He served five times as censor, and with the exception of Gasparo Malipiero in 1524, he was clearly the sole moving spirit for reform in the post. He was a censor when the Ten commissioned the office to eliminate gambling being carried on in small wineshops, much of which had to do with betting on elections, an activity so popular it was said to endanger family fortunes. Morosini's most interesting involvement was in the extension of the approach Marco Foscari and Gasparo Malipiero initiated toward *broglio* in 1517, an approach that Malipiero and Morosini himself then applied in 1524 to the Great Council's elections and to Senate *scrutinii*.[100]

---

98 On seatings: Sanuto, 49:456–457; 54:377. On the 1529 Zonta: Sanuto, 51: 610–611; 607. On Gritti's speech: Sanuto, 54:317; cf. 8, 103; 56:678; 58:541–542. On Senate nominations for censor: Sanuto, 43:628; 177, 627–628.

99 Sanuto, 51:607–608.

100 On gambling: Sanuto, 53:85–86, 87; 203, 375–376, 528, 593; ASV, Magistrato Censori, Capitolare, Reg. 1, fols. 33r–34r, 35r, 39r–39v; Enrico Besta, *Il Senato Veneziano*, p. 267.

Morosini's extension consisted of three reforms, which passed the Great Council and the Senate in May 1533. The first was an extension and refinement of the 1524 law allowing aspirants for office to give their names to the grand chancellor to be passed on to the nominating committees; the law now also allowed them to express their ambitions to close relatives, although lobbying in general was still forbidden. The injunction that the nominators must read the list suggests that the procedure was not popular with them, perhaps because it interfered with their freedom of selection. The second reform, apparently based on the 1524 law, involved a dual vote for *scrutinii;* the Senate's elections to the Collegio; and the Great Council's elections for state attorney, censor, and councillors. The first vote was the usual one for the office in question; the second was to determine who had been lobbied for the first. If a patrician's vote had been solicited, he was to put a ballot in the proper portion of an urn; and if the ballots so cast equalled one-fifth of those voting, the victor was disqualified and the election held again. The third reform was the modification of the 1526 prohibition against congratulations and condolences after elections, so that one was allowed at least to express happiness or sorrow, whichever was appropriate when the sovereign assembly made known its will.[101]

Morosini's reforms, as well as those of 1517 and 1524, show a new approach to the two extremes of electoral corruption. The "lobby vote" was aimed especially at the Switzers, who, however, could vote that they had been lobbied in order to swing an election to their employer. In any case, it was not an effective measure; patricians often refused to participate in the vote, which was, as a law of 1546 stated, "very lengthy and tedious."[102] The stipulation of formulas to be addressed to victors and losers was a mere face-saving accommodation to a practice that had gone unabated despite the 1526 law. However, the measures concerning expression of ambition and solicitation of friends and relatives were more significant, for they gave a formal, if ambiguous, role in elections to the gentler modes of electoral corruption.

The grand chancellor's list of *ambitiosi,* permission to request support from close relatives in the Great Council, and the right to approach five members of the Senate before an election legitimized the most widespread and uncontrollable aspects of electioneering. Lobby-

101 On the reforms: Sanuto, 58:151, 153, 154, 481–482.
102 ASV, Magistrato Censori, Capitolare, Reg. 1, fols. 12v–13r; cf. 12r–12v, 14r–15v.

ing remained forbidden; but asking a limited number of persons for votes, in certain circumstances, was to be tolerated. Perhaps this new official toleration is a measure of how deeply the disreputable modes of corruption penetrated Venetian political life during and after the war. Faced with organized vote peddling and rampant fraud, even strict traditionalists must have come to recognize that mere ambition and friendship were not unalloyed wickedness but could be formally integrated into the political system. The new procedures, limited as they were, represented an accommodation to *broglio honesto* and thus acknowledged the important function it performed in the politics of Venice.

The proliferation of offices and elections, the complex electoral procedures, the obligations of kinship, and division between rich and poor within the ruling class combined to make *broglio* an integral part of the Venetian system. With dinner parties, weddings, church services, christenings, and judicial meetings seized on as occasions to lobby for office, it is clear that electoral corruption was woven into the Venetian social fabric. The inefficacy of laws against electioneering is not surprising, for it was not a minor problem to be solved by more detailed legislation, closer surveillance, or exhortations to virtue and selflessness. Forbidding patricians to shake hands and embrace after elections can only be seen as an ineffectual, even comic, gesture when contrasted to the relentless ambition of Venice's office seekers.

Ambition for office was at the heart of the Venetian system, and that had the effect of lessening respect for the law within the patriciate. Those in charge of enforcing the law were reluctant to take action against patrician malefactors for fear of being defeated in the Great Council. Not only laws against electioneering went unpunished. Patricians owing money to the state were not forced to pay; the dissolute life in many of the city's monasteries went unchecked because the relatives of patricians were involved; and the petty tyrannies of officials governing the mainland proceeded with impunity. In such cases, *broglio* subtly spread its influence beyond the strictly electoral sphere into government and politics in general. "Fear of the ballot," Priuli says, governs Venice and prevents the execution of justice. Effective action by the Ten was inhibited by the web of personal interests and political debts that drew the ruling class together. Members of the Ten wanted reelection to the executive councils, a desire often at odds with enforcement of the law.[103] Because every patrician repre-

103 Priuli, 4:35; 2:77–78; 4:158, 161, 163, 232; Sanuto, 9:411; 25:357.

sented one vote, it was best to offend as few as possible. Balloting in the Great Council made for amiable administration in the Council of Ten. The Ten's political wisdom in dealing leniently with Alvise Soranzo's friends and relatives in 1511 when they rescued him from prison was highlighted five months later when the chiefs of the Ten suspended three state attorneys from office for halting the execution of a patrician, thereby angering the *terra* and meeting defeat in the next Great Council elections.[104] Of course, the Ten acted secretively and severely against Bon, Falier, and Minio, but that was precisely from fear of political retaliation by poor patricians in the Great Council. The speed and manner with which those men were shipped into exile testifies more to the Ten's political apprehension and timidity than to its institutional ruthlessness.

Caught between political ambition and official responsibility, those on the Ten frequently resorted to mere gesture to enforce the law against patricians. Thus, when they sent officials to the basilica to write down the names of those found electioneering, the intention was clearly to disperse the office seekers without the embarrassment of arresting them. Similarly, when the Ten issued a ruling that patrician state debtors must pay or face imprisonment, the threat was received with justified scepticism: "Many say," explains Priuli, "that the declaration was made to frighten those who will fear imprisonment and thus go to pay, but that otherwise the ruling will not be executed." When secrets were leaking from the Senate in 1496, the Ten appointed to look into the matter three investigators, who often met, Sanuto notes, "more to create fear than otherwise." After Padua was recaptured in July 1509, the mercenaries were quickly brought under control and prevented from looting; but patricians ran riot through the city, paying no heed to the chiefs of the Ten and state attorneys who, according to Priuli, "have great care in proceeding against and punishing Venetian patricians because of *broglio*, that is, honors." Finally, orders were sent to Padua to arrest one patrician "as an example to others and to create fear." Rule by fear and example usually only took bloody form when patricians were not involved, as when three foreigners caught brawling with weapons at the Rialto were beheaded and left in view for several hours: "This sentence has terrified the entire city," writes Malipiero, "so that everything was quiet during the jousting."[105]

---

104 Sanuto, 12:187, 188, 190, 193; Priuli, vol. 6, fols. 206v–207r.
105 On the basilica: Sanuto, 37:7–8. On the debtors: Priuli, vol. 5, fol. 120r; cf. 2:275. On secrets in 1496: Sanuto, 1:402. On Padua: Priuli, 4:161; ASV, Con-

Lack of respect for the law was a negative consequence of *broglio* and political ambition. A positive consequence was that hostility within the patriciate was channeled into place seeking and elections. Passions were expressed by excluding others from office, with ballots, not with blood. The tensions within the ruling class found expression in elections and had no ideological dimension, the conflict between the old and new houses being the most convincing evidence of this. Certainly some electoral maneuvers, such as contests for the Collegio and the Ten, were tactics in factional disputes over policy, especially foreign affairs, but concern for place and position far outweighed interest in programs and policy. The Great Council held out a promise to every patrician, and major differences within the assembly were submerged in the time-consuming and compromising business of getting elected. Offices and elections created a community of interest and a sense of complicity, dissolving the edge of factions and making political life less dangerous than it might otherwise have been. Priuli put the matter very succinctly, if cynically, when he asserted, regarding Venetian corruption, "A wolf never eats the flesh of a wolf."[106]

Because the ruling class was closed to outsiders, and because extensive and illegal cooperation was essential for gaining nominations and winning elections, reciprocal dependency and fluid alignments were the bases of factionalism. *Broglio* was in the foundations of the constitution, maintaining, as one patrician wrote, "the unity, affection, and mutual deference without which the system of government might perish." In this perspective, even the selling of votes may be seen as a form of commerce that welded together rich and poor patricians.[107]

Broglio's role in stilling discontent and insuring harmony was vital and of immense practical significance. It not only explains in part Venice's freedom from debilitating factionalism and the maintenance of civic concord. It also clarifies why patrician state debtors were not punished; why poor patricians worked out their frustrations in the Great Council; why the Ten was so reluctant to chastise patricians, so quick to absolve them; why stern actions were never taken to eliminate vote peddling and political entertainment; and why attempts to fight corruption were doomed to failure. As Sanuto caustically inquired

---

siglio di Dieci, Parti Miste, Reg. 32, fol. 126r. On the beheadings: Malipiero, 2:674–675.

106 Priuli, vol. 6, fol. 93v.

107 On *broglio* in the foundations: "Discorsetto," no pagination. On the selling of votes as a source of unity: "Istoria del governo di Venezia," c. 11.

when a patrician was elected censor who had lobbied for the office: "How can he punish others?" *Broglio* also explains why disgrace and condemnation did not mean the end of a political career, for in Venice, political memories—except in the matter of votes—were necessarily short. As Priuli remarks, "In Venice intrigue, which has very great influence, comes into play. With scheming and so on, the actions of wrongdoers are forgotten and no longer talked about. In Venice there is nothing that cannot be obtained and nothing that cannot be forgotten with time, lobbying and intrigue."[108]

Venetians were of two minds about their political system. Recognition of the need for corruption coexisted with a certain commitment to the principle of honesty in elections. None of the measures to eliminate corruption could have passed without the support of majorities in the Great Council and the Senate. Yet Venetians were not simply hypocritical regarding their ideals; rather, their ambivalence toward electioneering reflected the ambiguous status of *broglio* as a necessary evil. A speech Sanuto made to the Great Council in 1526 perfectly illustrates that ambivalence, for, despite his lifelong opposition to electoral corruption, when he unsuccessfully spoke against the law on handshaking and congratulations, he presented an eloquent defense of political ambition.

The proposed law, Sanuto told the Great Council, was an offense to the loyalties of kinship and to the force of civic affection, which required external signs to make itself known. It was also a break with the traditions of the Republic's founders, who saw in fraternal embraces after elections the harmony that was the secret of Venetian success. He argued that a patrician elected by the Great Council had a twofold mandate that warranted a display of public happiness: A victory was an honor from the sovereign assembly, an appointment as its "vice-regent"; it was also evidence of the bounty of God. The proverb that "offices come from heaven" was, then, more than a counsel of despair or a solace in defeat; it was also a tribute to the ultimate sanction of all government. Finally, pointing out that several offices were exempt from the law because of their great dignity and importance, he asserted that a lowly patrician might be as happy to gain a meager post as a leading senator to rise to procurator, for all offices were honorable, and the Republic itself was enhanced when anyone shared in the distribution of honors: "That one is the start of

---

108 On the censor: Sanuto, 54:90; cf. 44:43; 55:295, 601. On Priuli's statement: 2:29; cf. 1:192; 4:198.

honors, and this the culmination . . . but the clasping of hands has been forever; and thus is created love, generosity, harmony, and peace: today for me, tomorrow for you."[109]

Corruption, because it was considered a necessary evil, was regarded both as a disease that had but recently infected the Republic and as a natural force, induced by the air of the city, stronger than the tides of the lagoon. Priuli thought that "intrigue and lobbying will be the ruin of Venice, and I marvel that it has lasted this long." Yet he also records the sentiments of others:

> Some say that lobbying and intrigue for offices are the salvation of the Republic of Venice, that is, the principal reason for [Venetian patricians] not offending or displeasing one another and for their maintaining tranquillity, amity and peace. Without their intrigues, favors and enticements, there would begin among them the sort of seditions, parties and discords which exist in all the cities of the world. There would be such great conflict among patricians that the complete ruin of Venice would follow. But by reason of lobbying and offices, all [discords] remain subdued, and enmities, factions and sects are kept secret.[110]

This perception of the link between political stability and *broglio* was not shared by the entire ruling class. Some patricians, including Priuli and Sanuto, rejected electoral corruption; most voted to outlaw it even while busily pursuing office. Yet the sentiment recorded by Priuli is striking evidence that some patricians recognized the political and electoral foundations of their state's unique freedom from upheaval and civic conflict.

The myth of Venice has a place within an ancient tradition of judging republics by the extent to which they triumph over corruption, whether that corruption is seen as the decay of civic spirit or as the inevitable breakdown of constitutional forms. But in Venice certain modes of corruption performed a vital stabilizing function. The renowned harmony and stability of the Republic were founded upon a politics of compromise and conciliation made necessary by the demands of seeking office. *Broglio* was the oil that made the complex machinery of state function so smoothly for so long that it seemed that Venice was free from ambition and faction. A state luminous

109 Sanuto, 40:665–666.
110 Priuli, vol. 5, fol. 90r.

with corruption thus became a shining example of political wisdom
and public virtue.

It goes without saying that this is not the portrait of the constitution found in Gasparo Contarini's treatise, the primary work through
which the notion of Venetian political perfection spread through
Europe after its publication in 1543. In the context of the early Cinquecento, Contarini's masterpiece appears in a strange light indeed,
for his description of a state perfectly ordered according to the laws
of nature and surpassing the wisdom of ancient republics is at odds
with that contained in the diaries of his contemporaries. Contarini
was far from ignorant of political realities, even if he was not greatly
experienced when he wrote his book around 1524. The Mantuan ambassador described him as "a very learned man, though not very expert in matters of state" when he was elected ambassador to Charles V
in 1520.[111] Born in 1483, Contarini was twenty-six at the time of
Agnadello, thirty-four when the war ended, and forty-one when *De
republica* was written. His description of Venetian government is very
much a product of the War of the League of Cambrai when he alludes
to the rise of the Ten, the decline of the state attorneys, *giovani*
domination of posts on the Collegio, and the flaunting of ancient laws
for reasons of ambition. He also shows a keen eye for the realities of
power when he discusses the force of the ballot, the role of the young
and poor in the Court of the Forty, and the political significance of
nonpatrician institutions. At the same time, he paints Venice in ideal
colors, at a fair remove from reality; his praise for Venetian perfection
is almost wholly reserved for the time of "our great ones," the founding fathers who started the Republic on its history of virtue and
wisdom.

There is more involved in the disparity between the myth and the
reality of Venice in the Cinquecento than the obvious irony that the
literary work that launched the European career of the myth was
written not long after Venetian politics had begun to be less open and
more corrupt as a result of the most devastating defeat in the city's
history. With its portrait of saintly, altruistic, and wise founders, *De
republica* may have been intended as much for the education of Contarini's fellow patricians as for the edification of Christendom. The
book was, then, a product of the Cambrai crisis, as well as a solution

111 ASM, b. 1454, Giambattista Malatesta to the marquis of Mantua, October
3, 1520. Cf. Felix Gilbert, "The Date of the Composition of Contarini's and
Giannotti's Books on Venice"; James Bruce Ross, "The Emergence of Gasparo
Contarini."

for it—a return to the spirit of Venice's origins, a reform of the present by a return to the values of the past. During the war, Egnazio, a Venetian humanist and a friend of both Contarini and Sanuto, praised the simple virtues and piety of the founders as suitable models for the present; and Sanuto too believed that a renewal of traditional values and a return to a simpler life were Venice's only salvation. Similarly, according to Priuli, Venice was once in "an earthly paradise," lacking factions and dissent, blessed by peace and harmony, until luxury, immorality, and corruption caused a "fall from heaven to earth."[112]

Given Venetian notions about the Republic's providential destiny, defeat by the League of Cambrai was only comprehensible in terms of a prior decline from grace. Agnadello did not shatter the image of a perfect republic: The fall from paradise had already taken place, in slow motion as it were, as Venetians succumbed in peacetime to slack morals, foreign manners, and soul-destroying luxuries. The War of the League of Cambrai appeared to many as a confirmation of degeneracy, a just punishment for deviation from original virtue; God was using the barbaric but pure people of the north to punish the Republic for its ambition and vice, for losing the courage and resolve that had made the state so powerful. The strengths of Venice, Antonio Condulmer asserted in 1504, had been converted to debilitating weaknesses: "Four good mothers have given birth to four evil daughters: prosperity created envy; familiarity, complacency; truth, hatred; and friendship, corrupt justice."[113]

Providential conceptions also pointed the way out of the crisis, for it could not be assumed that God would chastise without hope of redemption. The War of the League of Cambrai was therefore seen as a purge. The very magnitude of the defeat in 1509 became part of the argument for the Republic's essential perfection and God's guiding hand in its destiny. Agnadello seemed to offer Venice a second chance at virtue, an opportunity to recapture the purity of its origins. Hence the turn to the past by Contarini, Sanuto, Egnazio, Priuli, as well as the government itself, which in 1516 established the post of official historiographer of Venice.[114] Taunted by the enemy that Venetians

112 On Contarini and Egnazio: Felix Gilbert, "Religion and Politics in the Thought of Gasparo Contarini," pp. 101, 114; idem, "Venice in the Crisis," pp. 280, 289. On Priuli: Priuli, 4:331; 29–35.

113 Sanuto, 6:97. On Venice's decline: cf. Sanuto, 1:514; 8:290–291; 11:686; 12:80; Priuli, 2:31; 4:24, 26–27, 29, 33–35; Luigi da Porto, Lettere storiche dell'anno 1509 al 1528, p. 26.

114 Felix Gilbert, "Biondo, Sabellico, and the Beginnings of Venetian Official Historiography."

would be forced back to their original profession, Priuli retorted that such vituperation was really extraordinary praise, inasmuch as the founders of the Christian religion, like those of Venice, the first Christian Republic, were also simple fisherfolk. Agnadello, wrote a patrician, returned Venice to its origins, to the time of Attila, whose army ravaged the shores of the lagoon, as did that of the Empire in 1513. Titian's grandest woodcut, *The Drowning of the Pharaoh's Army in the Red Sea*, produced soon after 1513, clearly refers to both the city's foundation and its present crisis: A chosen people watch the confounding of their enemy, while a Gothic spire looms across the protecting water.[115]

For Priuli the survival of the city was miraculous, inasmuch as the War of the League of Cambrai far surpassed the dangers of the dreadful War of Chioggia, when only Genoa opposed Venice; in 1509, all Europe joined in the assault. A Venetian merchant, writing to his brother in Beirut shortly after Agnadello, bitterly complained of "this harsh and brutal war started by a league—and I should not call it a league but a crusade against this poor state, the sort of crusade that Christians have always tried to send against the wretched, infidel Turks has been launched against poor Venetians!" Yet, while the vaunted Roman Republic crumbled before the threats of Julius Caesar, Venetians could express immense pride in having retained their form of government even though the mainland empire was lost and the enemy could be sighted from the rooftops of the city. According to Priuli, the secret of Venetian survival lay in the immortality of a republican government, for the princely allies of the league were merely men and quick to pass away. Even when Gritti was languishing in a Milanese prison after his capture at Brescia in 1512, he had the comfort of being told by a servant of Louis XII of France that the pope and the emperor "build on air," for they are human, but "His Majesty recognizes that the Signoria will never die."[116]

Still, although it was possible to rationalize the disaster of the war as a punishment and a purge and to see the recovery of the state as a

---

115 On enemy threats: Priuli, 4:424; cf. Sanuto, *Cronachetta*, pp. 7, 13. On return to origins: Sanuto, 9:220. On the woodcut: Michelangelo Muraro and David Rosand, *Tiziano e la silografia veneziana del Cinquecento*, pp. 80–83.

116 On Cambrai and Chioggia: Priuli, 4:326; cf. 314. On the Venetian merchant: Dalla Santa, *La Lega di Cambrai*, p. 8. On Rome and Venice: Antonio Giustiniani, "Orazione fatta in occasione della Lega di Cambrai (1515)"; cf. Daniele Barbaro, *Storia Veneziana dall'anno 1512 al 1515*, p. 951. On Venetian immortality: Priuli, 4:398. On Gritti in prison: ASV, Consiglio di Dieci, Parti Miste, Reg. 35, fol. 21v.

sign of providence and perfection, the changes wrought in the patriciate and the constitution during the long crisis could not easily be resolved. In 1517 it seemed that Venice could return to normality, perhaps recover its past glory, but that soon proved to be illusory. When Venice accepted the Peace of Bologna in 1530, finally relinquishing the Apulian ports and the Romagna, notions of glory were themselves a thing of the past.

The years of the Italian wars were, for Venice, ones of spiritual turmoil compounded of a crisis of confidence in the ruling class, in the institutions of state, and in traditional values.[117] Efforts were made to eliminate political evils, buttress religious orthodoxy, and revive commitment to the values of the Republic's founders. The year 1524 saw the recreation of the censors, Venice's first official stand against Martin Luther, and the writing of Contarini's book on the constitution. These all redounded to Venetian credit abroad but could do nothing at home to restore the politics of the city to its pre-Agnadello forms. Before 1509, with all its undeniable confusions and inefficiencies, the constitution was a working whole characterized by lively collaboration and competition among the councils; patrician discontents were translated into vigorous tension between and within the principal assemblies. In this context the Senate played a crucial role as the council that, mingling *Primi* and *poveri*, mediated between the exclusive committees and the Great Council. After the Italian wars, this was clearly no longer the case, although interest in offices and elections remained as high as ever, with perhaps an added touch of acrimony if the *case grandi* struggle of 1527 is any indication. "When the bell rings for the Senate," said the procurator Ferigo Corner in 1529, "it is to govern the *terra* and not to do nothing, as is done at present."[118] But the complaint was already old.

Contarini's generation entered the Great Council in the year of the League of Cambrai, so it never experienced participation in a government not dominated by the executive councils and in which offices

---

117 Cf. Cozzi, "Authority and the Law," pp. 337–338; Felix Gilbert, "Venice in the Crisis," p. 290. Also see: I. Cervelli, "Storiografia e problemi intorno alla vita religiosa e spirituale di Venezia nella prima metà del '500," pp. 461–462; Carlo Dionisotti, "Chierici e laici nella letteratura italiana del primo Cinquecento," pp. 167–185. L. Puppi, "La residenze di Pietro Bembo 'in padoana,'" pp. 41–44, 47–48, 52–55; Gigliola Fragnito, "Cultura umanistica e riforma religiosa," p. 91; Lester J. Libby, "Venetian History and Political Thought after 1509," pp. 7–45.

118 Sanuto, 50:369; cf. ASV, Consiglio di Dieci, Parti Secrete, Reg. 3, fols. 2r–2v, 3r–3v, 9r–9v, 11r, 15r, 25r–25v.

were not regarded as objects of commerce. One wonders what effect constant evasion of the law, avoidance of sacrifice, sale of offices, closure of the governing circle, and acceptance of corruption had on its perception of politics. Writing around 1525, Donato Giannotti noted that some Venetians feared that the political disorder attendant on selling offices would spell the decline of the Republic into tyranny, "if not in our own time, at least in that of our sons."[119] Giannotti and Contarini turned to study the constitution just as the reality of the Republic's politics clearly diverged from what Venetians liked to believe about themselves and their fabled constitutional order. They wrote at a time when it seemed to many that Venice had squandered its second chance in the very struggle for survival, and when control of the Republic began slowly to slip into the hands of the generation formed by the crisis of Cambrai.

119 Giannotti, *Libro de la Republica*, p. 93.

Chapter V

Conflict in the Councils

1. *The Tron: Dissent and the Governing Circle*

In March 1515 the Signoria received a number of costly presents from Sultan Selim I. The councillors and *savi* eagerly distributed the largesse, with Doge Loredan receiving a fur cap, Alvise Pisani an ermine cloak, and Giovanni Francesco Bragadin an inlaid saddle. The happy occasion was spoiled, however, by Antonio Tron, a *savio grande*, who informed the Full Collegio that he intended proposing to the Senate that the gifts be auctioned, with the proceeds going to expenses in the Arsenal. Immediately, the gifts were surrendered and the Collegio presented Tron's motion to the Senate, where it was easily passed.[1]

Trivial in itself, the episode indicates some of the difficulties encumbering dissent in Venetian politics. Only a politician of high stature who frequently won election to the executive councils could effectively and consistently dissent from government policies while maintaining a voice in the making of decisions. Despite the fierce arguments within the executive councils when they met to set the agendas of the Great Council and the Senate, differences of opinion generally became matter for public debate only when they assumed the form of opposing motions, because the presentation of a single proposal was merely an occasion for voting. A motion to delay a vote was a common method of registering disagreement with a policy without the necessity of proposing an alternative and of giving patricians an opportunity to speak against the Signoria or the Collegio. During

---

1 Sanuto, 20:41, 43, 47; Michiel, fol. 157r.

the War of the League of Cambrai, the practice arose of using one proposal to spell out the faults of another, a maneuver the Ten soon condemned as making for contention in both the executive councils and the larger assemblies.[2]

It was rare that a motion was passed unanimously by the Great Council or the Senate. A handful of patricians could invariably be found to vote against such uncontroversial measures as giving grain to the poor (as a thanksgiving for the victory at Marignano) or contributing money for Alviano's funeral monument in the church of Santo Stefano. Although a council could register a clear protest against a measure by defeating it, that did not happen very often. When a single proposal came before the Great Council or the Senate, it usually had the support of a majority on the Full Collegio and passage generally was assured. Moreover, the councillors and *savi* were very sensitive to a hostile atmosphere in the councils; the possibility of a rebuff usually meant withdrawal of the motion at issue. According to Priuli in 1500, "the whole Great Council made substantial noise . . . and seeing the will of the assembly, the councillors reversed their [earlier] determination."[3] When a disagreeable proposal appeared certain to pass, the *Primi* often sponsored it themselves to avoid embarrassment and preserve their honor. That was the tactic used against Tron regarding the sultan's gifts. Concern for patrician opinion by the councillors and *savi* made Tron's lone dissent effective, although sponsorship of his intended motion by those who were the objects of it both muted his opposition and concealed their greed. Appearances were thus maintained. The Venetian political system had a marvelous capacity for absorbing the forces of dissent and opposition.

Public speaking, the most important formal means of registering dissent, was restricted by regulations concerning the making of proposals, responses in opposition, and the content of speeches. The right of making proposals belonged only to the Signoria and the Collegio, although ex officio members of the Senate could present motions in the area of their own competence. An enterprising patrician, such as Sanuto, could persuade a friendly councillor, chief of the Forty, or *savio* to put forward his idea for him, but this was probably not a

2 ASV, Consiglio di Dieci, Parti Miste, Reg. 34, fols. 38v–39r.

3 On the rarity of a unanimous vote: Sanuto, 13:305. On rarity of defeat: cf. Sanuto, 34:140. On grain and Alviano: ASV, Senato, Terra, Reg. 19, fols. 44r, 54r. On withdrawing a motion: Sanuto, 3:35, 65, 646; 7:153; 12:287; 43:90; 58: 498–499, 521; Michiel, fols. 168r–168v. On 1500: Priuli, 1:315.

common practice. Presentation of proposals and speeches against them followed certain procedures. In the Senate the doge and the councillors first put forward their motions, followed in order by the chiefs of the Forty, the *savi grandi*, the *savi di terraferma*, and the *savi agli ordini*; within each group, the older members had precedence. Replies by the Signoria or the Collegio to speeches in the Senate were made according to the rank of the opposing speaker. For instance, a *savio grande* or a councillor responded to a procurator; a *savio agli ordini*, to a judge of the Forty. This hierarchy of response was not followed in the Great Council, and several times Doge Gritti honored Sanuto by replying to his arguments. Brief comments in the Great Council and the Senate could be made from one's seat, but lengthy remarks were delivered from the *renga*, a pulpitlike affair set along the walls of the council chambers. Finally, all speeches, which were delivered in the Venetian dialect, had to be directed specifically to the motions at issue; deviation into generalities or other topics was forbidden. General remarks were permissible in certain set orations and in the *relazioni* of returned ambassadors but were not allowed in debate; nor were attacks on other patricians or the expression of unpatriotic sentiments permitted.[4]

Grand oratory was not suited to the Venetian temperament; public speaking was not a highly developed art in the city's assemblies. The Ten, responsible for decorum in the councils, passed legislation iterating the need for order during debate and establishing penalties for excessive noise, especially as caused by moving from bench to bench and interrupting speakers. The Collegio itself added to the disorder. While a secretary was reading a proposal to the Senate, the tribune was sometimes deserted by the *savi*, who would wander about the chamber, perhaps even leave it. A constant buzz and hum accompanied speechifying; it was difficult to attract and retain the attention of hundreds of patricians more interested in upcoming elections than in the fine points of legislation. The size of the council chambers presented an obvious difficulty for the orator; a patrician with what Sanuto calls "a slight voice" was well advised not to address the Great

---

4 On persuading someone to present a motion: cf. Sanuto, 28:390; 19:416–417. On presentation and response: Giuseppe Maranini, *La costituzione di Venezia dopa la serrata del Maggior Consiglio*, pp. 238, 246–247; Enrico Besta, *Il Senato Veneziano*, p. 221. On Gritti and Sanuto: Sanuto, 43:205; cf. 48:300; 51:55. On the *renga*: Maranini, *Costituzione di Venezia*, pp. 235, 249–250; Besta, *Senato Veneziano*, p. 226; Sanuto, 3:406–407; 7:191.

Council, where his words would have been lost in the immense hall (180 feet long, 84 feet wide, and 47 feet high). Sanuto often emphasizes the attention the Great Council paid to him by noting that "no one spat" while he spoke.[5]

Speakers were fond of set phrases, and Sanuto collected a list of the favorite clichés of thirty-three *Primi*. Thus, Giorgio Corner often repeated, "I wish to say this . . . "; Marco Barbarigo, "On the one hand and on the other . . . "; and Paolo Pisani, "How inhumane this is!" These do not testify to a high level of oratory. In fact, little tolerance was shown by patricians to those who occupied the *renga* too often or too long, and Sanuto usually felt that an apology was necessary when he rose to speak. The impatience of the councils is comprehensible considering that most debates were heavily laden with citations of precedents and other technical matter. For example, a magistrate from the Water Office spent hours opposing the digging of a new canal by reviewing all the legislation on such matters since 1324. Even the famous *relazioni* to the Senate must have been a chore to sit through, as with Lorenzo Bernardo's approximately five-hour report on his tenure as consul in Istanbul. Sanuto claims that the Great Council willingly listened when he spoke because of his reputation for brevity, but when Francesco Bollani, a state attorney, entered the *renga*, "he was garrulous, boring and few listened to him. . . . he has a slight voice and expresses himself poorly."[6] In short, speaking in the councils was not a venture to be undertaken lightly; numerous restrictions hemmed in a speaker, whose audience was censorious, easily bored, and quick to make known its displeasure.

Still, the rights of debate and free speech were highly valued in Venice. No matter how restricted they were in practice, they provided a measure of participation in the governing circle's decisions. According to Sanuto, whenever a patrician entered the *renga*, he "placed his honor in peril," even though it was the duty of everyone to speak out when displeased with a motion. It was the responsibility of the Ten to protect such dissent. Minio had the misfortune (or lack

5 On legislation by the Ten: Sanuto, 3:64; 7:191; 9:292. On *savi* wandering: ASV, Consiglio di Dieci, Parti Miste, Reg. 32, fol. 178r. On "no one spat": Sanuto, 24:656; cf. 677; 20:286; 28:508; 36:122.

6 On the clichés: Marino Sanuto, "Miscellanea di Cronica Veneta," fols. 67r–68r. On apologizing for speaking: Sanuto, 23:511–512; 26:374; 27:680. On the Water Office: Sanuto, 27:443; 392, 393, 448–449, 450; cf. 20:243. On Bernardo: Donald E. Queller, "The Development of Ambassadorial Relazioni," p. 182. On Sanuto and Bollani: Sanuto, 20:284.

of discretion) to oppose vital legislation at a crucial time and to imply
while doing so that providence was siding with the Turks against the
Republic; he thus overstepped the limits of official toleration, and the
Ten acted accordingly. But when Doge Barbarigo persistently inter-
rupted Alvise Bragadin's arguments against a proposal in the Council
of Ten in 1497, "the chiefs rose and said quietly that His Excellency
must allow everyone to speak and say what he thought, for the good
of the city. And the doge said nothing more, though he occasionally
complained that he received little respect."[7]

In 1500 a speech by Gabriele Moro, a *savio agli ordini*, angered
Leonardo Loredan, a *savio grande*, who demanded that the Ten take
action; the chiefs replied that "everyone in the Senate is free fully to
state his opinion." Twenty-three years later, Moro told the Senate
that he was at liberty to criticize the executive councils because he
was "born in a free city." Alvise di Giovanni Priuli's criticisms of
Loredan's timidity after Agnadello roused the doge to fury ("You
deserve to be thrown off this balcony!" he shouted); but the Ten
rejected his demand that Priuli be punished for disloyalty to the state.
Similarly, in 1528 Alvise Mocenigo criticized Doge Gritti, asserting
"that none of the Collegio says anything against him because of fear,
[yet Alvise] fears nothing [when considering] the good of the state
and the welfare of the patriciate."[8] So long as they did not affront the
basic values and self-interests of the state, dissent and criticism received some protection. At the same time, because the line of permissible dissent was vaguely drawn and depended on the particular
occasion and on the individuals charged with guarding free speech, the
dissenter was always in danger of provoking a reaction that could lead
to severe punishment or exclusion from power.

Luca and Antonio Tron were masters at political maneuvering on
the margin between tolerated opposition and outrageous dissent. Almost certainly they escaped serious censure on occasion because they
articulated the views of other (intimidated) patricians and because they
were firmly placed in the ranks of the *Primi*. The Tron clan numbered
only twenty-six members in 1527. Luca and Antonio were first cousins
and belonged to the San Benedetto branch of their clan, which counted
only ten men in the Great Council. The other branch of the *casa*,

7 On placing "honor in peril": Sanuto, 27:681; cf. 23:341. On Bragadin:
Malipiero, 2:706.

8 On Moro: Sanuto, 3:1079; 27:296. On Loredan: Sanuto, 8:369. On Mocenigo:
Sanuto, 47:727.

resident at San Stae and seven generations distant from its fellows at San Benedetto, was politically insignificant in the early Cinquecento. A century earlier the San Benedetto branch had split, and the line descending from Luca di Donato (the father of Doge Nicolò), which included Filippo, Luca, and Antonio, became extinct with the death of Luca in 1540.[9]

Doge Nicolò established the political and economic fortunes of the family. Like Antonio Grimani and Andrea Gritti, he entered politics late in life after amassing a fortune in the Levant. His election to the dogeship in November 1471 was aided by the death of his elder son, Giovanni, in a heroic attempt to recapture Negroponte from the Turks in July. He had, however, to overcome the accusation of one patrician who said that "at Rhodes he had been an infamous usurer, and that he was not the man to govern Venice." In the Ducal Palace, Nicolò was a welcome contrast to his predecessor, Cristoforo Moro, who, according to Malipiero, had been "gloomy, hypocritical, vindictive, mendacious, greedy, and hated by the people." The diarist describes Nicolò as "a rich man, worth 60,000 ducats, along with goods valued at more than 20,000. He gained this fortune at Rhodes, where he was a merchant for fifteen years. He was a man of strong character, fat and with ugly features, similar to the figure on his tomb [to the left of the high altar in the Frari]. He was a generous man, holding public dinners in the Ducal Palace for all the city's guilds, at which the dogaressa came dressed in cloth of gold. He was a man of great spirit," whose only drawback was a distressing habit of spitting when he spoke.[10]

Doge Nicolò's liberality and exuberant nature made him a popular doge. Both characteristics were typical of his son and nephews, who were also well liked by the *popolo*. Filippo di Nicolò was already an important politician before his father's three-year reign, during which he illegally accepted election to the Ten, although he was soon forced to resign the seat. In the ducal election of 1476, Filippo, affronted at the idea of a grandson of a man admitted to the patriciate as recently as the War of Chioggia occupying the Ducal Palace, spoke against the elevation of Andrea Vendramin. After holding the usual series of important offices, Filippo was made procurator in 1492. Ambitious and

9 Barbaro, 8597, fols. 143v–146r; Capellari, vol. 4, fols. 139v–141v; "Arbore della Famiglia Trono."

10 On Giovanni Tron: Malipiero, 2:660; cf. Antonio Pilot, "L'elezione del doge Nicolò Tron." On the accusation: Malipiero, 2:646–647. On Moro and Nicolò: Malipiero, 2:660–661; cf. Marino Sanuto, "Cronica Sanuda," fol. 335v.

subtle, he was Doge Agostino Barbarigo's nemesis on the Collegio and the Ten, never missing an opportunity to oppose his policies or mock his pretensions. Barbarigo and Antonio Grimani were Filippo's foremost opponents between 1497 and 1499 when he was the leader of a group, including some younger patricians, that supported Venetian intervention in the Pisan rebellion against Florence. In 1491 and 1497, he championed the right of the Senate to make ecclesiastical appointments against the Collegio's willingness to accede to Grimani's frantic lobbying for his son, Domenico. In August 1499 Filippo urged the expulsion of state debtors from the Collegio and the Senate—a highly unusual suggestion for a member of the governing circle. The same month saw the battle of Zonchio, which gave Filippo and his allies the chance to send Grimani into exile. Filippo had a fearsome reputation in the councils, where, notes Sanuto, he "lacks reverence and openly speaks his mind, and very cuttingly. . . . without regard for anyone." When Barbarigo called him "a man of the devil," he remained unperturbed, rejoining that he feared only God. The Ferrarese ambassador reported that Filippo's opponents prayed for his early death, a request granted (in Venetian political terms) when he died at sixty-four, a few days after his old enemy, Barbarigo. Detested by many of the *Primi*, "the people liked him, since he always attacked when debating— however they do not elect the doge."[11]

Luca and Antonio were equally successful in high office and in evoking hatred and affection. Their combativeness was similar to Filippo's, and their feistiness in the councils, as well as their readiness to criticize the *Primi*, explains the acclaim they enjoyed in the city. Luca established a reputation for being "just and severe" from his tour of duty as a government inspector (*sindico*) in 1499. A fierce debater, impetuous and clever, he was quick to impugn the motives of his opponents, one of whom ruefully remarked in 1510 that "Tron always has his knife at hand" in the councils. He was not afraid of taking chances, and at crucial moments his eloquence often prevailed— although, when the Portuguese began to encroach on the spice trade, he was not successful in urging the Senate to turn the state galleys

11 On Filippo's election to the Ten: Sanuto, "Cronica Sanuda," fol. 339v. On 1476: idem, *Vite dei dogi*, fol. 35r; cf. Malipiero, 2:667. On Pisa: Malipiero, 1: 512. On ecclesiastical appointments: Sanuto, *Vite dei dogi*, fol. 330v; Sanuto, 1: 746–747; cf. 2:774. On state debtors: Sanuto, 2:1071. On Filippo's reputation: Sanuto, 1:984; 4:144. On "a man of the devil": Sanuto, 2:788–789. On the Ferrarese ambassador: ASMo., b. 10, c. 54, Pellegrino Prisciani to the duke of Ferrara, June 29, 1492; cf. b. 10, c. 23, November 30, 1491. On the people and Filippo: Sanuto, 4:144.

toward the West because, as he argued, "the world has changed . . . [and] following the times we must change our habits and set sail."[12]

Antonio was a calmer, more calculating, and perhaps more serious politician than Luca, with a sense of political theater, a liking for the grand gesture. He too was renowned for his biting sarcasm and eloquence and was considered "a fearsome man" for prosecuting a fellow state attorney for corruption in 1493. Vigorous in combating corruption and special interests, he was, according to his friend Sanuto, "always willing to make innovations and to order the Great Council and the city for the greatest public welfare."[13] Although Luca and Antonio were sometimes on opposing sides of issues, for the most part they coordinated their political activity. Luca virtually ceased dissenting from government policies in the early 1520s, at the same time that Antonio retired from political life—a coincidence that hints at Luca following the lead of his cousin. However, the death of Luca's leading enemies, Leonardo Loredan and Antonio Grimani, may equally well have contributed to the end of his contentiousness.

Luca was elected a government inspector for the Levant in 1497. Inspectors, like state attorneys, were commissioned to ferret out official misconduct, and Luca proved exceptionally diligent in the post. It was a critical time to enter the office because the towns of Dalmatia and Apulia were in turmoil over an expected incursion of the Turkish fleet and were angry as well over abuses of authority by Venetian officials. Apparently inspectors were also known for their misconduct, for Malipiero claims that Luca's predecessors during the previous thirty years had merely added to the problems of the colonies. Luca and his colleague, Pietro Sanuto, left Venice in June 1498, armed with a commission that gave them great latitude in carrying out their task. Luca made ample use of this authority, sweeping through Dalmatia and Crete, countermanding orders and levying charges against administrators of every rank. Officials of Modone and Crete wrote to Venice complaining of his excesses. Marchio Trevisan, the captain general of the fleet who had recently replaced Antonio Grimani, complained hotly that Luca had charged him with incompetence stemming

12 On Luca's reputation: Sanuto, 5:710. On "his knife at hand": Sanuto, 10: 229–230. On "the world has changed": Gaetano Cozzi, "Authority and Law in Renaissance Venice," p. 321.

13 On "a fearsome man": ASMo., b. 7, c. 85, Aldobrandino Guidoni to the duke of Ferrara, September 9, 1493; cf. b. 7, c. 103, October 7, 1493. On Antonio making innovations: Sanuto, 1:838.

from the advanced stages of syphilis. In fact, the two inspectors, who had separated after leaving Venice, even wrote to the Signoria attacking each other's conduct in office. Luca accused numerous important officials in Crete of maladministration; his proceeding against Bernardo di Pancratio Giustiniani, military governor of the island, shocked the government at home, for Bernardo was "a saint and of high reputation" (he was also the brother-in-law of Leonardo Loredan).[14]

An attempt was made in the Collegio to cut short Luca's tour of duty, and when Filippo Tron tried to read to the Senate a letter he had received from Luca, Barbarigo halted him. Finally, in June 1500, two years after leaving, the inspectors returned. Luca reported to the Collegio that he was bringing many patricians to trial and that "our maritime territories are being plundered" by Venetian magistrates. When he gave the Senate a report on his activity in Crete, "the chiefs of the Ten admonished him many times not to speak badly of these persons [in their absence]; but when he still continued, Zaccaria Dolfin, a chief of the Ten, stood up and insisted that he obey." Luca presented the voluminous records of his investigations to the Signoria, and the trials of more than ten important colonial officials began. His case load was so heavy that a law was passed prohibiting election of returned inspectors to other offices for eighteen months so as not to interfere with their activity in the supreme courts. The outcome of these trials was surely influenced by events in the *stato di mar*. News of the fall of Modone followed Luca to Venice by three months, and to many it seemed that the colonial administration had indeed neglected its responsibilities. A few days before the Great Council's rejection of the nominees to the Zonta, Luca was elected to the Senate for his services. He gained "a great reputation [in the Great Council] for having convicted many officials."[15] It is equally certain that he had made a number of new enemies and angered old ones.

Luca's zeal and impulsiveness brought him into conflict with his

14 On turmoil in Dalmatia and Apulia: Sanuto, 1:651, 741. On misconduct by inspectors: Malipiero, 2:706. On the commission: Sanuto, 1:741; 905, 963, 982. On complaints by officials: Sanuto, 2:182, 190, 650, 1235, 1254. On Trevisan: Sanuto, 3:526; cf. 407, 550. On attacking each other: Sanuto, 3:69. On Giustiniani: Sanuto, 3:52.

15 On Filippo in the Senate: Sanuto, 3:52; 788. On Luca's report: Sanuto, 3: 384, 406-407. On the trials: Sanuto, 3:531, 585, 652-653, 1240, 1498, 1510, 1573; 4:23, 52, 75, 83, 158, 273; Pietro Dolfin, *Annalium Venetorum (pars quatro)*, pp. 115, 253. On the law: Sanuto, 25:246. On Modone and the Zonta election: this book, Chapter II.2. On Luca's reputation: Sanuto, 4:86; cf. 5:710.

fellows on the executive councils during the War of the League of
Cambrai. He was one of the *Primi* who favored an aggressive military
policy. In general, the executive councils followed conservative and
defensive strategies, preferring to keep Venetian forces bottled up in
areas already recovered rather than risk them against the enemy. As a
member of the Ten, Luca was one of the strongest proponents of the
ill-fated punitive expedition against Ferrara in the winter of 1509.
Despite the destruction of the fleet, he remained a staunch supporter
of subsequent expeditions, even joining with his enemy Antonio
Grimani to oppose the Collegio, which wanted to limit such adventuresome moves. Luca was also an advocate of seeking military aid
from the Turks, a policy decisively at odds with that of the Collegio.
As a chief of the Ten, he was opposed to making concessions to
Francesco Gonzaga, the marquis of Mantua, who had been captured
by Venice in August 1509; this intransigent attitude, maintained vehemently and singlehandedly, was unsuccessful, and Gonzaga won
release from prison.[16]

Luca's most notable victory over the Collegio regarding military
affairs was in March 1514, when he insisted that Alviano's forces be
sent to relieve the fortress of Osoppo in Friuli. Some thirty miles
north of Udine on the Tagliamento river, the fortress controlled
access to the province from Austria and was thus of crucial importance
to war strategy. If imperial troops succeeded in taking Osoppo, they
would link with Spanish forces in the Veneto and menace Padua and
Treviso, thereby putting Venice in a position similar to that of the
autumn of 1513 when the enemy destroyed Mestre. The Collegio was
opposed to letting Alviano leave Padua, no doubt recalling that, in
October 1513 when he moved from the city against a weaker Spanish
army, he was routed, despite every expectation of success. On March
1 the Collegio won Senate approval of a proposal to keep Alviano in
Padua; but a week later, Luca, a councillor, succeeded in having the
Senate delay issuing further orders to Alviano. It is likely that Luca,
supported by Grimani, a *savio grande*, used the delay to have Alviano,
an adventuresome commander, bring pressure on the government, for
a few days later Alviano wrote to the Ten about the bright prospects

16 On Ferrara: Sanuto, 9:330; 11:172, 270, 305, 397, 626; cf. Robert Finlay,
"Venice, the Po Expedition, and the End of the League of Cambrai (1509–
1510)." On the Turks: Sanuto, 8:548; 17:366, 535. On Gonzaga: Sanuto, 10:200; cf.
249–250, 291, 292, 523–524; Alessandro Luzio, "La reggenza d'Isabella d'Este
durante la prigionia del marito (1509–1510)."

for victory if he were dispatched to Friuli. Still, the Collegio's cautious policy was upheld on March 12 by a vote of 104 to 81, a position unshaken by Luca's speech attacking the Collegio nine days later. But on the twenty-fourth, after a lengthy and eloquent oration, he finally swayed the Senate, which approved his motion (cosponsored by Grimani) sending Alviano to Friuli. In exactly a week, Alviano had lifted the siege of Osoppo and decisively defeated imperial forces, one of the few clear-cut victories Venice enjoyed in the war. For the first time since Agnadello, Friuli was wholly restored to Venice, and the military threat from the Empire was gone. Luca was the hero of the city for defying the Collegio, and on April 2 the Great Council rewarded him with the important office of captain of Famagusta in Cyprus, an honor he declined; a week later he was made *savio grande* for the first time.[17]

Affairs of the government also attracted Luca's attention. While a chief of the Ten in August 1510, he authored legislation prohibiting cousins from serving together on one branch of the Collegio. A month later, while a *savio di terraferma*, he objected to the other *savi* sending off a letter without consulting the Senate; he usually tried when on the Collegio and the Ten to stop the executive councils from usurping the proper business of the Senate. In the same year he and a *savio grande* joined together to defeat a proposal by the rest of the Collegio for new taxes. He was the only *savio grande* in June 1514 to unite with three *savi di terraferma* in proposing the elimination of *scrutinii* nominations, and in 1521 he wanted to increase the authority of the Great Council by having the final electoral college in the ducal election selected by the sovereign assembly. He also opposed the sale of procuratorships, the growth of the Ten's *zonta*, and the creation of the censors.[18]

Luca's opposition to the censors stemmed from his concern that the new office would detract from the authority of the state attorneys, which he considered essential to the proper functioning of the consti-

17 On Osoppo: Sanuto, 17:125, 126, 152, 158, 176, 192, 202, 203, 220–221; 18: 35–36, 38–41, 49, 51–54, 64, 69–70, 71–75. On Luca's speech and the victory: Sanuto, 18:61, 62, 63, 65–66, 70, 78, 81–82, 90; Daniele Barbaro, *Storia Veneziana dall'anno 1512 al 1515*, pp. 1037–1040. On Luca's elections: Sanuto, 18:91, 114, 116–117, 119–120.

18 On the Collegio: Sanuto, 11:232. On protecting the Senate: Sanuto, 11:397; cf. 19:335, 357, 402, 415, 416. On opposing new taxes: Sanuto, 11:493. On the *scrutinii* and ducal election: Sanuto, 18:291, 305; 30:395, 402. On the procuratorships, censors, and *zonta*: Sanuto, 22:215, 253; 24:654; 28:8–9, 11.

tution.[19] For the same reason, in 1518 he was against the creation of a new magistracy to combat immorality in the city's monasteries. A year later he was the force behind a new law creating three special state attorneys (*avogadori straordinari*) to ease the heavy work load of the office to increase the efficiency, and thereby the prestige, of the regular attorneys. During these same years, Luca's concern for proper justice prompted him to oppose new laws—harsh reactions to the banditry that increased during the war—which permitted the murder of outlaws by other outlawed murderers in return for mitigation of the latters' sentences.

In 1520 Luca aroused the wrath of the doge, the Ten, and the church. All the other *savi grandi* proposed a letter to Rome requesting Pope Leo X to revoke a monastery's title to certain land near the lagoon because it was needed for Venetian defenses. Luca objected that Venice did not need the papacy's permission to fortify itself and that the Signoria had razed churches in Padua during the war without such permission. Fearful that Luca was risking the excommunication of Venice, his fellow *savi* wanted the Ten to take action against him. When the papal legate was meeting some time later with the Full Collegio, Luca, now a councillor, shocked the gathering by casually suggesting that Venice appeal against the pope to a church council—a notion that put him in accord with Martin Luther regarding the pope's authority. Furious at this indiscretion, Doge Loredan called on the chiefs of the Ten to silence Luca, who was thereupon instructed to make no further interruptions.[20]

Clear themes emerge from Luca's various concerns: regard for the Senate's authority and opposition to a monopoly on decision making in the executive councils, concern for good administration and clean government, support for the state attorneys, a commitment to equality within the patriciate, and a pronounced assertion of the right to debate and dissent. Yet these themes were almost invariably expressed in such vitriolic terms, so mixed with savage attacks on individuals, that it is impossible to discern where principle ends and animosity begins. In January 1515 his concern over customs revenue from salt turned into an all-out attack on the Collegio in which he accused the *savi*, especially Grimani, of financial corruption and, at least implicitly, of

19 On what follows, see Cozzi, "Authority and the Law," pp. 322–323, 338.
20 Sanuto, 29:297–298, 468; cf. 41:196; 46:239, 259; Cozzi, "Authority and the Law," p. 322.

treason.[21] He was an exceedingly difficult person to deal with, as Doge Loredan discovered many times. On February 12, 1512, Loredan instructed Gasparo dalla Vedova, the Ten's secretary, to read a regulation against carrying weapons to the Great Council. Luca, a chief of the Ten, chastised Gasparo for not seeking the permission of his council before following the doge's orders. This annoyed Loredan, who publicly declared in the next assembly of the Great Council that the chief was an unruly and unworthy official. When Luca reasserted the Ten's right to order its own business,

> the doge became incensed and stood up, saying, "We wish the Great Council to know of this": that arrogance occasioned misfortune, and that it was no wonder that adversity befalls [the Republic] since obedience is not given to those to whom it is due; that the doge was the head of the state and was obliged by his oath to enforce the laws of the Ten; that [Loredan] having ordered the regulations regarding weapons to be read, Luca Tron, who is a private citizen, was overweening to rebuff Gasparo, saying he was a chief of the Ten, for having read his orders and those of the Signoria . . . [that Luca] deserves a substantial rebuke . . . and [Loredan spoke further] with like words, full of great fury, clutching his crimson, satin cloak and spewing fire all about. Luca Tron, head of the Ten, stood at his place and said nothing. And this episode caused considerable grumbling in the Great Council, for such anger against a chief of the Ten was uncalled for.[22]

A mingling of constitutional nicety, personal spite, and impetuosity also characterized the next recorded clash between Loredan and Luca, which involved recovering funds said to have been embezzled by a treasurer, Vittore Foscarini, who had fled the city. On April 19, 1518, Giovanni Dolfin, a state attorney, suggested in the Senate that Foscarini be given a safe-conduct so that his testimony could be heard, but Loredan retorted that Dolfin merely wished to obstruct justice. Luca, a councillor, entered the *renga* to defend the state attorney and the rights of the absent Foscarini. Someone objected that he was not speaking to the motion, that is, to whether or not Foscarini should be indicted, and that it was forbidden to defend an accused patrician in his absence. Luca replied,

21 Michiel, fols. 150r–151r.
22 Sanuto, 13:478–479.

"Show me the laws or have the Signoria so determine that I must
leave [the *renga*], for I wish to speak, not to defend Vittore Foscarini but for the good of the city. . . ." So he began to speak,
making a fine exhortation and employing great cunning. It seemed
that he didn't speak for Vittore Foscarini, yet he tacitly defended
him, saying that it would be good to recover the money of the
Signoria from those who have taken it.

When Luca went on in this vein for a while, despite several warnings
from the Ten to address the motion, Loredan broke in and attacked
him for aiding Foscarini. Luca replied that Loredan arrogantly believed that no one should oppose the doge; and he added that Foscarini
was ready to return to Venice if given a safe-conduct. Finally, Giovanni Venier, a chief of the Ten and Loredan's son-in-law, ordered
Luca to be silent. Noting that he did not want to fight both the doge
and his relative, Luca left the *renga*, after which the vote to indict
Foscarini passed overwhelmingly.[23]

Squabbling continued in the Senate the next day, this time centered
around a proposal by the Full Collegio to create a new magistracy,
three officials to investigate corruption in monasteries (*Correctori
sopra le biasteme et sacrilegi*). Again, Loredan and the state attorneys
came into conflict. Giovanni Dolfin insisted that his office would be
denigrated through the creation of a new magistracy; he also noted
that Loredan, clearly the force behind the legislation, was evidently
intent on obstructing the work of the state attorneys, citing his opposition to a safe-conduct for Foscarini. Luca joined in the dispute and
condemned the motion as harmful to the authority of the state attorneys. He also claimed that

> Eleven nuns were cited [for investigation] in the Collegio, and the
> state attorneys, wishing to do their duty, were enjoined [from act-
> ing] by the doge and Collegio. He attacked the doge for not sup-
> porting the state attorneys. And [Luca went on] yesterday he wanted
> to speak on matters pertinent to the state and was compelled to
> leave [the *renga*] by the chiefs of the Ten, although the chiefs don't
> have [such] authority in the Senate. And [he said] in this *terra* there
> are three sorts: great, middling and lowly; and one may not act
> against the great ones because of the favoritism they enjoy, for there
> are nuns who are daughters of procurators and others.

23 Sanuto, 25:354–355.

When Bartolomeo da Mosto, a *savio di terraferma*, protested that "all are equal in this *terra*," Luca turned his sarcasm on him, implying that he did not have the votes to become a state attorney. Luca and another councillor then proposed that the state attorneys retain authority over the monasteries, and this motion defeated that of the Full Collegio by a vote of 117 to 92. Immediately after the vote, da Mosto went before the Signoria and said, " 'For lesser words than these Giovanni Antonio Minio was exiled.' Luca Tron rose and said, 'Who is equal to you? Ser Bartolomeo wants me remanded to the chiefs of the Ten? Go sit down!' The entire Senate laughed over this." Sanuto, who was not present in the Senate, approved of Luca's speech, as his punning comment indicates: "In short, he made an excellent speech [*renga*] or, to put it better, indictment [*rengon*]."[24]

It is likely that Luca placed himself in some danger by attacking the doge and asserting the existence of inequalities within the ruling class. He was saved from Minio's fate by his eminence, the following he enjoyed, and the good humor with which the Senate greeted his sallies. Still, he found it expedient for the next three years to avoid attending the frequent banquets in the Ducal Palace that Loredan held for the Full Collegio. "He pretended that he was ill," says Sanuto, "not wishing to cause disturbance by going to dinner." For whatever reason, in the same years his dissent from policy and his attacks on *Primi* abruptly diminished. By the time of his election as a procurator in 1527, he was an almost unexceptional member of the governing circle.[25] Perhaps Luca's retirement from troublemaking is one way of gauging the changes that took place in the councils in the course of the second decade after Agnadello.

Antonio Tron's disagreements with the government were based on the same concerns that motivated his cousin, but he was more consistent in his dissent and less motivated by personal spite. The needs of the poor were one of his abiding preoccupations, an issue bound to bring him into conflict with the *Primi*, inasmuch as he was concerned especially, although not exclusively, with the plight of poor patricians. He was opposed to the creation of a separate political elite within the ruling class, and he clearly recognized how gross economic inequalities made for political difficulties. In 1498 he was against Venetian involvement in the Pisan rebellion (unlike Filippo) because it hurt both rich

24 Sanuto, 25:356–357.
25 On avoiding dinner: Sanuto, 25:364; cf. 398, 462; 29:492. On his election: Sanuto, 43:580, 582; cf. 623, 627, 658.

and poor within the patriciate. Three years later he sponsored legislation that revoked all appointments made by the Forty to the post of crossbowman on the galleys because they were being sold illegally and not used for aiding poor patricians as intended. Like Filippo, he supported legislation expelling debtors from the Senate, and like Luca, he opposed the 1501 measure cutting government salaries. In 1510 he vainly resisted a measure confiscating the property of debtors held in trust by the procurator's office, arguing that much of the income from that property went toward charitable causes and support of the poor. Ten years later, he put through legislation that forced the procurators to distribute the lodgings at their disposal in the *Procuratie* for the benefit of the poor. At the same time, he advocated legislation for improving the administration of almshouses and for diverting substantial tax revenues into a lending bank for aiding the poor.[26]

Antonio's ambition to reform the Venetian tax structure by means of a reassessment of the basic rate (*estimo*) was also aimed at helping the poor and was strongly opposed by many *Primi*. The tax structure was based on the *decima*, a direct tax on real property, which favored the rich, whose investments in trade and government bonds escaped inclusion in the basic assessments, which had been last calculated in 1463. Malipiero observes that the poor suffered greatly during the Pisan war, while the rich hindered reform of the *estimo* because they earned interest from bonds, money markets, and various investments. On May 25, 1500, Antonio, a councillor, suggested the creation of a five-man commission to draw up guidelines for a revision of the tax structure; he most likely intended this as an alternative to cutting official salaries, a measure that struck particularly hard at poor patricians. No one else on the Full Collegio supported him, and the measure never came to a vote. He brought it up again on October 11, but a proposal that the topic be excluded from debate was accepted instead. This happened once more on November 29, prompting Priuli to remark that the rich men of the Senate were concerned only with their own financial welfare. Antonio was not able to win approval of his measure until after the War of the League of Cambrai and subsequent

---

26 On opposition to an elite: cf. Malipiero, 2:688. On the Pisan rebellion: Malipiero, 1:512. On the crossbowmen: Sanuto, 4:104; Priuli, 2:168. On debtors and salaries: Sanuto, 5:7–8, 379, 410, 468. On confiscating property: Sanuto, 9: 448, 455, 461, 517. On lodgings: Sanuto, 28:317, 325. On almshouses: Sanuto, 28: 250–251, 319, 325. On a lending bank: Brian Pullan, *Rich and Poor in Renaissance Venice*, pp. 492–493.

exactions had exhausted the usual sources of funds. In August 1521, as Venice prepared to fight Charles V, all the *savi grandi* except for Antonio proposed another tax based on the *estimo*; Antonio put forward his old motion, and after long argument it finally passed, thereby creating a commission to review the city's tax structure for the first time in fifty-eight years.[27]

Antonio's principal interest throughout his political career was the functioning of government. Like Sanuto, he was well versed in law and had an eye for the political consequences of bureaucratic regulation. He was very active in fighting electoral corruption, and some of his reforms—the introduction of a new voting urn and nonpatrician *ballottini*—permanently altered the procedures of the Great Council. The city was full of rumors in December 1497 when the Ten and its *zonta* were closeted for three days; finally the chiefs produced new laws regulating dinners, weddings, registration of patrician births, corruption in elections, and graft in office. The moving spirit behind the legislation was Antonio, a chief of the council. In 1498 when he learned that an election he had won had been irregularly conducted, he arranged to have it annulled and held again. He was the most important politician supporting the creation of the censors in 1517, and he wanted them to act against all manifestations of electioneering. In March 1520 there was an intense *broglio* for the dogeship when Loredan seemed near death, and after his recovery Antonio wanted the censors to prosecute the men who had lobbied for the dogeship during the presumed deathwatch; he proposed abolition of the censors when they had taken no action within a week. In May, Antonio remarked in a Senate debate that "when the doge was ill, a preacher said in the pulpit that the doge is no longer made by way of grace [*colombina*] but by petition [*pregierie*]—a pun lost in English, for *pregierie* means both "prayers" and "lobbying." Antonio's uncompromising refusal to seek the dogeship in 1523, when he was the favorite, was unique among Venetian politicians, who could only regard such rectitude and indifference as tantamount to "Madness."[28]

27 On the poor during the Pisan war: Malipiero, 1:406–407. On 1500: Sanuto, 3:346, 891, 1003–1004, 1115; Pietro Dolfin, *Annalium Venetorum*, p. 47; Priuli, 2:77–78. On 1521: Sanuto, 31:196, 198, 206, 207, 209, 268, 270–271; cf. 12:593; ASV, Senato, Terra, Reg. 22, fol. 49r.

28 On December 1497: Sanuto, 1:835–838. On 1498: Sanuto, 2:108. On March 1520: Sanuto, 28:371, 390–391. On May 1520: Sanuto, 28:491. On Antonio in 1521 and 1523: this book, Chapter III.3.

Before the War of the League of Cambrai, Antonio was concerned with three aspects of government other than the needs of the poor and the control of electoral corruption: the Signoria's electoral authority in the Great Council, the composition of the Senate, and the procedures of the Great Council. Prior to 1500, the Signoria retained the significant prerogative of making separate nominations (called *voxe de la bancha*) to some of the Great Council's elections, a right that predated the reformation of the assembly in 1297. The signorial nomination had four important consequences. First, it provided a means of restoring a politician to office if he were bypassed in the regular nominating procedures. As such it had the same force as did the Senate's *scrutinio* authority: It put the weight of the *Primi* behind one of the nominees in the Great Council competition. Significantly, when Sanuto argued against a *scrutinio* nomination in 1521 because it would lead to elimination of the Great Council's power, he also warned that reinstating *scrutinii* might even lead to revival of the Signoria's nominating authority. Second, it was a way for a member of the Signoria to boost a relative into office. No doubt the bargaining and trading that characterized the work of the Great Council's nominating committees also took place when the Signoria met privately, perhaps over dinner in the Ducal Palace, to plot its nominations. Third, according to Pietro Dolfin, the signorial nominations could be secretly purchased, a practice that put the procedure into disrepute and probably contributed to its abolition. Fourth, nominations by the Signoria occasionally led to inefficiency because "doddering and decrepit" *vecchi* thereby entered the ducal council and were unable to bear the labor of the post. For example, a quorum of four councillors could not be gathered on the Signoria for two days in January 1500 because of illnesses, so the Ten and the Great Council could not meet. Sanuto grumbled that "because of the councillors, the affairs of the city could not be attended to yesterday and today. And it was bad to elect these old ones: the *voxe de la bancha* are the ruin of this city."[29] In short, the signorial nominations infringed on the Great Council's authority and were bound up with favoritism, bribery, and inefficiency.

Although Antonio had long wanted to abolish the signorial nominations, he first publicly announced his intention of submitting a pro-

---

[29] On *scrutinii* and signorial nominations: Sanuto, 30:159. On helping relatives: Priuli, 2:52–53. On purchasing the nomination: Pietro Dolfin, *Annalium Venetorum*, p. 164. On nominating "old ones"; Priuli, 2:52–53; cf. Malipiero, 2: 686. On January 1500: Sanuto, 3:87.

posal to do so in May 1500, a few days before he began trying to win acceptance of a new *estimo*. With exquisite political timing, he started his campaign in earnest in mid-August, as fears for the security of Modone mounted in Venice; his subsequent action against the Signoria's prerogative benefited from the same political atmosphere that aided the reception of Luca's indictments of colonial officials. The Great Council's anger with the *Primi*, which was to find vent in the September defeat of many *vecchi* in the Zonta election, provided Antonio, a councillor, with the opportunity to override strong opposition to his proposal within the Signoria. On August 16 the other councillors prevented him from putting his proposal to annul the signorial nominations before the Great Council. There was evidently considerable conflict within the Signoria over Antonio's plans, for six days later Giovanni Morosini, a councillor, complained to Doge Barbarigo that Antonio repeatedly proposed annulling the nominations no matter what motions were being debated. Morosini claimed that Antonio could not act on his own because the accord of four councillors was required for presentation of a motion to the Great Council—an interpretation of the law challenged by Antonio. The issue was resolved on September 12, during the first convocation of the Great Council since Venice learned of the fall of Modone. Morosini planned to nominate a relative as treasurer at Cremona, which caused some dissension among the other councillors. Antonio seized the opportunity to suggest once more that the signorial prerogative be annulled; the councillors, apprehensive that Antonio would succeed in presenting his motion, and recognizing the Great Council's hostile mood toward the *Primi*, adopted Antonio's proposal as their own. "This was a novelty to the Great Council," says Sanuto, "since it knew that Antonio Tron always wanted to propose this." It approved the Signoria's abdication of its own electoral authority by a vote of 1,005 to 249.[30] The abolition of signorial nominations was among the most substantial accomplishments of Antonio's long and busy career.

Between December 1499 and September 1500, while dealing with the signorial nominations and the tax structure, Antonio was also concerned with legislation affecting the composition of the Senate. He presented numerous proposals, some several times, reducing the number of officials who were elected by the Senate and entered it by virtue of their office; about forty officials were touched by this legislation.

30 Pietro Dolfin, *Annalium Venetorum*, pp. 137–138, 164–165; Sanuto, 3:770; 634, 661; Priuli, 2:52–53.

Antonio convinced the Senate to abolish offices concerned with customs, financial affairs, water control, and sumptuary laws, all of which
duplicated already existing magistracies. "Little by little," notes
Sanuto, "the Senate is being reduced," a process that aroused the opposition of officials whose jobs were at stake and of those patricians
who aspired to the posts. Most of the 140 ex officio magistrates in the
Senate had been added in the last fifty years. Some offices fell into
disuse in time, but because places in the Senate were prized, useless
and redundant positions were retained, even though they necessarily
lessened the secrecy and order of the Senate's deliberations. Antonio's
legislation intended to rectify this situation, making the Senate a more
efficient and orderly forum. The same motive was behind his legislation of October 1504, which limited for a number of minor officials
the prerogative of sitting in the Senate after completing terms of
service.[31] Antonio's ultimate intention was significant—to maintain the
Senate as the central governing council—although the results he obtained were not. To be sure, the size of the Senate was slightly
reduced, but his legislation ran counter to too many vested interests—
especially that "greediness to create offices" of which Sanuto complained in these same years. The Senate remained inefficient and
bloated, ripe for being shunted aside in the crisis that followed
Agnadello.

Antonio's interest in the detail of government, as well as his skill at
political maneuvering, were again evident in 1506 when he won passage of legislation altering the electoral procedures of the Great
Council. On May 24 the Signoria proposed to the patriciate that the
period of disqualification (*contumacia*) be abolished for the position
of lord of the Arsenal. Although all magistrates were presumably
prohibited immediate succession in the same office, there were many
exceptions to the rule. In fact, as recently as 1500 Antonio had won
acceptance of a motion iterating a 1450 law requiring universal *contumacia*. It was therefore no surprise when he countered the Signoria's
proposal with one calling for a period of disqualification with no
exceptions whatever; but he caused consternation among his fellow
councillors when he coupled this with a motion for changing the
procedures used in making up the nominating committees of the Great
Council. Before 1527 only one member of a clan was permitted to be

31 On the legislation: Sanuto, 3:63, 303, 509, 573, 659, 704, 786; 6:389. On re-
ductions of the Senate and the opposition: Sanuto, 3:62–63; cf. 704. On October
1504: Sanuto, 6:70; cf. 389.

among the thirty-six patricians of the four committees. Thus, when a Contarini drew a gilded ball from the first urn (containing sixty gold balls and the remainder silver), the rest of the Contarini house was excluded from further participation in the selection of committees. Antonio thought this procedure unfair because the only Contarini patrician with a chance of becoming a nominator could still be eliminated at the second urn (containing thirty-six gold balls and twenty-four silver). He proposed that the exclusion of a clan take place at the second urn rather than at the first; in other words, any number of Contarini could pass the first drawing so long as no member of the *casa* drew a gilded ball at the second. "This created equality for all," Sanuto approvingly remarks, and the *case grandi* were much in favor of it. However, Doge Loredan and the other councillors were displeased with Antonio's motion regarding *contumacia*, and they would not permit the new proposal to be voted on. The question of *contumacia* was settled, at least temporarily, when the Senate and the Great Council passed Antonio's motion.[32]

On September 29, when the Great Council met to vote on the Signoria's motion to elect the Zonta, Antonio again brought up his proposition concerning the urns. Technically, the Zonta was not a permanent part of the Senate, although it had been in existence since the early Quattrocento, and the initiative for its annual renewal had to come from the Signoria. Antonio, joined by the chiefs of the Forty, proposed that the Zonta be made permanent and that the suggested alteration in the selection of nominating committees be accepted; the Great Council easily approved both motions. The Zonta proposal was mainly of symbolic importance because the September 29 renewal was already a fixture of Venetian politics; but making the Zonta a lasting addition to the Senate removed any possibility of the *Primi* deciding to dispense with an electoral mechanism that occasionally caused them discomfiture. The change in the nominating procedures had more practical significance, as was seen in the nomination of five Contarini men on September 29. Seven months after Antonio's alteration was adopted, Sanuto observes that "eighteen hundred come to the Great Council every meeting, which is an extraordinary, unheard-of thing. This is done because of the law proposed by Antonio Tron, that is, not to expel [clan members] at the first urn." The large clans and

32 On *contumacia* in 1500: Sanuto, 3:970; Priuli, 2:66. On the electoral proposal: Sanuto, 6:432–433; 342. On electoral procedures: this book, Chapter II.3. On passage of the *contumacia* legislation: Sanuto, 6:390, 392, 397–398.

others were very pleased with the new procedure, and almost a year after the law was passed, the Great Council elected Antonio as procurator. He came before the Great Council to accept the honor, and after following the traditional ritual of expressing gratitude to the doge and councillors, and receiving the keys of his office, he once more surprised (and snubbed) the Signoria: "He turned [from the tribune] and thanked the Great Council: an innovation."[33]

This was little more than two years before Agnadello, the defeat that ushered in changes affecting the Senate, executive councils, and electoral competition, all of which worked against everything Antonio valued. He could do little to oppose the new modes of governing, and his reaction to them was itself a confession of impotence: During much of the remainder of his career, he boycotted offices in the executive councils. He remained active in government up to January 1510, until the defeat of the Po expedition against Ferrara made it clear that the war was going to be long and drawn out. He refused to accept election as captain general of the fleet after Angelo Trevisan's disgrace, not because of discontent with policies, but because, as he told the Great Council, "It is not right that fish go on land and horses on water." However, he was furious when the Senate passed a motion confiscating debtor property held by the Procuratia. In a meeting of the Ten on January 14, he asserted that the Republic would be troubled so long as Loredan occupied the Ducal Palace. After this outburst, he rarely attended the Collegio or the Senate for the next eighteen months. When he did make an appearance, it was usually to refuse election as a *savio grande* or to resist a measure under consideration. For example, on March 13, 1511, he came to the Senate to attack a motion by the Collegio for new taxes; in the course of the debate, "He said to the doge that under him the state had been lost, that he had a wicked heart, and that he would lose the rest if the laws weren't observed." He went on in this *renga da satiro*, as Sanuto calls it, to complain that the Great Council's electoral authority was being usurped when patricians paid to enter the Senate.[34]

33 On the legislation: ASV, Maggior Consiglio, Deliberazioni, Liber Deda, Reg. 25, fols. 28r, 29r–29v; Sanuto, 6:432–433. On nomination of Contarini: Sanuto, 6:432–433; cf. Consegi, 8893, fols. 324r–324v. On eighteen hundred in the Great Council: Sanuto, 7:42. On Antonio's election: Sanuto, 7:47. On Antonio thanking the Great Council: Sanuto, 7:146.

34 On refusing election as captain general: Priuli, vol. 5, fol. 57r; cf. Sanuto, 9:417–418. On January 14: Sanuto, 9:461. On March 13: Sanuto, 12:57–58.

Refusing to sit on the executive councils did not lower Antonio's reputation; indeed, it most likely enhanced it. Procurators were forbidden to attend the Great Council (presumably to prevent them from cultivating support for a ducal election) except when matters concerning the Procuratia were being discussed; and on July 13, 1511, the councillors planned to present a proposal already passed by the Senate allowing procurators special privileges in *savi di zonta* elections. Antonio was the only one of the nine procurators to attend the Great Council meeting, and when the Signoria realized that he intended to oppose them—according to Sanuto, "because he has no regard for anyone in speaking the truth for the good of the Republic"—it withdrew consideration of the proposal. Antonio gained "very great honor" from this silent victory, especially because a procurator had not sat on the benches of the Great Council in living memory. The next day he accepted election to the Collegio.[35]

Still, he remained at odds with government policy. During his terms on the Collegio after July 1511, he failed to have a period of disqualification uniformly applied to the Collegio, to win a tax revision of the city, and to prevent the Collegio from assuming full authority for negotiating with the Spanish ambassador.[36] After a second, briefer boycott of the Collegio in 1514, he entered the post of *savio grande* in December on the understanding that the Collegio no longer act improperly; but he resigned his post on February 16, 1515, when the Signoria prevented the Collegio from placing a motion regarding the grain trade. Two days later the doge and the councillors persuaded him to return to the Collegio, a gesture they may have regretted shortly after when he forced them to surrender the sultan's presents.[37]

Antonio returned to the Senate after another absence of some months on May 30, 1516, when the auction of procuratorships was being debated. He was consistently solicitous of the proper operation and prestige of the Procuratia. Shortly after his election to the office in 1507, he presented proposals for altering its procedures; and when auctioning of the post was well advanced in 1522, he insisted on stricter control of its funds, much of which were directed toward charitable causes. During the 1516 debate, Antonio shocked the Senate by saying that the proposal

35 Sanuto, 12:287, 288.
36 Sanuto, 14:613–614. On other dissents by Antonio between 1511 and 1513: cf. Sanuto, 11:66–67, 788; 12:301; 13:217; 14:53.
37 Sanuto, 19:438, 439; cf. 20:43, 47.

diminishes the reputation of the procurators, and that he wished to resign from the Procuratia in order to aid the city. He returned his keys [of office], saying, "Elect someone in my place and raise 10,000 ducats; and if I am elected to the *zonta* [of the Ten], I wish for nothing else . . . " He left the keys of the Procuratia on the *renga* and went to sit down—but not at the place of the procurators. The doge called for him to reclaim the keys, but he did not wish to.

Luca Tron, a *savio grande*, argued that Lorenzo Loredan should be declared ineligible for the post of procurator, citing the precedent of Filippo Tron's resignation from the Ten when his father was doge. Pietro Tron, a second cousin of Luca and Antonio, supported the motion to auction procuratorships because of the need for money. The long and acrimonious debate ended with passage of the motion and with Doge Loredan convincing Antonio to reclaim his keys of office.[38] Antonio's gesture thus proved ineffectual, as perhaps he knew it would; he may well have counted on Loredan's insistence that he not resign, just as the doge was aware that Antonio would take up his keys again. Impotence reduces dissent to mere gesture, conflict to ritual motion. Yet Antonio certainly knew that few actions would impress his fellow patricians more than the voluntary renunciation of the Republic's second-highest office.

Between May 1516 and January 1520, Antonio once more refused election to the Collegio and rarely attended the Senate. In January 1520 he reluctantly accepted election as *savio grande*, telling Loredan that "he would rather attend to his soul, as he had done for some time," than participate in a government in which "justice is not possible due to fear of intrigue."[39] Despite this hesitation, he was very busy in the subsequent eighteen months: He won acceptance of measures dealing with misuse of public funds, administration of the Procuratia, composition of the Collegio, tax assessment of the city, operation of almshouses, and abolition of the censors.[40] His only notable quarrel was with Luca Tron over whether "inferior" councillors (who presided over the Forty in the absence of the chiefs) should be eligible for election as *savi grandi*. Luca maintained that such elections were legitimate, evidently because he once entered the Collegio by that

38 On procedures in 1507: Sanuto, 7:162. On funds in 1522: Sanuto, 33:331–332; cf. 28:325–326. On 1516: Sanuto, 22:253–254; 258, 260.

39 Sanuto, 28:152. On refusing election: Sanuto, 25:323, 596; 27:412, 474; 28: 126, 144, 145.

40 Sanuto, 28:273, 279, 281–282, 317, 319, 325–326, 390; 31:206, 207, 209.

route; but Antonio argued that the councillors pandered to the Forty in the courtroom to gain its support in the Senate's election to the Collegio. After considerable argument, the Senate supported Antonio. One suspects that the assembly was bemused by the spectacle of Venice's most feared debaters, cousins and close allies, turning on each other. Sanuto notes that "today in the Senate there was a great tussle between the two Tron."[41]

Antonio ended his active political life in the late summer of 1521. Significantly, his last extended involvement in government took place in the brief interlude between the end of the crisis of Cambrai and the onset of new military and financial difficulties for Venice. Again, boycotting the executive councils seemed to be the only appropriate response to changes beyond his control. In May 1523 he was in Gritti's ducal conclave, but he had no ambitions for the dogeship himself and discouraged any lobbying on his behalf. The men carrying his effigy dressed as a doge around the Piazza di San Marco and calling his name in the basilica after the election were acclaiming a politician whose career had ended some years before by his own choice. On January 4, 1524, he came to the Ducal Palace for the last time to refuse election to the Collegio. As he told the Signoria, " 'I have always carried out the tasks given to me, but now I am old, over eighty-four since last April, and I have a chill in my bones that cannot be cured.' " A few days later, amid the worst winter Venice had known for years, he caught pneumonia. "He died," notes Sanuto, "with a reputation as an excellent patrician, and everyone wished that he had been doge." He was very wealthy but not ostentatious: "He gave much charity to the poor, but not to patricians. God grant peace to his soul."[42]

2. *Marino Sanuto, a Venetian Republican*

In all that was most important to him, Sanuto was not a success. For thirty-five years he aspired to high office—in vain. He never became state attorney or censor, the offices he coveted most; he longed to be in the Senate but was a member of that assembly for less than seven years. Striving to immortalize the Republic in his books, he was a

41 Sanuto, 28:491; 507–508.
42 On January 4: Sanuto, 35:314; 316–317. On his death: Sanuto, 35:324; 330. On charity expended in his will: ASV, Archivio Notarile, Testamenti, Giacomo Grasolario, Reg. 1183, no. 32.

mediocre writer and historian; the post of official historiographer always eluded him. Measuring his aspirations against his achievements, Sanuto may be accounted the most outstanding political and literary failure of his generation.

Sanuto wrote his first book, a summary of ancient myths, in 1481 at the age of fifteen; three years later he composed an account of his journey with government inspectors through the *terraferma*, as well as a commentary on the War of Ferrara. A minor legal post as one of the *avocati pizoli* gave him, in 1486 at the age of twenty, entrance to the Great Council and an introduction to Venetian law as well. The next decade was spent in study and in collecting material for future writing projects. He began his *Vite dei dogi* in 1493 (although it was unfinished till 1530) and his *Cronachetta* very shortly after. His account of Charles VIII's descent on Italy was begun soon after it occurred in 1494, and as his narrative caught up with events, it insensibly took on the form of a diary. Sanuto had discovered his métier. *La spedizione di Carlo VIII* ends with December 31, 1495, and the *Diarii* commence with the first day of the new year.[43]

Sanuto began his political career two years after he started his diary. In March 1498, at the age of thirty-two, he was elected to a police magistracy, the Lords of the Night, for six months. From October 1498 to April 1501 he served four consecutive terms as *savio agli ordini*, a post that did not have the burden of a disqualification period. He was then elected by the Great Council as treasurer at Verona, where he remained for sixteen months. Returning from Verona in September 1502, he was a *savio agli ordini* for two more terms. A hiatus of seven years then occurred during which, although he attended the Great Council, he held no office and his daily recording of events became generally skimpy; this was partly due to the distraction of squabbles with his brothers and to his marriage to Cecilia Priuli in 1505. His wife died in the month of Agnadello (perhaps that is why Sanuto barely notes her passing), and in March 1510 he was elected to his seventh term on the Collegio at the age of forty-four.[44]

In the ordinary course of events, Sanuto could have expected elevation to the rank of *savio di terraferma* or councillor, eventually even

43 On Sanuto's early works: Guglielmo Berchet's preface in Sanuto, 1:17–24, 35. On entering the Great Council: Marino Sanuto, *Cronachetta*, pp. 218; 221. On Sanuto: Mario Brunetti, "Marin Sanudo"; G. de Leva, "Marino Sanuto"; Gaetano Cozzi, "Marin Sanudo il Giovane."

44 Sanuto, 1:906, 1114; 2:537, 170, 849; 4:8, 321, 329; 5:89; 6:132; 10:56.

a seat on the Ten and a post as *savio grande*. Instead, he was never elected to office again, and it is no exaggeration to say that his career ended before it had really begun. His only subsequent victories were five elections to the Zonta and one (for a loan) to the Senate. His defeats and disappointments were legion, especially in elections for the Collegio, state attorney, and censor. In all but two years between 1514 and 1533, he was nominated at least once to the Zonta, but he won election only five times. He lost numerous contests for the Senate, magistracies in Venice, ambassadorial posts, and positions in the maritime and mainland territories. Some of these defeats were self-inflicted, for it was known that he would not accept many posts outside Venice, and he considered a number of city offices beneath his dignity. While he wanted to be a government inspector for the *terraferma*, he cursed an enemy who nominated him as inspector for the Levant. And he did not wish nomination to a customs office in 1516, "considering that I was nominated for state attorney [three days before] and did very well, and now this, which is a very meager post, although it lasts two years and permits entry to the Senate."[45]

Twenty-one men served with Sanuto as *savi agli ordini* between 1498 and 1503, and the diarist's failure may be gauged by comparison with their careers. Leonardo di Tommaso Mocenigo, Bartolomeo Priuli, and Giacomo Gabriel were dead by 1510; Giovanni Trevisan, Giovanni Moro, Andrea Suriano, Vicenzo Barbo, and Marco di Pietro Molin dropped out of politics. Marcantonio Calbo, Nadilino Contarini, Vittore Capello, and Marco di Francesco Molin settled into relatively important administrative posts in the colonies and Venice. Gabriele Moro, Francesco Morosini, Antonio Venier, Faustin Barbo, Marco Lando, Alvise Mocenigo, and Francesco Donato were highly success-

---

45 On defeats for *savio di terraferma*: Sanuto, 10:683–684; 12:104; 17:129, 428, 439; 18:308; 24:128, 130, 406, 408; 25:501, 505, 515, 516, 526, 616, 618; 26:320, 337; 28:392; 39:123, 173; 43:11, 30; 49:307; 54:423. On defeats for *savio grande*: Sanuto, 56:1029, 1031. On defeats for state attorney: Sanuto, 17:171; 22:7, 66, 149–150, 535–536, 538; 24:666, 668; 26:40; 27:320; 28:405–406; 29:566; 30:310; 31:42–43; 37:52–53; 38:328; 48:272, 500–501; 49:197–198; 50:90, 246; 54:240; 58:385, 571–573. On the Zonta defeats: Sanuto, 17:103; 19:97; 20:526; 25:12; 26:66, 72; 28:324; 29:217; 31:498; 33:466; 36:624–625; 39:487; 40:17, 21; 43:771; 46:124; 48:544; 51:611; 53:578; 54:541, 622; 55:368, 369; 58:750. On Senate defeats: Sanuto, 22:348, 399–400, 409; 24:677; 25:594; 26:52; 27:672, 679, 684, 689; 28:493; 31:311; 39:330, 481; 49:352; 56:875; 58:541–542. On government inspector: Sanuto, 13:407–408; 14:20, 207–208; 28:244, 274. On 1516: Sanuto, 22:157–158; cf. 11:403; 15:314, 315; 14:225.

ful, frequently entering the Signoria and the Ten and serving as *savi grandi*; Mocenigo became a procurator, and Donato was elected doge in 1545. Trojani Bollani was invariably elected to the Senate and defeated for the Collegio, so he must be counted a qualified failure. The only one of the twenty-one patricians who remained active in politics and ambitious for high office without the faintest success was Sanuto.

A large family, wealth, and influential contacts were the best guarantees of success in Venetian politics; yet Sanuto's misfortune was not conspicuously due to lack of these. The Sanuto clan numbered twenty members of Great Council age in 1527, although only fourteen were attending the assembly in 1531, the year in which the death of a brother made Marino the oldest male of his house. He notes in that year that, of the twelve older clan members who had died during his lifetime, nine had held the rank of senator and above. His father, Leonardo, was a prominent man of letters in the midst of a promising career when he died at the age of forty-nine while serving as ambassador at Rome in 1476. Sanuto was only ten years old at that time, and his father's death was doubtless a severe blow to his family's fortunes and to Marino's future in politics. Sanuto was taken under the care of his uncle, Francesco, who in 1482 also died at a relatively young age for a Venetian politician. Still, Sanuto was not as successful as his older brothers, Alvise and Antonio, both of whom eventually served on the Ten and its *zonta*. A first cousin, Marino di Francesco, called *il Grando*, was a *savio di terraferma* several times. It was a source of pride to Sanuto in December 1499 that his brother-in-law, Zaccaria Dolfin, was a chief of the Ten and a first cousin, Marco, was state attorney. A very close friend, Marco di Francesco, was an important politician and an aspirant to the office of procurator when he died in 1505 at the age of fifty-nine.[46]

Although not a wealthy man, neither was Sanuto one of the *poveri zentilhomeni*; he did not have a "social affinity" with poor patricians.[47] To be sure, it was difficult for him to raise money to serve at Padua

46 On the Sanuto: Barbaro, 8597, fols. 94v–95r; Capellari, vol. 4, fols. 55r–56v; Berchet's preface in Sanuto, 1:12–13; cf. Sanuto, "Cronica Sanuda," fol. 349r. On Francesco: Berchet's preface in Sanuto, 1:17. On Alvise and Antonio: Sanuto, 18:7; 54:597; 55:209. On Marino di Francesco: ASV, Segretario alle voci, Elezioni in Senato, Reg. 2, no. 16, fols. 17r, 18r. On December 1499: Sanuto, 3:66. On Marco: Sanuto, 23:343; cf. Marino Sanuto, *La spedizione di Carlo VIII in Italia*, pp. 603–604.

47 Cf. Cozzi, "Authority and the Law," p. 301; idem, "Cultura politica e religione nella 'pubblica storiografia' veneziana del '500," p. 227.

and to bid for office during the war. In fact, he had recourse to a loan to meet the latter expense, nonpayment of which led to his being put under arrest one morning as he set out for the Ducal Palace. However, income from family property at the Rialto allowed him to devote himself to his political and literary interests. He was part of the circle around Aldo Manuzio's famous press, and he haunted the bookstalls of the Mercerie, especially during the war when there were many bargains, such as the ornate Hebrew bible he bought in 1509. In 1520, in response to papal urging, the government seized books by Martin Luther being sold by a merchant in San Maurizio: "Yet I obtained one," brags Sanuto, "and I have it in my study." By 1533 he had a library of sixty-five hundred volumes, certainly one of Venice's largest collections, for which he must have spent at least 4,000 ducats; after 1533 he was forced to sell a large part of his library to pay his creditors.[48] However distressing his financial situation in his later years, lack of money was not an acute problem for Sanuto throughout his career. Some patricians were successful in politics by purchasing votes and good will; Sanuto chose to buy books.

Nor did Sanuto lack for important, politically powerful connections. He was friends with Giorgio Corner, Marino Morosini, Luca Tron (whom Sanuto calls *mio patron*), Antonio Tron, Lorenzo Loredan, Zaccaria Dolfin, Bernardo Bembo (the father of Pietro), Giorgio Emo, and Cristoforo Moro, grandnephew of the doge, whose wife was a Sanuto.[49] He was very close to Antonio Grimani, whom he supported for the dogeship as early as 1495 and for whom he shed "tears of joy" after the ducal election of 1521. He was likewise on very good terms with Agostino Barbarigo and Leonardo Loredan; Gritti was the only doge with whom Sanuto was not friendly, although they apparently

48 On Sanuto's arrest: Sanuto, 23:343; cf. ASV, Collegio, Notatorio, Reg. 18, fol. 36r. On Manuzio and Sanuto: M. J. C. Lowry, "The 'New Academy' of Aldus Manutius," pp. 388, 413. On bargains in wartime: Berchet's preface in Sanuto, 1:104; cf. Rawdon Brown, *Ragguagli sulla vita e sulle opere di Marino Sanuto*, 2:15–16; 65. On a book by Luther: Sanuto, 29:135; cf. Paul F. Grendler, *The Roman Inquisition and the Venetian Printing Press, 1540–1605*, pp. 71–72. On his library: Sanuto, 22:172; Berchet's preface in Sanuto, 1:104, 108; K. Wagner, "Sulla sorte di alcuni codici manoscritti appartenuti a Marin Sanudo"; idem, "Altre notizie sulla sorte dei libri di Marin Sanudo."

49 On Corner: Sanuto, 5:90; 7:577; 8:29. On Morosini: Sanuto, 57:490. On Luca Tron: Sanuto, 25:246; cf. 20:195, 197. On Lorenzo Loredan: Sanuto, 23: 262; 54:230; cf. 30:5. On Dolfin: Sanuto, 9:31, 34. On Bembo: Berchet's preface in Sanuto, 1:98. On Emo: Sanuto, 16:318. On Moro: Sanuto, 22:227; cf. 7:101.

came to respect each other. Finally, Sanuto was friends with two important secretaries of the Ten, Gasparo dalla Vedova and Giangiacomo Caroldo.[50]

Sanuto's lack of success was not somehow inherent in his social and economic condition; the small size of his clan and limited wealth did not doom him to failure. His career began respectably, if unexceptionally, with seven terms on the Collegio and a responsible post in *terraferma* administration; as *savio agli ordini* he performed admirably, first to arrive at the Ducal Palace every morning, diligent at his job, moderate in his policies, with the same fine eye for detail and procedure that is evident in his diary. The *savi agli ordini* were exempted from the obloquy that fell on the Collegio when Modone was lost in 1500; their attention to the needs of the besieged city and the fleet most likely stemmed from Sanuto's initiative, for, even allowing for his high opinion of his own excellence, the impression remains that he was the de facto leader of his branch of the Collegio.[51] He opposed the higher ranks of *savi* many times—notably on the question of Turkish policy—and he certainly offended some *Primi*; but the Collegio was by no means a unified body, and differences over policy were common. Such arguments did not damage his career, and it is significant that he won reelection so many times.

His political failure arose from an unfortunate conjunction of his personality and principles with the needs and impetus of government during the War of the League of Cambrai. His personality was not attractive. While learned, pious, and compassionate, he was also vain, arrogant, and self-righteous. Energetic and methodical, he combined pugnaciousness with unrelenting pedantry; he had little sense of discrimination, humor, or imagination, and his curiosity was at once insatiable and cheaply satisfied—in short, a magpie, obsessive collector and incessant scold. Judging from his own confused reports, he was capable of an eloquence in the councils that is wholly lacking in his writings. In January 1529 Giambattista Malatesta wrote to the marquis of Mantua some observations that throw further light on the diarist's character:

50 On Grimani: Sanuto, *Spedizione di Carlo VIII*, p. 130; Sanuto, 30:480; 31:7; cf. 6:132. On Barbarigo: Sanuto, 1:145. On Leonardo Loredan: Sanuto, 6:145; 22:90. On Vedova: Sanuto, 29:416–417. On Caroldo: cf. Caroldo's notebook, MCC, MS. Cod. Correr, 1336, cc. 222–223 and Sanuto, 26:64.

51 On arriving early: Sanuto, 2:392. On doing his job: cf. Sanuto, 2:37, 39, 52; 3:36, 44, 46, 47, 50, 51, 54, 56, 62, 66, 95, 98; 4:346–347, 491, 653; 5:890–891. On Modone: Sanuto, 3:733; and this book, Chapter II.2.

Sanuto is very refined, for having spoken three times with a person, he so confronts him [as if to] impale him. He is very learned and would have a higher reputation in this state if it were not for this vice. I used to have a servant to whom he gave three *mocenighi* [that is, about half a ducat] a week, but he was obliged "to run the lance" three times. He is notorious in the trade here.[52]

Malatesta was not above relaying salacious rumors to the young marquis,[53] but his remarks about Sanuto have a ring of authenticity about them: It is hard to wink at the detail regarding the servant's commerce with Sanuto. Assuming that Malatesta's report was accurate, one may agree that Sanuto's reputation would have been higher if he were not a homosexual without concluding that his sexual behavior was the cause of his political failure. By 1529 his hopes for high office were past, and perhaps he was less discreet than in previous years. Also, Michiel's comment in 1516 about the Ten's declaration regarding sodomy being directed against "important men" on the Ten and Collegio indicates that homosexuality was not necessarily a disqualification for the highest ranks of Venetian government.[54] Sanuto's personality as a whole, as well as the nature of his times, accounts for his frustrated career.

Given his character and dedication to republican principles, Sanuto was bound to come into conflict with the increasingly closed and corrupt government of post-Agnadello Venice. Commitment to debate and to participatory government were in contradiction to domination by the executive councils, and devotion to honest elections was a distinct liability in a milieu of unrestricted *broglio*. It was Sanuto's misfortune to reach the age when he could expect admittance to the Senate and advancement in office at precisely the time when Venice was experiencing rapid and fundamental changes antithetical to his character and beliefs. By contrast, Luca and Antonio Tron were

---

52 "Il Sanuto è gentilissimo, come ha parlato tre volte con una persona lo affrunta che lo impali, et è doto et saria in reputazione in questo stato se non fusse tale vitio. Io solea haver uno servitore al quale gli donava tre mozenighi la septimana, ma era obligato correre le lanze tre volte. Costui è famosissimo nel mestiere qui" (ASM, b. 1463, Giambattista Malatesta to the marquis of Mantua, January 29, 1529; cf. Alessandro Luzio, *Pietro Aretino nei primi suoi anni a Venezia*, p. 11, n. 1; Berchet's preface in Sanuto, 1:72).

53 Cf. ASM, b. 1454, Giambattista Malatesta to the marquis of Mantua, July 9, 1520.

54 Chapter IV.2, n. 54.

firmly established in the ranks of the *Primi* before the war began. Sanuto's defeats for office kept him from joining the *Primi*, but they also confirmed him in his convictions, thereby fueling his dissent from the governing circle and his opposition to the thrust of Venetian politics. At the same time, he turned many patricians outside the governing circle against him as well, for numerous voters were horrified at the prospect of an uncompromising political purist, with unlimited energy and unparalleled knowledge of law, in a position of power. For instance, the Switzers were no doubt unalterably opposed to electing Sanuto to the post of state attorney or censor. As perhaps his enemies recognized, Sanuto's dedication was less to the principles of equality and free speech in themselves than to the rule of law in every aspect of government. Deeply conservative in belief and character, he was still seen as too radical to be permitted to act in the name of the state. His very "wish to stay here [in Venice] and criticize" guaranteed that he would remain, as one patrician called him, a Cato, an unofficial, even somewhat eccentric, tribune of the law.[55]

Sanuto's last term on the Collegio was critical for his future career. After a seven-year absence, he entered the council as a *savio agli ordini* in March 1510. It was, in fact, something of a vote of confidence in him that he was elected at this time. In December 1509 Venice suffered its greatest setback since Agnadello when Angelo Trevisan's galley fleet was destroyed on the Po, and the Senate may have felt that maritime affairs needed the expertise Sanuto had shown as leader of the *savi agli ordini* in the past. Moreover, a month before Sanuto's election, Julius II broke with the League of Cambrai; and the prospects for a Venetian-papal attack on Ferrara, involving another expedition up the Po, were excellent. Shortly after his election, Sanuto proposed that a fleet be dispatched against Ferrara as soon as possible. When the fleet was assembled in the summer, he and two other *savi agli ordini* were given special authority for directing its movements, a responsibility that led the diarist into trouble. On August 22 he presented his plans for the attack on Ferrara to the Collegio, and meeting opposition from other *savi*, he insisted on a meeting of the Senate, which then voted his proposals: "And almost the entire Senate," he brags, "shook my hand." The next day, however, he learned that the Collegio had altered his plans. Infuriated, he told the *savi*, "Tomorrow we will see if the Collegio will be over the Senate!" At this point, Antonio

---

55 On criticizing: Sanuto, 28:247. On Sanuto as Cato: Berchet's preface in Sanuto, 1:72; cf. 34:24.

Grimani and Francesco di Filippo Foscari, two *savi grandi* who had backed Sanuto on the twenty-second, prudently withdrew their support, while the latter successfully rallied the Senate against the Collegio's illegal alterations.[56] Sanuto's original plans were restored.

It was a costly victory for Sanuto, for it is certainly no coincidence that he never again held office after humiliating the Collegio. His appeal to the Senate against his colleagues was no doubt considered sufficient evidence for the *Primi* that he could not be trusted to keep affairs of state within their circle. When the Collegio was usurping the prerogatives of the Senate (and allying itself with the Ten), the governing circle would not extend its confidence to a patrician liable to violate the secrecy of its deliberations and its monopoly of power. Sanuto was to spend the rest of his life in pursuit of the offices on which Antonio Tron turned his back. Both patricians were touchy and idealistic, both casualties of the crisis of Cambrai.

Although the August episode marked Sanuto's most dramatic dissent from the Collegio, he also opposed further *savi* motions regarding the Po expedition, as well as proposals to abolish *contumacia* while salaries were suspended and to hold Senate elections for posts that were the province of the Great Council. He contradicted the Collegio again on September 26—and this time without the support of the other *savi agli ordini*, who had followed his lead a month earlier. All the *savi* called for appointment of a captain of the Po by the Senate, but Sanuto proposed that a captain general be elected by the Great Council, a suggestion that was accepted by ninety-two votes to eighty-seven.[57]

Denied another term on the Collegio, Sanuto explained his defeat to himself by listing several considerations: "First, the Forty wanted to be solicited, as usual, and I didn't say a word . . . ; then, none of the Collegio wanted me [elected], so that I won't oppose them and their opinions, as I've done . . . ; also, the great lobbying carried on by these youngsters [helped defeat me]. . . . There was much murmuring throughout the city over this defeat."[58] For the next six and a half years, Sanuto remained outside the Senate, and frequent nominations

56 On the special authority: Sanuto, 10:376; 11:60, 102, 110, 111, 160. On August 22: Sanuto, 11:172; 169–170, 171; ASV, Senato, Secreto, Reg. 43, fols. 103r–103v. On August 24: Sanuto, 11:180; 178, 184; ASV, Senato, Secreto, Reg. 43, fols. 104r–104v.

57 On September 26: ASV, Senato, Secreto, Reg. 43, fols. 126r–126v. On Sanuto's other dissents: Sanuto, 11:223, 423, 446, 474, 601, 605, 621, 624, 627–628.

58 Sanuto, 12:92.

in that assembly, as well as in the Great Council, did not result in victory.

As with the majority of patricians, Sanuto found himself limited to the forum of the Great Council; unlike most patricians, Sanuto made himself heard in the assembly, although not for nearly three years after he left the Collegio. On July 10, 1513, Doge Loredan made an emotional appeal to state debtors to pay what they owed; the Signoria then presented a motion stating that debtors who served at the defense of Padua or Treviso could be elected to office during their terms of service (and for three months thereafter), although they could not take possession of their posts without paying their debts. The Great Council made known its displeasure with this parsimonious proposal, probably by booing and stamping of feet, so the Signoria amended it, stipulating that one-half the debt need be paid for eligibility. Sanuto went to the *renga* to urge rejection of the new motion: "This law is very bad because a poor patrician, for love of his fatherland, will be hard-pressed [but] will find money to go aid his country. . . . He will be honored with election but won't be able to enter office because of not having paid his debt. He will have endured expenses and endangered his life for nothing." Sanuto suggested that entrance to office be permitted regardless of debt, as was done with judges of the Forty the year before. The assembly's support for Sanuto's suggestion was so evident that the Signoria modified its motion accordingly, after which the Great Council passed it by a vote of 1,010 to 159. Sanuto exults that everyone lauded him for his speech, including the doge, who called him to the tribune and "praised my opinion, saying, 'We have always wished you very well.' "[59]

All this goodwill did not, however, translate into electoral victories for Sanuto. Three months after his triumph, Mestre was burned by the enemy, and he bemoaned his exclusion from the Collegio in such perilous times. In early October the "predators and arsonists" left the lagoon's shores, and Loredan again appealed to state debtors to pay or donate their service, although he did not offer to send his own sons to war. Sanuto was offended by Loredan's lack of patriotism and wished to address the Great Council; but proposals were not presented, so he was compelled to keep silent. In late October he served at Padua, motivated as much by hopes of an office as by desire to serve Venice; after returning home in December, his string of defeats remained unbroken.[60]

59 Sanuto, 16:491; 493.
60 On bemoaning exclusion: Sanuto, 17:108; cf. 103, 105–106. On early October:

On April 15, 1515, a few days after defeating a minor proposal of the Signoria and losing yet another election, Sanuto remarks that "toiling is of no value, nor making speeches in the Great Council and defeating their arguments, since that increases the spite and worse, which are in the *terra*." This was a fleeting perception, for a month later he was anxious to speak when the Signoria proposed that state attorneys be elected by Senate *scrutinii* as well as by Great Council election. He wanted to oppose the Signoria, but Francesco Bollani beat him to the *renga* and pointed out that the motion contravened the 1514 law that had eliminated *scrutinii*. The Great Council turned down the Signoria, and a few days later Bollani was elected state attorney for his defense of the assembly's authority.[61]

A month later Sanuto and Bollani clashed over the subject of nominations by the Senate to Great Council elections. On June 10 Bollani presented a proposal to the Great Council that called for *scrutinii* for some judicial offices, claiming that the law creating the offices required nominations by the Senate. Sanuto retorted that Bollani's proposal was in contradiction to the 1514 law against *scrutinii*, which the state attorney had himself defended so recently, and that it detracted from the sovereignty of the Great Council, which could "make and unmake [offices] as it pleases." The Great Council rejected Bollani's motion, an especially pleasing outcome for Sanuto because he had defeated Bollani using the same argument the latter had used to win the patriciate's plaudits and the office of state attorney:

> The entire Great Council shook my hand, as if I had been elected *podestà* of Padua; all praised me, enemies and friends alike, saying that they wished to make me the next state attorney. . . . And this lasted more than eight days, with everyone I bumped into congratulating me with a happy heart, saying, 'We must nominate you quickly, and for every post, so that the *terra* will honor you!' Some said: 'We'll submit a motion to impeach the state attorney [Bollani] and put you in his place.' Thus this was a great rebuff for the state attorney: he lost credit, and they are sorry they elected him.[62]

Sanuto, 17:120; cf. 18:251. On Sanuto's service and defeats: Sanuto, 17:246, 258, 261, 352, 357, 428, 439; 19:239.

61 On April 15: Sanuto, 20:119. On Bollani: Sanuto, 20:204–205, 206–209, 218–219; Michiel, fols. 167v, 169r.

62 Sanuto, 20:286–287; 283–284, 285–286; cf. 20:326.

A clear indication that the acclaim for Sanuto was not as universal as he asserts is that he continued to meet defeat in the councils. Even when loans for offices were inaugurated, his fortunes did not immediately improve. On March 30, 1516, he bid for nomination to the post of state attorney, but just before the election, important news of the war arrived, so "the whole Great Council rose up and caused great commotion, saying that a state attorney could not be created today. Yet I had more than 700 who would vote for me. And the doge said to me that I should regard this as a good omen: 'You will be state attorney.'" But when the election fell due again, Sanuto was not nominated. A further humiliation awaited him on April 23, when his brother Leonardo nominated him for commissioner of customs (*provveditore sopra i dacii*), a position Sanuto considered beneath his talents, even though it permitted entrance to the Senate. As he records, "When I went [to the tribune of the Signoria] to make an offer, I said these words: 'Most Serene Prince, against my wishes, my luck has determined that I have been nominated as customs commissioner, though I don't seek the office; yet I am prepared to enter it, and therefore I desire to serve the city with this loan of 400 ducats.'" To his embarrassment and chagrin, a patrician offering only 200 ducats easily defeated him.[63] No doubt the Great Council expected more enthusiasm from those desiring its honors.

Finally, Sanuto entered the Senate on August 6, 1516, after presenting a loan of 500 ducats. During his year in the assembly he spoke often, although he did not indulge in especially dramatic gestures against the Collegio. He opposed a motion that would have replaced *scrutinii* with straightforward bidding, and he spoke against the *savi* regarding nine other measures, touching such subjects as Turkish policy, galley voyages, and official salaries. His most important activity during his term in the Senate actually occurred in the Great Council, where he gave a lengthy and eloquent speech supporting the creation of the censors.[64]

Not only was Sanuto's diligence unrewarded with an office or re-election to the Senate; he was shortly afterward defeated on one day in contests for the Zonta, censor, and *savio di terraferma*—something of a record even for him. He attributes these defeats to quarrels with his family; he receives, he complains, no aid from his brothers, while

---

63 On March 30: Sanuto, 22:90; cf. 7, 66, 149–150. On April 23: Sanuto, 22: 156, 157; cf. 172.

64 Sanuto, 24:704–705; cf. this book, Chapter IV.3.

his first cousin, Marino di Francesco, an old enemy, "opposes me in every way." His resentment sparked new resolutions: "I'm always rejected, and I don't gain half the Great Council's votes, so I'll keep my opinions to myself, for I wish to live peacefully. . . . No one in the Senate has spoken in the *renga* for the benefit of this state as much as I have, yet everything ends in defeat."[65]

Perhaps because of depression or cumulative disappointment, Sanuto remained silent for seven months, until he opposed a very complicated proposal for reforming the state attorney's office on April 10, 1518. After reminding the Great Council that such ill-conceived legislation would never have passed the Senate if properly examined, he noted that the effect of the motion would be to allow persons to stay in the post of state attorney for as long as four years, an argument that impressed the patriciate as well as the Signoria, which did not respond to him. The proposal was turned down, and once again many said that Sanuto would be the next state attorney. The diarist was justifiably losing confidence in such prophecies, for his response when defeated for the post a week later was fatalistic: "One can't rail against heaven," he writes. "Whoever wishes to dissent must be crazy; all will be for the best."[66]

Yet Sanuto's next intervention in debate on September 26 won him a place on the Zonta. Francesco di Filippo Foscari narrowly defeated Francesco Donato in a contest for the Ten; but two councillors, Luca Tron, an enemy of Foscari, and Antonio Mula, an ally of Donato, ordered another vote on technical grounds and declared Donato elected when he surpassed Foscari's first and only vote. All three state attorneys objected to this maneuver as unfair to Foscari, and after some consultation the Signoria split on the issue, three councillors supporting the validity of the first vote, three the validity of Donato's second vote. The Signoria thus proposed that the Great Council decide the legality of the two ballots. Sanuto objected to this procedure on the grounds that it was unfair to Foscari and disrespectful of the Great Council's sovereignty, for it "gave authority to the councillors to elect whom they pleased, notwithstanding the will of the Great Council." He informed the state attorneys that the proper procedure was for them to submit a proposal annulling Donato's second vote; the officials agreed, the Great Council voted, and Foscari once more became the

---

65 Sanuto, 24:705; 128, 174. On enmity with Marino di Francesco: Sanuto, 10: 573; 25:516; 42:733, 777; 53:578.
66 Sanuto, 25:353; 342, 344–347, 349.

victor. Four days after his defense of the Great Council's authority, Sanuto was rewarded with election to the Zonta for the first time, "for which I am," says the diarist, "[the Great Council's] servant forever, and I consider myself repaid for all my labors, since I've been placed in the most excellent Senate with so much honor."[67]

Sanuto entered the Senate determined to moderate his dissent. When what he regarded as an unjust motion was presented to the Great Council in November 1518, he comments that "if I had not been elected to the Zonta, where it is necessary to exercise more gravity, I would have countered it." When the Collegio acted illegally a few days later, he was silent: "I leave the burden [of opposition] to the many others who are in the Senate." Similarly, although he wanted to oppose the Collegio in March, he refrained from speaking, "so that it won't be said that Marino Sanuto goes to the *renga* for everything." Yet the speaker's platform retained an irresistible attraction. In January 1519 he twice contradicted the Collegio on Turkish policy, and in March he successfully argued in the Great Council against a proposal by the Forty for taxing litigants to pay judicial salaries. A few days before his defeat for reelection to the Zonta, he spoke against a *savi* motion concerning galleys; and he noted that, while he was aware that his dissent damaged his political fortunes, he trusted that it aided the Republic.[68]

His relative discretion indicates that the Zonta term of 1518/1519 was a critical point in his career. He clearly tried to restrain himself and act the part of a sober senator respecting the wisdom of the *Primi*. When he did speak, he first excused himself "for entering the *renga* more often than is appropriate, since it is considered presumptuous to frequent the *renga*." He went on to tell the Senate that "love of country made me say these words [about the Collegio's Turkish policy], for I would not oppose others than to do good for the country; either due to divine will or natural instinct, neither regard for others nor anything else matters [to me]. If I must die poor, without sons or others, the gratitude of the state is sufficient." Reelection to the Zonta was more or less automatic if the Great Council was not annoyed with an individual or with actions of the *Primi*, and Sanuto's restraint was certainly dictated by that consideration. Excluded from

67 Sanuto, 26:64, 65; 72, 83.
68 On refraining from opposition: Sanuto, 26:215–216, 229; 27:9. On dissenting: Sanuto, 26:374–375, 392–393; 27:111, 672, 679, 680–681, 684, 689.

the Collegio, he could at least secure a regular place in the Senate.[69]

Still, reelection eluded Sanuto, perhaps because of his speeches during the year or because his reputation proved stronger than his self-imposed censorship. That reputation had by now become a fixture of Venetian politics. In January 1520 Francesco Morosini, a state attorney, felt the need for Sanuto's knowledge of law when the Collegio presented an improper measure. He took the occasion to lament that "the observer of the laws" was not in the Senate: "When he sees something proposed," said Morosini, "which is against the law, he doesn't let it pass, which deserves great praise. He must be in all the councils, for whoever observes laws maintains republics." Others evidently agreed with Morosini, for Sanuto was elected to the Zonta again in September 1520; and during a Senate debate in August, according to Sanuto, "Many looked around to see if anyone would respond [to the Collegio], and especially to the place where I, Marino Sanuto, listen, for when I see the best for our fatherland, I am not afraid to say what I think."[70]

During his 1520/1521 Zonta term, Sanuto lived up to his reputation. The moderation that characterized his previous service was gone, and he was more active in opposition to the *Primi* than at any other time in his career. His instinctive nonconformity had won out over a calculated, if feeble, desire for accommodation. Three weeks after his election, he argued against a motion by the Signoria for the continuation of three special state attorneys to supervise government accounts, an issue on which he was in agreement with Antonio Tron. Most likely both wanted to restore power to the regular state attorneys, as well as to stop an unnecessary multiplication of magistracies. After Sanuto's speech, four councillors withdrew from the motion, and it was defeated. However, in January 1521 his attempt (in alliance with Antonio Tron) to have the censors disbanded and their responsibilities given to the state attorneys was not successful.[71]

Sanuto's activity in the Senate began in earnest in the spring of 1521. On April 19 he helped defeat a motion that would have allowed Venetians to ship goods on foreign vessels, the sort of economic suicide, Sanuto argued, that well-ordered republics never practice. Two days later he successfully opposed a measure placing obstacles before Venetian merchants who wanted to send galleys to Lisbon for spices.

69 On Sanuto's reasons for dissenting: Sanuto, 26:374, 376.
70 On Morosini: Sanuto, 28:206–207. On the August debate: Sanuto, 31:230.
71 Sanuto, 29:312; cf. 28:666; 29:87, 279, 283.

But, as always, his principal interest was offices and government. On May 7 he spoke against a complicated proposal by the Water Office regarding proprietary rights to minor offices. The measure was shelved until July, when the Senate passed it over Sanuto's continued objections, although the Signoria refused to submit it to the Great Council for final approval, perhaps because Sanuto had defeated similar legislation in that assembly in 1515.[72]

On May 14 Sanuto defeated a motion, sponsored by Luca Tron, a friend and occasional debating opponent, whose effect would be, he claimed, to reduce an appeals court to impotence. Sanuto contends that Luca submitted a proposal a week later to elect state attorneys by a *scrutinio* vote in order to avenge that defeat. If Luca's intention was indeed to lure Sanuto into debate and defeat him, then he was successful. The diarist did not speak against the motion in the Senate but waited for a Great Council meeting on June 2. Despite the intense heat, sixteen hundred patricians were in attendance, "because," Sanuto asserts, "of the rumor that I planned to speak against the motion to elect state attorneys by *scrutinio*." Before addressing the motion, Sanuto felt compelled to explain two points to the assembly: First, his ambition to be state attorney had nothing to do with his opposition, and only his concern for "the public good" prompted him to enter the *renga*; second, he did not oppose the motion in the Senate because he would have been defeated, yet he knew that he could count on the wisdom of the Great Council. He went on to cite the numerous precedents against *scrutinii*, several of which he had helped establish, and to defend the prerogatives of the Great Council:

> This motion is nothing other than the beginning of the elimination of your freedom, that is, returning votes to the method of *scrutinio* as they used to be and forcing your excellencies to elect one of those nominated by scrutiny, as always was done. It is a poor notion to deny your excellent deliberations, as when you nominate some who are not *Primi di la terra*. But whoever says that those on the most excellent Council of Ten [for whom *scrutinii* were eliminated in 1501] are not of the best speaks against the truth.

He also warned that approval of *scrutinii* for state attorneys was only an opening wedge for the Senate, which would begin applying the procedure to a host of other offices. But neither his flattery of the

72 Sanuto, 30:154–155, 185, 198, 201, 457.

Great Council nor his warning of dire consequences availed; the motion passed by 1,097 to 512. At the next meeting of the Great Council, Sanuto was defeated for state attorney, he asserts, "for having opposed the motion." After arguing against the Collegio on several measures during the following summer, Sanuto left the Zonta and was not reelected for the next four years.[73]

Poor health kept Sanuto from attending the Great Council from late 1521 to March 1523. Absence from all the councils plunged him into despair and forced him to address his complaints to the pages of his diary:

Having already, with divine assistance, written thirty volumes of my history of events in Italy, wherein I have described what happens day by day throughout the world—a work which, put into final form, will be deserving of no little admiration—and having, with the greatest exertion, written about and truthfully sought out events worthy of being memorialized, I wanted to end [the diary] for two reasons. First, my age [of fifty-six years] weighs heavily on me. Second, having worked so hard, I believe that I deserved a reward, if not a public stipend, as others have who write nothing [that is, Andrea Navagero, official historiographer], then at least some honor from my country, which I have so extolled and enshrined to eternity —or if not more honored than I have been for some years, at least not more miserable, as [I am now] by my bad luck or by the malignity of those who wished me thrown out of the Zonta. And one may say that this will more quickly redound to their disadvantage than to mine, since, I swear to God, being in the Senate I have spoken many times and given my opinions on affairs for the welfare and benefit of my dearest fatherland; and usually they were approved by the senators with their votes. But this has excited hatred against me, seeing how stoutly I oppose the opinions of those who govern the state; hence I find myself outside the Senate because they and their relatives don't wish me elected—or perhaps it's the will of God. . . .[74] God has given me eloquence of tongue and an excellent memory, and [I have] knowledge of affairs for having described them already for so many years and for having examined all the books of our chancellery, so that it would seem to me a self-betrayal not to give my opinion when matters are dealt with. I know that those who propose motions complain if they are opposed, and so do

73 On May 14: Sanuto, 30:232, 253. On June 2: Sanuto, 30:158, 159, 310. On being defeated: Sanuto, 30:348; 31:145, 216, 230, 251, 252–253, 311, 498.

74 Sanuto, 33:5–6.

others if something is to their advantage; but I, concerned only for
the public welfare, care for nothing but to aid the Republic in any
way that I am able. Yet the upshot has been that those who don't
wish to be contradicted, with their sons and relatives, some my contemporaries and some older, are blinded by envy, not being able or
not knowing how to respond [to me] . . . while others are motivated simply to desire evil to whoever does good—all these col-
laborate to defeat me. . . . I confess that these rejections have given
me no little pain and have caused my illness. And in the renewal of
the Zonta this past year [1522], it's little wonder that I failed when
I was nominated, since many considered me moribund or so ill that
nothing could be done; nor had I left my house for many months
previously. Still, heavenly benevolence wished to preserve me. I have
completed the account of the past year, and even though quite ill, I
have not refrained from recording the news brought me daily by
friends, such that another volume is finished. Some thoughts of abandoning this burdensome project occur to me; but then I seem to see
those compatriots who love me and who say, "Marino, don't give up,
continue with the enterprise begun, for 'Offices and wives come from
heaven.' Go on writing about events in Italy and the world, since you
see great forces gathering against Christianity."[75]

Away from the Ducal Palace for the first time since he held office
in Verona two decades ago, out of the Collegio for more than twelve
years, deprived of plaudits in the councils, defeated yet again for the
Senate, his health broken, his debts increasing—it is hardly surprising
that Sanuto gave way, even more than usual, to self-pity, justifications,
complaints, and most significantly, to doubt about carrying on his
lifelong work, the diary. He sought resolution for his personal crisis
by looking beyond his own problems and failures to the travail of
Europe: the loss of Rhodes and Belgrade to the Turks, a burgeoning
revolt against the papacy in Germany, an intensified battle between
France and the Empire in Italy. This expansion of his horizons to some
extent assuaged his anguish, for even locked away in San Giacomo
dell'Orio, he could still feel himself in contact with events of tremendous magnitude.[76]

During the diarist's long illness, he drew up a list of proposals that
he would have liked to see enacted if he had the authority, a private
tinkering with the government that probably afforded him a sense of

75 Sanuto, 34:6–7.

76 Sanuto 33:6; 34:7; cf. Giorgio Martino Thomas, *Martin Luther und die
Reformations Bewegung in Deutschland vom Jahre 1520–1532 in auszügen aus
Marino Sanuto's Diarien.*

involvement with affairs at the Ducal Palace. Most of the fifty-two would-be laws and regulations dealt with minor procedural and ceremonial matters, but some concerned fundamental aspects of the Venetian political system.[77] Sanuto wished to restrict the Ten's power, thereby indicating his agreement with a patrician's assertion in May 1521 that "thirty alone want to govern the city."[78] Other proposals were also aimed at controlling the executive councils: The Collegio was to be forbidden to allow ambassadors to depart Venice for their posts without the permission of the Senate; the Signoria was to be prohibited from extending terms of office under any conditions; the Senate was to have a stronger voice in nominations for ecclesiastical positions; and one meeting of the Senate every week was to be devoted to the reading of dispatches. A typically Venetian anticlerical bias was expressed in his suggestion that the clergy be taxed, with the proceeds going to the Arsenal; another proposal simply states that "bishops and cardinals must reside in their cities." His concern for the law is revealed in the proposal that a commission be established to introduce order into the chaos of Venetian statutes.

Two propositions involved alterations in the Great Council's voting procedures: He wished to eliminate the first urn used in making up the nominating committees, thus eliminating a time-consuming stage in the selection process; second, and more important, he wanted to impose a disqualification period of one month on the patricians of the nominating committees, a measure designed to insure wider participation in the distribution of honors. Three proposals concerned the touchy issue of poverty within the patriciate: One stated that "the poor patricians must be provided for"; the other two made concrete suggestions—"That 100 patricians be sent to Cyprus and be given an income"; "That 30 patrician canons be created in San Marco, with 200 ducats each as a benefit from the state." Finally, a proposal provided for the creation of an official whose duty it would be "to oppose or to praise in the *renga* whenever a motion is presented giving money to anyone," a post that Sanuto no doubt found easy to imagine for himself.

These proposals embody a program that is of a piece with the notions expressed in Sanuto's numerous dissenting speeches: the value of participation in government, equality within the ruling class, the link

77 On the following proposals, see the document reproduced in Berchet's preface in Sanuto, 1:83–85.
78 Sanuto, 30:229.

between poverty and electoral corruption, rationality in law and administration, and the necessity for objectivity and selflessness in decision making. With the exception of those dealing with indigent patricians, none of the proposals were notable departures from tradition. Indeed, they expressed traditional republican values. Yet, in the context of Venice after Agnadello, they reveal a viewpoint inevitably at odds with the new tenor of Venetian politics. They help further explain why Sanuto remained an outsider in the politics of his city.

Sanuto returned to the Great Council in March 1523 and was welcomed back by crowds of friends; however, he continued to be plagued by illness, and it was not until a year later that his attendance at the Ducal Palace became regular again. He spoke in the Great Council for the first time since June 1521 on March 29, 1524, opposing a motion, passed by the Senate and authored by Luca Tron, that rescinded legislation requiring lawbreakers to present themselves for trial if cited by a court. Tron claimed that this law was much abused, while Sanuto argued that it was necessary to prevent greater violence and crime, a position that the patriciate finally supported. In his speech Sanuto said that he wished to expound the law for the benefit of the many *giovani* who had entered the sovereign assembly since 1514; a few days later, he claims, the young men supported him in an election, "however the *vecchi* did not want me because I oppose them."[79]

On April 23 Sanuto spoke against a motion passed by the Senate giving certain rights to an individual who had purchased a procuratorship. After noting that the motion had only passed the Senate by "very few ballots," he apologized for speaking against his many friends on the Full Collegio, but, he asserted, it was necessary to forego "every particular benefit and to defend the public welfare, as every good citizen must." Much to his pleasure and honor, the motion was decisively defeated. On September 25 he argued against a proposal to elect three procurators for loans. Bernardo Donato—"a very bestial creature," according to the diarist—replied that Sanuto was merely trying to impress the Great Council for the upcoming Zonta election, a slur to which Sanuto did not deign to respond. The motion was approved by the assembly, Sanuto reports, because "the crooked and the Switzers supported it in order to get some money from those whom they nominate." In any event, Sanuto had failed to impress the Great Council, for in a few days he again fell short in election for the Zonta.[80]

79 Sanuto, 36:149–150; 127–128, 129; cf. 34:7; 39:481.
80 On April 23: Sanuto, 36:251. On September 25: Sanuto, 36:613–614.

A month later Sanuto spoke once more against the ceaseless effort of the Senate to reinstitute *scrutinii*, but the Great Council was deaf to his warning that its liberty would be lost by acceding to that procedure. After this defeat Sanuto was silent until June 1525, when he successfully opposed the attempt to alter the order of the *Quarantie*'s rotation into the Senate, a measure intended to eliminate *giovani* from the latter assembly. His resounding and eloquent defense of the necessity to bring "youngsters" into the higher councils of government almost certainly won him election to the Zonta for the third time on October 4, four years after having ended his last term. "God be praised," he says, "who knows my heart is wholly [dedicated] to the welfare of our Republic and my dear country!"[81]

Although Sanuto was elected to the Zonta again in 1532 and 1533, his 1525/1526 term was the last in which he was especially active in opposition to the *Primi*. As in his first Zonta term of 1518, he was aware of the need for discretion. For example, when the subject of selling shops on the Rialto bridge came up, he remained silent, not wishing it to be said that "Marino speaks on vulgar matters." Again, however, his moderation was short-lived. In December 1525 he objected to the Collegio sending *savi* to the home of the papal ambassador and insisted that the latter should instead come to the Ducal Palace for discussions; the Senate agreed with him, and the Collegio altered its proposal without argument. His lengthy speech in the Great Council in January 1526 against the censors' measure to eliminate congratulations and handshaking after elections was without effect. But what eloquent orations failed to accomplish could occasionally be achieved with forbidding silence. According to Sanuto, when it was evident in March that he intended to object to some phrases in a letter to Charles V, the *savi* expunged the offending words: "I was praised by the whole council," boasts the diarist, "for having achieved my ends without entering the *renga*."[82] In the early Cinquecento, perhaps only Sanuto and Antonio Tron had such well-established reputations as critics that they could sometimes accomplish their ends without even voicing opposition.

Predictably, Sanuto's disagreement with the *Primi* during the rest of the year merely confirmed both the Collegio's opposition to him

---

81 On *scrutinii*: Sanuto, 37:80. On the *Quarantie* legislation: Chapter III.2. On Sanuto's election: Sanuto, 40:17; 21.

82 On selling shops: Sanuto, 40:888. On December 1525: Sanuto, 40:439–440; cf. 40:449. On January 1526: Chapter IV.3. On the letter to Charles V: Sanuto, 41:21; cf. 48:185, 187.

and his own sense of self-esteem. In April the Senate supported Sanuto against the *savi* in a matter regarding France, "and the Collegio was mightily astonished, not knowing what to do, and perhaps great hatred grew against me among them." His defeat of the *savi* two months later concerning a letter to England "satisfied almost the entire Council, and everyone saw how useful I am to the Republic." The final three months of his term were less successful, and his protests on a number of subjects, including the reinstitution of loans for offices, were not supported by the Senate.[83]

Even though he was elected to two more Zonta terms after 1526, Sanuto's final political years remained gloomy. Sixty years old in 1526, he saw his last hopes for office and recognition vanishing. A few days before he exited the Senate in 1526, he objected to the Signoria that seats on the Ten should go only to *Primi di la terra*, and Nicolò Bernardo cruelly replied, "Then why are you not nominated?" Naturally, Sanuto had no chance of entering the Ten (his only recorded nomination to that council came in 1527 when an enemy put his name forward), and in September 1526 he was even defeated in reelection for the Zonta. A week after that defeat he considered opposing a motion in the Great Council extending loans for offices, but "seeing that I was poorly rewarded and expelled from the Zonta, I did not wish to speak."[84]

Sanuto went to the *renga* infrequently after 1526. On July 30, 1527, he resisted the *case grandi* proposal; shortly after, the large clans defeated him for the Senate and the Zonta. In September 1529 he countered a motion to elect a captain general of the fleet, which later was approved by a vote of 1,216 to 110: "And I wish to God that I had not spoken," he moans, "for to go against such a mob is a weighty matter; but I said what I thought." Although partly a result of discretion and further illness, Sanuto's uncommon silence after 1526 was principally due to the reintroduction of loans for offices in the autumn of that year.[85] His scant hopes for office dwindled still further as money and lobbying once more dominated place seeking; protests

---

83 On France and England: Sanuto, 41:159, 487. On his last three months: Sanuto, 41:742; 42:184–185, 317–319, 417, 513.

84 On Bernardo: Sanuto, 42:716. On his nomination to the Ten: Sanuto, 48:473. On not wishing to speak: Sanuto, 43:32; cf. 39, 90, 105, 107.

85 On Sanuto and the *case grandi* proposal: Chapter II.4. On September 1529: Sanuto, 51:532–533; 605. On discretion and illness: cf. Sanuto, 50:92, 247. On reintroduction of office loans: Chapter IV.2.

against concentration of power in the executive committees made little sense when secretive government was clearly the norm.

Faced with familiar obstacles and disheartened by the politics of his city, Sanuto virtually retired from public life. He was elected to the Zonta in January 1532, most likely because he had just become the oldest member of his clan and a certain preeminence was therefore due to him. He spoke on several subjects in the Senate in this term, and his two principal actions were in keeping with his previous dissents. He forced the Collegio to withdraw a motion that called for a Senate election to an office under the Great Council's authority; and he won revision of a measure that substituted a Collegio election for one by the Senate, a victory that pleased the latter "but not the Collegio." These were the last protests of his career. He won readmittance to the Zonta in September 1532, but he seldom attended the Senate because of illness. Nine months after this election, he stopped keeping his diary; among the final notes of his thirty-seven–year project were reports on an election for censor (in which he was not nominated) and on one for the Zonta, which, he approvingly comments, proceeded "without any error." Slightly more than three years later, he died at the age of seventy and was buried in the church of San Zaccaria, where, in the course of later renovations, his tomb was removed and lost. In moments of great depression, Sanuto often bitterly quoted the Latin tag, "Ungrateful fatherland, thou shalt not have my bones!" —an ironically accurate prophecy.[86]

By any reckoning, Sanuto's was a pathetic career, characterized by a tremendous gap between ambition and achievement, capacity and accomplishment. His career almost exactly spanned the years of the Italian wars, during which he witnessed what he considered a steady erosion of republican principles in Venetian politics, an erosion he could only fitfully oppose excluded as he was from the centers of power. With the possible exception of Antonio Tron, Sanuto knew more about Venetian law, administration, and history than any of his contemporaries. Yet this remained a knowledge of the study, uninfluenced by the reality of Venetian politics, for which he had slight sympathy or understanding; his was the temperament of an ideologue, little given to the striving for consensus and compromise that characterized the politics of the Venetian Republic. Hectoring, lecturing, complaining, indeed demanding that the ruling class hew to his notion

---

86 On Sanuto's last protests: Sanuto, 58:498, 499, 521, 686. On his last entries: Sanuto, 58:750. On the Latin tag: Sanuto, 51:611; cf. 22:172.

of inviolable principle, he had only himself to blame for his failure.
On their own terms, patricians in the Great Council and Senate were
correct to reject him; he clearly did not fit the mold of a Venetian
politician.

Naturally, Sanuto could not accept the notion that he was a born
outsider in his city's politics; he needed a rationalization for his constant defeat and frustration. In fact, an overriding sense of religious
mission sustained the diarist in his long years of failure, a conception
of divine guidance that was not uncommon in his intensely devout age.
He was supported in his thankless opposition to the powers of the
terra by the sense that he was an instrument of providence, that in
upholding republican principles he was part of the transcendental
design that shaped the Republic's destiny: As God watches over the
Republic, so He also attends to those who labor for its salvation. Rejected by his peers, excluded from power, Sanuto thus justified his
failure by envisioning success on a sublime plane of endeavor. His
certainty, emerging slowly in the course of his career, that the Republic was in an advanced state of degeneration arose not only from
the corruption and illegalities he saw around him but from the ruin of
his own political fortunes. "Offices come from heaven": God was
punishing Venice by not granting success to His and its most faithful
servant. Sanuto's conceit was equal to his extraordinary perspective—
he would be a Job for Venice. And a Jeremiah: His oration of August
1526 against loans for office began with the lamentation of that
prophet, "*Veh civitas!*"[87]

It was, then, "pleasing to God" when Sanuto was in the Senate, for
He was aware of the diarist's devotion to the Republic, even if others
remained ignorant or uncaring. Addressing the Senate in August 1526
on a foreign policy question, Sanuto said "that it was determined by
God that I alone should enter the *renga*, since I see no one else who
would speak." He was pleased to record that "whoever does not want
me, above all, in the Senate is an enemy of God and of the Republic."
Offense to God, as well as "self-betrayal," would result if he ignored
his conscience and allowed an unjust measure to go unopposed. He
trusted in God's support and guidance in the councils and that He
would amply punish those who unjustly resisted him in debates and
elections. "I must have patience with those who go bawling against
me," he consoles himself, "for God will pay them back in the end."[88]

87 Sanuto, 42:317.
88 On "pleasing to God": Sanuto, 40:17. On entering the *renga*: Sanuto, 42:

Sanuto's toil "for the honor of God Eternal and the exaltation of the Venetian state" encompassed his production of a diary as well as his opposition in the councils. His literary activity was closely linked to his political involvement, and he suffered defeats concerning the former as sore as any he experienced in the Great Council. He aspired to the post of official historiographer of Venice, which in 1516 went to Andrea Navagero, who wrote nothing during his thirteen-year term. Sanuto was once more bypassed in 1530, when Pietro Bembo was given the office, possibly because the latter was supported by Doge Gritti.[89]

Sanuto's disappointment over this second defeat was compounded by events of the following year. In the winter after his appointment as official historiographer, Bembo visited Sanuto at his home. After taking a close look at the volumes of the diary, Bembo concluded that—"though they contained many superfluous things," as he later wrote to the Ten—they would be useful for his own composition. He therefore asked Sanuto for the loan of his diary, "to which he responded that these books were the concern and labor of his entire life and that he did not want to give [the product of] his sweat to anyone." By the summer of 1531, Bembo had decided that this reply was unsatisfactory, and he successfully appealed to the Ten and to Gritti to order Sanuto to turn over the volumes to him. The Ten—which included such friends of the diarist as Gasparo Contarini, Giacomo di Giorgio Corner, and Pietro Tron—compensated Sanuto for the indignity of loaning the diary to Bembo by giving him a 150-ducat annual pension, even though that was, as Sanuto wrote, "nothing compared to the very great labor I have had." He rather grandly asserted that his pension made him a "public historian," and he had the title *historiae venetorum ex publico decreto* carved on his tomb.[90] But these were merely rationalizations designed to salvage some self-esteem from

---

513–514. On "an enemy of God": Sanuto, 42:317; 319, 513. On offending God and "self-betrayal": Sanuto, 34:5; cf. 26:377; 42:752. On God's support: Sanuto, 40:17. On punishing enemies: Sanuto, 31:329; 42:319; cf. 49:308; 54:351.

89 On "God Eternal": Sanuto, 34:5. On the official historiographer: Cozzi, "Cultura politica e religione"; Felix Gilbert, "Biondo, Sabellico, and the Beginnings of Venetian Official Historiography." On Bembo and Gritti: Carlo Lagomaggiore, "*L'Istoria Viniziana* di M. Pietro Bembo," p. 31.

90 On Bembo, Sanuto, and the Ten, see the documents in Berchet's preface in Sanuto, 1:94–99. On members of the Ten: Sanuto, 54:572, 576. On a "public historian": Sanuto, 55:211. On his tomb: Berchet's preface in Sanuto, 1:110; cf. pp. 97, 99.

humiliation—in all, a defeat that demands sympathy for the diarist, for it was the only one he suffered that was not in some measure self-inflicted.

Sympathy also is required because of the critical role the diary played in its composer's self-perception, a role that subtly altered across almost four decades. In the beginning Sanuto considered that he was merely collecting source material that, "with time, if God gives me life, I will reduce to a brief history, eliminating many superfluous things." This remained his ambition until his protest-filled Zonta term of 1521 and his subsequent prolonged illness, the latter accompanied by doubt about continuing his record of events. As his list of political defeats grew longer and the volumes of his material multiplied, he came perforce to view his compilation as justified in its own right, "part vernacular history, part diary." Significantly, this altered view dates from about the same time he came to see his rejection by the councils as having transcendental import. A diary, he wrote to the Ten in 1531, "contains all the truth, which is very powerful in history," because in such a work "it is necessary to write everything." By contrast, Sanuto implies, Bembo would only write in Latin about noteworthy events, eviscerating the true matter of history for the entertainment of an elite. Sanuto was working in his "mother tongue" on "a history in the form of a diary," an account in a new and exhaustive mode of *rerum gestarum Venetorum*. As such, his many volumes possessed an excellence surpassing traditional forms of historical writing. Even while surrendering his work to Bembo, Sanuto was proud that his rival so badly needed it: "I will say this: certainly no writer can ever produce anything decent on modern history without seeing my diary, which comprises everything that happened."[91]

As the diary developed into the principal work of Sanuto's life, it became indissolubly linked with his career and ambitions. The labor and money he spent on the diary became for him an argument that he should be honored with office; he frequently laments that his efforts are not rewarded with election, "for having composed so many books in honor of my fatherland." In 1519 he told the Senate that he desired only "the gratitude of the state," but ten years later countless defeats

---

91 On collecting source material: Sanuto, 6:5; cf. 5:109; 8:5–6. On the diary in 1521: Sanuto, 30:5. On "vernacular history": Berchet's preface in Sanuto, 1: 96. On his 1531 statement: Berchet's preface in Sanuto, 1:96. On "history in the form of a diary": Sanuto, 29:255; cf. 26:52. On need for his diary: Berchet's preface in Sanuto, 1:96.

led him to condemn Venice and threaten to halt his record of events: "Seeing that I'm not acceptable to my fatherland, I won't write [my diary] anymore but will devote myself to what little time I have left. I am sixty-three and the son of one who died for his fatherland while ambassador at Rome, where his bones are. And I wish to say with him: *ingrata patria non habebis ossa mea.*" Yet he continued his diary, which had also become the one place where he could comment on everything, criticizing the doings of the councils from which he was excluded; he had his own private *renga.* Moreover, surveying European politics gave him a connection with the great events of his time, which he otherwise lacked.[92]

The introduction of remarks on his political fortunes becomes especially noticeable during the early 1520s, when he began to realize that high office was closed to him—and when he decided to continue his diary because of "great forces gathering against Christianity." During the same years, he reevaluated his composition, seeing it as worthy in its own right, indeed seeing it as his own best guarantee of "glory and perpetual renown," as insuring him the recognition by posterity that contemporaries denied. This renown would be posthumous retaliation for his political failure. Thus after recording a defeat for the Zonta, Sanuto adds that "I wanted to make this note here so that all may see how things are in republics." The record of his failure was enshrined in a work whose very magnificence would make evident how unjustly its author was treated by the Republic he wished to serve for its own glory and in obedience to divine dictates. The diary was to bestow immortality on both Sanuto and Venetian iniquity toward him.[93]

Political ambition, religious inspiration, and historical composition were inseparable for Sanuto. They reinforced one another and were all expressed through his admittedly cranky and intemperate personality; they shifted their respective weight and force as his career foundered and the crisis of Cambrai reshaped Venetian politics. His was an exemplary failure, revealing at once the limitations of his character, the nature of patrician dissent, and the changes he witnessed and recorded. His patriotism, righteousness, and perseverance stemmed

---

92 On "having composed so many books": Sanuto, 49:352; cf. 15:188; 22:172; 25:84; 26:52; 48:473. On 1519 and ten years later: Sanuto, 26:376; 51:611; cf. 41:540.

93 On "glory and perpetual renown": Sanuto, 30:5. On defeat for the Zonta: Sanuto, 24:704–705.

from his sense of providential support, while his diary served as an argument for reward, a place of refuge, a promise of renown, and an instrument of revenge. Only a politician sustained by a notion of divine election could reconcile himself to such complete temporal failure. At the same time, Sanuto retained his faith in republican principles and pursued his ambitions for so long because he channeled his frustrations and bitterness into a work that argued that the Republic itself suffered when he was forced into opposition and excluded from directing its destiny.

Sanuto was certainly the most outstanding opponent of the *Primi* who was not part of the governing circle. Within the *Primi*, Luca and Antonio Tron were exceptional in their eagerness to take issue with their peers. Of course they were not alone, for Gasparo Malipiero, Filippo Tron, Marino Morosini, Antonio Condulmer, and Alvise di Giovanni Priuli also often dissented from the governing circle of which they were a part. These patricians shared at least one assumption: All believed that the structure of the Republic was fundamentally sound, that the machinery of government did not require a complete overhaul. Implicit in their dissents was the notion that only more or less minor tinkering—reform of electoral methods, action against corruption, a different foreign policy or taxation program—was needed for the state to run as smoothly as it had in the days of the founding fathers. Even Sanuto often implied that all Venice required to right its course was to enlist him in the ranks of the governing circle.

All, too, were hampered to some extent by the strict limits set to dissent by the Venetian political and constitutional order. Had Sanuto and the Tron joined with like-minded patricians in maintaining a common front and presenting a coherent program, they might have been more effective; but this is speculation contrary to the reality of Venetian politics, which worked against the possibility of such unity by emphasizing accommodation rather than programmatic conflict, expediency rather than principle, place seeking rather than ideology. Sanuto and the Tron were opposed to the post-Agnadello changes in government; yet they were reduced to making isolated protests against particular measures. Sanuto's exclusion from the executive councils and his infrequent attendance in the Senate meant that he could rarely mount a concerted attack on the measures he opposed; the Great Council was a rare and inadequate forum for significant debate. In general, Luca Tron's disagreements with the government were fitful and intense, occasions when he strained against the limits of decorum and safety to rally support against disliked policies and personal enemies. Antonio Tron, perhaps the most respected politician of his generation, sporadically boycotted the Collegio when he despaired of reversing changes that the *Primi* believed were necessary for Venetian survival.

During the War of the League of Cambrai, an unusual unity of purpose was imposed on the governing circle; the men of the executive councils almost entirely agreed in reducing the effectiveness of the Senate as a center of debate and decision. There was, however, little else that the *Primi* agreed on. Disunity among those who dissented from the government was matched by fragmentation of the governing circle; patricians dominating the government were rarely united on issues that did not challenge their control of policy. Factions within the ruling class were diffuse and shifting, not neat groupings that invariably acted in unison. This reduced the effectiveness of dissent inasmuch as protests could seldom be addressed to a coherent group that clearly dominated the setting of policy across a wide range of issues. Patricians in accord on policy toward the Romagna or on the question of new taxes found themselves opposed to one another on conduct with the Turks or on a treaty with France. Political expediency cut across relationships of friendship and enmity. Leonardo Loredan and Filippo Tron were bitter rivals; yet they found common ground in disposing of Antonio Grimani and in supporting an alliance with France in 1499. Despite their enmity, Luca Tron and Grimani joined forces in urging military action in Friuli and against Ferrara, although they remained opposed on policy toward Spain. Grimani's antagonism toward Angelo Trevisan contributed to the latter's exile in 1510, but within a year they were united in urging a second galley expedition against Ferrara. Whereas they collaborated on most issues, the Tron were in different camps on such questions as the prestige of the state attorneys, the creation of the censors, and military tactics during the war. Sanuto fought with almost every major politician in Venice; yet he was on good terms with Luca Tron, Antonio Grimani, Giorgio Corner, and Lorenzo Loredan, all of whom struggled as well as cooperated with one another. With the exception of the extraordinary struggle between the old and new houses, expedient alliances and transient quarrels shaped the diffuse, shifting factions within the Venetian patriciate.

Patricians were drawn together by numerous ties resulting from electoral debts and familial obligations. In particular, as Priuli emphasizes, a patrician's concern for the welfare of his immediate descendants muted his passions and promoted compromise with his enemies. Dissenters within the ruling class did not fully engage in this search for accommodation and compromise, and it is no coincidence that of the

most prominent dissenters of the early Cinquecento only Gasparo
Malipiero had legitimate children. Andrea Gritti, the only doge of the
same period to attempt enforcing the laws against electoral corruption,
was "without sons." Priuli, intemperate and unyielding in his condemnation of the *Primi* within the privacy of his diary, also had no
children. The freedom and independence a patrician gained by not
having descendants made him more likely to act contrary to the con-
ciliating modes of Venetian politics.

Sanuto and the Tron were critics within a political society that did
not fully value their function. They were, finally, regarded as political
eccentrics, essentially unpredictable, prone to extravagant actions,
abrupt assaults, jeremiads. As Sanuto concluded after a defeat, "Whoever wishes to dissent must be crazy," and patricians thought that
placing principle before electoral victory, as did Antonio Tron, was
"Madness." In short, those who went against the grain of Venetian
politics were neither discreet nor anonymous. If the councils had been
dominated by such personalities, Venetian politics would have been
characterized by discord and tumult rather than by conformity and
passivity. As it was, Luca lapsed into silence, and Sanuto was barred
from the decisive assemblies. Antonio shunned the councils when expediency triumphed over tradition and principle; and despite the
popularity he enjoyed in the *terra* in 1523, he never came close to the
dogeship. The *Primi* knew better than to place in the Ducal Palace a
politician who thought that the doge must act as "a fourth state
attorney," as Antonio lectured Doge Barbarigo in 1500.[94] The Venetian
political system limited the force and muted the opposition of its dissidents; the councils were less arenas for conflict than buffers for absorbing dissension and reconciling differences.

Still, even if the role played by dissenters within the councils was
more often dramatic than effective, they helped keep alive the principles of the Venetian republican tradition: dedication to participation in
government, probity in public life, equality within the ruling class,
rule of law in elections and administration, and freedom of expression
in the assemblies. The ruling class seldom wholeheartedly heeded these
in practice nor were they permitted substantially to shape political
action. Yet their place in the Republic's politics was evident when they
were passionately defended by Sanuto in the *renga* and epitomized in
Antonio Tron's gesture of turning from the Signoria to thank the
Great Council for his new position of honor.

94 Sanuto, 3:952.

Conclusion

Venetian political history in the half millennium after the *Serrata* of the Great Council may be divided into three periods of roughly equal length, 1297–1450, 1450–1630, and 1630–1797. From 1297 to 1450, the implications of the *Serrata* were worked out: in particular, the formation of the patrician caste and the rise to dominance of the Senate. It was a tumultuous period for Venice, with rapid constitutional change at home and constant warfare abroad. During this century and a half, the crisis of the War of Chioggia (1378–1380) may have been of decisive importance for fixing the loyalty of the patriciate to the state. Triumphant over Genoa, Venice then turned to creating a mainland empire, which made new demands for service on the ruling class at the same time that it expanded the state bureaucracy.[1] By the mid-Quattrocento, the constitution was filled out and the sense of patrician self-identity solid and influential. Reflecting both developments, numerous writers turned to praising Venice during this period, laying out the particulars of the myth of Venice that would be further elaborated in the Renaissance.

Politics in Venice during the Renaissance (from 1450 to 1630) was characterized by change within the constitutional lines established earlier. The War of the League of Cambrai was the central episode in this period, confirming the dominance of the executive councils over the Senate as well as Venice's status as a second-rate power. Where Chioggia had confirmed Venetian self-confidence and launched the Republic into an era of expansion, Cambrai threw Venetian values and institutions into doubt and placed immovable limits to its international sway. The crisis of Cambrai initiated nothing wholly new in Venetian politics, for the executive councils, led by the Ten, had been expanding their power against the Senate since at least the last decades of the Quattrocento; but, as with the phenomenon of electoral corruption,

1 Cf. Stanley Chojnacki, "The Making of the Venetian Renaissance State: The Achievement of a Noble Political Consensus, 1378–1420" (Ph.D. diss., University of California at Berkeley, 1968); and this book, Chapter I.3.

the crisis greatly accelerated that expansion, substantially altering the tone and nature of Venetian political life. When the Ten bypassed the Senate in making peace with the Turks in 1540 and 1573–1574,[2] it was acting from an authority it had definitively arrogated to itself from the time of Cambrai. The much-discussed reform of the Ten in 1582–1583, in which the *zonta* was abolished, reduced that council's administrative power but otherwise amounted only to a slight reformulation of the governing circle's technique of domination. In the context of the 180 years from 1450 to 1630, the episode was merely "a brief flutter of largely personal animosities," after which "everything carried on much as before—the same men, the same methods, if anything worse abuses."[3]

Substantial change came to Venetian politics only in the first quarter of the seventeenth century; by no later than 1630, the political formula of the Republic had been recast. In the years from 1630 to 1797, the decisive episode was the War of Crete (1646–1669), which, following the plague of 1630–1631, struck hard at the patriciate and the economy. The plague caused a manpower shortage in the government, and a lack of qualified candidates for offices was already a problem in the 1630s.[4] The Venetian gerontocracy began to unravel as younger men entered high office. Whereas Cambrai had led to the auctioning of offices, Crete resulted in selling patents of nobility. After the war, eighty new families were admitted to the patriciate for 100,000 ducats each, the first additions to the Great Council since immediately after the War of Chioggia; forty-seven more were added between 1684 and 1718. Indeed, the last doge, Lodovico Manin, was from a *terraferma* family; and on his election in 1789, a Venetian exclaimed, "They have made a Friulian doge; the Republic is dead."[5] Yet given the crucial identification between the patrician caste and the form of government, both products of "the salty water," a patrician might just as reasonably have concluded that the Republic died when the first men from the mainland entered the Great Council more than a century before.[6]

Selling patrician status after the War of Crete was a drastic confirmation of changes already afoot in Venice in the first decades of

---

2 Cf. Fernand Braudel, *The Mediterranean and the Mediterranean World in the Age of Philip II*, 2:845, 1126, 1148.

3 M. J. C. Lowry, "The Reform of the Council of Ten, 1582–3," p. 306.

4 James Cushman Davis, *Decline of the Venetian Nobility as a Ruling Class*, pp. 75–76; 75–105.

5 Davis, *Decline of the Venetian Nobility*, pp. 117; 109–110.

6 See the discussion of patrician self-perception, Chapter I.1.

the century. Several events spelled the end of the Renaissance phase of Venetian politics. Always at the foundation of Venetian politics, the Great Council clearly registered this shift in its nominating committees. The average number of men naming themselves to office in the committees rose from four per election day between 1544 and 1605 to nine per day after 1607. On some days, self-nominations made up almost the entire work of the committees. For instance, on January 17, 1608, eleven of twenty-one competitors in the Great Council nominated themselves; on February 12, 1612, it was twelve of sixteen. At the same time, the number of uncontested elections rose dramatically. In the Cinquecento it was very rare for any office to go uncontested, but after 1605 it became common to have three or four every meeting of the Great Council. Thus on Feburary 21, 1608, seven of ten elections were awarded without competition; on January 22, 1612, one-third were uncontested, and 63 percent of the nominees were also in the nominating committees. In the Cinquecento there were usually thirty-six nominators to thirty-six nominees; after 1605 the same number of nominators generally produced less than half their number of nominees.[7] In short, the Great Council was merely ratifying the Senate's nominee or the single nominee issuing from its four committees. Electoral competition, the heart of the political system during the Renaissance, was thus transformed into a formal exercise. The Great Council ceased to be an arena of desired place and honors and became instead a distribution center for sinecures and governmental largesse.

Declining competition in the Great Council may be related to the breakdown of the old political unity of the *Longhi* in the sovereign assembly.[8] After 1605 the old families ceased concentrating their forces in a few elections every meeting. In other words, the "ancient discipline"[9] of the *Longhi* was relaxed before (and not after) Marcantonio Memmo, from a *Longhi* family, gained the dogeship in 1612, the first man from the old clans in the Ducal Palace since 1381. Perhaps, as Sanuto (writing of the 1486 ducal election) had hoped, "time, marriage, and kinship" had finally taken their toll of the rivalry between the clans. In any case, conflict between *Longhi* and *Curti*, a basic animating force in the Great Council and in ducal elections, was

---

7 These generalizations are based on examination of the Consegi volumes (8901–8917) for the January–February elections of 1544, 1550, 1560, 1570, 1580, 1589, 1597, 1600, 1602, 1604, 1605, 1608, 1612, and 1628; names of nominators are not given until 1544.

8 See Chapter II.3.

9 "Distinzioni Segrete che corrono tra le Case Nobili di Venezia," fols. 6v–7r.

not part of Venetian politics after 1612, although whether its disappearance was a cause or a consequence of changes within the Great Council is impossible to determine.

Other divisions assumed more importance within the patriciate. As the Mantuan ambassador wrote in 1609, "Here they no longer speak of old and new houses but of *Papalini* and *Republichisti*," a statement made shortly after the end of the great Interdict struggle between Venice and Rome. This was a new sort of politics for Venice, a division along ideological lines, and to some extent confirms the opinion of the English ambassador in 1612 that patricians "here change theyr manners, they have growne factious, vindicative, loose, and unthriftie."[10] Indeed, an "embryonic party system" seemed to be developing in the Great Council during the 1620s, when Renier Zen led a large number of poor patricians in demanding reform of the Ten.[11] They wanted that council's criminal jurisdiction transferred to the Forty and for the chiefs of the court to enter the Ten. The latter was minimally reformed in 1628, and the movement by *poveri zentilhomeni* petered out; but the turmoil and open agitation of the episode indicates that the Great Council was no longer adequately fulfilling its old function of subsuming differences within the patriciate in electoral competition.

A final hint of the new political scene emerging in the early seventeenth century is legislation that was turned down by the Great Council in June 1603. Without a Sanuto to give a blow-by-blow account of the political infighting, one is left with the legislation itself, an extraordinary attempt by the *Primi* to alter the fundamental relationship between the Great Council and the Senate. Briefly, the proposal called for the regular sixty senators to be elected as was the Zonta, that is, nominated in a group by the outgoing Senate and then approved by the Great Council.[12] The intention behind the legislation was apparently to broaden the gap between the Great Council and the

10 On the Mantuan ambassador: Alessandro Luzio, *La congiuro spagnola contra Venezia nel 1618*, p. 96. On the Interdict struggle: cf. Gaetano Cozzi, *Il doge Nicolò Contarini*; William J. Bouwsma, *Venice and the Defense of Republican Liberty*. On the English ambassador: Cozzi, *Doge Nicolò Contarini*, p. 15, note. On changing attitudes in the patriciate in the early seventeenth century: cf. Gaetano Cozzi, "Una vicenda della Venezia barocca."

11 On "embryonic party system": Frederic C. Lane, *Venice*, p. 405. On Zen: Davis, *Decline of the Venetian Nobility*, pp. 100–101; Charles J. Rose, "Marc Antonio Venier, Renier Zeno and 'the Myth of Venice.'"

12 ASV, Maggior Consiglio, Deliberazioni, Liber Vicus, Reg. 33, fols. 49r–50r.

governing circle, inasmuch as the effect of the law would have been to halt the Great Council's nominations to the Senate and to co-opt indefinitely the same coterie of men for that council. To be sure, this would have raised the prestige of the Senate, for the assembly would have been (with the exception of the Forty) entirely co-opted by *Primi*. Whatever the intentions behind the proposal, the fact remains that, just as the electoral procedures of the Great Council began to slide into disarray, the Signoria suggested that the sovereign assembly no longer bother nominating men to the Senate. Although the legislation was turned down (by 750 votes to 363, with 210 abstentions), its being drawn up and presented is symptomatic of changing perspectives in Venetian politics as the Renaissance neared its close.

In the three stages of Venetian political history—marked and formed by three crises: Chioggia, Cambrai, and Crete—the Renaissance stands out as particularly coherent and vital. In the first period, the patrician caste and the political system were forming; in the final period both were deteriorating, the caste breached by numerous additions, the political system short of manpower and sunk in lethargy. In "the long sixteenth century" of the Renaissance,[13] the Republic of Venice reached its most mature political form: a confident ruling class established in a highly competitive, plethoric assembly, attentive to popular opinion and jealous of its prerogatives; *Primi* anxious for their reputation within the *terra* and unceasingly covetous of the Ducal Palace; a silent, extended struggle for dominance between the executive councils and the "governing council" of the Senate. Above all, dominating the activity and shaping the perspective of the ruling class, there were offices and elections. Votes, indeed, were everything.

"It is very certain," wrote Alexis de Tocqueville, "that of all people in the world, the most difficult to restrain and manage are a people of office-hunters."[14] Although preeminently a people of office hunters, Venetian patricians were in fact restrained and managed by precisely that circumstance. Those seeking office were coterminous as a group with those bestowing offices. Membership in the Great Council was, in effect, an office that gave the right to vote others into office; patricians were simultaneously electors and candidates. The Great Council established the conditions that made Venetian politics so successful and that produced the peculiarly discreet patrician temperament. The *popolo* could affect the general policies and individual ambitions of

13 Braudel, *Mediterranean*, 2:893–898.
14 Alexis de Tocqueville, *Democracy in America*, 2:264.

those gathering in the Ducal Palace because the ruling class was permanently ensconced in an assembly whose major business was elections; contests for positions of influence within the caste thereby became, to some extent, barometers of public opinion.[15] The ceaseless elections of the Great Council provided the arena for struggles between factions, such as the old and new houses, as well as the means of communication between the majority of the patriciate and the *Primi di la terra*.[16] In the sovereign assembly, old age received its due and a gerontocracy was created as the patriciate voted its senior members into high office.[17] The hall of the Great Council (and its antechamber, the *piazza del broglio*) was the setting for the vote seeking, vote trading, and vote buying that fused the ruling class together, for the "whispers and backpatting" that Priuli asserts distinguished Venetian politics and government.[18] With all its drawbacks as a public forum, the hall was also the one place where every patrician could express himself on issues before the government, even if most seldom availed themselves of the *renga*.[19] As the *case grandi* controversy indicates, the Great Council remained an important site for parliamentary maneuvering; the *Primi* might be able to dispense with the Senate, but they could not do without the approval of the Great Council.[20]

The renowned harmony and stability of the Venetian Republic flowed from all these considerations. More than anywhere else, it is in the nature of the Great Council—or, to put it another way, in the nature of the patriciate as an office-holding caste—that the origins of the myth of Venice are to be found; for the sovereign assembly imposed its weight on all aspects of Venetian politics and constitution, shaping the political behavior and temperament that were praised in the *mito di Venezia*.[21] A reciprocal disposition to oblige, motivated by self-interest, was at the roots of Venetian politics, making patricians mindful of others and, it seems, forgetful of themselves. In seeking votes and maintaining goodwill, a patrician's pride and arrogance had to give way before need for others. In such a character, the line between cupidity and patriotism was well-nigh invisible, as is shown in Marco Foscari's report to the Senate in 1528. Decrying his humble

15 Chapter II.1.
16 Chapter II.2 and II.3.
17 Chapter III.2.
18 Priuli, 2:363; see this book, Chapter IV.3.
19 Chapter V.1.
20 Chapter II.4; Chapter IV.2.
21 See Chapter I.2.

service for Venice, Foscari proudly lists his terms as state attorney, ambassador, censor, *savio di terraferma*. The love of a citizen toward the state, he asserted, must be like that of a dog toward a cruel master, always "more humble, more amiable, and more faithful," despite occasional injustice and ingratitude.[22] Two years before, when Foscari was accused in the Great Council of lobbying for the Collegio, he threw himself on his knees before Doge Gritti (his cousin) and protested his innocence. Not surprisingly, the case was dismissed by the Signoria, with "little honor" to Francesco Valier, the censor; "and the following morning it spread through the city what a public fool he had been."[23] The publicity of the Great Council put every patrician's reputation at hazard; an ethic of sacrifice and subordination, so important a part of the myth of Venice, was a response to that threat. Serving the state, discreet and anonymous, the patrician's self-esteem was at once submerged and enhanced. Anxious for both approval and dignity, he willingly donned a mask of accommodation and amiability.

"Reputation," declared the 1516 measure reestablishing the post of official historiographer, "is one of the principal foundations of every state."[24] A product of state propaganda, religious faith, and wishful thinking, the myth of Venice was still considerably more than a distortion of the truth. The myth was, rather, an idealization of reality, as when one views a city from a distance, unaware of the clamor and dirt that fill its streets. In this sense, the myth of the perfect republic—loved by its people, governed by the wise, manifesting concord, transcending politics and faction, enduring and stable—is wholly relevant to the reality of Venice. In effect, the myth extolled as intrinsic to the constitution that which was an appearance produced by the politics that gave life to the constitutional order.

Thus the *popolo* were content with rule by a patrician caste, not because the latter was benevolent and provident, but because it did not barricade itself in the Ducal Palace and because it did in some measure seek the support and heed the moods of those without the right to vote. Although ducal power was crucial to the functioning of the regime, it manifested itself in ways that were not always obvious—and that patricians were pleased to overlook; the ducal oath thus papered over a perennial problem in the constitution.[25] Patrician character

22 Angelo Ventura, ed., *Relazione degli ambasciatori veneti al Senato*, 1:90, 180.
23 Sanuto, 43:770.
24 ASV, Consiglio di Dieci, Parti Miste, Reg. 39, fol. 39r.
25 Chapter III.1 and III.3.

was certainly far from self-sacrificing and temperate; but the politics of the city, in countless ways, rewarded the appearance of such behavior. So too the old men of the governing circle were not uniquely wise and prudent but, rather, the products of a prolonged apprenticeship to state service in which self-effacement and moderation were promoted, eccentricity and dissidence punished. Faction and conflict existed within the ruling class, although so channeled into electoral competition that a casual observer (or wishful thinker) might believe them absent; enmity and opposition were expressed through the quiet dropping of ballots into urns, and the orderly lines of patricians voting in the Great Council always impressed the foreign visitor. Republican values were constantly upheld in official proclamations and state propaganda; yet they were not allowed unduly to disturb the decorum of the councils that purportedly embodied such values.[26] Although the patriciate was divided by lines based on age, ancestry, and income, a common stake in the political system, manifested by electioneering, preserved the necessary measures of congeniality and solidarity. If all were not in fact equal within the ruling class, the power of the vote in the Great Council brought the *Primi* down to the level of the ordinary patrician. In short, while not the whole truth, neither was the myth of Venice a lie.

Because of the nature of the ruling class in the Great Council, the Republic was founded on a politics of compromise, conciliation, and consensus. Here, too, the myth accurately reflects an essential truth about Venice: Its political life was tranquil and moderate, composed of committee meetings, persistent vote seeking, humdrum debate, incessant elections, and discreet bickering. If Venetian politics was unexciting, even monotonous, at least it was not dangerous. This was something of which to be proud, and the myth of Venice is both an expression of patrician self-congratulation and a reflection of the achievement of the ruling class. The patrician republic gave Venice five hundred years of domestic peace and stability. Violence was kept from politics; electioneering and voting engendered collaboration and dedication; political behavior was conventional and restrained; pervasive corruption made for civic concord. A commonplace, entirely unexceptional political life thus gave birth to the extravagant and hopeful notion that at least one society had transcended the difficulties and dangers inherited by other political communities. Not all republics have been so fortunate.

26 Chapter V.2.

Bibliography

Primary Works

"Arbore della Famiglia Trono." MCCC. MSS. Prod. Div. 2250/7.

Aretino, Pietro. *Aretino: Selected Letters.* Translated by George Bull. New York, 1976.

Barbaro, Daniele. *Storia Veneziana dall'anno 1 12 al 1515.* Edited by T. Gar. *Archivio storico italiano,* 1st ser., vol. 7. Florence, 1843–1844.

Barbaro, Marcantonio. *Genealogie delle famiglie patrizie venete.* BMV. MSS. Cl. VII, 925–928 (8594–8597).

Capellari, Girolamo. *Il Campidoglio Veneto.* 4 vols. BMV. MSS. It. Cl. VII, 8306.

Caroldo, Giangiacomo. MCC. MS. Cod. Correr, 1336.

Commynes, Philippe de. *Mémoires.* Edited by B. de Mandrot. 2 vols. Paris, 1901–1903.

Contarini, Gasparo. *La Republica e i Magistrati di Venezia.* Venice, 1564.

"Discorsetto in propositione de' Broglio." MCC. MS. Cod. Cicogna (980) 3182.

"Distinzioni Segrete che corrono tra le Case Nobili di Venezia." MCC. MS. Cod. Gradenigo-Dolfin, 24.

Dolfin, Giorgio. "Cronaca Veneta dalle origini al 1458." BMV. MS. It. Cl. VII, 794 (8503).

Dolfin, Pietro. *Annalium Venetorum (pars quatro).* Edited by Roberto Cessi and Paolo Sambin. Venice, 1943.

Giannotti, Donato. *Libro de la Republica de Vinitiani.* Venice, 1564.

Giustiniani, Antonio. "Orazione fatta in occasione della Lega di Cambray (1515)." MCC. MS. Cod. Cicogna, 1537.

Guicciardini, Francesco. *Storia di Italia.* 3 vols. Edited by Silvana Seidel Menchi. Turin, 1971.

"Istoria del governo di Venezia." Vienna, Nazional Biblioteca. MS. Cod. CCCXXI, Fondo ex Foscarini.

"Le vesti e maniche ducali, 1636." MCC. MS. Cod. Cicogna, 3282.

Longo, Francesco. "Diarii, 1537–1540." MCC. MS. Cod. Sagredo, Prov. Div. 382-c.

Machiavelli, Nicolò. *Machiavelli: The Chief Works and Others.* 3 vols. Translated by Allan Gilbert. Durham, N.C., 1965.

Malipiero, Domenico. *Annali veneti dall'anno 1457 al 1500.* 2 vols. Edited by T. Gar. and A. Sagredo. *Archivio storico italiano,* 1st ser., vol. 7. Florence, 1843–1844.

"Memorie pubbliche della Repubblica di Venezia." BMV. Cod. It. Cl. VII, 811 (7299).

Michiel, Alvise. "Diarii, 1578–1586." MCC. MS. Cod. Cicogna, 2555.

Michiel, Marcantonio. "Diarii." MCC. MS. Cod. Cicogna, 2848.

——. *Notizie d'opere di desegno nella prima metà del secolo XVI.* Edited by T. Frimmel. Vienna, 1888.

Milledonne, Antonio. "Dialogo de Antonio Milledonne con uno amico suo: Che la repulsa dalli honori non sia cosa mala." BMV. MS. It. Cl. VII, 709 (8403).

Morosini, Domenico. *De bene istituta re publica.* Edited by Claudio Finzi. Milan, 1969.

Muazzo, Giannantonio. "Del Governo Antico della repubblica veneta, delle alterazioni, e regolazioni d'esso, e delle cause, e tempi, che sono successe fino a nostri giorni: Discorso istorico politico." BMV. MS. It. Cl. VII, 964 (7831).

——. "Storia del governo antico e presente della Repubblica di Venezia." BMV. MS. It. Cl. VII, 966 (8406).

"Naratione delle electione d'M. Nicolò da Ponte al principato di Venetia, 1578." BMV. MS. It. Cl. XI, 67 (7351).

Pius II. *The Commentaries of Pius II.* Translated by Florence Alden Gragg. Smith College Studies in History, vol. 43. N.p., 1957.

Porto, Luigi da. *Lettere storiche dall'anno 1509 al 1528.* Edited by Bartolommeo Bressan. Florence, 1857.

Priuli, Girolamo. "Diarii." Vols. 5–8. MCC. MSS. Prov. Div., 252–c.

——. *I diarii di Girolamo Priuli.* Vol. 1 edited by Arturo Segre. Vols. 2 and 4 edited by Roberto Cessi. Rerum Italicarum Scriptores, vol. 24, pt. 3. Bologna, 1912–1938.

"Raccolta dei Consegi (Nomine, ballotazioni ed elezioni alle cariche della Repubblica di Venezia)." BMV. MSS. It. Cl. VII, 813–871 (8892–8950).

Sabellico, M. A. *Del sito di Venezia città.* Translated by G. Meneghetti. Venice, 1957.

Sanuto, Marino. *Cronachetta.* Edited by Rinaldo Fulin. Venice, 1880.

——. "Cronica Sanuda." BMV. MS. It. Cl. VII, 125 (7460).

——. *I diarii di Marino Sanuto.* 58 vols. Edited by Rinaldo Fulin and others. Deputazione R. Veneta di Storia Patria. Venice, 1879–1903.

——. "Miscellanea di Cronaca Veneta di Marino Sanuto." MCC. MS. Cod. Cicogna, 970.

——. *La spedizione di Carlo VIII in Italia.* Edited by Rinaldo Fulin. Venice, 1883.

——. *Vite dei dogi: Dal 1474 al 1494.* BMV. MS. It. Cl. VII, 801 (7152).

Stringa, Giovanni. *La Chiesa di San Marco: Capella del Serenissimo Principe di Venezia: Descritta brevamente da D. Giovanni Stringa.* Venice, 1610.

Torre (?), Francesco della. "Relazione della Serenissima Repubblica di Venezia." BMV. MS. It. Cl. VII, 1553 (8826).

Venier, Giovanni Antonio. "Storia delle Rivoluzioni Seguite nel Governo della Republica di Venezia e della Istituzione dell'Eccelso Consiglio di X sino alla sua Regolazione." BMV. MS. It. Cl. VII, 774 (7284).

Ventura, Angelo, ed. *Relazione degli ambasciatori veneti al Senato.* 2 vols. Rome, 1976.

Vettori, Francesco. *Sommario della historia d'Italia.* Edited by E. Niccolini. Bari, 1972.

Secondary Works

Aldobrandini, N. P. *Le monete di Venezia.* Venice, 1907.

Baron, Hans. "Early Renaissance Venetian Chronicles: Their History and a Manuscript in the Newberry Library." In *From Petrarch to Leonardo Bruni: Studies in Humanistic and Political Literature*, pp. 172–195. Chicago and London, 1968.

Baschet, A. *Les archives de Venise: Histoire de la chancellerie secrète, le sénat, le cabinet des ministres, le conseil des dix et les inquisiteurs d'état dans leurs rapports avec la France.* Paris, 1870.

Berlan, F. *I due Foscari.* Turin, 1852.

Bertelli, Sergio. "Pier Soderini 'Vexillifer Perpetuus Reipublicae Florentinae' 1502–1512." In *Renaissance Studies in Honor of Hans Baron*, edited by Anthony Molho and John A. Tedeschi, pp. 335–346. Florence, 1971.

Besta, Enrico. *Il Senato Veneziano (origine, costituzione, attribuzioni e riti).* Miscellanea di storia veneta, vol. 5. Venice, 1899.

Bistort, G. *Il magistrato alla pompe nella Republica di Venezia.* Miscellanea di storia veneta, vol. 5. Venice, 1912.

Boerio, Giuseppe. *Dizionario del dialetto veneziano.* Venice, 1856.

Bonardi, Antonio. "Venezia città libera dell'Impero nell'immaginazione di Massimiliano I d'Asburgo." *Atti e memorie della R. Accademia di scienze, lettere ed arti di Padova* 31 (1915):127–147.

Borghi, L. C. "Del Broglio." *Nuove Veglie Veneziane* 9–10 (1895):3–16.

Bouwsma, William J. *Venice and the Defense of Republican Liberty: Renaissance Values in the Age of the Counter Reformation.* Berkeley and Los Angeles, 1968.

Braudel, Fernand. *The Mediterranean and the Mediterranean World in the Age of Philip II.* 2 vols. Translated by Sian Reynolds. New York, 1972.

Brown, Horatio. *Studies in the History of Venice.* 2 vols. London, 1907.

Brown, Rawdon. *Ragguagli sulla vita e sulle opere di Marin Sanuto.* 3 vols. Venice, 1837.

Brown, William Archer. "Nicolò da Ponte: The political career of a sixteenth-century Venetian politician." Ph.D. dissertation, New York University, 1974.

Brulez, Wilfred. *Marchands Flamands à Venise, 1568–1605*. Brussels, 1965.

Brunetti, Mario. "Il doge non è 'segno di taverna.'" *Nuovo Archivio Veneto* 33 (1917):351–355.

——. "Marin Sanudo." *L'Ateneo Veneto* 46 (1923):3–19.

——. "Due dogi sotto inchiesta: Agostino Barbarigo e Leonardo Loredan." *Archivio Veneto-Tridentino* 7 (1925):278–329.

Burckhardt, Jacob. *The Civilization of the Renaissance in Italy*. Translated by S. G. C. Middleton. London, 1965.

Burke, Peter. *Venice and Amsterdam: A Study of Seventeenth-century Élites*. London, 1974.

Cadoni, Giorgio. "Libertà, republica e governo misto in Machiavelli." *Rivista Internazionale di Filosofia del Diritto*, 39 (1962):462–484.

Cecchetti, B. *Il doge di Venezia*. Venice, 1864.

——. "I nobili e il popolo di Venezia." *Archivio Veneto* 3 (1872):421–428.

Cervelli, I. "Storiografia e problemi intorno alla vita religiosa e spirituale di Venezia nella prima metà del '500." *Studi Veneziani* 8 (1966):447–476.

Cessi, Roberto. *Storia della Repubblica di Venezia*. 2 vols. Milan, 1944–1946.

Chabod, Federico. "Venezia nella politica italiana ed europea del Cinquecento." In *La civiltà veneziana del Rinascimento*, pp. 29–55. Florence, 1958.

Chambers, D. S. *The Imperial Age of Venice, 1380–1580*. London, 1970.

Chojnacki, Stanley. "Crime, Punishment, and the Trecento Venetian State." In *Violence and Civic Disorder in Italian Cities*, edited by Lauro Martines, pp. 184–228. Berkeley and Los Angeles, 1972.

——. "In Search of the Venetian Patriciate: Families and Factions in the Fourteenth Century." In *Renaissance Venice*, edited by J. R. Hale, pp. 47–90. Totowa, N.J., 1973.

——. "Patrician Women in Renaissance Venice." *Studies in the Renaissance* 21 (1974):176–203.

——. "Dowries and Kinsmen in Early Renaissance Venice." *Journal of Interdisciplinary History* 4 (1975):571–600.

Cicogna, Emmanuel A. *Delle iscrizioni veneziane*. 6 vols. Venice, 1824–1853.

——. *Intorno la vita e le opere di Marcantonio Michiel, Patrizio veneto della prima metà del secolo XVI*. Memorie dell'Istituto Veneto di scienze, lettere ed arti, vol. 9. Venice, 1861.

Cipollini, F. "La Lega di Cambrai." *Rivista d'Italia* 13 (1910):59–85.

Cochrane, Eric. *Florence in the Forgotten Centuries, 1527–1800*. Chicago, 1973.

Cogo, G. "La guerra di Venezia contro i Turchi (1499–1501)." *Nuovo Archivio Veneto* 18 (1889):5–76, 348–421; 19 (1890):97–138.

Cozzi, Gaetano. *Il doge Nicolò Contarini: Ricerche sul patriziato veneziano all'inizio del Seicento*. Venice, 1958.

——. "Una vicenda della Venezia barocca: Marco Trevisan e la sua eroica amicizia." *Bolletino dell'Istituto di Storia della Società e dello Stato Veneziano* 2 (1960):61–154.

——. "Cultura politica e religione nella 'pubblica storiografia' veneziana del '500." *Bollettino dell'Istituto di Storia della Società e dello Stato Veneziano* 5–6 (1963–1964):215–296.

——. "Domenico Morosini e il 'De bene istituta re publica.'" *Studi Veneziani* 12 (1970):405–458.

——. "Marin Sanudo il Giovane: Dalla cronaca alla storia (nel V centenario della sua nascita)." In *Aspetti della storiografia veneziana fino al secolo XVI*, edited by Agostino Pertusi, pp. 333–358. Florence, 1970.

——. "Authority and the Law in Renaissance Venice," In *Renaissance Venice.* edited by J. R. Hale, pp. 293–345. Totowa, N.J., 1973.

Cracco, Giorgio. *Società e stato nel medioevo veneziano.* Florence, 1967.

Crowe, J. A., and Cavalcaselle, G. B. *Titian: His Life and Times.* London, 1877.

Dalla Santa, Giuseppe. *La Lega di Cambrai e gli avvenimenti dell'anno 1509 descritti da un mercante veneziano contemporaneo.* Venice, 1903.

da Mosto, Andrea. *L'Archivio di Stato di Venezia.* 2 vols. Rome, 1937.

——. *I dogi di Venezia nella vita pubblica e privata.* Rev. ed. Milan, 1966.

Davis, James Cushman, *The Decline of the Venetian Nobility as a Ruling Class.* Baltimore, 1962.

——. "Shipping and Spying in the Early Career of a Venetian Doge, 1496–1502." *Studi Veneziani* 16 (1974):97–108.

——. *A Venetian Family and Its Fortune, 1500–1900.* Memoirs of the American Philosophical Society, vol. 106. Philadelphia, 1975.

de Leva, G. "Marino Sanuto." *Archivio Veneto* 36 (1888):109–126.

Demus, Otto. *The Church of San Marco in Venice: History, Architecture, Sculpture.* Washington, 1960.

Diehl, Charles. *Une république patricienne.* Paris, 1938.

Dionisotti, Carlo. "Chierici e laici nella letteratura italiana del primo Cinquecento." In *Problemi di vita religiosa in Italia nel Cinquecento*, pp. 167–185. Padua, 1960.

Ell, Stephen. "Citizenship and Immigration in Venice, 1305 to 1500." Ph.D. dissertation, The University of Chicago, 1976.

Ercole, Francesco. *Da Carlo VIII a Carlo V: La crisi della libertà italiana.* Florence, 1932.

Fasoli, Gina. "Nascita di un mito (Il mito di Venezia nella storiografia)." In *Studi storici in onore di G. Volpe*, vol. 1, pp. 445–479. Florence, 1958.

Fedalto, Giorgio. *Ricerche storiche sulla posizione giuridica ed ecclesiastica dei Greci a Venezia nei secoli XV e XVI.* Florence, 1967.

Fink, Zera S. *The Classical Republicans: An Essay in the Recovery of a Pattern of Thought in Seventeenth-century England.* 2nd. ed. Evanston, 1962.

Finlay, Robert. "The Politics of the Ruling Class in Early Cinquecento Venice." Ph.D. dissertation, The University of Chicago, 1973.

——. "Venice, the Po Expedition, and the End of the League of Cambrai, 1509–1510." *Studies in Modern European History and Culture* 2 (1976): 37–72.

Fletcher, Jennifer. "Marcantonio Michiel's Collection." *Journal of the Warbug and Courtauld Institutes* 36 (1973):382–385.

Fragnito, Gigliola. "Cultura umanistica e riforma religiosa: Il 'De officio boni viri ac probi episcopi' di Gasparo Contarini." *Studi Veneziani* 11 (1969):75–190.

Fulin, Rinaldo. "Dell'attitudine di Venezia dinanzi ai grandi viaggi marittimi del secolo XV." *Atti del R. Istituto Veneto di scienze, lettere ed arti* 7 (1881).

——. *Diarii e diaristi veneziani*. Venice, 1881.

——. "Girolamo Priuli e i suoi Diarii (I Portughesi nell'India e i Veneziani in Egitto)." *Archivio Veneto* 22 (1881):137–248.

Gaeta, Franco. "Alcune considerazioni sul mito di Venezia." *Bibliothèque d'Humanisme et Renaissance*, 23 (1961):58–75.

Gallo, F. Alberto. "Musiche veneziane nel ms. 2216 della Biblioteca Universitaria di Bologna." *Quadrivium* 6 (1964):107–115.

Geanakoplos, Deno John. *Greek Scholars in Venice*. Cambridge, Mass., 1962.

Gilbert, Creighton. "When Did a Man in the Renaissance Grow Old?" *Studies in the Renaissance* 14 (1967):7–32.

Gilbert, Felix. *Machiavelli and Giucciardini: Politics and History in Sixteenth-century Florence*. Princeton, 1965.

——. "The Date of the Composition of Contarini's and Giannotti's Books on Venice." *Studies in the Renaissance* 14 (1967):172–184.

——. "Religion and Politics in the Thought of Gasparo Contarini." In *Action and Conviction in Early Modern Europe: Essays in Memory of E. H. Harbison*, edited by Theodore K. Rabb and Jerrold E. Seigel, pp. 90–116. Princeton, 1968.

——. "The Venetian Constitution in Florentine Political Thought." In *Florentine Studies*, edited by Nicolai Rubenstein, pp. 463–500. London, 1968.

——. "Machiavelli e Venezia," *Lettere Italiane* 21 (1969):389–398.

——. "Venetian Diplomacy before Pavia: From Reality to Myth." In *The Diversity of History: Essays in Honor of Herbert Butterfield*, pp. 79–116. London, 1970.

——. "Biondo, Sabellico, and the Beginnings of Venetian Official Historiography." In *Florilegium Historiale: Essays Presented to Wallace K. Ferguson*, edited by J. G. Rowe and W. H. Stockdale, pp. 275–293. Toronto, 1971.

——. "Venice in the Crisis of the League of Cambrai." In *Renaissance Venice*, edited by J. R. Hale, pp. 274–292. Totowa, N.J., 1973.

———. "The Last Will of a Venetian Grand Chancellor." In *Philosophy and Humanism: Renaissance Essays in Honor of Paul Oskar Kristeller*, edited by Edward P. Mahoney, pp. 502–517. New York, 1976.

Gilmore, Myron. "Myth and Reality in Venetian Political Theory." In *Renaissance Venice*, Edited by J. R. Hale, pp. 431–444. Totowa, N.J., 1973.

Giraldi, Philip M. "The Zen Family (1500–1550): Patrician Office Holders in Renaissance Venice." Ph.D. dissertation, University of London, 1975.

Grendler, Paul F. *The Roman Inquisition and the Venetian Printing Press, 1540–1605*. Princeton, N.J., 1977.

Guerdan, R. *L'oro di Venezia: Splendori e miserie della Serenissima*. Translated by A. Calesella. Verona, 1967.

Herlihy, David. "The Generation in Medieval History." *Viator: Medieval and Renaissance Studies* 5 (1974):346–364.

Hess, Andrew C. "The Evolution of the Ottoman Seaborne Empire in the Age of the Oceanic Discoveries, 1453–1525." *American Historical Review* 75 (1970):1,892–1,919.

Howard, Deborah. *Jacopo Sansovino: Architecture and Patronage in Renaissance Venice*. New Haven, 1975.

Kardos, Tibor. "Dramma satirico carnevalesco su Alvise Gritti governatore dell'Ungheria, 1532." In *Venezia e Ungheria nel Rinascimento*, edited by Vittore Branca, pp. 397–427. Florence, 1973.

Kedar, Benjamin Z. *Merchants in Crisis: Genoese and Venetian Men of Affairs and the Fourteenth-century Depression*. New Haven, 1976.

Kent, Dale. *The Rise of the Medici: Faction in Florence, 1426–1434*. Oxford, 1978.

Kent, Francis William. *Household and Lineage in Renaissance Florence*. Princeton, N.J., 1977.

King, Margaret Leah. "Personal, Domestic and Republican Values in the Moral Philosophy of Giovanni Caldiera." *Renaissance Quarterly* 28 (1975):535–574.

———. "Caldiera and the Barbaros on marriage and the family: humanist reflections of Venetian realities." *The Journal of Medieval and Renaissance Studies* 6 (1976):19–50.

Labalme, Patricia. *Bernardo Giustiniani: A Venetian of the Quattrocento*. Rome, 1969.

———. "The Last Will of a Venetian Patrician (1489)." In *Philosophy and Humanism: Renaissance Essays in Honor of Paul Oskar Kristeller*, edited by Edward P. Mahoney, pp. 483–501. New York, 1976.

Lagomaggiore, Carlo. "L'*Istoria Viniziana* di M. Pietro Bembo." *Nuovo Archivio Veneto* 7 (1904):5–30, 334–372; 8 (1904):162–180, 317–346; 9 (1905):33–113, 308–341.

Lane, Frederic C. *Venetian Ships and Shipbuilders of the Renaissance*. Baltimore, 1934.

———. *Andrea Barbarigo, Merchant of Venice, 1418–1449*. Baltimore, 1944.

——. "Family Partnerships and Joint Ventures." In *Venice and History*, pp. 36–55. Baltimore, 1966.

——. "Medieval Political Ideas and the Venetian Constitution." In *Venice and History*, pp. 285–308. Baltimore, 1966.

——. "Venetian Bankers, 1496–1533." In *Venice and History*, pp. 69–86. Baltimore, 1966.

——. "Venetian Shipping during the Commercial Revolution." In *Venice and History*, pp. 3–24. Baltimore, 1966.

——. "The Enlargement of the Great Council of Venice." In *Florilegium Historiale*, edited by J. J. Rowe, pp. 235–274. Toronto, 1970.

——. "Naval Actions and Fleet Organization, 1499–1502." In *Renaissance Venice*, edited by J. R. Hale, pp. 146–173. Totowa, N.J., 1973.

——. "Public Debt and Private Wealth, Particularly in Sixteenth-Century Venice." In *Mélanges en l'honneur de Fernand Braudel*, pp. 317–325. Toulouse, 1973.

——. *Venice: A Maritime Republic*. Baltimore, 1973.

Lazzarini, Vittorio. *Marino Falier*. Florence, 1963.

Libby, Lester J. "Venetian History and Political Thought after 1509." *Studies in the Renaissance* 20 (1973):7–45.

Liberali, Giuseppe. *Le 'dinastie ecclesiastiche' nei Cornaro della Chà Granda*. Documentari sulla Riforma Cattolica Pre e Post-Tridentina a Treviso, vol. 1. Treviso, 1971.

——. *Il 'Papalismo' dei Pisani 'dal Banco.'* Documentari sulla Riforma Cattolica Pre e Post-Tridentina a Treviso, vol. 2. Treviso, 1971.

Lowry, M. J. C. "The Reform of the Council of Ten, 1582–3: An Unsettled Problem?" *Studi Veneziani* 13 (1971):275–310.

——. "The 'New Academy' of Aldus Manutius: A Renaissance Dream." *Bulletin of the John Rylands University Library of Manchester* 58 (1976):378–420.

Lucchetta, Francesca. " 'L'Affare Zen' in Levante nel primo Cinquecento." *Studi Veneziani* 10 (1969):109–220.

Luzio, Alessandro. *Pietro Aretino nei primi suoi anni a Venezia*. Turin, 1888.

——. "La reggenza d'Isabella d'Este durante la prigionia del marito (1509–1510)." *Archivio storico lombardo* 38 (1910):5–104.

——. "I preliminari della Lega di Cambrai." *Archivio storico lombardo* 38 (1911):245–310.

——. *La congiuro spagnola contra Venezia nel 1618*. Miscellanea di storia veneta, vol. 13. Venice, 1918.

Luzzatto, Gino. *Storia economica di Venezia del XI al XVI secolo*. Venice, 1961.

——. "L'economia veneziana nei secoli '400 e '500." *Bergomun* 58 (1964): 59–71.

MacMullen, Ramsay. *Enemies of the Roman Order: Treason, Unrest, and Alienation in the Empire*. Cambridge, Mass., 1967.

Maranini, Giuseppe. *La costituzione di Venezia dopo la Serrata del Maggior Consiglio.* Venice, 1931.

Maria, Julìan. *Generations: A Historical Method.* Translated by Harold C. Raley. University, Alabama, 1970.

Marks, L. F. "La crisi finanziaria a Firenze dal 1494 al 1502." *Archivio storico italiano* 112 (1954):40–72.

Martines, Lauro. *The Social World of the Florentine Humanists, 1390–1460.* Princeton, N.J., 1963.

Matteucchi, Nicola. "Machiavelli, Harrington, Montesquieu e gli 'ordini' di Venezia." *Il Pensiero Politico* 3 (1970):337–369.

Mazzarotto, Bianca Tamassia. *Le feste veneziane: I Giochi popolari, le Cerimonie religiose e di Governo.* Florence, 1961.

McClure, Norman Egbert, ed. *The Letters of John Chamberlain.* 2 vols. Philadelphia, 1939.

Molho, Anthony. *Florentine Public Finance in the Early Renaissance, 1400–1433.* Cambridge, Mass., 1971.

Molmenti, Pompeo. "La corruzione dei costumi veneziani nel Rinascimento." *Archivio storico italiano* 31 (1903):281–307.

———. *La storia di Venezia nella vita privata.* 3 vols. Bergamo, 1910–1911.

Mousnier, R. "Le trafic des offices à Venise." *Revue historique du droit français et étranger* 30 (1952):552–565.

Mueller, Reinhold C. "The Procuratori of San Marco in the Thirteenth and Fourteenth Centuries: A Study of the Office as a Financial and Trust Institution." *Studi Veneziani* 13 (1971):105–221.

———. "Charitable Institutions, the Jewish Community, and Venetian Society: A discussion of a recent volume by Brian Pullan." *Studi Veneziani* 14 (1972):37–82.

Muir, Edward. "The Doge as Primus Inter Pares: Interregnum Rites in Early Sixteenth-Century Venice." *Essays Presented to Myron P. Gilmore*, edited by Sergio Bertelli and Gloria Ramakus, vol. 1, pp. 145–160. Florence, 1978.

———. "Images of Power: Art and Pageantry in Renaissance Venice." *The American Historical Review* 84 (1979):16–52.

Muraro, Michelangelo. "La Scala senza Giganti." In *De Artibus Opuscula XL: Essays in honor of Erwin Panofsky*, edited by Millard Meiss, pp. 350–370. New York, 1961.

———. "Ideologia e iconografia dei dogi di Venezia." In *Receuil de Travaux le Prince Lazar*, pp. 421–436. Belgrade, 1975.

———. and Rosand, David. *Tiziano e la silografia veneziana del Cinquecento.* Vicenza, 1976.

Musatti, E. *Storia della promissione ducale.* Padua, 1888.

Mutinelli, Fabio. *Lessico Veneto. Venice,* 1852.

Nallino, M. "L'Egitto dalla morte di Qā'it Bay all'avvento di Qānsūh al-Guri (1496–1501) nei *Diarii* di Marino Sanudo." *Atti Accademia nazionale dei Lincei* 20 (1965):414–453.

Newett, M. Margaret. *Canon Pietro Casola's Pilgrimage to Jerusalem in the Year 1494.* Manchester, 1907.

Occion-Bonafons, G. "Intorno alle cagioni della Lega di Cambrai." *Archivio storico lombardo* 4 (1955):1–39.

Pampaloni, G. "Fermenti di riforme democratiche nella Firenze medicea del Quattrocento." *Archivio storico italiano* 119 (1961):11–62.

Panofsky, Erwin. *Problems in Titian, Mostly Iconographic.* New York, 1969.

Papadopoli, N. "Una tariffa con disegni di monete stampata a Venezia nel 1517." *Nuovo Archivio Veneto* 17 (1899):102–104.

Pecchioli, Renato. "Il 'mito' di Venezia e la crisi fiorentina intorno al 1500." *Studi storici* 3 (1962):451–492.

Pieri, P. *Intorno alla politica di Venezia al principio del Cinquecento.* Naples, 1934.

Pilot, Antonio. "La teoria del Broglie nella Republica Veneta," *L'Ateneo Veneto* 27 (1904):176–189.

——. "L'elezione del doge Nicolò Tron." In *Nuova Rassegna di Letteratura Moderne,* pp. 1–17. Florence, 1906.

Plumb, J. H. "Venice: The Golden Years." In *The Penguin Book of the Renaissance,* edited by J. H. Plumb. pp. 227–244. Harmondsworth, England, 1969.

Pocock, J. G. A. *The Machiavellian Moment: Florentine Political Thought and the Atlantic Republican Tradition.* Princeton, N.J., 1975.

Preto, Paolo. *Venezia e i Turchi.* Florence, 1975.

Pullan, Brian. "The Famine in Venice and the New Poor Law, 1527–29." *Bollettino dell'Istituto di Storia della Società e dello Stato Veneziano* 5–6 (1963–1964):141–202.

——. "Service to the Venetian State: Aspects of Myth and Reality in the Early Seventeenth Century." *Studi Secenteschi* 5 (1964):95–148.

——. *Rich and Poor in Renaissance Venice: The Social Institutions of a Catholic State, to 1620.* Oxford, England, 1971.

——. "The Significance of Venice." *Bulletin of the John Rylands University Library of Manchester* 56 (1974):443–462.

Puppi, L. "Le residenze di Pietro Bembo 'in padoana.'" *L'arte* 7–8 (1969): 30–66.

Queller, Donald E. *Early Venetian Legislation on Ambassadors.* Travaux d'Humanisme et Renaissance, vol. 88. Geneva, 1966.

——. "The Civic Irresponsibility of the Venetian Nobility." In *Economy, Society, and Government in Medieval Italy,* edited by David Herlihy and others, pp. 223–236. Kent, Ohio, 1969.

——. "The Development of Ambassadorial Relazioni." In *Renaissance Venice,* edited by J. R. Hale, pp. 174–196. Totowa, N.J., 1973.

Rosand, David. "Titian's *Presentation of the Virgin in the Temple* and the Scuola della Carità." *The Art Bulletin* 58 (1976):55–84.

Rose, Charles J. "Marc Antonio Venier, Renier Zeno and 'the Myth of Venice.'" *The Historian* 36 (1974):479–498.

Ross, James Bruce. "The Emergence of Gasparo Contarini: A Bibliographical Essay." *Church History* 41 (March 1972):22–45.

Rossi, Agostino. "Gl'Inquisitori sopra il doge defunto nella Repubblica di Venezia." In *Studi storici*, pp. 282–382. Bologna, 1906.

Rubinstein, Nicolai. "I primi anni del Consiglio Maggiore a Firenze (1494–99)." *Archivio storico italiano* 112 (1954):151–194, 321–347.

——. "Politics and Constitution in Florence at the End of the Fifteenth Century." In *Italian Renaissance Studies*, edited by E. F. Jacob, pp. 148–183. London, 1960.

——. "Italian Reactions to Terraferma Expansion in the Fifteenth Century." In *Renaissance Venice*, edited by J. R. Hale, pp. 197–217. Totowa, N.J., 1973.

Sardella, Pierre. *Nouvelles et spéculations à Venise au début du XVIème siècle*. Paris, 1948.

Seneca, Federico. *Il doge Leonardo Donà: La sua vita e la sua preparazione politica prima del dogado*. Padua, 1959.

——. *Venezia e papa Giulio II*. Padua, 1962.

Sinding-Larsen, S. *Christ in the Council Hall: Studies in the Religious Iconography of the Venetian Republic*. Institutum Romanum Norvegiae, vol. 5. Rome, 1974.

Smith, Logan Pearsall. *The Life and Letters of Sir Henry Wotton*. 2 vols. Oxford, 1907.

Stella, Aldo. "La regolazione delle pubbliche entrate e la crisi politica veneziana del 1582." In *Miscellanea in onore di Roberto Cessi*. Vol. 1, pp. 157–171. Rome, 1958.

——. *Chiesa e stato nelle relazioni dei nunzi pontifici a Venezia: Ricerche sul giurisdizionalismo veneziano dal XVI al XVIII secolo*. Vatican City, 1964.

Stella, Antonio. "Grazie, pensioni ed elemosine sotto la Repubblica veneta." In *Monografie editate in onore di Fabio Besta*. Vol. 2, pp. 715–785. Milan, 1912.

Tenenti, Alberto. "La Sérénissime République." In *Venise au temps des galères*, pp. 161–183. Paris, 1968.

——. "The Sense of Space and Time in the Venetian World of the Fifteenth and Sixteenth Centuries." In *Renaissance Venice*, edited by J. R. Hale, pp. 17–46. Totowa, N.J., 1973.

Thayer, William Roscoe. *A Short History of Venice*. New York, 1908.

Thomas, Giorgio Martino. *Martin Luther und die Reformations Bewegung in Deutschland vom Jahre 1520–1532 in auszügen aus Marino Sanuto's Diarien*. Ansbach, 1883.

Tocqueville, Alexis de. *Democracy in America*. 2 vols. Translated by Henry Reeve and edited by Phillips Bradley. New York, 1945.

Trevor-Roper, H. R. "Doge Francesco Foscari." In *The Penguin Book of the Renaissance*, edited by J. H. Plumb, pp. 245–261. Harmondsworth, England, 1969.

Usteri, Emil. *Marignano: Die Schickalsjahre 1515/1516 im Blickfeld der Historischen Quellen*. Zurich, 1974.

Vecchiato, E. *I Foscari ed i Loredano*. Padua, 1898.

Venturi, Lionello. "Le Compagnie della Calza (sec. XV–XVI)." *Nuovo Archivio Veneto* 16 (1908):161–221; 17 (1909):140–233.

Wagner, K. "Sulle sorte di alcuni codici manoscritti appartenuti a Marin Sanudo." *La Bibliofilia* 73 (1971):247–262.

——. "Altre notizie sulla sorte dei libri di Marin Sanudo." *La Bibliofilia* 74, (1972):185–190.

Weinstein, Donald. *Savonarola and Florence: Prophecy and Patriotism in the Renaissance*. Princeton, N.J., 1970.

Wild, Johannes. "The Hall of the Great Council of Florence." In *Renaissance Art*, edited by Creighton Gilbert, pp. 92–132. New York, 1970.

Yriarte, Charles. *La vie d'un patricien de Venise au XVIème siècle: Marcantonio Barbaro*. Paris, 1874.

Zille, Ester. "Il processo Grimani." *Archivio Veneto* 36–41 (1945–1947): 137–194.

Index

A

Agnadello, battle of, 52, 54, 63, 72, 98, 119, 164, 167, 170–171, 196, 200, 222–224, 231, 237, 241, 246, 248, 252, 258, 270

Alviano, Bartolomeo, 54, 153, 177–178, 228, 236–237

Apulia, 165, 225, 234

Aretino, Pietro, 30

Arsenal, 269; administrators of, 66; commissioner of, 186; lord of, 186, 208, 246; workers of, 20, 47–49, 52, 119, 121

Arsenalotti. See Arsenal, workers of

avocati pizoli, 22, 252

B

Badoer, Giacomo, 100, 102–103

ballottini, 90, 201–203, 243

Barbarigo, Agostino, doge, 53, 56–57, 77, 115, 118, 121, 124, 134–135, 138, 149–151, 161, 209, 231, 233, 235, 245, 255, 280; complaints about, 111–112; election of, 145–147

Barbarigo, Marco, doge, 56, 114, 145, 161, 230

Barbaro, Francesco, 25, 84

Barbaro, Marcantonio, 131

Barbo clan, 83

Basilica di San Marco, 18–20, 29, 110, 121–122, 251

Bellini, Gentile, 19, 47

Bellini, Giovanni, 151

Bembo, Bernardo, 131, 255

Bembo, Pietro, 130–131, 255, 275–276

Bembo clan, 84

Bergamo, 165

Boldù, Antonio, 76–77

Bollani, Francesco, 62, 132, 230, 261

Bollani, Marco, 66, 131

Bolognetti, Alberto, 37–38, 46

Bon, Gabriele, 76–77, 79–80, 218

Botero, Giovanni, 41

bowmen, 69, 242

Bragadin, Francesco, 112, 131

Bragadin, Pietro, 101–102

Bragadin clan, 84

Brescia, 11, 156, 165, 173, 224

broglio, 28, 197–198, 200–201, 203–208, 210–221, 243, 257; growth of, 204–206; *honesto*, 199, 211, 217; influence of, 217–220; *piazza del*, 22–23, 26–29, 197, 286; significance of, 221. *See also* electioneering; electoral corruption; Switzers

C

Cadore, battle of, 29, 153

Calbo, Francesco, 101–103, 105

Cambrai: allegory of the War of the League of, 163; crisis of, 194, 222–223, 226, 251, 259, 277, 281; League of, 54, 163–164, 197, 224–225, 258; War of the League of, 3–4, 58–59, 63, 72, 120, 138, 156, 174, 181–182, 188, 195, 200, 209, 222–224, 228, 236, 242, 244, 256, 279, 281–282, 285

Campanile, 18–20, 164

Capello, Paolo, 56, 66, 86, 131, 172, 191

Capello, Pietro, 62–63, 159, 186

Capello clan, 86